APPALACHIAN
Home Cooking

APPALACHIAN
Home Cooking
History, Culture, and Recipes

MARK F. SOHN

THE UNIVERSITY PRESS OF KENTUCKY

Publication of this volume was made possible in part by a grant from the National Endowment for the Humanities.

Scholarly publisher for the Commonwealth, serving Bellarmine University, Berea College, Centre College of Kentucky, Eastern Kentucky University, The Filson Historical Society, Georgetown College, Kentucky Historical Society, Kentucky State University, Morehead State University, Murray State University, Northern Kentucky University, Transylvania University, University of Kentucky, University of Louisville, and Western Kentucky University. All rights reserved.

Editorial and Sales Offices: The University Press of Kentucky 663 South Limestone Street, Lexington, Kentucky 40508-4008 www.kentuckypress.com

Photographs by Mark F. Sohn www.marksohn.com

Library of Congress Cataloging-in-Publication Data

Sohn, Mark F.
  Appalachian home cooking : history, culture, and recipes / Mark F. Sohn.
        p.   cm.
  Includes bibliographical references and index.
  ISBN 0-8131-9153-X (pbk. : alk. paper)
  1. Cookery, American.
  2. Cookery—Appalachian Region, Southern.
  I. Title.
  TX715.S678115 2005
  641.5974—dc22   2005015814
  ISBN 978-0-8131-9153-9

*I dedicate this work to Appalachians everywhere,
as well as to Appalachian cooks and food writers
who have shared their food, stories, and recipes.*

*Specifically, I dedicate this book to two
Pike County women, now deceased,
who influenced my cooking:
Bill "Doc" Newsom of Robinson Creek and
Alice Kinder of Upper Chloe Creek.*

Contents

Part One: Appalachian Foodways

Part Two: Appalachian Food

Foreword

Cooking my way through this book made me want to prepare huge portions of food to share with friends. The recipes made me hungry for flavors I haven't enjoyed in years. They made me remember to tell my little girl the stories and songs I learned from my grandfather and to feed her the recipes I learned from my grandmother. This book and this food made me want to go home.

Historical cookbooks are much more than collections of recipes and menus; they show not only what people eat, but also how they live and what they value. The best cookbooks convey a region's concept of home and place, which is exactly what this book does as it delves into the heart of Appalachian food and culture. I had the pleasure of testing most of the recipes in this book, and I enjoyed talking about them with Mark Sohn.

For mountain people, the homeplace is not just a house, but also a sense of place, of origin, of belonging. Their beloved mountains are not just where they live, they are where they are from. I grew up in the Blue Ridge Mountains eating many of these same dishes, and I found that Mark Sohn's stories capture the Appalachian people's fierce devotion to and reliance on their land. For many years, the isolated region forced mountain cooks to rely on what was local, but they were blessed with rich, diverse, natural abundance. Meals echoed the patterns of the season because mountain cooks used the best of what was at hand, and they left little to waste.

Many ethnic groups have settled in the mountains, each bringing foods from their home countries and making the region less isolated, both geographically and culturally. Current tastes have mingled local, traditional favorites with the vast variety of foods available at any grocery store. The result is a new batch of family favorites to add to the collection handed down from previous generations.

Mountain cooks have always embraced new foods and conveniences, particularly store-bought foods that enabled them to produce meals with less work. The first packaged goods were a simple respite from a lifestyle that included little leisure time. For most people, work was constant, but not always drudgery. An evening of sitting on the porch stringing and snapping beans became a social event of storytelling, singing, and laughing. You can taste that heritage and hospitality in this book.

I had a wonderful time making these recipes. Some of them, I make often. Others, I hadn't made or tasted in years. My favorites were the Sweet Potato Pie, Stack Cake, Fresh Apple Cake, and anything you can eat with a hot, fresh biscuit or crusty cornbread. Those dishes instantly transported me back to my grandmother's kitchen, returning me to the exact aromas, the familiar flavors, and the sense of well-being that food prepared with love can convey.

I've traveled to many places around the world, dined in fabulous restaurants, and now earn my living as a professional cooking teacher, so I've eaten many different foods. But when people ask me about my favorite meal, I answer without hesitation "soup beans, mashed taters, garden vegetables, and cornbread." When I was a child, I didn't know that my grandmother was raising us on food with a rich, cultural heritage. For us, it was just supper.

Sheri Castle,
Recipe Tester,
Cooking School Instructor
Chapel Hill, North Carolina

Preface

Behind the negative hillbilly stereotypes associated with the Appalachian people, I find a culture of pride. One by one and family to family, many mountaineers cook the foods that combine history, religion, and environment and reflect a glorious heritage. However, what were once daily routines are slowly becoming memories. This book documents the passing food culture of Appalachia.

Food is integral to mountain life. Today as much as ever, Appalachian cooking expresses diverse patterns of culture, and one pattern that has been particularly informative is dinner on the grounds, a traditional covered-dish meal held in a church setting. Another is expressed in community festivals (see the listing in Part Two). At these public events, groups celebrate food history as they create the current imagination of what once was. In addition, for convenience and often to celebrate, cooks carry their favorite dishes to schools, churches, and halls of government. For Thanksgiving, Christmas, and summer picnics, families gather around their cooking.

I find this indigenous food to be balanced, flavorful, and often healthy. Boiled beans. Chicken and dumplings. Garden vegetables. Mashed potatoes. Fresh fruit. Cornbread. Fruit cobblers. And fudge. These are foods that lend themselves to family dining and healthy living. In addition, they often provide a foundation on which professional chefs build imaginative dishes and exciting menus.

When mountain home cooks gather for a dinner, they spread dishes of salad, bread, vegetables, meats, and desserts across tables, and in this book I collect both their memories and their recipes. I use narratives to present the stack cake (a many-layered apple cake), poke plant, and country ham; and I use lists to identify mountain nuts, coffee preparations, methods of preservation, and wild greens. The reference list includes almost 200 citations, and the 30 or so mail-order sources link readers to mountain ingredients. The 75 recipes are in a style that allows cooks of the twenty-first century to carry on the traditions of the mountain kitchens.

How did I go about studying Appalachian food? For more than a decade beginning in 1978, I taught a Pikeville (Kentucky) College class in Appalachian studies. As part of that class, I organized Appalachian dinners, and my students and their parents or grandparents prepared traditional dishes. With as many as 50 students in a class, these dinners were grand affairs that offered great choice. Semester after semester and year after year, my Appalachian dinners were an education in mountain food, and I took notes. I learned about moonshine, shucky beans, pawpaws, and cushaw. I tasted and talked and made mental notes.

Then, in 1988, knowing my interest in regional food, the Pike County newspaper, *The Appalachian News-Express,* asked me to write a food column, and with this column I began to document foods of the region. From the start, my goal was to relate the food to history and culture. In the early years, my interest combined recipe traditions and kitchen applications. I measured, stirred, and baked, and always I developed recipes. In the kitchen I used my French cooking school training, and at my desk I used my academic research skills. One ingredient or one recipe a week, I studied and cooked. For most recipes, I prepared a spreadsheet on which I listed the ingredients and methods of from 10 to 30 recipes. I wrote the recipe name and source for each one down the left margin; across the top, I listed the ingredients; and working from left to right, I listed the quantity of each ingredient. At the end, the spreadsheet included every ingredient from each recipe, and by reading from top to bottom I could compare what others had done with each ingredient. The recipes I developed from this information reflected the most common ingredients, quantities, and methods. In the kitchen, I tested and re-tested. At my desk, I wrote recipe headers that reflected the various approaches the different cooks used.

However, when I left the kitchen, the recipes were not enough. Recipes are like frostings on cakes. They hide from sight the textures, colors, and ingredients found below. As frostings cover a cake, recipes give no hints of their long histories, and, in fact, reflect no more than a moment in time. With every cook and every generation, recipes change. The fluid nature of food makes the search for its history exciting. However, this book is both a search for the past and an attempt to extend that past into the future. While the topic essays look back, they also move our food habits forward. Change is constant, and this book is part of that process.

The recipes included here are intentional updates of long-standing traditions. In preparing these recipes, I did not use butter churns, heavy crocks, or whole hog livers because I believe that accessible, tested, modern recipes will preserve this vital food tradition and serve those who take an interest in cooking.

I studied the indigenous ingredients, storage methods, utensils, combinations, and pairings. I followed the recipe changes through history and season. I learned how the mountain specialties presented at my Appalachian dinners were grown in a garden, cooked on a hearth, or preserved for winter. Through reading, I traced the frontiersmen as they stalked, killed, and prepared a buffalo, and then I went deer and elk hunting. For 25 years, I kept a vegetable garden, and I always raised fruit. From experience and observation, I learned how hill folk lived on their farms, what their children ate at school, and how shiners made moonshine. I talked, cooked, tasted, read, and observed. I crisscrossed the region and gathered data. At home I collected cookbooks and paid particular attention to community cookbooks. Appalachian food became my passion.

But there is no single definition of "Appalachian food." The food boundaries of Appalachia, or any region for that matter, are not drawn on a map like state and county lines. Just as people move around, food also travels, and it knows no political demarcations. While the Mason-Dixon line may separate the North from the South, food does not stay on one side or the other. Therefore, by arbitrary definition, the Appalachia of this book lies south of the Mason-Dixon line, but that does not mean the food customs of Appalachia are confined to a political region.

In addition, the Appalachian region has been without clear boundaries, because the map of Appalachia has been drawn and redrawn. In 1910, John C. Campbell drew the first important map of Appalachia, and he excluded all of Pennsylvania, Mississippi, and Alabama. In 1950, other scholars added about 25 percent of Alabama to that definition of Appalachia, and in 1965, the Appalachian Regional Commission added another 25 percent of Alabama, as well as parts of New York, Pennsylvania, Ohio, and Mississippi. There is no state of Appalachia and no Appalachian Land Grant University.

State boundaries are political. Every state has a capital and every county a seat. Food boundaries, on the other hand, are a matter of both individual habit and cultural tradition. While some claim a collards line, others who live north of that line swear by collards. Like so many ingredients, collards travel.

Furthermore, Appalachian food is not limited to a climate zone, although climate does influence the food of a region because it dictates what local foodstuffs are available. But foodstuffs can travel. When railroads were built into the Appalachian interior, oysters became popular, and while sugar cane will not grow north of the frost line, northerners enjoy white sugar as much as anyone in the South.

Another challenge with any attempt to trace food origin stories and regionally specific cuisines is that in the last 150 years, every 25 years or so food styles, habits, and expectations have changed. If a food generation spans 25 years, then since 1800 mountain food has passed through eight generations. Recently, the pace of change has been dramatic. For example, today the microwave oven and salad bar are taken for granted, but they are only about 25 years old. The service station food mart is a relatively recent phenomenon, but more recently the country has been overwhelmed by Starbucks. What was eaten 25 or 50 years ago may be unacceptable or even unavailable today. Children used to go to the garden and dig potatoes; they carried water, fed pigs, and killed chickens. Today they want a trip to McDonalds. While French cooking was popular across this country in the 1970s and 1980s, Japanese food is popular today. Tastes change. In the 1940s, Appalachian cooks began making yeast dinner rolls, while in recent times they have enjoyed cornbread salads. Advances in retailing, genetics, technology, and manufacturing push these changes.

A few foods, however, find a place and emerge as icons of culture. Appalachian soup beans (a bean soup), stack cakes, and chicken and dumplings are good examples. In the pages that follow, these opposing trends will enlighten our view of Appalachian foodways.

This book is important because it not only preserves a style of cooking, but it also describes an active culture. For 12,000 years Appalachian food patterns have been changing, and the goal of this book is to summarize, preserve, and engage this evolution. Appalachian food may be a stereotype, but the food of Appalachia is not.

Mark F. Sohn
Pikeville, Kentucky

Acknowledgments

Because my roots have strongly influenced my study of Appalachian culinary traditions, I must first thank my parents, Fred and Frances Sohn, of Roseburg, Oregon. I am a grateful beneficiary of their life-long fascination with flavors, recipes, and cooking methods. As I grew up in the 1950s, not only did they give me an appreciation for the aesthetics of food, they were also models as they approached food from a critical perspective. In addition, they were, as I am now, motivated to eat well and to find authentic and pleasing tastes. At many family meals of my childhood, one topic of conversation was what we were eating, and we often planned the next meal before finishing the last one. Because of my parents, food became a script in my life.

I must also thank my wife, Kathy, not only for sharing the kitchen, but also for editing much of this material. Kathy was caring and supportive throughout the project. And I thank my children, Laura and Brian, for eating and critiquing a continuous stream of recipes as they grew up.

Since 1988, the *Appalachian News-Express* and the Images Editor, Nancy Goss, have provided me with a public forum, a sort of workshop, for these recipes. Without my column, "Class Cooking," these recipes and this story would not be on paper. While this work is in no way supported by Pikeville College, I also thank the college, which since 1975 has provided the opportunity to live and work in eastern Kentucky.

I am indebted to the staff at the Santa Fe (photography) Workshops, especially my teachers, Douglas Merriam of Santa Fe and Arthur Meyerson of Houston, Texas. They taught me about lighting and composition and encouraged me to exhibit my work.

I received invaluable support, editing, typing, and proofreading assistance from my friend, Tina Rae Collins of Berea, Kentucky, who has worked with me on various projects since 1978. Sheri Castle, a food professional from the mountains of western North Carolina who grew up eating foods similar to those discussed here, tested the recipes, and I appreciate her effort and comments.

In the summer of 2002, Jennifer Peckinpaugh, an acquisitions editor at the University Press of Kentucky, invited me to submit a proposal for this book. At the time, I was not looking for this project, but Jennifer's enthusiasm was contagious. Jennifer supported the project through July of 2003, when she left the Press to be a full-time mom for her new son, Jack. I thank Jennifer for her support.

Without being specific, I want to thank my neighbors, students, and acquaintances who cook and share their food. I am also grateful to the foragers, gardeners, farmers, food writers, school and restaurant cooks, and church members with whom I have had either direct or indirect contact and who have helped inspire this writing.

Grateful acknowledgment is given for permission to reprint previously published material from the following works:

"Buttermilk Pie" by Susan L. Helwig originally appeared in *Catch the Sweet* published by Seraphim Editions in 2001 and © 2001. Used with permission of the author.

From *The Edible Tao: Munching My Way Toward Enlightenment* by Ruth Penningon Paget. Copyright 2003 by Ruth Pennington Paget. Reprinted with permission of iUniverse, Inc., and Ruth Pennington Paget.

Quote from Exie Dils on pp. 185 reprinted with permission. © 1984. *The Foxfire Book of Appalachian Cookery,* pp. 185–186. The Foxfire Fund, Inc. Mountain City, Georgia.

From *Head o' W-Hollow,* by Jesse Stuart. Published in 1936. Reprinted by permission of The Jesse Stuart Foundation, Inc., P.O. Box 669, Ashland, Kentucky 41105.

"The Old Homeplace" by Laura M. Lauderdale originally appeared on Chuck's Page of the Texans R Us web site, *www.texans-r-us.com.* Copyright 2000. Used with permission of Laura Lauderdale.

"Ramps" by Jeff Mann originally appeared in Vol. 29, No. 3, of *Appalachian Journal* (Spring 2002). Copyright 2002, Appalachian State University. Used with permission.

Recipes from the Heart, http://www.rootsweb.com/~kyfloyd/recipes.htm, by Libby Preston. Reprinted with permission of the author.

"Soup Beans and Cornbread" by Rick Neal. Reprinted by permission of Rick Neal.

From *Sitting Down to the Table: A Collective Memoir of Appalachian Food,* by Anna Ellis Bogle. © 2000 by Anna Ellis Bogle. Reprinted with permission.

"Tomato Gravy" by Glen Simpson from *Sycamore,* a CD by Glen Simpson. Tomato Gravy Records, 1996. Courtesy BMI/Glen Simpson.

Material on honey and sorghum in Chapter 10 from the forthcoming *West Virginia Encyclopedia,* by the West Virginia Humanities Council, Charleston, West Virginia. Reprinted with permission of Debby Sonis.

"Grits-Lover's Prayer" appears on page 97 of *Martha White's Southern Sampler,* by Martha White Foods, Inc., 1989, and is reprinted with permission of the Rutledge Hill Press, Nashville, Tennessee.

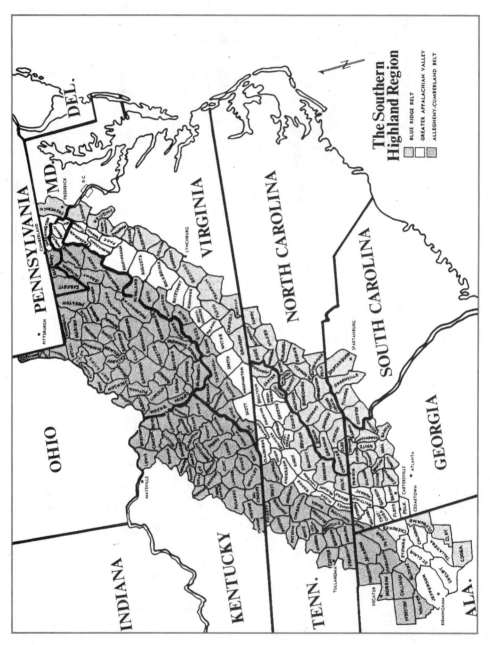

The Southern Highland Region

BLUE RIDGE BELT
GREATER APPALACHIAN VALLEY
ALLEGHENY-CUMBERLAND BELT

For purposes of this book, Appalachia is defined using the 1910 John C. Campbell definition, and like Campbell, this discussion will focus on the mountains south of the Mason-Dixon line and exclude New York, Pennsylvania, and Mississippi. From *The Southern Highlander and His Homeland,* John C. Campbell, University Press of Kentucky.

PART ONE

Appalachian Foodways

ONE

Food Origins

Regional and Cultural Roots

Appalachia, reflecting the diversity of its people, does not have a homogeneous style of food and cooking. Its food has neither a linear history nor a predictable shared taste. Certain ethnic foods are Appalachian because Africans, Asians, and Europeans migrated to the region. Other foods became popular because the region's climate supported their growth. For example, settlers arriving from Ireland in 1860 traded an island for mountains and sheep for pigs. Ireland offered opportunities for fish and seafood, while the mountains offered large and small game. In order to survive, the settlers adapted quickly. They needed food, and they ate what was available. In addition, they wanted to eat as easily and efficiently as possible. This continuous, natural human tendency to adapt gives rise to the many regionally specific foods that interest those studying the culture.

Mountain food may not have a homogeneous style, but it is distinct. It is distinct because the region's people were independent, its mountains offered an abundance of natural resources, and because its settlers mixed with the Native Americans. In short, the region was both isolated from the outside and firmly connected to foreign cultures. Food does not know county seats, state lines, or foreign boundaries. On some occasions, foreign settlers were able to recreate their root foods, and sometimes they could not. By working with what they had, and by adapting their native food traditions to the new environment, they developed rich food traditions.

In this chapter, we introduce the foods that have become most closely associated with Appalachia, and we also trace the ethnic, cultural, and geographical influences on the development of the region's food traditions.

The Most Common Appalachian Foods

One way to get a sense of a region's palate is to explore its most common traditional foods. While there is no absolute list of Appalachian favorites, several people, using a variety of methods, have tried to identify the region's most authentic foods, and the overlaps among their choices give an indication of popularity. First, consider an average shopping list of the early to mid part of the twentieth century: Mountain families regularly bought 50-pound bags of pinto beans, Irish potatoes, and wheat flour. To these staples they added corn, pork, and apples.

Fifty-odd years later, much of that list might still be valid. A recent focus group held in Pikeville, Kentucky, listed a "top ten most authentic Appalachian foods" in order of importance. Topping the list was chicken and dumplings. The other nine items were cornbread, apple stack cake, biscuits and sausage gravy, soup beans, fried potatoes, pork chops, fried chicken, deviled eggs, and green beans.

In her spring 2000 senior thesis on Appalachian foods, Anna Ellis Bogle of eastern Tennessee focused on 12 recipes she considered important. In alphabetical order, her selections were: biscuits, cornbread, fried chicken, grits, pork, country ham, souse (a cold cut made with pork parts and gelatin), kraut, peas, poke, stack cake, soup beans, and venison.

And had you attended the Mountain Heritage Festival of Whitesburg, Kentucky, in the fall of 2000, you would have seen a more extensive list of traditional mountain foods displayed on the chests of your fellow fair-goers. The souvenir tee shirt sold at that event listed the following: shucky beans, fried pies, cornbread, gravy and biscuits, fried potatoes, chicken and dumplings, bread and butter pickles, apple butter, stack cake, pickled corn, fried green tomatoes, pickled eggs, hominy, wilted lettuce 'n' onions, soup beans and cornbread, mustard greens, fresh peas, fried okra, corn pones, pickled beans, watermelon pickles, corn fritters, molasses, drop biscuits, corn cob jelly, kraut, boiled cabbage, cooked ribs 'n' potatoes, rhubarb, souse, blackberry cobbler, baked sweet potatoes, fat back, gingerbread, deviled eggs.

These four lists help us identify important food of Appalachia. But they really don't go quite far enough. To both focus the definition and to suggest the breadth of Appalachian food, consider the following list of about 100 items. Foods are included here because they are popular, have historic roots, and elicit strong emotions.

These foods are of Appalachia not only because the region embraces them, but, more importantly, because Appalachians prepare them and recall them with joy. Of the foods listed below, some are symbolic while others are daily fare. Although food preparations have changed dramatically over the last 50 years, some elements of taste, styles of cooking, and cooking utensils persist causing traditional mountain foods to endure.

First 10: bacon, biscuits and breakfast gravy, chicken 'n' dumplings, cornbread, coffee, fried potatoes, green beans, soup beans, stack cakes, vegetable soup

Next 15: apple butter, chili, coleslaw, corn on the cob, deviled eggs, dumplings, fried apples, fried chicken, gingerbread, kraut and wieners, moonshine, peanut butter fudge, pork chops, sausage gravy, sweet potatoes

Second 25: apple pie, banana pudding, blue cheese dressing, boiled greens, bread pudding, broccoli casserole, buttermilk, chow chow, cornmeal muffins, cracklings, cream pull candy, dinner rolls, fresh apple cake, fried chicken livers, fried mush, macaroni and cheese, peach cobbler, peanut brittle, ramps, shuck beans, sweet tea, turnips, venison, wilted or killed lettuce, country ham

Third 25: barbecue, cherry cobbler, chocolate fudge, chocolate gravy, corn meal gravy, corn pudding, corn relish, cushaw, dried apples, dry land fish (morels), fried liver mush, ham biscuits, hominy, honey, peach pie, pecan pie, pickled beets, poke, prune cake, pumpkin roll, sorghum syrup, souse, squirrel, tomato gravy, wild greens

Fourth 25: bean patties, blackberries, black walnut cake, bread pudding, cabbage rolls, cheese biscuits, cold pies, egg butter, fat back, fried apple pies, fried sorghum syrup, gritted cornbread, lard, mustard greens, pawpaws, pecans, pork ribs, potato cakes, potato roll candy, rabbit, rape, rhubarb pie, salmon patties, salt-rising bread, sassafras tea, sauerkraut, stuffed green peppers, succotash, trout, wine

Traditional Appalachian Meals and Seasonal Menus

While the previous section lists individual dishes, menus are also significant because a knowledge of food combinations is essential to understanding the culture's foodways. Menus provide insight into the context of recipes. Rather than being served alone, recipes have a place that should not be separated from the farm, farmhouse, or the kitchen. Menus also reflect the season. For example, many cooks serve winter vegetable soup as the core of a winter dinner, as suggested in the second menu below.

Brief Summer-Fall-Winter Menus: Each of these might be a simple, home-cooked meal or dinner for a traditional Appalachian family. Notice the emphasis on meats and starches and that some menus include not only two potatoes, but also corn, baked beans, and biscuits.

Soup beans, kraut with wieners, fried potatoes, cornbread, greens, sliced fresh onions, coffee, buttermilk

Winter vegetable soup, cornbread or grilled cheese sandwiches, buttermilk, soda pop

Fried chicken, macaroni and cheese, fried potatoes, mashed potatoes, gravy, green beans, baked beans, biscuits, corn or corn pudding

Fried catfish, coleslaw, skillet corn (rake off cob, add cornmeal, fry), hush puppies, fried potatoes

Chicken 'n' dumplings, green beans, mashed potatoes, sweet potatoes, hot rolls, pone bread (skillet cornbread)

Fried pork chops, fried green tomatoes, biscuits, sliced red tomatoes, fried apples

Steak, baked potato, green salad, dinner rolls

Summer barbecued pork ribs, buttermilk, cornbread, coleslaw, fresh sliced tomatoes, fresh cucumbers, sliced onions, cantaloupe

Desserts tend not to be matched with particular main dish items. In addition, for the last 50 years or so freezers and other means of preserving have allowed storage of rhubarb picked in the spring, blueberries gathered in late summer, and apples from the fall. Thus, many desserts are served out of season. A typical list of mountain desserts might include banana pudding, biscuits with beehive honey, blackberry cobbler, blackberry dumplings, bread pudding, cut-out watermelon, molasses stack cake, peach cobbler with ice cream, strawberry dumplings, strawberry-rhubarb pie, strawberry shortcake, rice pudding, vinegar dumplings, and vinegar pie. Popular cakes include burnt sugar cake, gingerbread served with sorghum, pineapple upside-down cake, pound cake, prune cake, red velvet cake, and scripture cake (a pound cake where each ingredient is paired to a Bible verse).

Seasonal Celebrations: At times mountaineers gather to enjoy more extensive meals. When the family drives up the hollow to the old homeplace for the last warm-weather gathering of fall, or for a mid-season meal to break winter's monotony, the cooks will bring dishes such as those listed below. These menus illustrate traditional food combinations Appalachian families have come to expect.

Fall Menu I: Vegetable soup, chicken casserole, chicken and dumplings, fried chicken, ham, green beans, mashed potatoes, corn pudding, sorghum biscuits, white and pumpkin rolls, loaf breads, blueberry pie, black walnut cake, sugar cookies, fried apples, persimmon pudding

Fall Menu II: Chicken and dumplings, Southern fried chicken, soup beans, cabbage stew, green beans, shelly beans, pickled beets, sweet potato casserole, hash brown casserole, buttermilk cornbread, pumpkin rolls, pecan pie, dried apple stack cake, popcorn balls

Winter Menu: Buttermilk biscuits and country ham, squirrel gravy and biscuits, venison chili, broccoli casserole, shuck beans, scalloped potatoes, blackberry dumplings, lemon butter bars, coffee and hot cocoa.

Comparing Appalachian and Southern Food

Countries such as India, France, and Italy have long histories, but the United States is a young nation, and, not surprisingly, its food traditions are relatively newly formed. Even so, today America enjoys ethnically distinct foods, regionally distinct foods, chef-created foods, and even nationally symbolic foods. These flag-raising foods are potato salad, hot dogs, hamburgers, meat loaf, pancakes, and apple pie. From coast to coast, the nation embraces chili, chuck wagon stew, baked beans, brownies, and bread puddings. From the Atlantic to the Pacific, foods travel.

However, history, culture, geography, and climate do influence regional cooking styles, as is apparent in Southern and Appalachian cooking. Perhaps because of the region's long growing season and mild climate, one of the nation's richest food heritages developed in the South. Southern styles include soul food, Cajun, Creole, plantation, Ozark, Florida-Spanish, low Charleston, and coastal cooking. Traditional Southern crops such as rice, cane sugar, citrus fruits, peas, beans, soybeans, and sweet potatoes find their way into recipes in all of these traditions. And where the land touches the sea, recipes for oysters, shrimp, crabs, and crayfish are common.

Many of the iconic foods of Appalachia are equally common in the South (cornbread, biscuits and gravy, fried apples, and chicken and dumplings, to name a few), and regional commercial beverages and foods such as Jack Daniel's, Mountain Dew, Moon Pies, and Goo-Goo Clusters have crossed regional lines to become common to both food traditions. But geography and climate limited the spread of other foods. For example, seafood is uncommon in land-locked Appalachia, and rice—associated with Charleston, South Carolina, and regions farther south—could not be grown in the mountains. The same is true of cane sugar, which grows in frost-free climate zones but not in Appalachia. This suggests why sorghum, honey, and maple syrups are the sweeteners found in cooler climates including Appalachia. Similarly, Irish potatoes are more popular in Appalachia than in the South. It is simply too warm in the Deep South for farmers to hold seed potatoes over from one season to the next.

However, one Southern tradition—soul food—is well represented in Appalachia. Soul food's collard greens, hominy, cracklings, and ham hocks are popular, as are sweet potato casseroles, corn pudding, pork chops, coconut cream cakes, and peanut brittle. But cultural differences may have prevented the wholesale adoption of soul food traditions in Appalachia. During the time of slavery, Blacks were cooking in the big house, the center of life on great plantations. There, for the pleasure of their masters, slaves cooked beaten biscuits, fried okra, and stuffed ham steaks. They made French-style desserts such as *crème brûlée, pears belle Hélène,* and chocolate mousse. The grand plantation home was not only a farm center, but also a center for balls, barbecues, and soirées, and, at these special events, the host offered distinctive foods. In contrast, in Appalachia there were few slaves, smaller farms, and little of the food associated with slavery and plantations. Like other agrarian cultures, most Appalachians raised, gathered, and prepared foods within the family, and mothers passed these traditions down to their children.

Despite these differences, neither food nor food writers stay within state lines. Southern cookbooks are a mix of coastal and mountain, Spanish and Cajun, African-American and Native American, and Maryland and Georgia. This homogenization is normal and reflects the openness of American culture. Indeed, it is more difficult to separate the Appalachian from Southern cooking traditions than to combine the two into a monolithic whole.

The British Connection

Both ingredients and recipes are obvious venues for cultural understanding. On both sides of the Atlantic, foods such as moonshine, buttermilk, and potatoes suggest links between Appalachia and the British Isles.

Moonshine: The word "moonshine" was first used to describe white brandy that was smuggled on the south coast of England in Kent and Sussex. Early settlers from Scotland, Ireland, Wales, and England came to the Appalachian Mountains with distilling tools and quickly replaced oats and barley with corn. In fact, on the American frontier they made whiskey with almost every imaginable crop, including pears, peaches, apples, grapes, elderberries, pumpkins, and parsnips. For the Scots-Irish, whiskey-making was linked to freedom. They came to Appalachia in search of freedom, and they brought not only their whiskey-making knowledge but also their worms and stills.

Buttermilk: For much of their history before the year 1500, the Irish were a pastoral people who kept enough goats, cows, and sheep so they could practically live on milk (called "white meat") gathered from their herds. They used fresh milk to make cream, curds, cheese, and butter. They also drank milk fresh, sour, and clotted. And they made buttermilk.

The earliest settlers of Appalachia valued milk and milk products equally highly—when the mountains were a frontier, cow's milk could mean the difference between life and death for children. The tradition of keeping cows for milk persisted until about 1950, when rural homes that were served with electricity slowly began buying milk rather than keeping cows.

Today in Appalachia, some mountain people drink buttermilk while eating soup beans or killed lettuce, the traditional dish of hot grease and wilted greens. Others crumble cornbread into buttermilk, and of course, many others do not drink buttermilk. (See Part Two for a recipe for buttermilk pie.)

Potatoes: White Irish potatoes, the standard grocery store potatoes, are basic to the mountain diet. Mountaineers grow them in gardens and buy them in 5-, 10-, 25-, and even 50-pound bags. Mountaineers have an expression that supports the importance of potatoes. "A meal is hardly worth coming home for if potatoes are not on the table."

Just as the English, Scots, and Irish eat them baked, boiled, and fried, so do mountaineers. Potatoes are native to South America, but many people associate them with Ireland. Mountain families bake them in bread, fry them in oil, and boil them in soup. They serve them hot and enjoy them cold. Sometimes they boil them in milk and serve them with gravy as is done in the recipe, new potatoes and gravy in Part Two.

Breakfast: In continental Europe, breakfast might be a roll and a cup of coffee, but breakfast fare in the British Isles is much heartier. For example, according to Mary Kinsella, author of *An Irish Farmhouse Cookbook,* an Irish breakfast consists of rashers (bacon), sausages, eggs, porridge (hot cereal, usually oatmeal, but also a mixture of grains), and grilled tomatoes. Compare that to the traditional Appalachian breakfast, which may include scrambled eggs, biscuits, pork chops, bacon, sliced tomatoes, fried potatoes, fried apples, and gravy. Both offer two kinds of pork, fresh tomatoes, biscuits, and eggs. If the menus included special occasion foods, the overlap would be greater. See Chapter 2, Breakfast Traditions.

Biscuits: On both sides of the Atlantic, quick breads made with baking powder or baking soda (soda bread, scones, and biscuits) are served all day long—for breakfast, morning tea, or Sunday dinner. The ingredients in the triangular, raisin-studded Irish scone are very similar to those in the cathead biscuits that mountain cooks break into odd shapes or the baking powder biscuit formed with a biscuit cutter. See the recipe for baking powder biscuits in Part Two.

Dumplings: Andre Simon believes that dumplings are "one of the most characteristically English contributions to cookery." The "hard dumplings" from Sussex (southern England) he describes in his *Encyclopedia of Gastronomy* bear a marked resemblance to Appalachian slick dumplings. It certainly is possible that our flat, sinking dumplings originated in Sussex. See the recipe for mountain dumplings: slick runners in Part Two.

Apple Pie: The double crust, all-American apple pie is generally not found in the traditional cookery of continental Europe, but it is popular in Ireland. The Irish apple pies have less filling than do their American counterparts, and are cut into squares, not wedges. And while the American pie crust is savory and flaky, the Irish crust is just slightly sweet, smooth, and rich, much like the dough on a fig Newton.

Gravy: Flour-based gravies—tomato gravy, chocolate gravy, brown gravy, sausage gravy, and more—are among the great Appalachian foods. They are valued equally highly in the British Isles, where, as Alan Davidson says, "Should gravy be lacking, the voice of the chief male at the table will be raised in that most terrible and touching of remonstrances: 'Where's t'gravy, then?'" See the three recipes for white sausage, chocolate, and tomato gravy in Part Two.

Native American Food History: Hunting, Gathering, and Modern Feasts

About 12,000 years ago, as the earth warmed and glaciers retreated, a nomadic people, likely arriving from Asia, settled the southern Appalachian region. These first human inhabitants developed food traditions that continued until the Industrial Revolution.

In the early years, they ate mastodon and giant tortoise. They hunted, fished, and gathered. Then, the earth warmed again, the mastodon and tortoise moved north, and the southern diet changed. About 10,000 years ago, native Appalachians in the southern region ate bear, elk, white-tailed deer, turkeys, squirrels, and raccoons. They also enjoyed hickory nuts, black walnuts, acorns, grapes, berries, and persimmons.

The climate differences between northern and southern Appalachia produced cultural differences between the tribes of the two regions. Life north of Virginia and Kentucky was more difficult, and anthropologists say these groups were more egalitarian and less dependent on agriculture. The smaller populations of northern tribes, those from the Maryland panhandle north, were more nomadic than those in the south, with the men who hunted eating more meat and the women who farmed eating more vegetables.

Unlike their northern counterparts, the inhabitants of the middle Appalachian regions that now include Kentucky, Tennessee, and Ohio gradually abandoned the hunter-gatherer traditions in favor of agriculture. They settled in one area and began to plant crops such as squash, corn, and beans. Domesticated squash was first grown as early as 5,000 years ago; corn became a dominant crop about 1,000 years ago; and the common bean arrived in southern Appalachia 800 years ago. By the sixteenth century, agriculture was well developed. In 1549, Spanish conquistador Hernando de Soto recorded that Cherokee tribes were cultivating seven food plants: beans, corn, grapes, mulberries, potatoes, serviceberries, and roman squash.

As the practice of gardening matured, the population increased, particularly in the warmer southern regions of Appalachia. The stability produced by access to a dependable food supply influenced the development of hierarchies, chiefdoms, and an elite class. It also gave the Cherokees the time to develop a written alphabet and tribes in Florida time to build temple mounds. But the development of agriculture was not an unmixed blessing. The diets of the men, who continued to travel and hunt for game, remained high in meats, nuts, and wild greens, while the women, who tended the crops, consumed greater quantities of starchy foods such as corn. This increase in starches is partly to blame for an increase in dental problems among women, and as villages developed, these populations experienced a general decline in health.

Whether using starches or meats and vegetables, these women also developed a distinct cuisine. In their 1951 volume, *Cherokee Cooklore,* Mary Ulmer and Samuel E. Beck identified historic Cherokee recipes, including the following one for succotash: "Shell some corn, skin it with wood ashes lye. Cook corn and beans separately, then together. If desired you may put pieces of pumpkin in, be sure to put the pumpkin in in time to get done before the pot is removed from the fire." Ulmer and Beck's book also includes directions for preparing such dishes as bean bread, chestnut bread, hominy soup, barbecued fish, ramps, bean salad, dried cabbage, dumplings, parched corn, hominy corn drink, honey locust drink, succotash, and parched yellow jackets (made with bees).

Native Americans also adopted American, African, and European foods. European foods that eventually became popular were pork, wheat, barley, apples, turnips, cabbage, and various kinds of liquor including beer, wine, brandy, and rum. Europeans also brought horses, cattle, sheep, and chickens, while Africans brought cowpeas, okra, watermelons, and collard greens. From Central and South America came potatoes, tomatoes, lima beans, and chocolate.

This admixture of styles is reflected in the menus of the Indian feasts the Museum of the Cherokee Indian in Cherokee, North Carolina, sponsored in the 1950s. Including the Native American foods that were often dominant, these dinners were a melding of the food of four continents. The menus included: boiled corn mush, baked cornbread pones, cornmeal gravy, rolled flat flour dumplings boiled with dry beans or chicken, boiled chestnut bread, succotash, flavorful dried leather breeches (dried green beans) boiled with side meat, fresh ramps (a type of wild onion) fried with crease greens (a leafy spring green), and squirrel gravy served over biscuits, as well as dishes made with wild and cultivated fruits and berries.

The Appalachian Frontier: History, Attitudes, Tools, and Food

Appalachia might be considered America's first frontier. Those who struck out from the established coastal colonies in the eighteenth century were among the first Europeans on the trail, the first to see the new territory, and the first to settle. For those who settled, the frontier became a way of life that, Joe Gray Taylor maintains, lasted into the twentieth century. They established communities, built churches, and, at times, fought the Indians.

These European immigrants brought wheat, cattle, pork, guns, and cast-iron cookware to the area. They also brought the technology required to smelt iron, and its impact on the frontier was vast. Eventually they used iron not only to cast cauldrons, ovens, and fryers, but also to forge rails, tools, and rifles.

Even more significant than the technology and goods they brought, these settlers also brought attitudes and values. From the beginning of the nineteenth century and until the coming of railroads and industry 80 to 120 years later, Europeans were drawn west for land, freedom, and challenge. For them, conquering the frontier was a goal much like space exploration was for Americans of the latter part of the twentieth century. Frontiersmen were isolated and their survival took hard work, but those challenges allowed the expression of values that included self-reliance, industry, and individualism. If one accepts William Jackson Turner's thesis that the frontier shaped democracy, then the early settlers of Appalachia had an enduring impact on the American spirit. Like those who conquered the western frontier, fur-trade frontier, the gold-rush frontier, and the grazing frontier, the settlers of the Appalachian frontier contributed to the formation of the American character. For some people, this Appalachian-American spirit was embodied in Daniel Boone, for others it was country ham or moonshine, and for others it was the enduring spirit of the Cherokees and the beauty of their mountains.

These first settlers also brought food traditions that persist to this day. Pork, because it was easily preserved, was a valued frontier food. Farmers killed mature pigs, laden with lard, in late fall or winter. They boiled the fat for use in cooking and soap making, and they salted and dry-cured the meat, boiled bone and head parts to make souse, and simmered pigs' feet for soup. The pork lard that settlers used on the frontier dominated mountain cooking until the end of the twentieth century, and today, pork remains a favorite meat. In addition to pork, frontiersmen raised cattle and used the milk to make cheese, buttermilk, butter, and cream. They planted corn, beans, and squash, picked apples, peaches, and grapes, and gathered nuts, berries, and greens.

In the early homesteads, the stone fireplace was central to the cabin; it provided heat for both the house and the cooking. Around 1825 in progressive areas, wood-burning or coal stoves began to replace the hearth; stoves did not become common in most of Appalachia until well after the Civil War.

A grand mountain dinner during the mid-nineteenth century might include elk backstrap steaks, venison stew, greens fried in bear grease, and ashcakes—cornbread rolled in ashes and baked directly on the coals on the hearth. Corn on the cob, as well as Irish and sweet potatoes, were cooked in the same fashion. After a dessert of fruit pie or sweet cake, pioneers passed a jug and enjoyed a splash of corn whiskey. While the environment was harsh, Appalachian settlers prided themselves on quality foods, and often included with this "high-fashion" frontier dinner were hot biscuits, fresh butter, honey, strawberry preserves, mixed pickles, rich milk, cream, teas, and coffee.

A dinner of this style might be prepared in, and served on, cooking and tableware crafted by the pioneers themselves. The well-established frontier home was equipped with items crafted from stone, wood, tin, clay, and iron. Pioneers used wood to make boxes, bowls, barrels, churns, trays, spoons, stirrers, hooks, rolling pins, and mashers. Tinware was light and easy to fashion, and tinsmiths made cups, candlesticks, graters, simple saucepans, cake pans, and pie plates. The round tin cup with its flat bottom and curved handle was the standard vessel for cold beverages.

In areas either to the east or west of the mountains, early craftspeople also mined clay and made pottery. In some ways this material was not as durable as cast iron, tin, or wood, but items such as crocks, bowls, and pitchers found a place on mountain farms. Settlers made pottery with redware, a kind of clay, or the stronger gray stoneware clay. Wealthier settlers also had more valuable materials such as pewter, copper, and silver in their frontier homes. Pewter was associated with the wealthy and given for wedding gifts. Between 1750 and 1800, pewter was most commonly used for dinnerware such as plates, but pitchers and other tableware such as cups were also made.

The Appalachian Frontier: European Settlement

While we might associate frontiersmen with independence, they were in fact quite dependent on other settlers. In many cases, newcomers owed the very roofs over their heads to the efforts of established families, who helped them build cabins and provided other support. To establish their land position over the Indians, they built quickly, and, as they worked, they kept their rifles close at hand in case of Indian attack. The first log cabins were single-room dwellings that may have measured a mere 16 by 20 feet. The fireplace and open hearth provided heat for both the house and the cooking.

Once established, families were able to take advantage of Appalachia's rich soil and its abundance of wild game. As they prospered, they added rooms onto their cabins and worked hard to preserve food. For emergencies and hunting trips, they made jerky and hardtack, a hard biscuit made with flour and water. At home they used the popular food storage methods such as drying, salting, and pickling. In addition, frontiersmen stored dry foods such as corn, flour, and beans aboveground, and in cool underground storage areas they saved potatoes, beets, turnips, carrots, and parsnips. From this period, dried apples, peach leather (a sheet of dried fruit purée), and shuck beans have remained popular.

From the Native Americans, settlers learned to identify wild greens such as creases, fiddleheads, lamb's quarters, poke, purslane, ramps, and watercress. However, wild meat and animal fats were more important to the pioneer diet than greens. Wild game remained abundant well into the nineteenth century. In the late eighteenth century, J.F.D. Smythe toured the region and in his book, *A Tour of the United States of America,* said that he saw wild turkeys in flocks of 5,000. However, to supplement wild game, even the early settlers raised pork and beef that, for most of the year, could forage in the wilds.

Industrial Period: Steel, Logging, and Ethnic Foods

Industry came early to Appalachia. First, the region was close to the population centers of the East and products were easily shipped to the east coast. Second, Appalachia's abundant resources of water, timber, and coal attracted manufacturing. And finally, its many hot springs and other resources for leisure attracted the wealthy.

In about 1750, when Englishmen Thomas Newcomen and James Watt were inventing the steam engine, a new wave of settlers began their push into Appalachia. Often they were looking for resources to support the industrial development. Appalachia held an abundance of fossil fuels, and after 1840 coal was used as fuel for making iron. From 1750 to about 1850, forges were small and charcoal was used for heat. Once coal became the fuel source, however, Appalachia became a magnet for industrial development. Towns such as Johnstown and Altoona in Pennsylvania, and Morgantown, Fairmont, and Clarksburg in West Virginia, fed supplies to Pittsburgh, allowing it to become one of the world's leading cities of the time. The development of the Carnegie Steel Corporation in the 1870s and 1880s was dependent on Appalachia's coal and iron resources.

At about the same time—1870 to 1910—the systematic cutting of Appalachia's gigantic hardwood forests began, and timbering provided many jobs. Those who farmed in the warm months of the summer could cut and float timber in the cool rainy months of the winter. After 1910 forests continued to provide employment, but at a lower level.

Working loggers were served by male bull-cooks or boilers who prepared large meals that were served from early morning to late evening. Loggers' food reflected the common fare of the region and included smoked ham, squash, cabbage, potatoes, and corn-bread. Breakfasts included pies, biscuits, eggs, tomatoes, pota-toes, and pork chops. Those moving logs down river carried foods such as cornbread, bacon, smoked ham, sausage, chow chow, fox grape jelly, sorghum syrup, and moonshine. In *The Encyclopedia of Appalachia,* Deanne Moskowitz notes that the loggers of this pe-riod coined terms for many foods, and coffee became "jerkwater" and milk was "white line." Donuts were "fried holes," and apple butter was "Pennsylvania salve." The term "sawmill gravy" may have been coined by a logger who was eating country gravy with cathead biscuits and about a dozen fried eggs.

Like the logging camps and unlike the large industrial centers such as Pittsburgh, most of Appalachian industrialization took place in small towns. As industrialists built mines and factories, new work centers attracted farmers who left their land for better jobs and places to live. While some miners and factory workers moved to company towns, others stayed in the country and worked in mines. Those who moved brought with them their agri-cultural skills, and they planted gardens.

Food in these communities reflected the nationalities of not only those who had been living in the mountains, but also of new immi-grants. During the Industrial Period, the Appalachian region at-tracted people from eastern and western Europe, Africa, and the In-dian subcontinent. The myriad ethnic influences on the cuisine are illustrated over and over in community-based cookbooks. The Poles who came to work in the mines and mills brought recipes for *pierogies,* crullers, and pickled herring; Russians brought sweet nut and poppy seed breakfast rolls; Italians cooked gnocchi and strom-boli; and many other nationalities added their own favorites. Many of these recipes, while associated with particular ethnic groups, are still available in Appalachia as well as other parts of North America.

As the new immigrants were bringing new foods to the region, new kitchen equipment was entering the market. Between 1840 and 1870, hundreds of foundries began making ranges used in hearths as well as freestanding stoves. In addition to a range or stove, well-equipped kitchens now included large worktables, china closets, pie safes, and dry sinks, and, after the 1860s, perhaps even ice chests. The Industrial Revolution also brought changes in kitchen gadgets. Cast-iron apple peelers and cherry pitters, as well as tools used to squeeze lemons, stuff sausage, crack nuts, chop onions, shell peas, and slice beans made work at home more efficient. Because they simplified a number of tasks, the new appliances were referred to as "servants" and contributed to the reduction of human servants in large homes.

Typical of the gadgets and the changes associated with the Industrial Period were ice cream churns. Ice cream was fashionable in town and popular in rural homes. In 1864 Nancy Johnson invented a home-style ice cream freezer that included a wooden tub, tin lining, and hand crank.

But more important than ice cream makers was enameled ware. First made of enamel-coated iron and later of enameled sheet steel, these graniteware pans were safe, durable, and easy to clean. The 1895 Montgomery Ward & Co. catalog had an extensive listing of enameled kitchen ware known as granite and agate, including pots, pans, buckets, plates, kettles, pitchers, and measuring cups.

Equally important in the Appalachian household were the glass canning jars kept in the can house (a small building or cellar) for food storage. From 1860 to 1900 canned food largely replaced drying as a means of food storage, and mountain families canned meats, fruits, vegetables, and juices. About 50 years later, they began to purchase deep freezers for food storage.

Postmodern Appalachia: Packaged, Haute, and Hispanic Foods

During the last 25 years, some Appalachian foods have emerged in unexpected places. The legacy food of valley farms and mountain hillsides is now found in the larders of some fine restaurants and even a few fast food outlets. Mountain food today is both fast and slow, and it ranges in cost from high to low.

Foods sold at quick-stop, gas-and-go service stations suggest a range of tastes that is largely homogenized yet also diverse. These stores sell not only gasoline, but also the fastest of fast food—packaged chips, beef jerky, snack sausage, candies, coffee, beer, and sandwiches. Next to the brand-name, all-American, plastic-wrapped offerings you might also find pickled eggs, pepper sausage, pork souse, pigs' feet, and fried pork skins. Deli counters may offer sausage biscuits, potato wedges, cheese sticks, and pizza rolls, but more often the hot food is brand name such as Cinnabon and Burger King.

But these mini-marts are not the only quick food sources. As recently as 1975, small rural towns had few fast-food restaurants, and venues such as McDonalds, Burger King, and Taco Bell were found in larger cities. Today, however, these brands and others such as Dairy Queen, Wendy's, KFC, and Pizza Hut have become primary family destinations with even small towns having as many as 20 outlets.

In a parallel development, large department stores such as K-Mart and Wal-Mart established presences. Later they became mega-stores that contained large food markets. As was true in rural communities all over America, when these stores opened, many small Appalachian markets closed, and the food shopping patterns changed. These changes in retailing affected what families ate. In this case, the stores offered a greater selection of standard items but fewer foods that reflected only local tastes. When large commercial food outlets dominate within a region, tastes tend to become homogenized, and only a few regional items such as fried pork skins might gain attention and become regional symbols.

At the other end of the spectrum from quick markets are upscale, expensive restaurants. Here, chefs create dishes using ingredients from around the globe, across the country, and down the road. Appalachian chefs often look to regional traditions to inspire their "invented" food. Several years ago, for example, the Terrace Restaurant of Grove Park Inn in Asheville, North Carolina, offered an appetizer of fried bean cakes that reflected a century-old tradition. For more than 100 years, mountain cooks have been using leftover soup beans or boiled pintos to make bean patties, but the Grove Park Inn bean cakes expanded on those traditions. The chef used black, pinto, and white beans and added extensive garnishes. Diners were served tiny bean cakes adorned with sour cream, chow chow, fox grapes, raisins, and chives. In short, the chef transformed the simple bean cake into a multi-layered, mixed-textured, complex dish with visual appeal.

Today, while they usually do not announce their heritage (they may fear the hillbilly stereotype), talented Appalachian chefs have been successful in cities from Pittsburgh to Charlotte. In *The Encyclopedia of Appalachia,* Jean Haskell noted that many of these chefs cook in a style inspired by traditions from Appalachian home cooking. They add flourishes to green beans, fried potatoes, and boiled beans. They enhance biscuits and prepare relish. They place fried pies and pumpkin rolls on the dessert menu. In addition, they are making purchases from local producers. Economic and social forces have come together to create a new style of Appalachian slow food where chefs create dishes with care, serve them beautifully, and present them in refined settings.

Far removed from the fancy tradition-inspired chefs are Hispanic workers who have served Appalachia for more than 100 years. The recent increase in Mexican foods available in the region has roots that go way back. Hot chilies, dry beans, lard, and corn are among the foods common to both Appalachian and Hispanic traditions. In addition to these foods, mountaineers are enjoying new Hispanic foods from the many Mexican restaurants and groceries that have become part of today's Appalachian food experience. Since 1980, Hispanics have come to Appalachia in large numbers to work in agriculture and construction, and they have developed communities and opened restaurants. As is true across the nation, even small towns have several Mexican restaurants, and Mexican dishes have become so common that it is no longer necessary to translate Spanish terms such as *tacos, guacamole, burritos, tostadas, mole, enchiladas,* and *chimichangas.* To flavor their potato chips, soup beans, and fried chicken, Appalachians pour hot sauce from slim bottles with names like Gary, Tabasco, Pickapeppa, and Tapatío. Imported Mexican beers such as Negra Modelo, Dos Equis, Sol, and Corona are common. At high school sports events, concessionaires sell cheese nachos along with hot dogs.

In addition to Mexican restaurants, larger towns have small grocery stores that are much like those seen in Latin America. These stores offer imported brands of groceries, spices, and chilies, as well as tee shirts, music videos, and DVDs. These family-operated businesses may also offer native-language television and limited menu items. Roast pork, five-way chili, eggs with red sauce, and chili-dipped candy may be served. Families and older children watch Spanish-language shows, and American customers may not hear a word of English.

Just as the last 25 years have brought a new wave of Hispanics, Wal-Mart super centers, and fast-food outlets, attitudes regarding the sale of alcoholic beverages have also changed in the last few decades. Some communities that were dry since Prohibition have voted to allow liquor sales. Medium-sized towns in some Southern states that went for 80 years without the legal sale of liquor may now have several liquor stores. Before liquor sales became legal, residents of many rural communities had to drive to a large city or go to a bootlegger to buy beer, wine, or spirits.

Beyond ethnic and cultural influences, Appalachian food of today reflects national concerns for the environment and good health. On the health side of this, the 25- to 50-pound buckets of lard once common in local stores are now almost nonexistent. In some areas, farmers have witnessed a decrease in tobacco production and an increase in trout and catfish farming.

Over the last 50 years, Appalachians' relationship to the mountains has also changed. Years ago, hill country highlanders went to the woods to pick, hunt, or dig. Industrialists cut forests, and miners removed coal. All of them left scars. Today, the public is organizing to reestablish the living wilderness and protect it for future generations. Mountaineers seek back-country isolation to four-wheel, picnic, or hike. In addition, the environmental movement has spawned organic foods and farmers' markets. In the Asheville, North Carolina, area, the Appalachian Sustainable Agriculture Project promotes locally grown food, vertical integration, organic certification, environmental awareness, and sustainability. They lobby for land-use laws that protect small farms, and they promote the health value of local foods. Today, public restoration programs are reestablishing the elk, bear, and bison that frontiersmen wiped out, and the developing herds are the pride of ardent followers.

Within the parameters of current history, Appalachian food continues to be a mix of slow home cooking, simple restaurant food, and new ethnic influences. As ethnic groups arrive, the food landscape, while influenced by the past, changes again. The traditional foods such as pure sorghum, fried greens, squirrel gravy, and boiled groundhog are important, but for most Appalachians these foods are an occasional treat or perhaps only a memory. Just as the mastodon and giant tortoise died out due to global warming, some Appalachian foods have disappeared due to changes in culture while a few others continue to dominate daily fare.

Sources

Richard Blaustein. *The Thistle and the Brier: Historical and Cultural Parallels Between Scotland and Appalachia*. Jefferson, North Carolina: McFarland & Co, Inc., 2003.

Anna Ellis Bogle. *Sitting Down to the Table: A Collective Memoir of Appalachian Food*. Amherst, Massachusetts: Self-published thesis, Hampshire College, 2000.

Joseph E. Dabney. *Smokehouse Ham, Spoon Bread, & Scuppernong Wine: The Folklore and Art of Southern Appalachian Cooking*. Nashville, Tennessee: Cumberland House, 1998.

Alan Davidson. *The Oxford Companion to Food*. Oxford: Oxford University Press, 1999.

Kandace R. Detwiler and Amber M. VanDerwarker, "Native American Foodways," in *The Encyclopedia of Appalachia*. Knoxville, Tennessee: The University of Tennessee Press, forthcoming, 2006.

Paul B. Hamel and Mary U. Chiltoskey. *Cherokee Plants and Their Uses—A 400-Year History*. Asheville, North Carolina: Hickory Printing, 1975.

Jean Haskell. "Restaurant Haute Cuisine and Cooking Schools" in Jean Haskell and Rudy Abramson, Co-editors. *The Encyclopedia of Appalachia*. Knoxville, Tennessee: The University of Tennessee Press, in press, 2006.

Deanne Moskowitz. "Loggers' Foods" Article in Jean Haskell and Rudy Abramson, Co-editors. *The Encyclopedia of Appalachia*. Knoxville, Tennessee: The University of Tennessee Press, in press, 2006.

Michael Montgomery. "The Idea of Appalachian Isolation." *Appalachian Heritage*. Vol. 28, No. 2, Spring 2000, pp. 20–31.

Ellen M. Plante. *The American Kitchen 1700 to the Present: From Hearth to Highrise*. New York: Facts on File, 1995.

Andre L. Simon. *A Concise Encyclopedia of Gastronomy*. Woodstock, New York: Overlook Press, 1981.

Mark F. Sohn. *Mountain Country Cooking: A Gathering of the Best Recipes from the Smokies to the Blue Ridge*. New York: St. Martin's Press, 1996.

Joe Gray Taylor. *Eating, Drinking, and Visiting in the South: An Informal History*. Baton Rouge, Louisiana: Louisiana State University Press, 1982.

Mary Ulmer and Samuel E. Beck, Editors. *Cherokee Cooklore: To Make Bread*. Cherokee, North Carolina: Mary and Goingback Chiltoskey and The Stephens Press, Inc., 1951.

TWO

Breakfast Traditions

Biscuits, Gravy, Apples, and Grits

Mother and daughter or father and son may argue about what to serve for an old-fashioned mountain breakfast, but on one issue many agree: The early mountaineers ate gigantic breakfasts. But mountain lifestyles have changed, and mountain breakfasts have gone through a three-phase evolution. First, 75 to 150 years ago, as the settlements became communities and as railroad companies pressed their steel tracks into mountain coalfields, breakfast was extensive. Cooks loaded the table with sliced side meat, sausage, and pork chops—all at one breakfast. In the absence of pork chops, they served pork ribs and backbones, fried chicken, or country ham. With this they often offered fried potatoes or hash browns, buttermilk biscuits, white sausage gravy, homemade wild blackberry jam, hominy or hominy grits, and eggs, eggs, eggs. Finally, mountaineers enjoyed wedges of blackberry, apple, or pumpkin pie and milk, juice, and coffee. They called these foods "victuals" because they supported workers' labor until the midday lunch. In the early industrial period, workers needed a big breakfast because work breaks were short and hours on the job long.

Then, in the 1950s breakfasts became smaller. Some mountain families replaced biscuits with toast, pies disappeared, and bacon, sausage, or ham often stood alone with eggs. Hot cereal and sweet potatoes occasionally found places on the table, and milk, juice, and coffee were constants. Old standbys such as biscuits held a spot with manufactured cold cereals such as puffed rice and corn flakes.

Now in recent years, phase three, the modern era, mountaineers share concerns about calories and fat. Mountain cooks, like others in North America, tend to reserve eggs and bacon for special occasions, and they use egg substitutes as well as boxed and frozen pancakes, waffles, and sausage biscuits. They pop them in a microwave and eat them in the car. Today, most families are concerned about diet, blood pressure, and cholesterol. As available time shrinks, folks of all ages replace home-cooked bacon and eggs with drive-thru or fast-food breakfasts. Home "cooks" cover dry cereal with skim or low-fat milk, microwave a bagel, slice a banana, or toast a pop tart. Fast. Quick. The pastry is crisp. The cereal has crunch. The bagel is soft and warm. Few take the time to boil hot cereal, and, except for those who are "doing Atkins," eggs are gone and so are the pork chops. Breakfast is pastry and coffee from Starbucks or a blended fruit smoothie. For many Appalachians, phase three is a breakfast on-the-go. Indeed, mountain food and culture have changed.

However, from the general trend, opposing patterns emerge. As large, old-style breakfasts have slipped from the daily routine, memories grow, and many seek a break from the weekday hustle, the drive-thru, stand-up, speeded-up, and thoughtless routine. On weekends and national holidays, some highlanders make the time and find a place for traditional country breakfasts. Both men and women cook.

Today, special-occasion mountain breakfasts may include biscuits, grits, pork chops, white gravy, and fried eggs. These breakfasts are reserved for late Saturday morning or Sunday after walking the dog and drinking a glass of juice. When the sun is high in the sky and the weekend house guests have finished their wake-up routine, an occasional mountain family sits down to an Appalachian breakfast from the 1950s. As was done in times past, they set the table, gather the family, say a blessing, enjoy a cup of coffee, talk about people, and discuss the weather. They may serve grits, linger at the table, read the paper, and then skip lunch. Breakfast can be a meal or a party. Cover the table with linens, flatware, dishes, and flowers, and then try one of the breakfast menus listed below.

Traditional Mountain Breakfasts

Fried apples, home fries, fried eggs, bacon or sausage, butter-milk biscuits, fresh butter, hot sorghum, and pear honey

Spiced applesauce, biscuits and gravy, scrambled eggs, pork chops, grits, orange juice, and coffee

Red-eye gravy with country ham, angel biscuits, fried apples, fried potatoes, sliced fresh tomatoes, toast, eggs, and orange juice (Note: red-eye gravy is made with the drippings from fry-ing country ham)

Apple pie or dried apple stack cake, fried green tomatoes, breakaway dinner rolls, fresh fruit, and black coffee

Gingerbread-apple upside-down cake, sausage casserole, fried mush, fried eggs, buttermilk cornbread, sorghum butter, and mixed fresh fruit

These breakfasts differ from those served in, say, the Pacific Northwest or California. In the Northwest, breakfast might include fresh or smoked salmon, huckleberry pancakes, or even Dunge-ness crab cakes. An old-fashioned Appalachian breakfast does not have a French flavor—the tastes of baguettes, brioches, scones, and *café au lait* (hot milk poured into black coffee). Nor is moun-tain tradition anything like an Israeli breakfast of corned beef hash, hard-boiled eggs, pickled onions, and smoked white fish, an Alpine buffet of sweet pastries, yeast breads, farm cheeses, sa-lami, hard sausage, hams, honey, and marmalade, or a New En-gland spa menu of yogurt, mangoes, and granola. In the reality of today's food experience, an Appalachian breakfast may encom-pass any of the above, but the iconic Appalachian breakfast is hearty and robust.

Biscuits: A Common Mountain Treasure

In the early 1980s a wrinkled mountain woman, Exie Dils, sitting at her kitchen table, talked about biscuits. "I was eighty-five the twenty-second of October, so it's been eighty years since I started making biscuits. At first I was so little I couldn't reach the table to work the dough. Mommy had a bread tray, and I'd put that on the floor and work up my dough. I made up biscuits that way a many a time, and there never was one refused to be eat. And I don't say it to be bragging, but I've never been beat in making biscuits" (recorded in *The Foxfire Book of Appalachian Cookery*).

Bread is basic to the mountain diet, and the bread of choice is quick, fresh, steaming, hot, and crusty. The flavors linger. Mountain bread is baked in cast-iron skillets and served by those who prepare it. From every oven and every cook the breads are different, and they vary from region to region and season to season. Biscuits and cornbread are common, not because mountaineers don't like yeast bread, but rather because in rural areas in the mid-nineteenth century, there were few if any bakeries, and by using baking powder or soda mountaineers could prepare breads quickly. Light bread—white, sliced, bagged, and commercial—was a development that came to Appalachia later, and then it was only for those who could afford it. In school settings, when children sat down to eat, they were embarrassed by biscuits. They wanted white sliced bread from the store, and they envied their classmates whose families could afford to buy it. Today, at family gatherings this attitude has changed: Homemade biscuits are the treasured exception while store-bought bread is a commodity that may be scorned.

Beans, corn, and flour have been mountain staples for more than 100 years. Evidence of this remains today where rural grocers sell these commodities in bags reaching 25 pounds. One hundred years ago, however, the bags of flour may have weighed 50 to 100 pounds, and biscuits were served two and three times a day.

In the early history of Europe, biscuits were twice-baked. Roman legions, medieval crusaders, and the armies of Napoleon ate the old-style, keep-forever, twice-baked, hard-as-rock hardtack or stone bread, or in French, *bis-cuits*, which means twice-baked. But today, even east of the Atlantic, few biscuits are twice-baked. Biscuits should be eaten fresh, but mountain cooks might reheat leftovers by frying them. Here in the mountains, twice-baked biscuits are monkey biscuits. Cooks prepare day-old biscuits by frying them in a mixture of sorghum, honey, and butter. This process crisps the outer crust, softens the center, and results in a honey bun—a warm and sweet treasure.

When Europeans first settled the South, cornbread was dominant because maize was the New World grain, and because the climate was too damp for wheat. Later, in the years following the Civil War, transportation improved, wheat was shipped from the Midwest, and commercial flour milling developed. Wheat flour became commonplace, and, for those who could afford to buy it, biscuits became a welcome variation to cornbread.

An important event in the transition from cornbread to biscuits was the invention of baking soda around 1840 and baking powder in 1856. As the nineteenth century closed, the baking powder was often Arm & Hammer, and the flour was packed in barrels which sold for as little as $3.00 for 100 pounds. In the early 1880s, the White Lily flour company of Knoxville, Tennessee, began making flour with soft winter wheat. This flour, which has some properties of cake flour, has remained popular because it makes up into light, tender, and almost fluffy biscuits. These light biscuits have dominated breakfast tables ever since. (See the Mail-Order Sources for White Lily Foods.)

Using barrels of flour and, later, 25-pound bags of self-rising flour, mountain cooks served biscuits with flour gravy, but their biscuits were not alike. Some were tall, others flat. Some were tough outside and soft inside while others were the opposite. Indeed, some biscuits reflect the personalities of their makers: gentle, delicate, and softly scented; or big, high-rising, and arrogant. Other biscuits and biscuit makers are small, slight, and humble; but a few are hard, dry, prickly, and wry with humor. Regardless of personality, biscuits covered with chocolate, sausage, or red-eye gravy are a delight, a moment of calm, a source of pleasure.

The history of biscuits is also tied to shortening, which evolved from lard, to butter, to Crisco, to oil. Eighty-year-olds recall that the biscuits of their childhood were made with lard that was rendered on the farm. Later, many of these cooks switched to Crisco, and recently, as they have aged and followed the advice of their doctors, they have switched again. Now, they stir their biscuit dough with a heart-healthy oil.

With each change in ingredients, the biscuit itself changed. It morphed from beaten biscuits, to baking powder biscuits, to biscuits raised with yeast. The first Southern biscuit was really a cracker. Known as beaten biscuits, these biscuits became tender as a result of hours of hand beating. In this labor-intensive process, as the cook beats flour, lard, salt, and milk with a mallet, iron pestle, or even the side of an ax, the ingredients become elastic, and the beating creates blisters in the dough. Once the dough is ready, the cook rolls it flat, cuts it in rounds and pops it in the oven. Under high heat, the blisters expand and become air pockets that tenderize the cracker. Today, bakers prepare the dough by machine, and home cooks split them open and serve them with a slice of country ham. (See Mail-Order Sources, The Jackson Biscuit Company.)

However, for most mountaineers beaten biscuits are a thing of the past. By the mid-twentieth century, self-rising flour, electric stoves, and large families created an Appalachian biscuit culture complete with a unique vocabulary, fair competitions, and many variations. Biscuits became standard fare with common recipes.

Within the genre, however, those who eat biscuits find vast differences. For example, cathead biscuits are uneven and hand-pulled while angel biscuits are uniform. Angel biscuits are lightened by yeast and baking powder, while sweet potato biscuits are made heavy with the addition of spiced sweet potato casserole. Biscuits made with flour and cornmeal are, as you would expect, called cornmeal biscuits. Cheese biscuits contain grated cheese, cream biscuits are moistened with heavy cream, and buttermilk biscuits are made with buttermilk. Ham biscuits are filled with ham, and sausage biscuits are filled with fried pork sausage. Most biscuits are patted flat and cut into small rounds, but all-together biscuits are baked in a single piece like a loaf or pone, and drop biscuits like drop cookies are formed with a spoon and pushed onto a baking sheet.

However it is prepared, any biscuit—pulled, rolled, dropped, or cut—is the Appalachian base for shortcake and cold pie. To make shortcake, mountain cooks split biscuits to expose the soft center; cover them with cooked blackberries, fresh peaches, or fresh strawberries; and top them with vanilla ice cream, a big dollop of whipped cream, or maybe both. In addition to shortcake, mountain cooks use biscuits to make a breakfast sweet called cold pie. To make cold pies, they split leftover biscuits, cover them with berries and sugar, and place them in a pie safe for the night. By the next morning, the ingredients have come together and the day-old biscuit is a soft, sweet treat.

Biscuits are connected with so many foods that in some Appalachian families, no food, no meal, no day would be complete without them. They are made at home and eaten on the road, or for those who are on the road, chain restaurants such as McDonald's, KFC, Biscuit World, Lee's Famous Recipe, and Dairy Queen sell them warm and packed in a bag with napkins, butter, and honey. Indeed, biscuits balance the meal, fill the box, and warm the soul.

With the recipe found in Part Two, you can begin your search for the immortal best biscuit. The directions yield baking powder biscuits that are light in the center and crusty on the top and bottom.

How Many Biscuits
Traditional, first recorded in 1939

How many biscuits can you eat this morning
How many biscuits can you eat this evening
How many biscuits can you eat
Forty-nine more and a ham of meat
This morning this evening right now

I love my wife and I love my babies this morning
I love my wife and I love my babies this evening
I love my wife and I love my babies
Love my biscuits sopped in gravy
This morning this evening right now

Make my coffee good and strong this morning
Make my coffee good and strong this evening
Make my coffee good and strong
Keep on bringing those biscuits on
This morning this evening right now

Ain't no use in me working so hard this morning
Ain't no use in me working so hard this evening
Ain't no use in me working so hard
Cause I got a gal in the boss man's yard
This morning this evening right now

There's an old hen sittin' in a chimney jam this morning
There's an old hen sittin' in a chimney jam this evening
There's an old hen sittin' in a chimney jam

Keep on throwin' those biscuits down
This morning this evening right now

Mountain Gravies: Sausage, Chocolate, and Tomato

Like a coat of fresh paint, gravy brings out the best of what it covers. Throughout Appalachia, traditional cooks enjoy squirrel gravy, chocolate gravy, and sausage gravy. While these sauces moisten and flavor, they also add unity to plates of eggs, potatoes, biscuits, and fried apples.

Traditional hill country highlanders have many names for flour-based gravies. When they bring to mind the old days, the gravies are country gravy. When they are ladled over biscuits, they become biscuit gravy. When made with fruit and sugar, they are jam gravies. Soaked up with bread, they are soppy, and in the morning they are morning gravies. Loggers and sawyers make sawmill gravy flavored with pan drippings.

However, mountain gravies are not just served for breakfast. Gravies are a big part of any Appalachian meal, and the common options for gravy include chicken, beef, turkey, ham, bacon, bologna, and venison gravies, but mountain cooks also make gravies with vegetables such as tomatoes, morels, onions, and ramps.

In hot skillets coated with the dregs of fried meats or vegetables, the drippings are moistened, stirred, and scraped—in short, the pan is deglazed—to loosen the drippings and melt them into gravy. Highlanders make these gravies after they fry sausage, rabbit, pork chops, chicken livers, or pork middlings. When the meat is cooked and set aside, the extra oil is poured off and flour is stirred in. Flour that is cooked lightly becomes a white roux; flour cooked long becomes a brown roux. Brown roux pastes yield a dark gravy with a nutty flavor, and white roux pastes yield a lightly colored gravy called "white gravy."

Once the roux is ready, the paste is thinned with milk or water. Sometimes coffee or even a cola drink is used. Mountain gravies are flavored with salt and pepper and, as they simmer, the flavored flour pastes become sausage, liver, or chicken gravy.

In addition to these gravies made from the dregs of fried food, mountaineers make other gravies using fruit, butter, sugar, and flour. Like chocolate gravy, these sweet fruit gravies are ladled over biscuits. Recalling her childhood, Ruth Pennington Paget in *The Edible Tao* talks about her dad's raspberry gravy.

> [The] meal began at the grocery store when dad would buy a 15-ounce can of raspberries. . . . He would make a tray of biscuits. While the biscuits baked, dad would make the jam. First he would melt a stick of butter. Next he would add the raspberries with their juice followed by 6 tablespoons of sugar and 4 tablespoons of flour that had been mixed together. The flour never clumps if you add the sugar to it. He'd let this mixture simmer until it thickened. I would crumble the warm biscuit on my plate and let dad ladle this delicious . . . mixture over them.

For gravies like tomato gravy, a roux is thinned with the flavoring that gives the gravy its name. Tomato gravy is a mild tomato-based flour gravy. It is not like tomato sauce, which is made with tomatoes, tomato paste, onions, garlic, basil, and oregano. Tomato sauce is a marinara sauce, thickened by reduction, and served over pasta; it does not generally contain flour, milk, or cream. Tomato gravy, on the other hand, starts with a roux and becomes a white sauce, cream sauce, or milk gravy. This gravy is made with tomato juice or cubed, peeled, and cooked ripe tomatoes. Tomato gravy is thickened with flour and served over biscuits, fresh tomatoes, or fried green tomatoes.

The term tomato gravy is also applied to a second tomato gravy, one that is similar to sausage gravy or chicken cream gravy. In this case, tomato gravy is made with the pan drippings left after making fried green tomatoes. Once the tomatoes are removed from the frying pan, flour is stirred into the drippings, the pan is deglazed with milk, and the mixture is simmered until thick. Rather than being red, this is a white gravy.

To make these gravies, begin with a cast-iron skillet, bulk pork sausage, pan drippings, or tomato juice. (Part Two contains recipes for white sausage gravy, chocolate gravy, and tomato gravy.)

Tomato Gravy
From Glen Simpson's 1996 CD, *Sycamore*
Lyrics by Glen Simpson

Give me an old fashioned breakfast
Continental's not for me
I want food that sticks to your ribs

For all the world to see
Give me big cathead biscuits
To sop the gravy up
And thirty weight coffee
In a saucer to sup

I loved what mom fed me
A sturdy full course meal
Now breakfast is the best food
You can beg, borrow, or steal
Rich, firm and chunky
Bright red and wavy
Wake up in the morning to
Mom's tomato gravy

Chorus

Mom's tomato gravy
Is a treat and a delicacy
I'm no longer anorexic
As you can plainly see
I ain't missed many meals
I'm looking quite swell
I eat tomato gravy
I love that smell

You can have your bagels and croissants
Flapjacks that's my style
Sick of bran and fiber
Makes me run a country mile
Pour the gravy over bacon
Sausage or ham
Give me eggs full of cholesterol
I don't give a spam

Chorus

Repeat chorus

Breakfast Side Dishes: Fried Apples and Grits

Fried apples and grits are also part of mountain breakfasts. At one time, fried apples were as common in some mountain homes as biscuits, gravy, and sausage. They were served in Scout camps, tourist homes, and large resorts. At home, cooks served them from the skillet while restaurants served them on a buffet line in warming trays. This practice continues today. In spiral cookbooks, fried apples are listed as a vegetable, and, indeed, when served as a side dish, they become a vegetable.

The confusing thing about fried apples is that they are not fried. You do not dip them in batter or fry them in oil. Fried apples are not candied or glazed, and you do not caramelize the sugar or thicken it with long, slow cooking. Instead, fried apples are braised. Most cooks fry their apples at low heat on top of the stove in a covered cast-iron skillet. Cooking the apples covered releases moisture, steams them, and melts the sugar. Because apples release liquid after they start to cook, many cook them covered first and then uncovered. Covered cooking draws moisture while uncovered cooking evaporates it, and for fried apples both steps enhance the dish.

Traditional country cooks prepare fried apples with pork flavoring. They fry the apples in a pan of bacon grease, the drippings from pork sausage, lard, or even margarine. Others use just a little grease. Some add lemon juice, and others add brown sugar, or sorghum. Home cooks make delicious fried apples with any full-flavored, in-season cooking apple. Years ago, the apples of choice were June apples. Picked green, they were a firm, sour apple. Today, mountain favorites also include Granny Smiths, Macintoshes, Winesaps, Jonathans, and Rome Beauties. Fried apples are so popular that mountain markets sell them canned, fully cooked and seasoned. Unfortunately, the commercial "country style," apples are a poor substitute for apples fried at home.

As for grits, *grits* is the shortened term for ground hominy grits that mills manufacture from white corn hominy. Most markets offer three kinds of grits: old-fashioned, quick, and instant. Old-fashioned grits cook for 20 to 30 minutes. Quick grits cook in five to seven minutes, and instant grits "cook" as soon as you stir them into boiling water.

Old-fashioned grits are stone-ground, whole kernel grits such as Callaway Gardens Speckled Heart Grits. Having been processed less, the old-fashioned grits are more robust, fuller, coarser, and less smooth than quick grits. Order stone-ground hominy grits from Callaway Gardens, listed in the Mail-Order Sources. Cook as directed on the package, and serve alone as a hot cereal with fresh cream or butter and sorghum, or serve as a side to breakfast with bacon, eggs, toast, and jelly.

Grits-Lover's Prayer

From *Martha White's Southern Sampler*

Our Father, watchin' my kitchen,
Please help me understand
Why some folks just don't take to grits
Like I know you planned.

Perhaps it's 'cause they missed out—
Through no fault of their own,
Their mamas served 'em oatmeal
'Til they were nearly grown.

For that I cannot blame them
And since it's not too late,
I pray some good soul finds them
And puts grits upon their plate.

I'm sure there are grits in heaven
And angels are eatin' right.
But there are no grits below us
'Cept those burned black as night.

Traditional Coffee Preparations

No discussion of mountain breakfasts would be complete without a look at coffee, and while coffee is not unique to the mountains, it is central to the mountain way of life. Offering coffee is a sign of courtesy, hospitality, and friendship, and most hill country highlanders appreciate coffee morning, noon, and night. The earliest settlers sat at kitchen tables and poured the black brew into pewter cups. Today, driving to work, highlanders reach for a thermos or fill a Styrofoam cup at a quick-stop market. Coffee is a constant companion, and it fits today's fast pace of living. But coffee is not new.

Waverley Root and Richard de Rochemont, authors of *Eating in America,* report that "in the year 1725 coffee houses, a social phenomenon of considerable importance, were booming. There were nearly two thousand of them in London. . . ." The Scots-Irish and English that settled the southern highlands brought coffee with them, and they appreciated good quality. Mountaineers want coffee that has a clean aroma, fresh flavor, and full body. They know the difference between instant and brewed, fresh-perked or reheated, and quality beans versus supermarket specials.

Highlanders enjoy some variety in their coffee, and they serve it many ways.

Black coffee: Boiled, percolated, pressed, or filtered, black coffee ranges from a light tea-like drink to deep black brew. To make black coffee use 1 to 2 tablespoons of ground coffee per cup of water.

Once you have made black coffee, use it to prepare the following Appalachian variations:

Light coffee: To black coffee add milk, cream, or canned cream (evaporated milk).

Sweet coffee: To black coffee add sugar, honey, molasses, or sweet sorghum.

Cinnamon coffee: Another name for this is "Mexican coffee," and you make it in a percolator. Use 1 (3-inch) cinnamon stick for every 3 tablespoons of coffee and 2 cups of water. Let the coffee and cinnamon perk for 10 minutes, and sweeten it to taste. Alternatively, pour black coffee into a cup and add a cinnamon stick or sprinkle ground cinnamon.

Chocolate coffee: To a cup of black coffee add a piece of Mexican coffee chocolate, ½ teaspoon of cocoa, or an envelope of hot cocoa mix.

Moonshine coffee: To a cup of black coffee add 2 tablespoons of moonshine.

Southern Comfort coffee: To a cup of black coffee add 2 tablespoons of Early Times, Jack Daniel's, Wild Turkey, or Maker's Mark sour mash or bourbon whiskey. Lighten with cream.

Hard times coffee: When money was short, mountain cooks replaced coffee with a variety of flavorings, but in most cases the process they used to prepare the drink was like making regular coffee. These creative hot drinks were made with chicory, bran, dandelion roots, and even acorns. The recipes that follow suggest a pattern of roasting, grinding, and brewing.

Bran coffee: To make bran coffee, oven roast 2 cups wheat bran and ½ cup cornmeal, at 400°F on a large cookie sheet until they dry and brown. Into 2 cups of boiling water drop ½ cup of the roasted bran mixture, an egg, and 2 tablespoons of 100 percent pure sorghum. Boil 5 minutes, filter and serve.

Dandelion coffee: For dandelion coffee, gather and clean about 1 pound of dandelion roots. Let them dry. Roast the dry roots at 400°F, and when they get brittle and turn brown, after 6 to 15 minutes, pound them with a mortar or process in a food processor. Use this as a coffee additive, adding the dry ground roots to coffee in a ratio of 1 part dandelion to 4 parts coffee.

Chicory coffee: Chicory is a plant with a blue flower and, like the dandelion, is a member of the composite family. The plant is called blue sailors, and coffee made with chicory is New Orleans or Luzianne coffee. Dried, ground chicory root is a popular addition to coffee because it counteracts coffee's caffeine. To make chicory coffee, use a ratio of 1 part chicory to 4 parts coffee. Community Kitchens of New Orleans sells a coffee-chicory blend. (See Community Kitchens in the Mail-Order Sources.)

Acorn coffee: For acorn coffee, heat the oven to 500°F. Hull and roast 2 cups of white oak acorns. In a separate pan, roast ½ cup wheat. Cool and pound with a mortar or process in a food processor. Combine. Boil ¼ cup of the mixture in two cups of water and pour the mixture through a coffee filter. Makes a reddish-brown coffee.

Sources

The Foxfire Book of Appalachian Cookery. EP Dutton, 1984.
Ruth Pennington Paget. *The Edible Tao: Munching My Way Toward Enlightenment.* New York: iUniverse, Inc., 2003.
Waverley Root and Richard de Rochemont. *Eating in America: A History.* New York: The Ecco Press, 1981.
Martha White's Southern Sampler. Nashville: Rutledge Hill Press, 1989.

THREE

Vegetable Delights

Green Beans, Cushaw, and Chow Chow

Green Beans: Shellies, Shuckies, and White Half-Runners

Today, the bean that was once a primary Native American food—the pole bean—includes green beans, half-runners, shuck beans, and shelly beans. The beans can be made up into countless dishes, such as three-bean salad, pickled dilly beans, and green beans boiled with pork. But more on that later.

Even today mountaineers pick beans by the bushel. Then they retire to the porch and, sitting on padded rockers, hanging swings, wooden benches, or hickory bark chairs, talk and snap the beans. Everyone helps. When the washtubs are full, they carry the beans to the stove and ignite the burners. Some families own one, two, or three stoves, and soon an army of cauldrons begin to bubble. This goes on for hours, day and night, and day after day. In the end, when the cooking and canning are done, families enjoy announcing to anyone who will listen the number of quart-sized glass jars (often referred to as cans): 100, 300, or even 500 cans. Two hundred quart jars is common. Whether the beans were broken or snapped, the jars are ready for the can house and the winter.

However, green beans, like other modern vegetables, are available in many varieties. Plant breeders have changed their colors, shapes, flavors, textures, shelf life, and skin thickness. The new varieties look brighter, ship better, last longer, bruise less, feel more tender, and taste sweeter. They may also be bigger, or they may adapt better to mechanical pickers. However, they don't appeal to every palate, and some vegetable enthusiasts make a great effort to save the old varieties. For them, the new varieties do not compare in flavor. Bill Best of Berea, Kentucky, is typical of those who collect old varieties, and he has his favorites. Best's favorite all-round green bean is the big, tender greasy, so called because of its oily-looking seeds, and he grows about 20 varieties of greasy beans. His second favorite is cut shorts or greasy cut shorts. Finally, he likes regular cornfield beans.

In all, Best raises about 150 different kinds of green beans each year. Years ago he started with the beans his mother grew. Now, most of his beans are historic Appalachian varieties. Like his mother, he grows beans that are tender. He finds many half-runners to be too tough, and he says that old mountain varieties are the best. It bothers him when friends say they have lost their family's special beans, and he worries that they will become extinct.

To understand the complexity of Appalachian beans, one must consider not only bean varieties, but also stages of growth, types of plants, and mountain varieties. First, green beans are classified as bush, half-runner, and pole. Bush beans grow in the shape of a bush and may be 2 feet tall, but are not traditionally grown in the mountains. Half-runners are the most popular Appalachian bean, and they send out 3-foot-long stems or runners that twist and curl around a trellis usually formed from cut pieces of brush. Finally, pole beans grow tall and are supported on poles 6 to 8 feet in height.

Regardless of the bean variety, most green beans are eaten at different growth stages. The term "growth stage" refers to the bean's maturity, and the easily identified stages include immature pods, mature-but-green, full beans, mature seeds, and seed only. The least mature beans are French-styled *haricots verts*. These beans are small, immature, and less than a quarter of an inch in diameter. They contain no trace of a seed. While the French often prefer tiny green beans, here in the mountains gardeners let the beans grow until they are thick. When the pod thickens and the seed is partially formed, they pick the beans. Then, at the house they snap the beans and prepare them fresh, canned, frozen, or dried. Dried green beans are called shucky beans.

Many mountaineers also like to let the beans mature further and pick them when the seed is significant and the pod has started its decline. These shelly or shelled beans are a mixture of pods and seeds. This stage borders on dry beans, but holds onto some green bean shells. In preparation, some of the bean seeds fall from the pod, and pods that are too old are discarded. Other pods are young enough to prepare with the beans. Cooked shelly green beans include both seeds and pods. Finally, in the last growth stage the green pod is gone and what remains are beans or dry beans—the fully mature seeds. In central Appalachia, the most popular variety of dry bean is the pinto.

More Green Bean Varieties: Among green beans, growers choose from hundreds of varieties. Most beans sold today are uniform, tender, and stringless. What distinguishes highland green bean cookery is the robust character of the beans. Our mountain beans are thick, full-seeded, mottled, stringed, and meaty. Several bean varieties are truly robust, resulting in the heartiness mountaineers treasure. Bean varieties are specific to a particular area, and they vary in size, texture, color, and flavor.

In addition, different green beans parade through the summer. In the spring, families that plant summer gardens buy seeds for mountaineer half-runners, state half-runners, and genuine half-runners. From spring into summer, they look for the peanut bean, a pink-striped half-runner bean. In full summer, the most popular bean is the white half-runner (a light green pod with white seeds). In addition you'll find that in the summer mountain cooks treasure white McCaslans, Kentucky wonders, white greasies, colored greasies, and other large, robust string beans. Pole and wonder beans are favorites. Three other important summer beans are contender (prize winning), Roma II, and Romano (Italian in origin, pole beans with wide, flat pods). Starting in September, many markets also sell colored (red spots on a white surface) and white fall greasy beans. Later, mountaineers crave greasy cut shorts, also called shortcuts (short pods), and fall white half-runners. Greasy cut shorts are packed so tightly with seeds that they square off on the ends. Later in the fall, mountaineers buy October shellies, October reds, and greasies.

Many bean varieties are named for their region. For example, Logan Giants are from the area around Logan, West Virginia. Letcher beans are from Letcher County, Kentucky, and Pine Mountain beans were grown in the valleys near the Pine Mountain range on the Kentucky-Virginia border. To save time, farmers plant the lazy wife bean, a bean without strings. Realize too that these names are not specific, and beans sold by a name may be of different kinds. What you see is what you get.

For families that keep gardens (remember that 50 to 100 years ago all rural Appalachian families kept gardens) this number of varieties is not a concern. Each region has its favorite varieties, and gardeners usually plant the same varieties year after year. The only real solution to consistency is to find beans you like, save the seed, and plant them. If, however, you don't keep a garden, you might become acquainted with a farm producer or farmers market. In Appalachia, many markets offer the ever-popular white half-runners most of the year. Special varieties such as October shellies and October reds may be in and out of season in three weeks.

At the store, some mountaineers don't look for the greenest, straightest, cleanest beans. In some cases it seems that the worst looking, most mottled beans are the old varieties that have the best flavor. The best beans may have brown spots, shriveled ends, large seeds, stems, and leaves, and in some markets they were picked by hand by the farmer who grew them. However unlovely these beans are, after they're washed, broken, stringed, and sorted, then simmered over low heat with pork, the end result is a treasure.

The end, however, does not come until the beans are cooked for as long as four hours. Robust green beans require long cooking. Mountaineers boil or braise the beans, and they may allow the water to evaporate to the point that the pot likker is thick, dry, or "down to the grease." By reducing the water, they fortify the pork and bean flavor. Some cooks include sugar or a dried hot pepper, others cook green beans with potatoes, and still others add okra. Finally, some cooks prepare the beans ahead, allow them to rest, and reheat them at serving time.

Beans are cooked with many cuts of cured pork, but the cuts with the most flavor are preferred and include bacon, ham hocks, salt pork, and country ham. These cuts are salted, flavored, cured, and smoked differently, and each variation changes the bean dish.

Another variation results from seasonal plantings. For example, gardeners may plant spring, summer, and fall beans, and at some point both the varieties and seasons overlap. Then when beans are picked, they include different varieties and ages, but they all end up in one pot, resulting in a delicate mixture of young tender and older shelly beans. (See Part Two for two green bean recipes: The first includes bacon and the second is dressed with a hot vinaigrette.)

Shuck Beans for Intense Flavor

Shuck or shucky beans are also called leather breeches, leather britches, and fodder beans, and they are nothing more than dried green beans. Drying is both old-fashioned and modern, and drying is a healthy and natural, environmentally friendly method of preserving without preservatives. Whether fresh or dried, green beans are a staple of the Appalachian diet, and their significance is reflected in the music culture.

"Leather Britches" is the title of a fiddle tune that Tommy Dundurand played in the 1920s. Legend has it that he played the song in Chicago's Sherman Hotel, and that radio station WLS attributed its success in country music to the song. Other country music stars are big fans of shuck beans.

In *Shuck Beans, Stack Cakes, and Honest Fried Chicken* by Ronnie Lundy, Dwight Yoakam, the country music star, recalls his childhood when he helped his grandmother prepare shuck beans. "My granny (Earlene Tibbs) would come to the back porch with a big laundry basket full of beans. Friends gathered, and we would sit down and snap 'em and string 'em and crack 'em and throw 'em in the pan. We would sit there snapping and stringing for the whole afternoon. It could become a social event complete with fiddle or guitar music and singing."

While you can string beans of any maturity, mountaineers prefer to use well-filled, mature beans, getting more bean for their effort. After cleaning the beans, they break off the ends and pull the strings from both spines. With the strings removed, the beans are ready for drying.

The traditional drying method is to thread the beans on a string and hang them up. The process is like making popcorn Christmas tree garlands. To string beans, mountaineers take a large needle and heavy thread and run the needle and thread through the center of the beans. When they have filled a string, anywhere from 2 to 5 feet long, or enough to prepare one to two recipes, they tie a loop in the end of the string and hang it from a nail. Some hang their beans in the sun on the side of an outbuilding. Others say sun-drying changes the flavor, and use an upstairs hallway, rafters in the attic, or planks in the barn, or they may use a warm smokehouse, in a kiln, or even in a food dryer.

When the beans are dry enough to "crimp or rattle," cooks transfer them to wood barrels, paper bags, jars, or even flour bags. Today, some families freeze them, but as any old timer will tell you, "They should not be allowed to get damp with rain or fog, and they must be protected from insects and mice."

Winter Vegetable Soup: In mountain homes today, through the cold months of December, January, and February, soup pots simmer on the back of the stove. Made with tomatoes, potatoes, beans, and corn, these soups are not the uniform, consistent, tinny-tasting soups that come from some manufactured 11.5-ounce assembly-line cans. Mountain soups are not heavy, and they are not processed, fried, creamed, or egg-based. These soups are a staple. Highlanders of central Appalachia call them vegetable soup, winter soup, and country soup. In other parts of Appalachia, the names include homemade soup, lunchroom soup, ground beef vegetable soup, thick vegetable soup, and tomato-beef vegetable soup. Throughout the region, a large bowl of winter vegetable soup is a dinner favorite, and some homemakers don't make any other soup.

Quite often today family cooks select this recipe not only because of the long tradition associated with it, but also out of concern for health. High in fiber and low in fat, these soups satisfy the appetite, stick to the ribs, and warm both body and soul. If there is flu in the family or a bit of depression around the house, vegetable soup may be the magic, the cure, or the secret potion that brings the family back to health.

Winter vegetable soup is not only healthy, but it's also a convenience. For working families and those with commitments all over town, this soup can be made on the weekend and served all week. The soup is prepared in giant pots, and then reheated in individual servings or packed into plastic tubs and, in a typical mountain expression of friendliness, given to neighbors and family. Containing beef, beans, potatoes, and cabbage, as well as a little help from tomato juice, this soup is a complete supper. Add grilled cheese sandwiches, hot rolls, or cornbread and it's a celebration.

Almost as big as the soup pot is the list of possible ingredients. Homemade winter vegetable soups have a base of stewing beef, cubed beef, lean ground beef, corned beef, or even bologna. To this base, cooks add tomatoes, tomato juice, V-8 vegetable juice, carrots, onions, celery, corn, and potatoes. Some highlanders add cabbage, green beans, lima beans, northern beans, kidney beans, peas, cauliflower, broccoli, green peppers, and even macaroni. Others use parsnips, parsley, and salsify.

Hill country soups are thick, and like stew, they have little broth. However, from each season and every cook comes a different variation. Some don't like green beans and others omit the cabbage. Others refuse to include potatoes. And asparagus? Some can't imagine it, while others call it the crowning glory of vegetable soup. Vegetable soups, like stews, salads, and stir-fry, are a source of pleasure, a meal in a pot, and a medium for creative cooks.

But even after the soup is on the table, the cook does not have the last word. Around the table some of those eating will fill their bowls with crackers while others add crumbled cornbread. Mountain soups are as independent as mountaineers are. For a classic winter vegetable soup see Part Two.

Striped Monsters: Cushaw Squash

In early July, cushaw vines come into sight throughout Appalachia. In gardens and on small farms, the long green vines with high-growing leaves seem to cover everything. As the summer progresses and the temperature and humidity rise, so do the cushaws. They grow long and tall. At first the fruits are soft and small, but in July they gain size and become firm. Then, starting in September, farmers load their pickup trucks with the green-striped squash and move the crop to market. At produce markets, farmers sell cushaw from gigantic boxes supported by wooden pallets or spread them on flatbed trailers. A month later, at the foot of fodder shocks (gathered corn stocks) and arranged with hay bails, pumpkins, and gourds, this squash appears as an ornament. From the first of October until Thanksgiving, these monsters decorate businesses and front yards, and sometimes they make it to the kitchen.

Cushaw squash is a large, smooth, and hard-skinned winter squash. Some mountaineers identify two kinds of cushaw—green cushaw and white cushaw—but the two may not be botanically related. Both cushaws are related to pumpkin, and southern highlanders occasionally call the squash Indian pumpkin, which is appropriate because Europeans learned about squash from Native Americans.

Imagine the yield of 30-inch-long, 20-pound cushaw. The squash will be bigger than two basketballs and heavier than three bags of groceries. Fortunately, an open cushaw will last quite a while in a cool cellar and even longer in a refrigerator—if there is room. One 20- to 25-pound cushaw will yield enough squash to prepare five to ten different recipes, and rather than thinking about making a cushaw recipe, consider a three-course cushaw dinner.

For a first course, serve cushaw soup along with cushaw bread and pear honey. Follow this with a main course of savory cushaw pie and a cushaw cavity filled with tender chicken goulash. For dessert, serve cushaw cake topped with a scoop of vanilla ice cream and creamy caramel bourbon sauce. You'll find the recipes for this cushaw dinner in *Mountain Country Cooking* by Mark F. Sohn.

When Betty Fussell, the author of *I Hear America Cooking,* visited the Southwest in the mid 1980s, she found her Indian friend, Tony Garcia, growing cushaw squash. He called it "tewa." Fussell describes Garcia's squash as a green and white striped cushaw, one of the oldest Indian squashes and one of the oldest Native American vegetables used today. Native Americans have cultivated about 25 squashes for some 9,000 years, making squash cultivation far older than cultivation of corn or beans.

When the settlers arrived, the first Appalachians were using cushaw flesh for food and cushaw skin for containers. They make efficient containers because after about three years of storage in a dry area, the squash dries out, and the skin becomes as hard as plastic. When the Spanish explorer Hernando de Soto first came to the mountains in 1549, he found the Native Americans using the dried shells to carry water and dried beans. He also observed

Native Americans using small winter squash as dippers. Cushaw is not very different from other winter squashes, but its size and the fact that it grows prolifically in humid climates have made it the dominant mountain squash.

More About Cushaw: Cushaw is a large, mild, earthy-flavored, hearty winter squash. When baked, the squash is moist, meaty, and tender. Either during or after cooking, the squash readily absorbs sugar, honey, sorghum, butter, and spices. Mountain cooks combine the squash with fruits such as pear, apple, and pineapple and, occasionally, they combine cooked cushaw with pork chops, bacon, and cracklings. When cooked, the flesh is generally not as dense as a turban or butternut squash and not as loose-textured as spaghetti squash. However, around the seed cavity the flesh is slightly loose, and in the crookneck end, the flesh is firm.

Comparing green and white cushaw, the green cushaws are shaped like yellow crookneck squash and colored with uneven green and white stripes. One 20-pound squash could easily yield enough for 60 servings of baked squash, but a small 8-pound squash might serve as few as 10.

White cushaw is larger, growing up to 30 pounds. It is not crooknecked, but shaped like a squat pumpkin, and it is white to beige in color. Both green and white cushaws have hard shells. They may have some bumps or ridges near the stem, but the surface is almost completely smooth. Part Two of this book includes a traditional four-ingredient cushaw casserole recipe, as well as recipes for butternut squash and potato soup and puréed butternut squash.

Preserving: Salting, Canning, Fermenting, and Making Cheese

Throughout history, human survival and population increase has been dependent on food availability. Food preservation is the primary means of extending the life of food after harvest. Older methods of preserving food include drying, smoking, salting, pickling, fermenting, burying, and in the case of milk, using rennet to make cheese. In 1858, the Mason jar became available and changed food preservation. Freezing and sulfuring are among the newer methods of food preservation used by hill country home-steaders over the last 200 years.

As in other parts of the world, life in rural Appalachia has always reflected some worry of food shortage. In the mountains even today, when the weather forecast calls for flash floods or heavy snow, grocery stores are packed with fearful individuals stocking up on shelf-ready food. This normal concern causes mountaineers to keep large gardens, can houses, root cellars, and emergency supplies. In addition, extra large, filled-to-the-brim food storage areas are a source of pride and security.

Thus it was with pleasure that families added deep freezers to their home food storage facilities. The home deep freezer, a large electric-powered food storage appliance, became popular about 100 years after the invention of canning jars. But the freezer never fully replaced canning jars.

Canning: While the word canning suggests the use of some kind of metal can in which to store food, in Appalachia today the term canning is a reference to preserving food in glass jars. Those who use the jars then store them in a can house.

In urban Appalachian cities such as Pittsburgh and Knoxville, canned foods, especially soups, became available after the Civil War. In the 1860s and 1870s, well-known companies such as Borden, Heinz, Campbell, Van Camp, and Libby began selling food in metal cans. In 1896, for example, *The Ladies' Home Journal* carried an ad for Van Camp's Boston Baked Pork and Beans.

Over the years, mountaineers used three methods of canning in glass jars: open-kettle, water bath, and pressure. With the open-kettle method, they boiled food in a saucepan, transferred it to a jar, and sealed the jar. When it cools, the food contracts and further seals the jar. When using the water bath method, sealed jars of food are fully submerged in water and boiled. Finally, with the pressure cooker method, sealed jars are cooked under pressure. This method is good for low-acid foods that spoil easily.

While southern mountaineers sometimes can meats and fruits, vegetables are the most popular canned foods, and among vegetables, fresh beans and tomatoes seem to be most common. Pickled vegetables such as beans and corn are also popular. Sauerkraut, cucumber pickles, beets, corn relish, and chow chow also fill the shelves of can houses. Some families also make fruit jams, jellies, and butters.

Salting: Salting is using salt to draw liquid from meats and fish. As the liquid moves out, salt or sodium chloride moves in and acts as a preservative. In the case of pickling, the salt in a brine extracts plant juices. Most Southern farms used salting as the first step in preparing country ham.

Drying: Among the oldest methods of food preservation, drying is the removal of moisture from food. When placed in warm, ventilated areas, foods dry, and once the moisture level drops below about 12 percent, they can be stored for years. Apples and beans are the two most common Appalachian dried foods. However, historically, Appalachians dried most foods including fruits, vegetables, mushrooms, grains, and meats. In the southern mountains, they dried pumpkin, sweet potatoes, corn, okra, and peas. Once foods were dry, they had to be stored in such a way that they were protected from enemies such as rodents, bugs, and dirt.

Freezing: Venison, squirrel, chicken, turkey, nuts, blueberries, rhubarb, beans, bread, and other foods are easily stored in freezers. In rural Appalachia, large food storage freezers became popular in the 1950s and 1960s after electricity became available. Since that time, it has become standard practice for families to have a small freezer attached to the refrigerator and a large storage freezer in a garage or on the back porch. Experience has taught mountain families that some foods such as blackberries, when cooked with sugar and frozen in their juices, will keep frozen for years and years. Recipes that are ideal to store frozen include stuffed bell peppers and stuffed cabbage rolls.

Pickling: Pickles and relish are popular today because they add intriguing textures and flavors to any meal, but historically they were important because they allowed farmers to preserve a variety of foods. Pickling preserves food with salt, brine (salted water), or vinegar. To this, Appalachians add flavorings such as sugar, herbs, and spices, and, depending on the flavorings, their pickles are sweet, sour, hot, or dill. Pickling spice is popular and the mixture may contain allspice, bay leaves, cardamom, ginger, mustard seeds, and peppercorns. Cucumbers make perfect pickles, but pickled cabbage—sauerkraut—is equally important.

Other pickled vegetables include okra and green tomatoes. Chow chow, further discussed below, is a popular mixture of garden vegetables such as cabbage, cucumbers, green tomatoes, onions, corn, bell peppers, and even apples. The exact mixture depends on what is available and the cook's preferences. Corn relish, pickled beans, and pickled beets are common, but boiled eggs and pigs' feet are also pickled. Relish, a diced and highly seasoned pickle or sauce, is made with apples, peaches, cherries, onions, corn, and cucumbers.

Highlanders store pickles and relish in wooden barrels, stone crocks, churn jars, and glass jars. In recent years pint- and quart-sized glass jars have largely replaced crocks because they yield crisper pickles and provide more convenient quantities. Recipes for chow chow and corn relish are included in the recipe section in Part Two.

Burying: To bury food, mountain families would select a high, sloping area, dig a hole or trench well below the frost line, line the hole with straw or corn shucks, fill it with cabbages, potatoes, or apples, and cover them with straw and dirt. "Holing" vegetables was a cost-effective, efficient, and resourceful way to preserve a large crop. A second way to bury crops was to mound them on straw, cover with straw, and then cover with soil, forming an above-ground mound. In *Smokehouse Ham, Spoon Bread, & Scuppernong Wine,* Joe Dabney says cabbages were given "an upside-down burial" and sweet potatoes became a "sweet potato hill."

Root Cellars: A root cellar is a big and more permanent hole in the ground. Mountain families dug root cellars into the sides of hills, under farmhouses, and off basements. The cellars stayed warm in the winter and cool in the summer. In comparison to can houses, root cellars are more moist, and the moisture helps preserve roots. Root cellars had stone, concrete, or wooden walls and were used to store apples, pears, carrots, turnips, green tomatoes, onions, cabbages, potatoes, and sweet potatoes.

Cheese: In 1839, Lettice Bryan in *The Kentucky Housewife* described how to preserve milk by making cheese. She used dried rennet, water, brandy, and fresh milk. With the correct amount of rennet, curd would form in half an hour, and the water would then be drained and pressed from the cheese. Then, according to Bryan, adding flavorings such as salt and butter, further pressure, and aging could produce an excellent home cheese. Bryan advised her readers that too much rennet would make the cheese tough and too much pressure would make it crumbly. In her book, Bryan says it like this,

. . . If you use dried rennet, cut a piece four or five inches square, according to its strength; pour on a gill and a half of lukewarm water, add two large table-spoonfuls of brandy, cover it securely, and set it by to steep till next morning: then, having your milk fresh from the cows, strain it into a large pot or kettle; throw round it a few embers to make it about blood warm, and stir into it the prepared rennet water, allowing a table-spoonful to each quart of milk. Much depends on the strength of the rennet . . . if the milk should not conglomerate and form a firm curd in half an hour, mix in more of the rennet water.

Fermentation: The first step in making beer, wine, and moonshine is to ferment fruits and grains. Moonshiners begin to make moonshine by fermenting corn, barley, rye, and sugar. In the mountains, fermentation is also used to make sauerkraut, cheese, and vinegar. During fermentation, a microorganism such as yeast breaks down an energy source such as corn or sugar in the absence of air.

Smoking: When meats and other foods are hung on racks over wood smoke, the smoke helps to preserve them and adds flavor. In the mountains, most families built smokehouses that they used to make country ham, bacon, and sausages. Smoking is used in combination with drying, salting, brining, and slow roasting. Hot smoking involves the use of some heat while cold smoking is done at temperatures that range from 70 to 90°F.

Sulfuring: Sulfuring or bleaching is also a form of smoking. Sulfur is a mineral used in food preservation, and mountain homesteaders often burned sulfur to create sulfur smoke and bleach apples. Sulfur smoke preserves the apples so they stay light, almost white, in color. Without sulfur, sliced apples oxidize, turn brown, and spoil.

One method of sulfuring was to sprinkle sulfur over live coals and then place sliced and peeled apples in a basket over the coals.

Farmers covered both the coals and the basket with a quilt to hold in the fumes. They repeated the process several times before sealing the fruit for storage.

Another method was to place the apples in a tub, put sulfur in a small bowl or saucer in the tub, light the sulfur, and cover the tub with cloth, again to hold in the strong, foul-smelling fumes. After about half an hour, they stirred the apples and repeated the process.

A butter churn was an ideal container to sulfur a small quantity of apples. Here, farmers placed a single coal in a teacup with sulfur and layered the prepared apples on the dasher over the teacup. They then covered the churn with cloth. They repeated the process three times, and the apples were ready to be sealed and stored in a cool area for use as much as six or nine months later.

Bleached apples taste and feel like fresh apples. Today, commercial food processors use sulfites to preserve flavor, repel insects, and prevent bacterial growth, spoilage, and oxidation. Unfortunately, sulfates can cause allergic reactions, and in 1986 the Food and Drug Administration prohibited their use on ". . . fresh fruit and vegetables intended to be served raw . . ." and required the words "contains sulfites" on any food packaged with sulfites.

Packaging: Packaging keeps food fresh by sealing out moisture, dirt, and pests. It also facilitates handling and packing. For example, a small package of cookies is easily moved from the freezer to a lunch box. While commercially packaged crackers and potato chips are common, mountain cooks always wrapped and packaged their cookies, cakes, and candies. They used a variety of papers, boxes, cans, and wood containers. Later, when grocers started selling lard in large plastic tubs, farmers reused the tubs for food storage.

Today, preserved foods are a big business and most of the foods mentioned above, as well as the many of the different methods of preservation, are available by mail (see the Mail-Order Sources at the end of this book).

Pickles and Relish: Chow Chow and Beets

While today homemade pickles are treasures, years ago they were part of a rural lifestyle oriented toward survival. At the beginning of the twentieth century, pickling was a highly favored means of food preservation. Rural Americans in every region prepared pickles, and mountaineers were particularly fond of sauerkraut, pickled beets, corn relish, dilly beans, and chow chow. In can houses, they proudly displayed bread and butter pickles, dill pickles, mixed pickles, watermelon rind pickles, and pickled beans, pickled corn, pickled eggs, pickled grapes, pickled onions, pickled pears, and even pickled pigs' feet.

Chow Chow: Also called chowchow, chow-chow, and chou chou, this preserve is an important and popular relish. Evidence suggests that Chinese laborers introduced it into this country about 1850 when they worked on the railroads. Its Chinese origin is evident, not only in its name, but also in the seasonings that include a mixture of turmeric and various mustards.

Late in the nineteenth century, this odd mixture of fall garden produce became popular among mountain families, and it has remained a favorite. Today, those who travel find chow chow sold up and down the Appalachian Mountains, but less frequently to the east or west.

Chow chow is a highly variable vegetable relish. While most recipes call for five to 12 vegetables, an exception is the recipe published in 1879 by Marion Cabell Tyree in *Housekeeping in Old Virginia*. This simple recipe includes only onions and cabbage. Another simple Tyree recipe, one of six chow chow recipes she presents, calls for onions, green tomatoes, and cucumbers. More typically, recipes for chow chow include these as well as several of the following: celery, hot red peppers, green beans, lima beans, ripe tomatoes, apples, and corn. Chow chow ranges in heat from mild vinegar flavor to hot spicy to red-hot. Finally, the various Appalachian regions and even families enjoy variations with some chow chows being like pickles and others being like relish or even sauce.

Every edition of the Boston Cooking School cookbook, the *Fannie Farmer Cookbook*, starting in 1896 and through to the thirty-second edition of 1990, includes a chow chow recipe. The recipe published in 1896 calls for 2 quarts small green tomatoes, 12 small cucumbers, 3 red peppers, 1 cauliflower, 2 bunches celery, 1 pint small onions, and 2 quarts string beans. Seven flavorings, including mustard seed, turmeric, allspice, pepper, and cloves, are added to these vegetables, and vinegar is the pickling ingredient. By 1990, the number of ingredients had grown to 16 and included such odd items as whole white pearl onions, cloves, and whole allspice. The recipe for chow chow in Part Two of this book calls for ten ingredients. The corn relish recipe in that section is an easy, modern update of an old farm standard.

Beets. The beet family is a diverse group of vegetables that include table beets, Swiss chard, and sugar beets. A century ago, table beets were popular in Appalachia, while the sugar beets and Swiss chard Europeans preferred were less common. Today, in the cool temperatures of high elevations, Swiss chard has become almost as popular as beets.

Red ball and dark red are the most common table beet varieties. Another variety, golden beets, does not bleed, and the tops are succulent and tasty. Red and golden beets are harvested either when quite small or fully mature. Long beets, a variety that has been popular since Colonial times, are sweet and flavorful. When boiled and served cooked but not pickled, beets have an earthy, slightly sweet flavor.

Beets are often prepared with sauces that include citrus juices or vinegar because acid helps the beets retain their red color. However, more often than not, Appalachians serve their beets pickled. Pickled beets are spicy-hot or sweet or both hot and sweet, and they become bigger in flavor when cooked with allspice, garlic, celery seed, dry mustard, and peppercorns. Some areas prefer a sweet and spicy flavor, adding sugar, cloves, and cinnamon. To these flavorings some cooks add onions and green peppers. For a simple preparation, try the recipe in Part Two.

Sources

Bill Best, CPO 42 Berea College, Berea, KY 40404. Phone: 859-986-3204.

Lettice Bryan. *The Kentucky Housewife.* Cincinnati, Ohio: Shepard and Stearns, 1839. Facsimile Edition: Columbia, South Carolina: University of South Carolina Press, 1991.

Joseph E. Dabney. *Smokehouse Ham, Spoon Bread, & Scuppernong Wine: The Folklore and Art of Southern Appalachian Cooking.* Nashville, Tennessee: Cumberland House, 1998.

Fannie Merritt Farmer. *The Boston Cooking-School Cook Book,* The Eighth Edition, revised by Wilma Lord Perkins. Boston: Little, Brown and Company, 1947.

Betty Fussell. *I Hear America Cooking: A Journey of Discovery from Alaska to Florida—The Cooks, the Recipes, and the Unique Flavors of Our National Cuisine.* New York: Viking Penguin, Inc., 1986.

Linda Garland Page and Eliot Wigginton, Editors. *The Foxfire Book of Appalachia Cookery: The Regional Memorabilia and Recipes.* Garden City, New York: Doubleday, Anchor Books, 1984. This volume offers recipes for cushaw pie, lemon cushaw pie, and pumpkin or cushaw stack pie.

Mark F. Sohn. *Mountain Country Cooking: A Gathering of the Best Recipes from the Smokies to the Blue Ridge.* New York: St. Martin's Press, 1996.

Sue Strickland. *Heirloom Vegetables.* London: Gaia Books, 1998.

Marion Cabell Tyree. *Housekeeping in Old Virginia: Contributions from Two Hundred and Fifty of Virginia's Noted Housewives, Distinguished for Their Skill in the Culinary Art and Other Branches of Domestic Economy.* Louisville, Kentucky: John P. Morton and Co., 1879. Facsimile Edition, Louisville, Kentucky: Favorite Recipes Press, Inc., 1965.

Willing Woys Weaver. *Heirloom Vegetable Gardening.* New York: Henry Holt, 1997.

Order cushaw seed from Gurney's Seed and Nursery listed in the Mail-Order Sources.

FOUR

Dinner Side Dishes

Macaroni and Cheese, Cornbread Salad, and Fall Greens

It may seem that "everyone" is eating out, but rural Appalachians still gather for large dinners of home-cooked food. Some come together for church and family reunions; others enjoy Sunday dinner at the home of "mamaw and papaw." Families partner with food to celebrate births, graduations, weddings, and retirements. They eat together at club meetings, school events, award banquets, and funerals and graveyard reunions. Holidays such as Christmas, Easter, the Fourth of July, and Labor Day weekend, as well as the regular Sunday church service, are also occasions for large gatherings where they serve home-cooked, covered-dish dinners.

Food for the Spirit: Dinner on the Grounds

In Appalachia, one type of gathering is particularly noteworthy. A variation of the potluck supper, dinner on the grounds follows morning worship service, creates a break between morning service and afternoon singing, or serves those who traveled some distance. The event may also be a prelude to a memorial service in the church cemetery; or in churches where members volunteer to maintain the cemetery, the dinner comes before or during "graveyard workings."

Dinner on the grounds gets its name from the fact that food is eaten on church property on temporary tables, retaining walls, church steps, quilts laid on the ground, or any spot that one can sit on or lean against. Shade trees are popular. Sometimes, however, the dinner resembles football tailgate parties: After the service the members set up lawn chairs, open vans, empty coolers, and cover picnic tables with tablecloths. The event takes place next to the parking lot, in a graveled yard, or on an athletic field.

At rural churches years ago, the pastor, elders, and volunteers built serving tables under permanent, open-air shelters. Sometimes they built the serving table in the churchyard between two old oak trees and used metal folding chairs or picnic tables. With the advent of air conditioning and large prosperous churches, church elders began holding the dinners in fellowship halls.

In some churches today, dinner on the grounds is an annual homecoming event held in the fall, while in other churches women organize the dinner each month with the communion service. Sometimes they give the dinner as part of an all-day shapenote or sacred harp singing. In the Methodist church, dinner on the grounds is a congregational event, meaning that many churches gather. The dress at these events ranges from somewhat casual to the more formal attire expected in church. Many men wear a white shirt and tie, while women wear suits and dresses. In some churches, the dress is more casual, with men wearing polo shirts and women wearing slacks. This range of dress reflects the different standards among different churches.

The various traditions related to dinner on the grounds reflect different origin stories. Dinner on the grounds may have originated in Presbyterian churches when the Synod of Philadelphia sent an ordained minister to serve communion. The event was occasional, and the members of several churches gathered at one location. Dinner on the grounds may also be a reflection of the Old Regular Baptist Church practice of annual association meetings and monthly services. These services last all day or even two days. Old Regulars, as they are known, have a service once a month, and on other Sundays, if they go to church, they travel to another location where dinner on the grounds will be served.

Today, the tradition of dinner on the grounds has spread to many denominations and even schools. In Appalachia and throughout the South, dinner on the grounds is held among Methodists, Baptists, Presbyterians, and Pentecostals. Among the schools that have annual dinners on the grounds is the Highlands School in Birmingham, Alabama, which has such an event to celebrate the fall.

A great variety of foods is offered because churchwomen prepare dishes at home, bring them to the church, and place them on long tables. Church members describe dinner on the grounds as an event where "the men often sit and talk while the ladies set the food out." Always, churchgoers enjoy abundance. Glass and foil-covered casseroles, Tupperware boxes of raw vegetables or deviled eggs, baskets of bread and dinner rolls, as well as cake pans and pie plates, hold a cornucopia of goods. Guests form a line, wait for a blessing, visit with friends, and then pass along both sides of the tables selecting their favorite foods. Starting with a disposable dish and plastic cup, they choose from pasta salads, potato salads, vegetable salads, apple salads, and molded salads. The eggs are dressed or deviled, and the bananas are served as croquettes or in peanut salads. Cold salads are followed by hot vegetables, casserole starches, sliced meats, home-baked breads, and mixed pickles. The breads are yeast rolls or corn griddle cakes. Then, on a separate table or perhaps at the end of a long table are the desserts: cookies, bars, pies, cakes, and candies. These may include banana or persimmon pudding, and jam cake or buttermilk pie. Beverages include the always-present 1- and 2-liter bottles of pop and iced tea.

Sometimes the foods within these categories represent the varied ethnic backgrounds of those present whether they are African-American, Eastern European, English, German, Hispanic, Italian, Native American, Scots-Irish, or Swiss, all of whom have contributed to the region's food traditions. But more often than specialty ethnic foods, the guests bring foods that are all-American such as potato salad, chocolate chip cookies, macaroni and cheese, and chicken salad. In some churches, the event is an annual affair and the menu, like a Thanksgiving dinner, is highly ritualistic. On the other hand, when only a few volunteers prepare the dinner, the choices are limited and may include items such as commercially fried chicken and hot dogs.

Dinner on the grounds is integral to the region's Christian tradition. For some churchgoers, both the meal and the space are sacred. Others see the meal as a continuation of the Last Supper, and in some churches the members hold dinner on the grounds with communion. In this case, the communion service is held occasionally, maybe once a month, at a host church, which provides the meal. These meals reflect the integration of Christian life with the family and community. Finally, some pastors talk about how the various food dishes brought to dinner on the grounds are like the talents members bring to the church. Dinner on the grounds, they say, reflects church service with tables for singing, teaching, praying, or preaching. But whatever the symbolism, members leave dinner on the grounds saying, "We feasted and fellowshipped."

Casseroles: Casseroles are among the most popular dishes served at dinner on the grounds, and like so much mountain cooking of the late twentieth century, they are loaded with goodies from fat to sugar to cheese. Specifically, cooks create tempting dishes by enhancing grains, vegetables, and meats with milk, cheese, cream cheese, eggs, Velveeta cheese, butter, bread, and rich crackers. To one cheese mountain cooks add another, and to cream soup bases they add cheese. Cheese not only thickens sauce, but it also enhances flavor and texture. For example, broccoli baked in a casserole with crushed crackers, cream soup, and cheese becomes a tasty vegetable most unlike the original. Some casseroles are one-dish meals in that they combine protein, starch, and vegetables.

Mountain cooks prepare meat, seafood, poultry, grains, and vegetable casseroles. With rice or pasta, they use casseroles to stretch proteins. Baked in a single dish, casseroles are often the main event at a home-cooked meal. At a dinner on the grounds or community suppers, however, casseroles are more often side dishes in that they supplement the meat. A topping of cracker crumbs and cheese adds flavor and texture, while green bell peppers and tomatoes add color and moisture. The garnish or topping reflects casserole ingredients or enhances the texture. For example, if the casserole contains hard-boiled eggs, the cook might add a garnish of sliced hard-boiled egg. In a macaroni and cheese casserole, Parmesan cheese is used as a topping.

In addition to toppings, casseroles include binders. When cooks stir eggs, cheese, milk, cream, or flour into a hot liquid, the liquid thickens and forms a binder or sauce. Common binders include white sauce, cheese sauce, and canned cream soups. Binders hold casseroles together, and they contain the many signs of traditional Appalachian cooking such as mayonnaise, cheese, and cream.

Broccoli casseroles as well as other vegetable casseroles may be rich or light. Some cooks make them cheesy by adding Velveeta, Cheese Whiz, or American cheese; others add grains, especially rice, and others keep them light—light on salt, starch, or fat.

Are these casseroles made with canned soup? Yes and no. Many cooks make broccoli casseroles with commercially prepared cream of mushroom soup, and some use canned cream of chicken, Cheddar cheese, or cream of celery soup. But others make broccoli casseroles without help from cans, binding the dish with crackers, white sauce, cheese, or cornstarch. Depending on their goals, they might choose liquids such as skim milk, yogurt, whole milk, cream, or eggs.

Those who prefer rich casseroles use real cream, butter, eggs, bacon, crushed potato chips, mayonnaise, salad dressing, French fried onions, and buttered Ritz crackers. For light casseroles, others use skim milk, fat-free cottage cheese, and dry bread crumbs. Some make the white sauce without cheese. (The broccoli casserole recipe in Part Two is a compromise between rich and light.)

Another popular casserole, saucy macaroni and cheese (the recipe is also in Part Two), is less well documented, but no less frequently served, than items such as red-eye gravy or biscuits and gravy. In Appalachian homes, schools, restaurants, and family and church gatherings, as well as across America, macaroni and cheese is ever-present daily fare. In fact, no Appalachian menu would be complete without mac and cheese.

Finally, casseroles are not only the prepared foods in the dish, they are also the dishes themselves. Casseroles are oven-proof baking dishes made from china, ceramic, glass, stainless steel, cast iron, or copper. Most casseroles are decorative dishes so that when the food is removed from the oven, it can be served without being transferred to another dish. In support of this practice, large markets sell casserole dishes that have fitted serving baskets or serving stands. Another useful device is the insulated carrying case that holds the dish snugly, keeps it warm, and includes handles.

Appalachian Community Cookbooks

Mountaineers not only like to share their casseroles, but they also like to share the recipes in small plastic-bound books. Casseroles, as well as other mountain foods, are well documented in community cookbooks. For example, *Our Daily Bread* is a community cookbook published by the Island Creek Old Regular Baptist Church of Pikeville, Kentucky. It includes six broccoli casserole recipes. Like other community cookbooks, the recipes reflect the community's most popular and most prized dishes. The six broccoli casserole recipes suggest the popularity of the dish in Pikeville. The index also lists four recipes for cranberry salad, three for sweet potato casserole, and three for peanut butter fudge. Another book has two for hot dog chili, three for pumpkin cakes, and three for raw apple cakes. In Appalachia, community cookbooks are loaded with sweets.

Like the restaurant ratings in a Zagat survey, the entries in these cookbooks suggest recipe popularity. While some cookbook committees develop recipes around a theme, others refuse to leave out any submissions, and in so doing create books that are a democratic form of history. Just as a recipe is only a moment in time, the contents of community cookbooks mirror both a place and a time. The books include volunteer submissions, and the volunteers tend to submit recipes they find exciting or in demand.

While the individual recipes are secular in nature, Appalachian community cookbooks reflect a focus on religion. In some cases, the community cookbook is an outgrowth of dinner on the grounds; in other cases the book is a fund-raiser for a group within the church such as the women's prayer circle. In Appalachia, as elsewhere, the books are often prepared by churches, but many are also prepared by schools, sports booster clubs, extension homemakers clubs, Rotary-Anns (wives of Rotarians), women's clubs, extended families, community theater groups, 4-H Clubs, and the Junior League. The religious context of these books is reflected in their titles: *Sharing Our Best, Saint Francis in the Kitchen, Come and Dine, Heavenly Fare,* and a title that is typical of many, *The Robinson Creek Old Regular Baptist Cookbook.* Other titles also reflect themes of time or place: *Let Freedom Ring,* a tribute to America; *How to Feed a Panther,* a football boosters club; *Barter Seasonings,* a community theater; *Newsome Branch*

Kitchen Kanfusion and *The Crisp Family's 7th Reunion, Pumpkin Creek Lodge, Thanksgiving, 1991*, family cookbooks.

Usually, the motivation to produce these recipe collections is profit, and to make a profit organizing committees seek a large number of recipe contributors. In some cases, however, the primary goal seems to be to make a point about cooking, family history, school spirit, cultural diversity, or geographic identity. However, even the books that do not aim to record history or press a social theme do it exceptionally well. When prepared for a family reunion or a fiftieth wedding anniversary, the books preserve family traditions. When prepared for a sorghum festival, they emphasize sorghum, and if prepared for a cranberry festival, they emphasize cranberries. So while the books are not written as memoirs or public relations pieces, they serve these functions, and they represent the collective memory of a church, family, or community.

While some community cookbooks show evidence of a strong editor, others are especially representative of the cooks that submit recipes. This means that while the recipes may be included untested, the organizers always compile the best of what the church has to offer. Once the recipes are collected and put in order, the committee sends them to a community cookbook publisher. These printers-publishers then put the books into a standard format and add section dividers as well as stock pages of cooking tips. When published in the standard format, community cookbooks are small books with color covers and plastic spiral bindings. They usually measure 5½ by 8½ inches in size and have a single printing with a typical number being 750 copies.

Once the books arrive back from the printer-publisher, the committee becomes the sales team and sells the books person-to-person as opposed to by mail or Internet. Only the most dynamic committees get these books sold at Amazon.com or Barnes and Noble. More often, the books are found on the checkout counters of local drug stores or in the back of the church. After they are collected at home, and when families move or clean out, the books are given to younger family members, sold at garage sales, or even tossed in the trash.

For every generalization one might make about these books, exceptions exist. As an example of a church-published community cookbook, *Our Daily Bread* includes about 450 recipes on 165 pages. The brief recipes are signed, and the publisher develops an index. Appalachian community cookbooks, however, may have as few as 70 recipes or as many as 1,000.

Characteristic of the books is what may be missing. *Our Daily Bread* does not include a publication date or price. Others omit the names of the committee or the editor (they do not want to show off), and many omit the address of the church or organization. *Our Daily Bread* includes information about church history, officers, and worship times. The introductory material suggests strong dedication to the church as well as strong church leadership. In addition, these books tend to omit certain common foods such as soup beans, greens, or cornbread. These most common mountain recipes are omitted because cookbook committees do not give them any thought or no group member submits them.

Once the recipes are collected, a committee of volunteers compiles the books. That, however, is easier said than done. Some churches produce a book once and never again. Others attempt to repeat the project every five to ten years, and sometimes the project gets a start and then peters out. In the case of one church, a problem with the pastor caused the cookbook committee to stop work. Some of the committees publish recipes from about ten contributors while other committees include submissions from more than 100. Rural churches are small while larger organizations such as universities can draw on more volunteers, pushing the number of contributors to several hundred.

Not only does a committee prepare the book, but the committee also reflects the economic status of the church. Sociologists tell us that different churches, civic groups, and social clubs in this country attract different social classes, and like the difference between Wal-Mart, Target, and Bloomingdale's, these books represent the interests of different socioeconomic levels. For students of traditional culture, working class churches such as the Old Regular or Primitive Baptists provide the best recipes. Other groups tend to value exotic foods or follow food trends. The simpler books are loaded with recipes that reflect the immediate community, and what they lack in graphics or color, they make up for with recipes that work.

In Appalachia, the process of developing cookbooks by committee has been going on for more than 100 years. Among the early fund-raiser cookbooks, the First Presbyterian Church of

Paris, Kentucky, published *Housekeeping in the Bluegrass* in 1875, and the book flourished through nine printings and 20,000 copies. Another important but newer book is the 1907 *Knoxville Cook Book* developed by the Knoxville Women's Building Association. *Smoky Mountain Magic* compiled by The Junior League of Johnson City, Tennessee, Inc., was first published in 1960 and is still in print.

In the highlands of central Appalachia, several of these cookbook titles stand out. These books are larger and more permanent than most community cookbooks but still fit the genre. *What's Cooking in Kentucky* and its companion *What's Cooking for the Holidays* got their start in a church in Floyd County, Kentucky, and were bought by Irene Hayes who has kept them in print since 1970. With 750 pages, a large format, and hundreds of photos, *Home and Away: A University Brings Food to the Table,* published in 2000, traces the food and alumni of East Tennessee State University.

An example of a book developed by an extended family is the *W-Hollow Cookbook* published by the Jesse Stuart Foundation in 1990. This book is not a standard, spiral-bound community cookbook; it is bound in a hard-cover, 8½ by 11-inch format, and includes photographs, poetry, and chapter introductions. In spirit, however, the book is a community cookbook in that about 175 of Jesse Stuart's relatives contributed, and each recipe is signed. The book has about 1,000 recipes and is indeed a treasure of Appalachian cooking as well as a tribute to a famous Appalachian author (for a discussion of Jesse Stuart see Chapter 6). The inclusions are extensive, with 13 cornbread recipes, four stack cakes, four applesauce cakes, and many more. The book is available from the Jesse Stuart Foundation (see Mail-Order Sources).

Fall Greens, Rape, and Country Ham

Popular fall greens include collards, turnips, rape, and kale. Mountain cooks cut and wash masses of these green leaves, and then boil them with cured pork for long periods. When the dish is on the table, diners sop up the pot likker (broth) with cornbread. In fact, hearty fall greens differ from the tender spring greens such as lettuce, spinach, mustard, creases, poke, lamb's quarters, Swiss chard, and watercress in that spring greens are more tender and require less time to cook. Other common wild spring greens include chickentoe, dandelions, dock, fiddleheads, purslane, ramps, shepherd's purse, and watercress.

In restaurants all across North America today, many chefs serve undercooked, almost raw vegetables. Yes, the vegetables are bright in color; however, they are also tough to chew, hard to digest, and lacking in flavor. For traditional hill folk, the process is different. They simmer fall greens with country ham, salt pork, or smoked ham hocks for one, two, or three hours. Slow cooking develops the flavor and tenderizes both the meat and greens. The result is a muddy-green, drab olive, almost brown color, and it is full of taste and easy to chew and digest. Slow-cooked greens are an example of simple mountain cooking that requires patience.

About Rape: One of the less common fall greens is rape. Rape is a leafy cabbage-like green with a long history in the South. In 1941, Mrs. S.R. Dull in *Southern Cooking* discussed rape and suggested cooking it as you would kale. Rape plants produce tall, spreading, broad-leaf greens and scattered flower clusters or broccoli-like florets. Many mountaineers enjoy this wonder green for its flavor, which is rich, warm, spicy, and aromatic.

Because of its popularity and wide distribution, rape is known by many common names including broccoli rabe, broccoli Arab, rapeweed, broccoli raab, and in Italian, *brocoletti di rape,* and *rapini.* The Latin name for rape is *Brassica napus,* an herb of the brassica family.

Under the name of broccoli rabe, rape is making a comeback. David Rosengarten, writing in the trendy New York *Dean & Deluca Cookbook* talks about rape's flavor as being controversial. He says people either love or hate it, and he describes the flavor as a cross between collards and kale but cleaner and with a slight sting. Many a mountaineer, however, would argue with Rosengarten about rape's flavor being strong enough to be controversial. Mountaineers who have enjoyed rape greens for generations cherish the flavor, but do not think of it as strange, strong, or as Rosengarten says, controversial.

Mountaineers prepare rape like other fall greens including turnips, collards, and kale. Indeed, they frequently cook these greens in the same pot. Mountaineers raise rape because it grows easily, produces an abundant crop, tastes good, and, of course, because this green is a regional specialty that is not found on the menu of many restaurants.

Wilted Greens and Killed Lettuce

Darrel Rose, the postmaster of Pikeville, Kentucky, tells a story about killed lettuce. "An old fellow once told me that killed lettuce put him to sleep. The old man said, 'When I eat kilt lettuce I have to go straight to the couch and to sleep.' Perhaps," Darrel continued, "the combination of bacon grease and onions has an anesthetizing quality." Others remember killed or kilt lettuce because their grandmothers kept a grease pot on the back of the stove and used the bacon drippings for cooking. These drippings were easily heated, and then poured over the lettuce.

When this salad was served, the new-season harvest had begun. Historically, mountaineers looked forward with excitement to the first spring salad known as kilt, killed, wilted, or smothered lettuce. After a long winter of eating foods such as soup beans and cornbread, they gathered wild greens or garden lettuce and green onions. Today, many appreciate lettuce that is picked fresh from the garden while others prefer wild greens such as dandelion greens, poke, or tanglegut. Some use spinach or another leaf lettuce such as buttercrunch, red sails, or bib. Others use romaine or iceberg, but these long-growing, late-season varieties were not grown in the mountains and are not the best for these salads.

Once a cook has picked the greens and washed them carefully, he or she pours a stream of hot bacon grease over the greens, killing or wilting the lettuce. Some use hot buttermilk or hot vinaigrette in place of bacon grease. Others talk about killing the lettuce for two minutes while still others do not pour the grease, but prefer to stir the lettuce in the hot skillet with the hot grease.

Killed lettuce is a mountain variation on the theme of wilted salads. The use of hot bacon grease to wilt greens is widely adapted in this country and abroad. In the 1946 edition of the *Joy of Cooking,* this salad appears as wilted lettuce and wilted lettuce with cream dressing. To make the cream dressing, Irma S. Rombauer instructs you to add heavy cream to the bacon grease, and vinegar, salt, and pepper. In the 1973 *Joy of Cooking,* Marion Rombauer Becker changed the name to wilted greens and suggested using head lettuce, shredded cabbage, or spinach. Today, some cooks add mushrooms. Others use only lettuce and call the dressing bacon dressing or hot salad dressing. A quick but also modern adaptation is to heat a bottle of Italian dressing and use it to wilt lettuce.

Simone Beck, in her 1991 book *Food and Friends,* discusses a hot vinaigrette. Beck, the co-author of Julia Child, calls the dressing Lorraine dressing, and adds dandelion greens to a pan of hot pork grease, stirs them, and then serves the whole mass tepid. In Alsace, France, a similar wilted salad is popular. In this case, according to Richard Olney's *Simple French Food,* the Alsatians wilt cabbage in hot water, and then douse it with hot bacon fat, vinegar, and olive oil.

While Simone Beck uses dandelion greens and Richard Olney suggests cabbage, many mountaineers grow a traditional variety of lettuce. Up and down the Appalachians from the Savage in the north to the Snowbirds in the south, the lettuce of choice is a fragile, leafy, early spring lettuce known as black-seeded Simpson. Simpson is an heirloom lettuce, one that grows quickly and then goes to seed. Some hill folk call it cut-and-come-again lettuce because when the leaves are cut off at the base, the plant sprouts again. If planted on the first day of March, the lettuce is ready 45 days later or in mid-April. To extend the season, gardeners force the lettuce, planting it in cold frames or covering seedlings with plastic on cold nights. They also plant new seeds at two-week intervals from early March to mid-April. In most of southern Appalachia, the season cannot be extended because this lettuce cannot grow in hot weather. But black-seeded Simpson is ideal because it grows fast and matures early.

While killed or wilted lettuce is a traditional mountain salad, the recipe for Appalachian pork salad in Part Two is a hearty composed salad that combines hot pork with cold lettuce. To prepare it, select several different cuts of pork including diced raw side meat, fried salt pork, or crispy cooked bacon. You can add the trimmings from smoked ham hocks or use 1-inch strips of cold biscuit-style fried country ham, hot fried bologna cut in strips, fried pork link sausage, fried bulk pork sausage patties, slices of boiled pig's feet, or even pork loin medallions. Combining various cuts of pork, lettuce, and tomatoes with cornbread and buttermilk results in a hearty meal.

Sources

Julia Child and Simone Beck. *Mastering the Art of French Cooking,* New York: Alfred A. Knopf, 1961.

Mrs. S.R. Dull. *Southern Cooking*. New York: Grosset & Dunlap, Inc. 1968. (First published in 1928.)

Elkhorn Old Regular Baptist Church. *Let Freedom Ring: Recipes from Elkhorn and Friends*. Jenkins, Kentucky: Elkhorn Old Regular Baptist Church, 2002.

Irene Hayes. *What's Cooking for the Holidays*. Hueysville, Kentucky: The T.I. Hayes Publishing Company, Inc., 1984.

Irene Hayes. *What's Cooking in Kentucky*. Hueysville, Kentucky: The T.I. Hayes Publishing Company, Inc., 1982.

Island Creek Baptist Church. *Our Daily Bread*. Collierville, Tennessee: Fundcraft Publishing, circa 1995.

Arlene Johnson, Alvin Little, and Virgil Mullins. *Newsome Branch Kitchen Kanfusion: From the Descendants of Henry and Martha Ann Isaac Mullins*. Olathe, Kansas, 1992.

Junior League. *Smoky Mountain Magic: A Superb View of Treasured Recipes*. Johnson City, Tennessee: The Junior League, 1960.

Glennis Stuart Liles, Compiler, and Chuck D. Charles, Editor. *The W-Hollow Cookbook*. Ashland, Kentucky: The Jesse Stuart Foundation, 1992.

Richard Olney. *Simple French Food*. New York: Macmillan Publishing Company, 1974.

Pikeville Cheerleaders. *How to Feed a Panther*. Kearney, Nebraska: Morris Press, 1998.

Robinson Creek Old Regular Baptist Church, Robinson Creek, Kentucky. *Robinson Creek Old Regular Baptist Cookbook*. Kearney, Nebraska: Morris Press, 2001.

Irma S. Rombauer. *The Joy of Cooking: A Compilation of Reliable Recipes with an Occasional Culinary Chat*. Indianapolis, Indiana: The Bobbs-Merrill Company, Inc., 1946.

Irma S. Rombauer and Marion Rombauer Becker. *Joy of Cooking*. Indianapolis, Indiana: The Bobbs-Merrill Company, Inc., 1973.

David Rosengarten. *Dean & Deluca Cookbook*. New York: Random House, 1996.

Elizabeth Ross. *Kentucky Keepsakes*. Kuttawa, Kentucky: McClanahan Publishing House, Inc., 1996.

St. Francis Episcopal Church. *Saint Francis in the Kitchen*. Greensboro, North Carolina: St. Francis Episcopal Church, 1974.

Fred W. Sauceman. *Home and Away: A University Brings Food to the Table*. Johnson City, Tennessee: East Tennessee State University, 2000.

Order black-seeded Simpson lettuce seed from Gurney's Seed and Nursery Co., listed in the Mail-Order sources.

FIVE

Farm Starches & School Lunches

Soup Beans, Potatoes, and Slick Runner Dumplings

Dry Beans, Pintos, and Soup Beans

When the first frost nips the poke leaves and the sun is so low in the sky it fails to reach deep mountain hollows, soup beans come into their own. Fifty years ago they often simmered on the back of the stove all winter, and in the eighteenth century when hill country householders were truly pioneers on the frontier, the combination of soup beans, fried potatoes, and cornbread provided sufficient protein for healthy survival. Initially, the original Americans gave the settlers knowledge of beans and corn. The native people were successful farmers, and early European settlers learned from them how to grow, dry, and store pinto beans. In later times, grocers imported the beans from the Midwest, Southwest, and even Mexico.

Like stores across America, mountain markets today sell pinto beans, white beans, black beans, red kidneys, and great northerns in one-pound bags. In the fall, however, mountain markets also sell pinto beans in 10-, 25-, and even 40-pound bags. Forty pounds. This size bag suggests a diet staple.

Pinto beans, also called soup beans or brown beans, and known in Latin as *Phaselous vulgaris L.,* are an Appalachian specialty served at home, school, and work. Along with cornmeal and wheat flour, dry beans are a first choice, a winter choice, a traditional food. The dominance of the pinto may not be so dramatic north of Kentucky and north of southern West Virginia, but generally this bean is common in central and southern Appalachia. The recipes calling for soup beans will work with any large dry bean, but the choice in Appalachia's central highlands is often pintos. Both tradition and taste dictate their use for mountain chili, bean cakes, bean dumplings, baked pinto beans, and pinto bean pie. Once prepared at home, children and miners carried the same beans into deep mines and small schools.

Of all of the bean dishes, the most popular is soup beans. To a native of Appalachia, soup beans is just a name for a soup everyone makes; to outsiders it is an exotic specialty. Simple, traditional, and mountain through and through, soup beans are a silky smooth, pork-flavored dish of pinto beans usually free of bean soup ingredients such as peas, potatoes, parsnips, tomatoes, carrots, and celery. This is not a complex mixture like vegetable soup, stew, or chili—one recipe in Part Two uses just three ingredients: pork, beans, and water. Others use lard, salt pork, ham hocks, or smoked ham hocks. Elvis Hatfield, of Pinson Fork on Pond Creek in Pike County, Kentucky, makes soup beans with five ingredients: water, pinto beans, lard, salt, and pepper. First, he soaks the beans overnight. Then, he puts the ingredients in a saucepan and simmers them all day. For a more complex Appalachian-styled bean soup, make the U.S. Senate bean soup (see Part Two).

Bean soups vary greatly from region to region. Cooks from the Pacific to the Atlantic make bean soups with navy beans, lima beans, fava beans, black beans, and great northern beans. They add beef bones, sausage balls, rabbit parts, preserved duck, or chorizo sausage, and their soups are brown bean, Dutch navy, or Spanish bean. The recipes call for a variety of herbs and spices, and the soups are known as cowpuncher's, cassoulet, and chowder; they are called minestrones and 15-bean.

Soup beans, on the other hand, are pork and pintos, and they merit a place on the list of famous Southern soups. They are a distinct part of a Southern tradition that includes burgoo, peanut, pine bark, and she-crab soups. But in the mountains when the sky turns gray and the sun is low at noon, the delicate aroma of boiling beans fills the house. Walking in from the cold out of doors, you enjoy the fragrance of smoked pork and earthy beans. The next day there are usually some left and they are cooked again.

Boiled dry beans are so common in the mountains, you would expect to find cooks using the leftovers to make fried bean patties or cakes. And they do. Highlanders also use cooked beans to make chili, and they may even mix them with coconut, butter, eggs, and sugar to make a bean pie, which is something like a pecan pie.

Like bean patties, potato cakes are made with leftover mashed potatoes, fried mush with leftover boiled cornmeal, and fried dressing with leftover stuffing. However, among these various fried cakes gracing cast-iron skillets, bean patties stand out. Some large families like pinto bean cakes almost as much as soup beans. For an updated bean patty recipe see Part Two.

Soup Beans and Cornbread
Rick Neal

I promised myself
that I would never eat
soup beans and cornbread
again, when I grew up.
That pancakes and homemade syrup
would never be served in my home.
That I would never wear
patched blue jeans
or crew cut ever again!
Such is the promise of youthful
naiveté of the real world,
in which my mother
raised nine children by herself.
She made it look easy,
as though wood cook stoves
and hand sewn quilts
were her lifestyle choices
As though working in a coal mine
was her decision
and not the requirement
for earning a decent wage
in an Appalachian man's world.

Yes, I promised these things
as I squeezed in between
my 8 brothers and sisters
at the dinner table,
and watched mom fill my plate
with soup beans and cornbread
before gathering her hard hat,
boots, and breathing apparatus
to work the 2nd shift
in a West Virginia coal mine.

One-Room Schools and School Lunches

At the beginning of the twentieth century, the school year was not only short, but also relatively insignificant. In many isolated mountain communities planting, caring for, gathering, and preserving crops—working at home—was more important than school. School years commonly lasted three to four months, with some districts offering as many as seven months. Indeed, students often thought of school as a good break from work. Schools offered not only lesson time, but also playtimes, which included morning recess, afternoon recess, and free time after lunch. Children spent these breaks playing games such as tag, leapfrog, needle's eye, hopscotch, marbles, and jump rope. They also played round town and straight town, which are popular schoolyard versions of baseball.

While children fashioned lard can lids into basketball hoops, their mothers used the lard to cook soup beans, pork and beans, or wieners and beans. Then, children carried beans to school and warmed them for lunch on the edge of potbellied stoves. Many children walked home for lunch, but those who stayed at school carried their lunches in lard buckets, coffee cans, flour sacks, and paper bags. A few children carried metal dinner buckets that included a section for water, another for hot food, and a third for breads or sweets. In addition to soup beans, school lunches at the beginning of the twentieth century may have included cold fried chicken, ham-filled biscuits, cornbread, and even green beans or whole kernel corn. Leftover breakfast pancakes and pork chops were rare treats. Cornbread was crumbled into buttermilk, and other treats included pie wedges, cake slices, and candy brittles.

By 1930, the Pike County Board of Education (Kentucky) served 198 districts, and each district had at least one school. Most of these schools had a single room and one teacher. There were no principals, janitors, or cooks. In fact, until the schools got larger, there were no cafeterias. What students today take for granted was often missing. Bonnie Roberts recalls being cold in her one-room school on Red Creek in Pike County in the mid 1950s: "I can remember winter mornings when the older boys did not build a fire before we started school. We would spend half the morning freezing until the big potbellied stove in the middle of the room finally started putting out heat." Others recalled the double-seat desks. Until the 1950s when individual desks were introduced, double-seat desks with ink holders were common. These desks were built with a bench-like seat on the front and a desk top attached to the back, behind which another unit would be placed, so the student's desk was actually the back of the seat in front.

At these schools, Fridays were set aside for competitions and demonstrations. Math contests, spelling bees, poetry recitations, Bible stories, and oral reading changed the pace. Teachers gave prizes. In a 1982 class essay, Jan Tackett recalls the story of her grandmother's first doll, which was a gift from her teacher for "standing first" in the class an entire year for Friday spelling matches.

While most students were enthusiastic about Friday's special events, some had reservations about lunches packed at home. As one student stated in an interview given to Katherine Hackney in 1982, "I recall very well hating whole kernel corn, and our teacher would not let us go out to play until we ate our dinner. So I would wait until all the others went out to play, and I would put my corn in a piece of paper and hide it from the teacher." But more often than hiding food, students traded it. For example, one child traded a sausage biscuit for another's jam cake while another child traded blackberry pie for cornbread. While some teachers attempted to keep the trading fair, others did not allow it. Some parents took a different view and aided in the sharing by packing extra food. Lunchtime was not only a time for playing, it was also a time of give and take.

But the home-packed lunch did not remain universal. By the 1950s, some one- and two-room schools began offering government-supported hot lunch programs. Unfortunately, the already-busy teacher had to pick up the food, prepare and serve it, record who ate it, and collect money from those who paid. In the early years, students paid as little as 10 cents for a lunch that may have included milk. Later, when the lunches cost 20 or 25 cents and larger schools hired cooks, the school menus included meat loaf, carrots and peas, macaroni with tomatoes or cheese, pinto beans, and cornbread. Many students ate these lunches because it was the only choice their parents gave them.

As rural areas became more developed, school lunches reflected family differences in taste and opportunity. Some students ate the school's hot lunch; others walked to small stores to buy a pack of Nabs cheese crackers, a chocolate-covered Eskimo Pie, a cherry Moon Pie, or even a box of Barnum's Animal Crackers. These stores sold Pepsi and RC Cola, which students combined with peanuts. For those who used a meal ticket at school, the "store-bought" snack lunches were a point of desire, and they caused feelings of conflict between those who could afford to buy from a store and those who had to eat the school lunch or, even worse, a lunch made at home.

Even among students who ate homemade lunches, some preferred "classy" factory-made white bread to home-cooked biscuits. Ironically, today the made-from-scratch home-baked biscuit is a treat, and the factory-made white bread is less desirable.

These preferences are reflected in today's large school cafeterias. In Pike County as a result of consolidation and more consolidation, the Johns Creek School serves lunch in a large, modern cafeteria. With 940 students and about 100 employees, this school is among the largest in the area, and meals, rather than costing 25 cents as they did in the 1950s, were costing $3.00 by 1999. At Johns Creek, new steamers, new fryers, and new warming ovens add up to better lunches and more service. The large picture windows, steel and concrete walls, shiny tile floors, and fresh paint are inviting. The school celebrates holidays such as Thanksgiving, Christmas, and Easter with dinners that may include sliced fresh turkey, cornbread dressing, brown gravy, cheesy sauced broccoli, potato salad, hot rolls, and a holiday pudding.

The lunchroom seats 450, and the manager and her staff serve home-style, from-scratch meals. "From scratch" refers to preparing fresh turkey and making cornbread dressing from cornbread that they baked. Biscuits are baked fresh. Food at Johns Creek School is not fast food, but it is not slow home-cooked food either. These lunches are a mixture of home and school styles. First, children choose what they take, and second, the prepared foods are low in sugar, fat, and salt. Students select from choices such as meat loaf, pizza, country-fried steak, or a sandwich such as a hamburger or chicken breast sandwich. To offer these options the cooks place large trays of food on four cafeteria-style lines. Children pass by, make their selections, and serve themselves. The Johns Creek cafeteria manager, Mrs. Maynard, explained the system. "Up to the third grade," she said, "we serve the children, but they tell us what they want. From the fourth grade up our children serve themselves." Recalling the 1970s and 1980s, Mrs. Maynard said, "We used to fix the trays, and they accepted them whether they liked it or not. All trays were the same." Now most schools do it differently. The system is "Offer versus serve; we offer, they serve." The choices are many with children choosing from various drinks, main dishes, vegetables, and desserts.

Over the last 100 years, both the school and the food have changed, but Appalachian school children today are still bringing bag lunches, going to the store off campus, and eating a hot school lunch. The school lunch of today is no longer warmed on the edge of potbellied stoves, but within the schools, soup beans, as well as potatoes, are on the menu.

Irish Potatoes and Sweet Potatoes

Potatoes are essential to the mountain diet. Close observers know this from seeing long rows of potatoes in mountain gardens, from hand-crafted potato casserole displays at covered-dish suppers, and from 25- and even 50-pound sacks of potatoes sold in supermarkets. In mountain diets, potatoes are more popular than apples or beef.

Irish Potatoes
How did potatoes become so popular in Appalachian cooking? Maybe because they taste so good. Cissy Gregg, former food editor

of the Louisville, Kentucky, *Courier-Journal,* wrote in 1960, "Anyone can get tired of family, husband, or friends. But who gets tired of a good, luscious baked potato—stuffed, twice-baked, or plain?" Gregg was talking about baking mature Russet, Kennebec, Idaho, or Maine potatoes, all of which yield a desirable mealy texture.

These white potatoes are an indigenous American food. Long before Columbus discovered America, the Inca people of the Andes Mountains were using potatoes. Historians say their potatoes were small because they ate the big ones and planted the small ones. With this process of selection in use for hundreds of years, their potatoes were, perhaps, the size of a quarter.

Within about 80 years of Columbus' journey to America, Europeans were growing, but not eating, potatoes. For a long time they viewed them as a novelty, but by 1610 both the English and Irish were eating potatoes. The Germans were also quick to adopt the potato, but the French did not use them, believing potatoes would cause leprosy.

Finally, the potato became popular, and its availability was one cause of the population explosion that occurred in the eighteenth century. Potatoes were easy to plant, quickly stored, and highly productive. In fact, potatoes grown on two acres could feed nine to ten people for a full year, whereas ten acres of wheat were required to support the same number. The problem of the potato was that, unlike grains, it could not be stored from year to year. If the potato crop failed, people starved. This happened in Ireland in the 1840s and 1850s.

It is ironic that Irish settlers, forced out of Ireland by the potato famine, brought white potatoes back to America. In the minds of Irish emigrants, the potatoes were from Ireland, and they called them Irish potatoes. (That is not too surprising considering the fact that the English named a native American bird "turkeys" after the Turks because Turkish traders brought turkeys to English ports.)

So while the Irish grew potatoes in Ireland and brought them to the mountains, white potatoes are not native to Ireland, and Irish is not a potato variety. However, to distinguish between sweet potatoes and white potatoes, many North Americans refer to white potatoes as Irish potatoes.

Before they depended on potatoes, the Irish produced milk. Years later, when the potato arrived in Ireland from America and the English forced the Irish to live on smaller plots, the potato replaced much of that milk. So it's not surprising that, more than most cultures, Irish foodways combined milk and potatoes. Mountaineers, too, are fond of milk and potato recipes including scalloped, mashed, and twice-baked potatoes. They also frequently serve potato soups, the most popular of which are cream of potato, corn chowder, pork chowder, butternut squash and potato, bacon potato, cheesy potato, and cauliflower potato.

Scalloped potatoes, or potatoes *au gratin,* are cooked in milk, broth, or cream. As the potatoes cook, either the starch in the potatoes thickens the sauce, or flour, cheese, or egg yolks are combined with the liquid to make a cream sauce. The sauce is then poured over the potatoes. In addition to potatoes and sauce, some cooks add onions, mushrooms, sausage, or even pork chops to this dish. Many use cans of cream soup for the sauce. One of the most important tricks in making scalloped potatoes is to use new potatoes instead of baking potatoes. New potatoes add a waxy texture, and, when cooked, are firmer, less mushy, and less grainy than mature bakers.

The scalloped potato recipe in Part Two is fuller, smoother, richer, and more complex than most scalloped potato recipes. At family gatherings and community suppers all age groups rave about this dish, and even though the amounts called for in the recipe are large, it disappears quickly.

Irish stew is another traditional potato dish, a one-step affair that combines lamb and potatoes. Its clear ties to Ireland, use of potatoes, low-fat modern style, and forthright pure flavor make it an ideal recipe for today's Appalachian kitchen.

About 200 years ago, the Irish made this stew, but they did not call it Irish stew, and it's a fair guess that the recipe was not printed in cookbooks. Then, about 125 years ago, after the Civil War, cookbook authors working in this country began writing recipes for Irish stew. According to the Time-Life series, *The Cooking of the British Isles,* Irish stew is a close relative of hot pot, also a stew made with lamb or mutton and potatoes. But that is not the whole story. In Lancashire and Yorkshire, the English make hot pot with the neck chops of Pennine sheep, as well as potatoes, onions, and oysters. This stew was also a staple of millworkers because in the nineteenth century both oysters and mutton were inexpensive. In old Gaelic this "peasant food" was called *ballymaloe* or *stobhach gaelach*. Sheep were raised for wool, milk, and meat, and root vegetables were the norm.

The French, too, made this type of stew and called it a *daube*. Their stew combines layers of lamb and potatoes and uses red wine to braise the ingredients slowly in a covered pottery casserole. They also made a *baeckaoffa* with various meats, layered together with carrots, turnips, and cabbage, covered with water, and baked slowly for three hours.

Today, Irish stew combines lamb, potatoes, carrots, and onions. The stew is thickened by long slow cooking, and many cooks layer it in a large pan. They place potatoes on the bottom, then add a layer of lamb, and finally they add a layer of onions. They repeat the layering two or three times and finish with a layer of potatoes. Modern chefs have added new seasonings such as hot sauce and vegetables such as tomatoes, but these were not used in Ireland 200 years ago.

What the Irish used were large earthenware pots. Fortunately, in today's kitchen cooks simmer the stew in a saucepan, slow cooker, or pressure cooker. Others layer and bake it in a covered casserole or Dutch oven for 5 hours at 300°F. (A recipe for Irish stew appears in Part Two.)

Sweet Potatoes

While Irish potatoes are the most-consumed mountain potato, sweet potatoes are also significant in the mountain diet.

By the mid-1950s, ten-year-olds had not learned about World War II, the nation was booming, and cars had fins. Tomato aspic, chicken divan, and rice pilaf were in vogue. The following description, also from the mid-50s, is of an Appalachian woman serving dinner to a large family. As Harriette Arnow describes in *The Doll-maker,* the dinner is replete with mountain favorites, including baked sweet potatoes.

Gertie, sitting at the foot of the table with a lard bucket of sweet milk on one side of her, buttermilk on the other, a great platter of hot smoking cornbread in front, and other bowls and platters within easy reach, was kept busy filling glasses of milk, buttering bread, and dishing out the new hominy fried in lard and seasoned with sweet milk and black pepper. It was good with the shuck beans, baked sweet potatoes, cucumber pickles, and green tomato ketchup. Gertie served it up with pride, for everything, even the meal in the bread, was a product of her farming.

In central Appalachia in February and March, sweet potato sprouts fill jars and line windows. Roots form and the plants gain vigor. Then, in May when danger of frost has passed, farmers plant these starts; when September arrives and the heat of summer begins to moderate, the crop is ready. Even today, a few old-timers use a horse and plow to lift the tubers to the surface. Then, by hand, they gather the potatoes into piles and toss them onto wagons.

On small farms, hill folk fill wheelbarrows and then store the potatoes in boxes, baskets, or bins. Driving along country roads in October, one sees the potatoes for sale. Next to mailboxes at the end of driveways, whole bushels are sold for $5.00, and in small farmers' markets and commercial settings, sweet potatoes, fresh from the garden or shipped from the far side of this continent, are a symbol of fall, a staple of winter, and an alternative to beans and Irish potatoes.

Sweet potatoes are, of course, a root vegetable. The flesh ranges from dry and less sweet to moist and more sweet. Sweet varieties range in color from white to orange to purple, so the color of the pulp tells little about sweetness. In addition, there is confusion because people use the terms sweet potatoes and yams interchangeably, yet the two are different botanically. The yam is a starchy, African root vegetable that is popular in Central and South America. Yams are members of the genus *Dioscorea;* sweet potatoes, like morning glories, belong to the species *Ipomoea batatas*, are native American, and are popular in the United States. And sweet potatoes have a long tradition in North America. Years before the arrival of Europeans, the Cherokee Indians and other tribes throughout the South cultivated sweet potatoes. For example, Tater Hill, Georgia, located on the North Carolina-Georgia border, is named in memory of Cherokees who are said to have dug sweet potatoes in the region. Unfortunately, some markets mislabel sweet potatoes, calling them yams, but in reality few yams are sold in this country.

Appalachians use sweet potatoes to make pies, pones, puffs, and casseroles. They serve sweet potatoes baked, puréed, and glazed. These tubers have many uses, but Appalachian cooks combine them with apples, pecans, pork, and marshmallows. The amount of sugar added depends on the cook's preference and the potato variety.

From a plant that is native to America, American farmers now grow some 40 different varieties, and about 500 varieties are grown around the world. Popular varieties include Georgia jet, Puerto Rico, Nemagold, Big Stem, Yellow Jersey, vineless Vardaman, and Golden Maryland. But these potatoes are neither potatoes nor yams.

This crop not only has a long history in Appalachia, but today, developing nations around the globe consume 95 percent of the sweet potato crop. For example, in India a *poori* puffed bread is made with sweet potatoes, and in China sweet potatoes are so popular that big-city vendors sell them roasted from carts just as vendors sell pretzels in New York.

Indeed sweet potatoes are sweet, and mountaineers tend to gravitate toward sweet food. It almost seems that those living in the South and in Appalachia have a special gene that draws them to sweets. In Appalachian communities, Pepsi is preferred over Coke, possibly because Pepsi is sweeter. Community cookbooks are loaded with desserts, and sugar is added not only to vegetables such as carrots, but also to sweet potatoes, which are naturally sweet. It should be noted, however, that not everyone likes sweet foods, and today desserts are less sweet than they used to be. For example, some cooks are make apple pies without adding sugar to the apples; those cooking in the traditional style add 2 cups of sugar per pie.

Sweetness is only one element of sweet potato cookery. Another is hearth cooking. Sweet potatoes are well suited to hearth cooking, and 75 to 100 years ago living without electricity mountain families baked them in ashes. Ashes protected the potatoes from red hot coals. However, more endearing than that, baking sweet potatoes was a Friday night social event. Like renting a video today, gathering around hearths and baking sweet potatoes was a family tradition. In large households, family and friends would come and go. They sat in front of the hearth, watched the flames, told stories, argued, and waited for sweet potatoes to cook. Then, they pulled the potatoes from the coals, cleaned off the ashes, and began the tasting.

While today hearth cooking is seen mostly at folk festivals, an oven-baked sweet potato is an easy prize. Baking a sweet potato takes no fuss—the potatoes are simply washed in water, wrapped in foil, baked in a moderate oven, and served with butter, cinnamon, and brown sugar. While Irish potatoes are baked at 400°F, sweet potatoes do well at 350°F. Fresh sweet potatoes come from the oven moist and soft so that gravy is not needed, but in true Appalachian tradition, highlanders might dress them up with molasses or hot sorghum syrup, or moisten them with chopped pineapple or applesauce, or add texture with seeds, raisins, or nuts. This taste lasts all winter.

Sweet potatoes and casseroles go together like summer and baseball. When cooks mash or purée sweet potatoes and then add other ingredients such as persimmon pulp, crushed pineapple, orange juice, sweet milk, and brown sugar, the result is a home-style casserole. Sweet potato casseroles contain the traditional sweet potato spices including cinnamon, cloves, allspice, mace, and nutmeg. They might include fruits such as raisins, apples, lemon, and orange; dairy products such as cream, butter, milk, yogurt, and sour cream; and sweeteners such as honey, molasses, sorghum, and sugar. For added flavor, some cooks add a liquor such as brandy, sherry, and cognac. Like baseball cards and batting averages, the variations are endless, and your fun is in combining the ingredients you like. Run the bases. Catch fly balls. Make a sweet potato casserole, and garnish it with black walnuts, pecans, raisins, and fresh pineapple. This casserole is as old as baseball and as Appalachian as mountains; a recipe for it appears in Part Two.

In the not-so-distant past during the summer and fall, traditional mountaineers lived out of their gardens. For breakfast, lunch, and dinner, they ate what they produced or what they had stored. Keep in mind that most rural families had a hen house for chickens, a smokehouse for cured pork, a can house for preserved fruits and vegetables, and a root cellar for fresh roots and fruits.

The recipe for sweet potatoes and apples in Part Two is an example of how they combined fresh fall produce. To make this dish, the ingredients were simmered on top of the stove, and served from a large bowl like mashed potatoes. Today, mountain cooks continue the tradition using a cooking apple such as Rome Beauty or Granny Smith and sweet potatoes from the market. Looking at the recipe, it may seem like there are too many apples, but they sweeten the dish, add moisture, and shrink during cooking. When the dish is ready, the sweet potatoes will be almost mushy-soft, while the apples remain firm. Like the chicken and dumplings that follow, the sauce melds the ingredients.

Chicken, Dumplings, and Slick Runners:
Dough Balls, Slicks, and Slickers

Sweet or savory, dumplings thicken sauces, and sauces moisten dumplings. It's a cozy relationship comparable to pasta and tomato sauce. And Appalachian dumplings are a special breed of dumpling. They don't resemble the pasta-like dumplings served in Chinese restaurants or the mashed potato dumplings—*Kartoffelkloss*—favored by German-Americans. In Appalachia, cooks prepare dumplings with flour or cornmeal, and they cook them by boiling. Sometimes they use leavening, but more often they do not. Leavened dumplings are spongy and tender while those without leavening are firm and flat. Leavened dumplings are like biscuits, and the dough is formed with a spoon or pulled into pieces and then dropped into a bubbling pot. Leavening lightens the dumplings, and they float. The more common Appalachian dumplings, unleavened dumplings, are rolled like pie crust and cut with a pizza cutter or flattened on a floured surface and cut into uneven strips with a knife. These flat slickers or slick runner dumplings are like pasta and are served either filled or not filled. They are called slick dumplings because, like egg noodles, they are slippery when touched. The effect of plain dumplings on whatever broth they are boiled in is tremendous. Adding raw dough to broth is like adding heavy cream to soup. Dumplings thicken, smooth, and cream. What was broth becomes gruel.

Dumplings, whether leavened or not, improve many foods, but because the styles are so different, they are the cause of arguments. Cissy Gregg, writing her weekly food column in the Louisville *Courier-Journal* in 1946, believed the debate between flat slickers or "sad flats" as she called them and raised rounds or "pillows" is not a matter of geography. The preference "is a family affair and we'll hold on to our type, come what may." Cissy Gregg was grouping people by their cultural origins. "Those who call fat bits of fluff-duff with stewed chicken by the name of dumplings are one kind of people, while those who make slick dumplings to go with their chicken are another kind."

Gregg continued the column with three recipes for flat dumplings:

Dumpling one: Make the same kind of pastry you would for pie crust. Use more flour than usual on the board when rolling them out. Roll the dough very, very thin. Cut in strips and drop them into the broth.

Dumpling two: Make a richer-than-average biscuit dough. Go to the halfway place between biscuits and pastry and then you'll find the perfect proportion for a dumpling. Cook the same as dumpling No. 1.

Dumpling three: Place in a bowl the amount of flour you want to make, perhaps two cups. Add salt to taste—we use a good teaspoonful. The chicken has been cooked until it is at the place of doneness that, if it had to take one more simmer, it would suffer a complete breakaway from the bones. At this point, tenderly lift it from the stew pot to a serving bowl and keep hot. If the chicken was fat, with a large serving spoon stir up the broth, pushing back the fat a little, then dip up a spoonful of the hot liquid and add it to the measured flour in the bowl. Add enough of the chicken broth to make a rather stiff dough. Roll out thin on a well-floured board, cut in strips, I'd say an inch wide, and drop them into the boiling stew. Cover the pot and cook about 10 to 15 minutes.

One can only wonder about the regional source of the all-American folk song, "She'll Be Coming Round the Mountain." Consider the first lines of the song:

> She'll be coming round the mountain, when she comes. Toot toot!
> She'll be driving six white horses, when she comes. Whoa back!
> Oh, we'll all go out to meet her, when she comes. Hi babe!
> We'll be sippin' sarsaparilla, when she comes. Slurp slurp!
> And we'll kill the old red rooster, when she comes. Hack hack!
> We'll all have chicken 'n' dumplings when she comes. Yum yum!
> She'll be wearing green pajamas when she comes. Ha ha!

Given the verses on chicken 'n' dumplings and sarsaparilla, couldn't it have roots in Appalachia, and can't you imagine the chicken 'n' slick dumplings? Can't you see the green pajamas and poke bonnet?

Like other elements of American culture, dumplings can be associated with their geographic and ethnic origins, and the history of mountain dumplings tells us more than that family traditions are different. This history also supports the notion of an English and Scots-Irish connection to Appalachian culture. From legends, cookbooks, and observation, historians trace Appalachian culture back to the British Isles. Andre Simon, writing in *A Concise Encyclopedia of Gastronomy,* described dumplings as "one of the most characteristically English contributions to cookery." He goes on to discuss the English Norfolk raised dumpling, known colloquially as swimmers, and the "*hard* dumpling" from Sussex (southern England) that is much like Appalachian slicks. While Simon wrote his

Encyclopedia in 1981, an early English cookbook from 1747 by Hannah Glasse, *The Art of Cookery Made Plain and Easy,* includes eight kinds of dumplings. Glasse offers two for hard or unleavened dumplings, two for apple dumplings and one each for Norfolk, yeast, bread, and suet dumplings.

With this long history and these many dumpling variations, it is not surprising that immigrants continued the tradition. Dumplings are served in central Appalachia as a main course dish with chicken or as a dessert with blackberries. While chicken is the most common savory dumpling, mountaineers have been known to make tomato dumplings, green bean dumplings, greens and dumplings, and ramps with slick dumplings. In addition, mountain dumplings are boiled with dry beans, ham hocks, and squirrel gravy.

Other dumplings such as the Scottish green did not make their way into traditional Appalachian kitchens. In Scotland, a flour and suet dumpling is prepared in the spring with dandelion and nettle leaves as well as hawthorn buds.

Even though these particular Scottish dumplings did not make it to America, the term *dumplings* carries wide variations, and almost every ethnic group that settled the mountains brought dumplings ranging in style from soup dumplings to savory stew dumplings to sweet dessert dumplings. Among the dessert dumplings, the Pennsylvania Dutch enjoy apple dumplings that resemble apple pie: A whole apple is wrapped in pastry dough and baked in a sweet sauce. Historians trace this dumpling back to England where a recipe was published in Hannah Glasse's 1747 book.

Other dumplings known in the Appalachian region include biscuit dumplings served with pigs' knuckles and sauerkraut; buckwheat dumplings with cheese and also called *pierogi z kaszy;* farina balls made with cream of wheat, milk, butter, and eggs; liver dumplings made with rice, onions, and raisins and served in a clear soup; matzo balls often served in chicken soup; and Italian bread dumplings made with stale bread, cheese, eggs, and spices. Moistened stale bread is also the dominant base for dumplings in the area of Bavaria, Austria, and Bohemia or Central Europe. Of course, the best known Italian dumplings are gnocchi or dumplings made with potatoes, flour, or farina, shaped in little balls, and served as a side dish with butter or a savory sauce.

With these variations, dumplings balance the diet and add contrast to foods. Appalachians tend to associate savory dumplings with chicken. Some cooks flavor them with pepper, celery, onion, caraway, nutmeg, or sage. To the flour, others add cheese, farina, eggs, butter, bread crumbs, cracklings, and crackers, but the common dumpling is made with flour, shortening, and water. These dumplings are served in savory stews. Plain flour dumplings are also used in sweet fruit sauces with fresh fruits such as pie cherries, blueberries, strawberries, blackberries, and rhubarb.

The dumpling recipe on page 245 is similar to Gregg's third dumpling. It was adapted from Olga Latta's 100-year-old recipe published in Irene Hayes' 1970 book, *What's Cooking in Kentucky*. Latta's chicken and dumplings recipe calls for "a medium fat stewing hen, . . . lard the size of an egg, . . . and simmering the dumplings 15 minutes or until they are done."

Once the dumplings have been prepared, the pot is ready, and the combination is called chicken and dumplings. According to five-year-old Claire Fish of Pikeville, Kentucky, chicken and dumplings are the best part of Sunday dinner. After church, her family goes out to eat, and on the restaurant's long buffet table she may find 30 choices. However, Claire says, "I go straight for those chicken and dumplings." She is not alone. She skips the molded salads, vegetable casseroles, and pork ribs. Chicken and dumplings are her first choice.

To make the chicken and dumplings she likes, you stew and debone a whole chicken, or you simplify this by using chicken parts such as legs and thighs. Traditionally, highlanders went to their hen house and selected a mature stewing hen to use for chicken and dumplings. In place of the whole chicken, cooks today might use six breasts or eight thighs. Then, rather than cooling and deboning these chicken parts, they cook the dish in one easy step and serve the chicken parts whole. See Part Two for the recipe.

While Claire was speaking as a five-year-old, Libby Preston is an adult living in Ohio. Here, she recalls her childhood.

Well, when I was a child, every Sunday we went to our grandparents' home for Sunday dinner. My grandmother, Fannie Mae Davis Preston, born on October 27, 1907, frequently made chicken & dumplings. She would fry chicken & make a pot of dumplings & gravy. We called the dumplings slickers.

She boiled the chicken parts (backs, wing tips) for broth. She would remove the parts & add dumplings to the broth. To make the dumplings, she cut up, flattened & floured biscuits (she in later years used the canned version) & dropped them into the boiling broth. They float to the top while they are cooking & if you allowed them to gently cook they were the "fluffy" style of dumplings.

When my grandmother wasn't looking, my sister would always sneak in and stir them—when you stirred them they weren't as fluffy, they got semi hard & we called them slick runners. We (my sister & I) preferred them that way over the fluffy version. My grandmother used to 'threaten' her with bodily harm if she stirred them. But we knew she was safe—it was an idle threat!

By the way—it's 40 years later & my mother now threatens my sister since she still stirs them for the slick runner variety.

Sources

Hannah Glasse. *The Art of Cookery Made Plain and Easy,* First Edition. London: Mrs. Ashburn's China Shop, at Fleet and Dish, 1747. Facsimile Edition: Totnes, Devon: Prospect Books, 1995.

Irene Hayes. *What's Cooking in Kentucky*. Hueysville, Kentucky: The T. I. Hayes Publishing Company, Inc., 1982.

Andre L. Simon. *A Concise Encyclopedia of Gastronomy*. Woodstock, New York: The Overlook Press, 1981.

Mark F. Sohn. *Education in Appalachia's Central Highlands*. Pikeville, Kentucky: Self-Published, 1986.

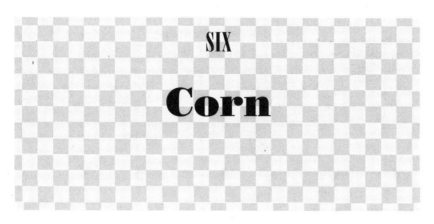

SIX

Corn

Gritted Corn, Cornbread, and Custard Corn Pudding

Corn, Cornpone, and Cornshucks

When Europeans arrived in America, native people had been growing corn for 6,000 years, and they enjoyed a diet that also included beans, tomatoes, potatoes, sweet peppers, and pumpkin, as well as smoked wild game and an abundance of fresh and saltwater fish. The environment had a large variety of foods to offer the new settlers; however, over time, it was corn that became dominant. Europeans soon learned that corn is a high-volume, high-energy grain that can be used to make cereal, livestock feed, and bread. Cornbread has evolved with our culture and tastes. Before the Europeans arrived, Native Americans made a bread they called suppone. Their cornpone (the batter) was a combination of cornmeal, water, grease, and salt; however, as time passed, the recipe evolved into ashcakes, hoecakes, griddle cakes, and corn dodgers.

When settlers came to the Appalachian Mountains, they brought Indian maize and native know-how with them, and, after clearing the heavy, jungle-like growth of timber, they planted corn in the narrow valleys and up the sides of hills. Corn was better adapted to mountain topography than wheat or barley, and, over time, settlers learned to use it in many ways. Early in the growing season when the ears began to fill out, mountain farmers picked and used what they called "roasting ears." They roasted or boiled the young ears and ate the corn out of hand and from the cob. When the corn matured and got firm, farmers or their wives grated the corn from the cob and used this "gritted" corn to make a moist cornbread. When the corn dried, they ground it into corn-meal or boiled it with lye to make hominy. Millers then ground hominy to make grits. Finally, moonshiners sprouted dry corn and used it to make mash for moonshine. Occasionally, farmers fed dry corn to chickens and pigs.

Corn, however, was more than food. Mountaineers used the shucks to make chair bottoms. They also made cornhusk mats, hats, and horse collars. When there was time to spare, they used their creative skills to make a mountain craft, the cornshuck doll.

Cornshuck dolls range in height from 4 to 15 inches. Craftspeople make them by moistening dry corn shucks, dying the shucks, cutting them with a scissors, forming doll parts, assembling the parts with thin strips of cornshuck, and painting the faces. They use corn silks for hair and small sticks for stands, broom handles, or logs. However, cornshuck dolls are not the only Appalachian corn-based toys. *The Foxfire Book of Toys and Games* lists many others, including corncob pipes, corn guns, corncob darts, corncob dolls, cornstalk airplanes, cornstalk fiddles, cornstalk sleds, and cornstalk slings.

More than a raw material for toys, the early varieties of corn were the bases of many variations. Those who grow corn know that corn varieties have different textures, colors, flavors, and keeping qualities. Not long ago, a common mountain corn variety was Hickory King corn, a traditional, open-pollinated, white corn. It grows tall, up to 16 feet high, and mountaineers feed it to livestock and use it to make hominy and pickles. However, by today's standard, Hickory King corn lacks the sweetness genes that geneticists developed in the late 1950s. The first sweet hybrids were varieties such as Sunglow and Golden Cross Bantam. A little later, agronomists developed Silver Queen, which was the standard hybrid for more than 30 years. More recently, corn geneticists have developed sugary enhancer hybrids such as Breeder's Choice,

Miracle, and Kandy Korn E.H. (Everlasting Heritage). These varieties often retain the texture of traditional varieties; however, they have a higher sugar content and will remain sweet for a week if left on the plant. Finally, today mountaineers enjoy the super-sweet hybrids such as Early Xtra-Sweet, How Sweet It Is, and Honey 'N Pearl. These new varieties, as well as others that become available every season, may be twice as sweet as older varieties, and when left on the cob, the corn retains its sweetness for a week or more. Highlanders still grow some Hickory King and Silver Queen corn, and they use them to make gritted cornbread, hog feed, and hominy. However, most Appalachians who garden now grow sweet corn and include a row or two of the newest varieties.

For those who don't keep a garden, markets offer many choices. While fresh corn on the cob is available in the market much of the year, the months of July and August offer the pick of the season. Buy freshly picked ears. The husks should be snug and green, and the stalk ends should look fresh, not dried up and chalky in color. The silks should be dark brown.

The ultimate, sure-fire, and guaranteed test of fresh corn is the taste. Fresh, raw, sweet corn should taste sweet, tender, crunchy, juicy, and delicious before it is cooked. If you can't taste the corn in the market, check the kernels to be sure that they look plump and juicy. They should be filled out, but not indented. If the kernels are dented or indented, they are dry and past their prime. Avoid wormy ears, and if possible, taste.

Fresh corn on the cob is cooked by boiling, steaming, roasting, or microwaving. Keep in mind that partly because they have more sugar, the new, sweet varieties cook faster than older ones. Boil them hard for two minutes and they are ready. For a sweet corn recipe that calls for corn that has been cut from the cob, see custard corn pudding in Part Two.

Writing in 1936 in *Head o' W-Hollow,* Jesse Stuart talks about planting and plowing corn. This paragraph is representative of the book and Stuart's hill-country interests.

We planted corn. We plowed it the first time and chopped the weeds out of it. We plowed it the second time and the third time. It was soon over the mule's back. When it got that high we quit plowin it. I'd lay in my bed at night and look at it. I'd look at the moon-light on the cornfield bright as day. I would think:

> The night is pretty.
> The night was made for man and the fox.
> The night was made for silence.
> The stars in the sky.
> The silver-like dew-drops on the corn.
> The night is pretty, whoever made it and whatever it was made for.
> I like the night.
> I love the night.

I watched the moonlight flicker on the corn blades. . . .

Jesse Stuart was an author, teacher, and school superintendent who lived from 1906 to 1984 in the hills of northeastern Kentucky. He was the son of tenant farmers and lived much of his life in a farm setting, supplementing his teaching salary with farming and writing. *The Chronological Bibliography of Works by Jesse Stuart* includes 62 works and his most famous book is *The Thread That Runs So True,* first published in 1949. For further information see the Jesse Stuart Foundation in the Mail-Order Sources.

Cornbread

In addition to enjoying corn fresh from the cob or baked in pudding, mountaineers store it dry and use it ground. Ground cornmeal is the primary ingredient in mush and cornbread.

Cornbread is so popular and so important that some mountaineers view it as a gift from God. Divine and spiritual, cornbread is a manna. From the time settlers reached the frontier and built cabins, corn and cornbread were a treasure like the one that sustained the Israelites for 40 years in the desert. Cornbread nourished mountaineers through the Great Depression, coal booms and busts, and mountain isolation. When mountaineers grew their own corn, they made cornbread three times a day, and today, no country restaurant in Appalachia would serve dinner without offering cornbread. Cornbread continues to be a mountain staple, a daily food, and a primal joy.

This popularity is due at least in part to the fact that cornbread is a quick, home-baked bread made with ground cornmeal and fast-acting leaveners. The batter is leavened with baking soda and buttermilk or with baking powder. An occasional fancy cook leavens cornbread with yeast, but this is rare.

Cornbreads include puffy corn fritters, gritted bread, crusty cornbread, fried corn pones, jalapeño cornbread, and quick cornbread. To this add recipes for hush puppies, johnnycakes, and corn dodgers. Other cornbread names suggest ingredients: hot water cornbread, mayonnaise cornbread, crackling bread, and buttermilk cornbread. Still other descriptors, such as muffins, sticks, griddle cakes, ashcakes, and skillet cornbread, tell us about the cooking utensil used. Muffins are baked in a muffin pan. Corn sticks are baked in a cast-iron corn stick pan, and griddle cakes are cornmeal pancakes fried on a griddle. Ash cakes are baked on a hearth in ashes while skillet cornbread is baked in a cast-iron skillet. Spoonbread is also a cornbread named after a utensil; however, rather than being baked in a spoon, the soufflé-like batter is baked in a casserole dish and served with a spoon like stove-top stuffing.

A most important cornbread shape is the pone, a round "loaf" of baked cornbread. When the batter is baked in a round cast-iron skillet, the bread is a pone. Mountain cornbread is not typically baked in a rectangular pan. Square loaf pans do not yield pones, and they do not yield the traditionally pie-shaped wedge of cornbread. A pone is also a small, round cornbread cake or a corn cake. These pones are biscuit-sized and biscuit-shaped individual servings of cornbread. Using thick batter, some bakers shape small pones between their palms, and bake them on a cookie sheet. Cornmeal muffins are also called pones.

While a loaf of cornbread is a pone, "cornpone" is the term used by early Native Americans for cornbread batter. They called it *apone* or *apan*. If the cornpone is thin, it can be poured onto a griddle and fried to make griddle cakes, hoecakes, Johnnycakes, or cornmeal pancakes. If the batter is thick, it can be dropped by spoonfuls onto a cookie sheet and baked like drop biscuits. Cooks also drop thick cornbread batter into stews to make dumplings or what mountaineers call cornmeal dodgers. When this same batter is deep fried, it becomes hush puppies.

A seasonal variation of cornbread is gritted cornbread. Cooks prepare the batter with corn they grate from the cob. Using the milky mixture of fresh corn and hull in place of cornmeal results in highly flavored, moist cornbread. When baked, gritted cornbread develops an outside crust while the center remains like pudding.

Other cornbreads are full of goodies such as bacon, cheese, chopped peppers, and cracklings. Today, cornbread can be thick or thin, robust or tender, sweet or savory, and rich or light. Through its evolution, the old Native American cornpone has been changed to include flour, baking powder, eggs, bacon grease, butter, vegetable oil, buttermilk, yogurt, and sugar. To the batter, cooks also add creamed corn, diced green peppers, red-hot peppers, onions, and diced ham. They bake cornbread in the oven, fry it in oil, and boil it in water. The many cornbread variations reflect the talents of hill country highlanders from Georgia to Maryland.

In her book, *Shuck Beans, Stack Cakes, and Honest Fried Chicken,* Ronni Lundy catches our attention when she says, "If God had meant for cornbread to have sugar in it, he'd have called it cake." Lundy grew up south of the Mason-Dixon line, and she knows that cornbreads are not all the same. She holds a bias against cornbreads baked from a package as well as commercial-style breads. Large establishments often make soft, thick, crumbly, and yellow cornbread. Staff cooks bake them in large, rectangular pans and cut them into squares. The top and bottom are soft and the four edges center-cut. This cornbread is a commercial excuse for fresh, home-baked mountain cornbread, and it may be so soft that you cannot spread it with a pat of butter.

Indeed, this style may please some, but the form is not traditional wedges, sticks, pones, or muffins. Furthermore, the bread is tender and sweet. Commercial cornbread is not only like cake, it also lacks coarse cornmeal and has little trace of old-fashioned, brash mountain country spirit.

While large-scale kitchens may bake cornbread as much as 3 inches thick, homemade breads are thinner. Thinner bread cooks more quickly and has more crust. Mountain cooks decrease thickness by adjusting the size of the recipe, using a larger pan, or baking the batter in two pans. A traditional thickness is 1½ inches, as it gives a good balance between crust and crumb.

Cornbread crumb is also important. Crumb is the center part of the bread. Cornbread centers range from crumbly to substantial. As cornbread batter gets richer and the cornmeal more refined, the crumb becomes more tender and more like cake. The addition of oil and eggs to the batter also adds tenderness. Many cornbreads are too rich. Traditional mountain cooks prefer a more primitive, more substantial, and less rich bread with a tough crumb.

The crumb stands in contrast to the crust. Cornbread crusts have three parts: top, bottom, and edge. When country cooks bake cornbread in a heavy cast-iron skillet and in a preheated 450°F oven, their cornbread comes out with a wonderful crusty brown top and a crunchy, golden-brown bottom. If the top is pale in color, it should be broiled; if the bottom is pale, it was baked too far from the heat source. To develop a crispy, crusty edge, preheat the oil and skillet until just before the oil starts to smoke. Then pour in the batter and bake.

Although a high oven heat can create a dry and crispy crust, moisture will soften it. Left in the pan, sealed in plastic, or covered with foil, crusty cornbread softens quickly. Moisture is the enemy of crispness. Careful cooks treat fresh cornbread so that it does not become soggy. To do this, they serve the cornbread as soon as possible after taking it from the oven. The longer the bread sits, the more the moisture moves from the center to the crust. To reduce this transfer of moisture, as well as the impact of hot steam, good cooks first turn the pone out of the cast-iron skillet and onto a wire cooling rack. Then, they flip it back onto a cutting board and listen to the crunch as they cut through the crispy top and hardened bottom. Finally, they return the wedges to the cooling rack or place them uncovered in a serving basket with an absorbent cloth lining. In a restaurant setting, chefs serve cornbread from a heated serving pan equipped with a top hot light. The hot pan and heat light draw steam away and help keep the crust fresh.

Biting into a crunchy cornbread crust is just one of the pleasures associated with this treat. Some diners find pleasure in holding the wedge and dipping it while others prefer to crumble it into soup beans, pot likker, or sour milk. Even within families, some argue the merits of cornbread wedges eaten out of hand and cornbread crumbles eaten from a bowl of likker with a fork or a glass of buttermilk with a spoon.

Dipped or crumbled, spoons or fingers, the traditional cornbread experience includes buttermilk, pot likker, wild greens, and soup beans. This combination is available at country restaurants along the Country Music Highway. US Highway 23, the north-south route that winds its way from Portsmouth, Ohio, to Kingsport, Tennessee, is dotted with a fast-food chain called Dairy Cheer. At

Dairy Cheer restaurants during the winter, you can get a lunch special of cornbread muffins, soup beans, and diced onion. This lunch special is a balanced meal, an art form, an Appalachian tradition, and honest cooking.

At restaurants such as the Windmill in Pikeville, Kentucky, or the Rusty Fork in Elkhorn City, Kentucky, mountain chefs serve cornbread with country fried steak, meat loaf, fried chicken livers, vegetable soup, roast pork, and fried chicken. For old-fashioned mountain eating, a wedge of cornbread served with a wilted lettuce salad and a glass of buttermilk makes a complete meal. So do soup beans, cornbread, and chow chow. For a feast, the kitchen staff adds fried potatoes and a thick slice of onion. This combination is as basic to the mountain spirit as squirrel hunting, poke sallet, and bluegrass music. An order of cornbread and soup beans (recipes for both can be found in Part Two) is both a culinary feat and feast for the spirit. Leftover cornbread makes good bread pudding, cornbread stuffing, and cornbread salad, and it can be fed to the chickens or fried in lard!

Now, let's ponder going to the kitchen, measuring ingredients, mixing batter, and baking cornbread. Simple. Quick. Thin. Not fancy and not complicated. The recipe for simple cornbread in Part Two, as well as the variation for kernel cornbread, represent the good that comes from old-style mountain cooking, and the two recipes appeal to modern minimalist-style chefs who want to serve unadorned cornbread. With four ingredients, one mixing bowl, and a trusty black iron skillet, this recipe is easy to prepare. The pone should be crusty and 1 inch thick.

The recipe for the more robust mountain country cornbread found in Part Two produces a light, low-calorie, quick bread. Not like a muffin, the bread is not sweet, not greasy, and not tender. Bread flour and egg whites hold it together so that it crumbles less than other recipes. The stone-ground cornmeal poured in the skillet and over the top gives the crust a bit of crunch as well as a primitive country appearance.

Finally in Part Two, you'll see the recipe for jalapeño cornbread. This recipe has become popular in recent years. The cornbread is almost a meal in itself, and, hot from the oven, a slice is crusty, moist, heavy, and full of goodies. If it were not baked in a cast-iron skillet, some would say it did not taste like true mountain cornbread. To develop a crusty cornbread surface, consider cast iron.

Cast-Iron Cookware: Cauldrons, Firedogs, and Spiders

Mountain cooks rely on cast-iron cookware. While evidence exists that early settlers used other materials such as tin, for certain tools iron was dominant, and it has remained popular for frying and baking. Indeed, cast-iron cookware has become almost symbolic of the Appalachian kitchen, and among the symbols are the skillet, cauldron, and Dutch oven. With these cooking utensils and an outfitted hearth, a frontier cabin was well equipped.

But equipping a cabin on the frontier was not easy. These pans were so highly valued that many settlers brought them from Europe. Others purchased them in eastern cities such as New York or Philadelphia. Sometimes several families shared cast-iron cookware. Frequently and even today, these pans were passed on from one generation to the next.

As fundamental to the mountain kitchen as corn or pork, cast-iron cookware continues to be prized by cooks and chefs because it distributes heat evenly, quick-seals meats, and slow-cooks stews. In country kitchens, the highly durable cast-iron skillet is the pan of choice for cornbread and biscuits, and in using these tools, cooks are part of a tradition as old as iron.

As Appalachia was settled, industrialists moved to the area and built foundries and forges. Cold blast furnaces eventually became hot blast furnaces, and they produced wrought iron, pig iron, and steel. At some iron works, molten iron was cast into cookware such as skillets and cauldrons, and others produced iron for general purposes, which included steel beams, pipes, plates, and rails. For every furnace, the demand for these products supported a number of small forges where artisans used iron to hammer out tools.

Iron production, casting, and blacksmithing are three steps along a continuum of iron work that produces a great variety of tools from rifles to skillets. While iron-making goes back 4,000 years and began as a crude process of hammering carbon or soot into iron to make steel, the Iron Age gained preeminence about 3,000 years ago. Later, the Industrial Age produced tools that further advanced civilization. For example, farmers shaped plow blades, farriers made horseshoes, builders used froes to split shingles, and blacksmiths made steel tools of all kinds. Today's hot blast furnaces produce various grades of iron, and these grades contain as many as 20 different elements that result in many types of steel.

Cast iron is an alloy of iron and 3 percent carbon that is both soft and strong as well as hard and brittle. Carbon strengthens iron. Industrialists make cast-iron cookware by heating the iron to 2,800°F and then cooling it in various molds. Each mold is in the shape of a pan or utensil.

Cast-Iron Utensils

Central to frontier cabins were small hearths. Settlers outfitted these cooking areas with cast-iron firedogs, or andirons, and cast-iron cookware. They used trammels to adjust pot height and swinging iron cranes to move pots to and from the fire. In addition, they used a variety of hand-forged tools including pothooks, fire shovels, fire pokers, fireplace tongs, and two-handled grips. For hot hearth cooking, settlers used long-handled skimmers, ladles, spoons, and forks.

Their cast-iron cooking utensils included pots that hung and pans with feet. For example, cooks used long-handled, footed skillets called spiders. Because they had feet, spiders could stand directly on the hearth, and their three legs held them above the hot coals.

In addition to the spider, the Dutch oven was popular. A Dutch oven is a large, all-purpose pot with a rounded or flanged lid, three legs, and a round wire handle. Cooks use the handle to carry the pot or hang it above the fire. While cooks hung the Dutch oven over the fire and used it for boiling, in early homes they also used it for baking bread. This is because early rural Appalachian cabins did not have brick or tin bread ovens. To bake cornbread in a Dutch oven, the woman poured batter directly into the pan, placed the lid on top, and moved the oven over the heat. If the oven had a flanged lid, she could also place burning coals on the lid. As its name implies, Dutch ovens were indeed baking ovens, and because they had both feet and hanging rings, they were more versatile than spiders or cauldrons.

A third essential frontier vessel was the cauldron, a large hanging pot used to boil stews or make apple butter. Mountaineers called this pot a rendering pot because at hog killing time they used it to render lard from fat. Because cauldrons were large, old-time cooks used them to make burgoo and Brunswick stew as well as to wash clothes on wash day.

Slowly, during the latter two-thirds of the nineteenth century and the beginning of the twentieth century, hearths gave way to wood and coal stoves, and the cookware that once had feet on the bottom or hanging handles on top was modified for use on a flat stovetop. While cooks still used fire stokers, spiders lost their feet and became skillets, and cauldrons became saucepans. Today, the skillet is the most common cast-iron utensil.

Once cooks had adapted from the hearth to wood or coal stoves, the next transition to gas or electric ranges was even easier. The cast-iron cookware that was used on wood stoves was also used on modern ranges. Even today, cooks are using cast-iron pans that were made for wood and coal stoves.

To summarize, the different pieces of cast-iron cookware reflect three periods of cooking history. Settlers used spiders, Dutch ovens, and cauldrons in hearths; later mountaineers used skillets, saucepans, and loaf pans in stoves, and today some restaurant chefs use specialty shaped pans such as fajita sets, chef's platters, and oval serving griddles. In addition, restaurants and some home cooks have a need for specialty cornbread pans shaped as serving-size perch, cactus, and stars. Lodge Manufacturing makes these items as well as over 100 others (see Mail-Order Sources).

Cast iron is heavy, natural, and durable. In modern kitchens outfitted with countertops of granite, tile, or wood, cast iron contributes to the feeling of permanence. In the age of reflective All-Clad and light Club Aluminum, cast iron is unique. By the same token, steel cookware does not seem to fit with Formica, fiberglass, or plastic. In modern kitchens, cast iron looks old, binds the present with the past, and might be the source of arguments when the estate is settled. Cast iron is not shiny like stainless steel, does not heat quickly like aluminum, and does not carry the status of copper, but cast iron is Appalachian to its core.

Rather than buying new pans, many cooks prefer to buy the smooth, well-used and -seasoned old pans. Collectors find the pans in country stores and antique malls, at flea markets and yard sales, and, of course, on the Internet. Many brands, including Wagner, Griswold, Filley, Merit, and Victor, are available. Some old skillets have a major build-up of baked-on grease, and you can clean the pan by baking it in a self-cleaning oven. After you bake the pan through the self-cleaning cycle, the crust comes off with a wire pad. Then, the pan is better than new, and it needs to be seasoned (directions for seasoning pans are provided in the next section).

Cooks looking to buy new cast-iron cookware will find that the pans are not expensive. Adding to their attractiveness, the pans last forever and they retain their value. Small new skillets are priced around $20.00 while large ones may cost under $50.00. Lodge Manufacturing sells a five-piece set of cast-iron cookware for about $65.00. In performance, these pans are competitive with other cookware choices, and they may be half or even one-third the cost.

Buying new cast-iron pieces today means buying imports or pieces from Lodge Manufacturing. Lodge is a good choice in that it is not only an American company, but since 1896 it has been located in Appalachia, specifically in South Pittsburg, Tennessee. Lodge offers a huge variety of cast-iron cookware for kitchens, grills, and camps. Its price list includes some 200 different pieces. These range from the common skillet to a line of seasoned cast iron to another line of items for the restaurant kitchen. Among the special items are two-sided griddles, deep fryer kits, and covered chicken fryers. While any cast-iron cookware is ideal for car camping or outdoor camps, Lodge makes special camping items such as tripods for hanging pots, lid lifters, outdoor grills, charcoal starters, and cookers with griddle lids (see Lodge Manufacturing in the list of Mail-Order Sources).

With so many items of cast-iron cookware available, it is not surprising that this old and simple material has many benefits. The big advantage of cast iron is its ability to conduct and hold heat. Conduction means that the iron material draws heat in and spreads it out, creating even heat that beautifully browns cornbread, biscuits, and cakes. Another benefit of cast iron is that, if it is well cured, baked cornbread and biscuits do not stick. Well-seasoned pans have a natural non-stick surface. Because cast iron holds heat, the material is ideal for browning meats. Drop meat into a kettle, and rather than the meat cooling the pan, the pan browns the meat.

Cast-iron cookware is made of a single piece of pure molded integral steel. Manufacturers do not coat, paint, shine, bolt, or piece the pans. Arms, lids, pulls, and handles are part of the pan, and this one-piece construction allows pans to be placed in hot ovens, directly in the fire, or on coals. The steel is thick enough that it will not warp over high heat.

Cast-iron cookware not only lasts for generations, but it is a joy to use. When it is stored or used, cast iron feels secure and permanent, and the material is cool to touch. The surface is smooth and with its imperfections it reflects a beautiful, soft, uneven black with a tinge of brown. Using cast iron is a different experience from using aluminum, copper, or stainless steel. Each has a place. Copper glistens and stainless steel casts a mirror image, however, cast iron is primitive, mountain, and homey to the core.

Another benefit of cast-iron cookware is that it adds iron to the diet. Iron is a necessary nutrient, and with each use, a microscopic amount of cast iron wears off the pan. Some of this enters the body, and if too much iron is taken in, the body eliminates it. Because cast iron is composed of natural elements, these pans are chemically active, magnetic, and good conductors of electricity. Finally, some cooks are so fond of their cast iron that they use the cookware as serving ware. These cooks buy beautiful old pans and cauldrons, and cook with them in the kitchen and serve from them at the table. In this case, cast iron is competing with those gleaming white decorated oven-to-table Corning Ware casseroles.

Iron's many advantages also cause four disadvantages. First, cast iron discolors acid foods such as lemons and light-colored foods such as carrots. This is because cast iron is reactive, meaning that highly acidic foods, such as pickled beets, react with the metal. Second, cast iron conducts heat slower than copper or aluminum does. However, once heated, it heats more evenly and retains heat better. Third, cast-iron cookware is heavy. A frequent complaint from older women is that they cannot hold their cast-iron skillets. While the new skillets have handles on both sides, these women must lift the old ones with a single handle that requires a strong grip. Finally, cast iron corrodes. Left out in the rain or soaking in the sink, it rusts. Because cast iron rusts, it must be seasoned.

To Season Cast Iron

To prevent rusting, cooks season or cure cast-iron cookware. This process embeds oil into the pores and fissures of the iron. To season a new pan, coat it with oil or Crisco. If the pan is warm, Crisco will spread easily. Once a pan is coated, experienced cooks bake it upside down on a large baking sheet at 350°F for an hour or so. The baking sheet catches the drips and keeps the oven clean.

Then, a paper towel and a couple of wipes will keep the pan clean. With use, this process is repeated, the oil finish builds, and the pan becomes not only more durable but also more resistant to rust. Old pans become smooth and reflective. Eventually they glisten, and, like old family Bibles, they improve with age.

Once cast-iron pans have been seasoned, cooks find them ideal for frying, blackening, boiling, and baking. Many Appalachian cooks designate a cast-iron skillet for one purpose: to make cornbread or bake biscuits. This is good because each time the pan is used, oil is added, the baked items release easily from the pan, the pan does not get dirty, and it requires no soap or water. Once the cornbread or biscuits are out of the pan and the pan cools, the cook wipes off the excess oil with a paper towel and puts the pan away. Other cooks use Dutch ovens as well as roasters for oven baking. Roasting in cast iron is excellent for stews, roasts, and vegetables because these pans aid in caramelization.

If a coated, fried food such as fish or chicken starts to stick to the pan, it needs to be cooked a bit longer. Then, the pan releases it with the coating intact. A browned crust sticks less than one that is undercooked. This of course is like making pancakes. If you turn a pancake too soon, it gets very messy, but if you let it cook until the bottom browns, the pancake will flip easily.

As mentioned above, some cooks will face the problem that the acid in wine, tomatoes, and lemons interact with cast iron and may cause an iron flavor. However, this occurs only after prolonged contact. Normally, if these items are in the pan for less than ten minutes, it will not cause the food to taste of iron.

Like pans of any material, cast iron must be cleaned. Cast-iron cookware can be soaked, washed, scoured, scraped, and filed. Cast iron is steel and can be treated roughly. If a pan has rough or sharp edges, a steel file or grinding stone will smooth them. No cleaning material will cause harm. Cast iron is the tough one against steel wool, copper pads, steel brushes, and abrasive sponges. Use them forcefully and cast iron is the winner. Some cooks realize that because they use cast-iron skillets for high-temperature baking and hot frying, the pans do not require the sterilization of soap or detergent. High heat sterilizes.

For those who wash cast iron with soap and water, once it is clean, they dry and oil it. Any oil coating brings a shine and eliminates rust. If cast iron is left wet, it oxidizes, and the resulting rust looks bad. When this happens, wipe off the rust, coat the pan with oil, and rub the oil with a paper towel. The long, slow soaking and soaping process of a dishwasher penetrates cast iron, and while dishwashers will not damage the iron, they will remove the build-up of oil and leave some rust. Soaking in a sink of hot, soapy water has the same results: It removes oil and causes rust. After soaking, some cooks cure the pan while others simply wipe on a light coat of oil. Then, when the pans shine, home cooks store them stacked on a shelf, back in the oven, or hung above the stove. Skillets come in various sizes from 6 to 15 inches, and five or six skillets will stack or nest on a shelf.

More Corn: Moonshine or Skull Cracker, White Lightning, Mountain Dew

While moonshine is not as old as cast iron and the beverage is not as widely consumed as cornbread, it holds a central role in the history and lore of Appalachia. The word moonshine entered the English language around 1600 when smugglers traded white brandy on the English coasts of Kent and Sussex. Like many who continued the tradition, these moonshiners were evading English taxes, and to do so they made or transported the beverage under moonlight to escape the law. "Moonshine" continues to be an appropriate reference to high-proof whiskey produced illegally and kept hidden from the law. Moonshine is illegal because producers do not abide by the laws regarding manufacture, distribution, sale, or taxation.

In Appalachia, mountaineers enjoy a proud, however hazardous, tradition of making what is perhaps the finest pure corn whiskey in the world. This beverage is both an Appalachian tradition and a negative Appalachian stereotype. Appalachian connections to the beverage are both natural and cultural. Clear streams, deep valleys, dry corn, soft water, and industrious farmers come together in the production of whiskey, the almost magical mountain dew or white lightning. Those who know the drink call it corn squeezin's, skull cracker, thump whiskey, happy Sally, stumper wine, blockade whiskey, tiger's sweat, rotgut, or busthead.

In addition, they may also know "revenuers." From the early frontier days and continuing today, as long as revenue agents did not cause trouble, making moonshine was an efficient, profitable, and pleasurable way to sell corn. Making the 100-proof whiskey was what farmers did to add value to their corn. During the process, one and a half bushels of corn were reduced to a gallon of whiskey, or put differently, a mule could carry only four bushels of corn. However, when that corn was made into whiskey, the same mule could carry the whiskey made from 24 bushels of corn or what was called "liquid corn." How profitable was moonshine? In the 1930s during national Prohibition, selling a bushel of corn after converting it to moonshine might have been 100 times more profitable than selling the bushel of corn. Two hundred years earlier, when Appalachia was first being settled, a good copper still and worm had the same value as a 200-acre farm.

Among the reasons corn whiskey had such high value was that making it required hard work and great risk. First, most moonshiners built their stills. Then, they built furnaces, stills, and condensing units, and when the mash was ready, they built fires. The work required moving huge amounts of corn, wood, sugar, and whiskey, each of which could attract the attention of the law. And then, working around a fire in the dark on the side of a hill was dirty, and always it seemed that moonshiners got burned on the blistering hot metal. Some "shiners" say that skin sticks to copper better than glue holds paper, and once it sticks, it must be torn off. This struggle adds to the glory. Moonshiners had to be among the toughest of men equal at least to pirates, cattle rustlers, drug dealers, or marijuana farmers.

Today, those who grow marijuana have a simpler task than does the moonshiner. They grow a crop, let it dry, and pack it in plastic bags. They do not build stills or assemble fuel, buy sugar, grow corn, or bottle the product. In comparison to quart jars of moonshine, dry marijuana is light and easy to carry. Today, marijuana and other drugs have largely replaced moonshine as sources of illegal income. However, moonshine is still available, and serving it brings to mind its long and colorful history.

Moonshine History

Early settlers from Scotland, Ireland, Wales, and England came to the mountains with distilling tools and quickly adapted their old recipes to include corn. They called it whiskey, and it became more valuable than the Continental Dollar. They used whiskey to barter for salt, nails, and even taxes. Some used it to buy property.

Soon after the colonies became a nation, specifically on March 3, 1791, Congress imposed taxes on stills and whiskey. This new law caused the 1794 Whiskey Rebellion, an uprising in western Pennsylvania. The settlers, mainly Scots-Irish, saw the tax as unfair and rebelled. President Washington was forced to engage troops to stop the rioting, and the tax remained in force for 11 years. Sixty years later, in 1862, the government again began controlling production by requiring a license for production.

With government restrictions came the American use of the term *moonshiner*. Once again, farmers who refused to buy the license or pay the tax started doing their work at night in the shadows of the law. These backwoods traders continued to sell moonshine freely from New York to Atlanta until around 1910, when states such as Tennessee and Georgia began enacting prohibition laws. These state laws outlawed the production, transportation, or sale of alcoholic beverages. In West Virginia, prohibition took effect in 1913, seven years before the beginning of the great national drought. Then, from 1920 until 1933 when national Prohibition was adopted, there was a dramatic increase in moonshining. Once again, this work of folk heroes and backwoodsmen was hidden from view and incurred the risk of arrest. In Kentucky alone, government agents seized an average of 675 stills per year during the 13 years of Prohibition. Even when national Prohibition ended, many Southern states remained "dry," meaning that it was illegal to sell alcoholic beverages, and from 1960 through 1969 still seizures in Kentucky averaged 379 per year.

Over the last 30 years as voters struck down local prohibition laws, regions became "wet," and economic conditions improved, moonshine production declined. However, in early March 2000, in the town of Rocky Mount, Virginia, a new task force of state and federal agents, headed up by Bartley H. McEntire, made an arrest. As the *New York Times* reported on March 23, 2000, Operation Lightning Strikes shut down a 1,000-gallon still and, in so doing, reduced the flow of inexpensive high-proof liquor to the East Coast. According to McEntire, the leading target of his agents was 60-year-old moonshiner, Ralph D. Hale, who could have been producing about 180,000 gallons of illegal liquor per year. For this new breed of business-style moonshiners the term may expand to include 150-proof pure corn whiskey or a variety of berry-flavored brandies.

A significant offshoot of moonshining and prohibition is stock car racing. Today's popular National Association of Stock Car Automobile Racing—NASCAR—circuit got its start when some drivers worked through the night using World War II-era Ford coupes to carry moonshine to Atlanta. Then, on Saturday night, they gathered at a speedway to race. However, long before NASCAR, stills were in use, and moonshine was transported. In some mountain regions, stills were almost as common as smoke houses and hen houses.

Making Moonshine

How do moonshiners produce whiskey? They ferment, distill, and condense. To do this, they need a still, which consists of a source of heat or a fire box, a large sealed copper pot or vessel to hold the mash and create the vapor, and a condensing coil or worm. To these major elements, the moonshiner adds various pipes to move water, steam, beer, faints, and slop. He also uses mash sticks to break the solid cap that forms on top of the mash as it ferments in the barrel and glass proof vials (glass tubes) to check proof. As each run ends, alcohol flows out of the condensing worm and into a jug.

However, before Appalachian moonshiners can set up stills and start fermentation, they must find a protected area or a hollow deep in the hills. They locate in an area that has cool, clean water and protection from revenue agents. The water is important. Good moonshine water is soft, and moonshiners know the water is limestone softened if they see red horsemint growing on the banks. Second, the hollow must be deep or well protected and far from the main road so it won't be discovered by revenue agents.

Years ago to avoid discovery, careful moonshiners didn't let cattle or hogs eat slop or mess in the creek water, and they didn't burn wood that made smoke. Why? Tradition and common sense tell us that water scented by animals and smoky fires attract agents. In addition, moonshiners don't spread gossip, and they don't tell anyone except family about their still.

While those who make whiskey can use all foodstuffs including vegetables, fruit, and grain, mountain farmers generally rely on dry corn and water. Once they locate the still, farmers move dry corn from the barn to the still, and at the still they sprout it under moist conditions. Next, they crush the sprouted corn and mix it with additional water to make mash, which then begins to ferment. However, good mash includes more than corn and water. Moonshiners make the mash (fermented corn) from about 80 percent ground corn and some barley, rye, sorghum syrup, or sugar. If they add yeast, the fermentation is fast, taking as little as four days; if they don't add yeast and if the temperatures are low, fermentation takes longer, maybe two weeks. The formula used by moonshiners varied greatly, as they were free to combine ingredients to suit their needs or tastes. This is in contrast to legal corn whiskey which, according to government standards, is made with 80 percent corn mash.

Then, moonshiners use the fermented mash to "run off" the whiskey, distilling it twice with cold running water, and not letting the still get too hot or too cold. When the drink is ready, they check the proof, and if the proof is too high, they temper or reduce it. Skilled moonshiners make a drink that they know is good, and when it is ready, they'll look in your eye and say with a slight smile, "This is the best whiskey in the world." Today, it is common practice to make clear, flavored, and charred moonshine. Flavors of moonshine include blackberry, grape, peach, and cherry. Burned or charred moonshine is caramel in color and has a slight burned flavor.

Making moonshine is an art, and a few men continue to work in the shadows of deep hollows where they run the "water" through copper worms. Unfortunately, they also work in fear of the law. Violation of federal liquor laws, as you would expect, can result in severe fines and imprisonment. In place of moonshine, many state-approved liquor vendors sell pure grain alcohol or a substitute such as bourbon, cognac, or sour mash whiskey. Government-approved beverages are not only legal, they are also safe.

Drinking Moonshine
Those who live in the mountains usually serve moonshine straight without ice or water. Some mix it with coffee, Coke, or Pepsi. Others serve moonshine before dinner in a brandy snifter with salty snacks, or serve as you would an after-dinner drink. While the possibilities are endless, moonshine also makes a fine cocktail when mixed with grapefruit juice and served over ice.

Sources

Joseph Earl Dabney. *Mountain Spirits: A Chronicle of Corn Whiskey from King James' Ulster Plantation to America's Appalachians and the Moonshine Life.* New York: Charles Scribner's Sons, 1974.

Foxfire 5: Ironmaking, Blacksmithing, Flintlock Rifles, Bear Hunting, and Other Affairs of Plain Living. Eliot Wigginton, Editor. Garden City, New York: Doubleday, Anchor Books, 1975.

Foxfire Book of Toys and Games, The, Reminiscences and Instructions from Appalachia. Linda Garland Page and Hilton Smith, Editors. Garden City, New York: Doubleday, Anchor Books, 1985.

Ronni Lundy. *Shuck Beans, Stack Cakes, and Honest Fried Chicken: The Heart and Soul of Southern Country Kitchens.* New York: The Atlantic Monthly Press, 1991.

Jesse Stuart. *The Chronological Bibliography of Works by Jesse Stuart.* Ashland, Kentucky: Jesse Stuart Foundation, 1997.

SEVEN

Herbs and Game

Dry Land Fish, Greens, and Wild Game

Dry Land Fish: Mountain Morels

Morels are one of the great luxuries of Appalachia. Mountaineers gather them in abundance and collect them with pride. Morels are earthy in flavor and robust in texture, and perhaps because the mushrooms are collected so frequently and by so many, Appalachians know them by various names including: markels, dry land fish, hickory chickens, molly moochers, dog peckers, sponge mushrooms, pine cones, and spring mushrooms. Some mountaineers say they call morels dry land fish because they taste like fish, while others use the term because they fry them like fish. In *More Than Moonshine,* Sidney Farr says that her family calls them hickory chickens because when cooked they remind them of chicken, and they grow under hickory trees.

Woodsy in nature and reminiscent of trolls, morels are totally void of green. In the spring they push their ribbed bodies through grass and leaves when the blue violets peak, apple trees lose their blossoms, and dandelions go to seed. Wild turkey season and morels come together and, when they pass, the spring is about half over.

Morels grow in open fields, old orchards, and overgrown pastures. In markets, the season for fresh wild morels is April, May, and June. In parts of Kentucky, however, the morel season is short, maybe just two weeks; however, if you were to follow the spring from northern Georgia to northern Canada, the morel season would last from March to June. Morels and ramps (wild leeks, discussed in the section that follows) are in season at the same time, and uptown chefs often combine them in preparations as varied as pizza, grits, smoked salmon, vichyssoise, and scrambled eggs. Even though morels are widely collected, the novice collector must be careful because, like many wild mushrooms, the morel has a poisonous look-alike, the wrinkled thimble cap (*Verpa bohemica*). Other popular edible wild mushrooms include boletus, chanterelles, and truffles. Today, growers cultivate many of these "wild" mushrooms and sell them in markets.

The scientific name for the common yellow morel is *Morchella eculenta*. Two other morels, the small black morel (*M. elata*) and the half-free morel (*M. semilibera*) also grow in Appalachia and are sold in specialty food stores. The various morels have excellent flavor, a flavor often described as "smoky, earthy, and nutty."

In the kitchen, Appalachian cooks cut dry land fish lengthwise, dip them in buttermilk, roll them in cornmeal, and fry them like catfish. Others in the southern highlands fry morels after soaking them in salt water. Some roll morel halves in flour or meal, dip them in beaten egg, and then fry them in lard. (A recipe for morels appears in Part Two.)

For creamed morels, cooks boil small pieces with a touch of diced onion, butter, salt and pepper. They then reduce the broth and thicken it with flour, add heavy cream, and serve over fresh biscuits or puff pastry. Call it morel morning gravy; creamed morels are mountain to the bone.

Ramps

In April of 1984, Oliver and Anne Walston traveled from their farm in Cambridge, England, to Richwood, West Virginia, to eat fresh fried ramps. Why? They went for the flavor: tangy, whole, and spicy hot. Ramps (*Allium tricoccum*) are a mixture of onion, garlic, and leek, yet different. In West Virginia as in other parts of Appalachia, mountaineers eat ramps raw, fried, boiled, stewed, and scrambled with eggs. Boiled ramps can be fried with bacon, sausage, country ham, and potatoes. Cooks then offer the fried ramps (see the recipe in Part Two) with cornbread, biscuits and gravy, soup beans, and sassafras tea. In addition, some mountaineers make ramp pie, ramp chili, and ramp meat loaf. Glen Facemire (see Ramps in Mail-Order Sources) sells ramps dried, pickled, and in jelly and candy.

However, the various community-wide ramp celebrations are more significant than is any individual ramp entrepreneur. Tradition, flavor, novelty, and profit explain some of the enthusiasm behind the dozen or more Appalachian ramp celebrations found in the mountains of West Virginia, Tennessee, North Carolina, and Virginia. Communities hold these events toward the end of April well after the peak of ramp season, but this allows the organizers to rely on volunteer help and to prepare and then freeze the ramps ahead of the event. (See Feast of the Ramson in the Festivals and Events section at the end of the book.)

Ramps
Jeff Mann

It's a craving at this point.
Mid-April, the hand-lettering signs
show up on country storefronts, roadside stands.

I seize the last decent batch
from the bottom of a cooler at Capitol Market.
"You'll reek for three days!"

my grandmother used to warn,
but it's only onion apocalypse
if you eat them raw, I promise.

In the sink I shake off forest mulch,
black mountain earth, I trim off the hydra-
headed roots, dirty diaphaneity of outer skin,

then rinse the leaves, so like lilies
of the valley my mother grew once
by the Greenbrier River, within a grove

of pines. Chopped coarsely, they pop
and sizzle in the bacon fat before I add
sliced potatoes, patience, scrambled eggs.

Then finally taste that earthy, spicy, garlic edge.
We love ramps because they're rare, only once a year,
taking spring's evanescence between our teeth

after months of hillside pewter, hoarfrost pasture,
paralyzed ponds, breathing gray
in and out, in and out. We love them because

ramps remember the wild asleep
beneath our skin, a rich green wild
we hungrily take in and taste again,

while another Wal-Mart goes up,
another well runs dry,
mastectomies slice off another mountaintop.

Poke: Green Stems, Purple Rain, Spring Potherb

Poke is undoubtedly Appalachia's most popular, most available, and most eaten wild potherb. This tall perennial plant is both strange and uniquely beautiful. During much of the growing season, parts of the plant are poisonous, but in the spring it sprouts tender, edible shoots and leaves. Then, the flowers come.

The early sprouts are tasty. Poke shoots resemble asparagus shoots, except they are larger. In addition, poke is sweeter, more succulent, more tender, and lacks the strong flavor of asparagus. From a grand tuber, sometimes the size of a man's arm, poke sends up sprouts that are large, abundant, and easily gathered. These shoots emerge from March through May, depending on the climate. When the shoots get 5 to 10 inches high, foragers cut them a few inches above the ground.

Poke is then boiled, fried, canned, and pickled. Vintners ferment it to make wine, and home cooks scramble it with eggs. According to a once-popular source, Euell Gibbons' *Stalking the Wild Asparagus,* some foragers use a diluted pokeberry tea as tonic or medicine to protect children from boils and pimples. Gibbons also recalled that in his childhood his parents put pieces of poke root in the chickens' water to "protect them from disease."

This, however, is misleading, as parts of the plant are poisonous. Even though the young poke shoots and leaves are wonderful greens, the mature leaves and shoots as well as poke roots and berries are poisonous. Even so, while it may be against the law to sell dried poke root, some health food stores sell it for tea, and label it "not for human consumption." Other plants such as rhubarb also have poisonous parts. With rhubarb, the stems are edible, and the leaves are discarded because they are poisonous. Poke is also like apples. Apple seeds are poisonous, but people don't eat apple seeds because in large quantities (several cups) they might be fatal.

Rodale's *Illustrated Encyclopedia of Herbs* supports the conventional wisdom on the subject of poke by saying that "children who've eaten the inky pokeberries have died." But Rodale's *Encyclopedia* is vague in that it does not say whether the children ate three berries or three cups of berries. Caution is good, but you don't need to avoid the entire plant when the young stems and leaves have value and a long history of use.

Poke greens are good food, but when the plants mature, the stems and greens become tough. This is no different from green beans that are too old or rhubarb stems that become hollow and dry. When poke stems are young and filled with pith, you'll find them tender and succulent.

Because of its availability over a wide climatic zone and popularity, the poke plant, *Phytolacca americana,* has many common names. Poke is also called pokeweed, poke sallet, pigeonberry (eaten by pigeons and mockingbirds), inkberry (a common source of ink), garget (causing inflammation of the udder of a cow), and cancer jalap (a cure for cancer). It grows in disturbed and acidic soils, fence rows, road cuts, and around barns from Maine to Florida and west to the Great Plains.

Poke also thrives in basements, can houses, and warm cellars. In the fall after the big frost, industrious gardeners dig or "grub" the roots and plant them in large containers. (Grub is the common word for the labor-intensive process of digging the roots with a shovel and maybe a pick.) Root gatherers leave the tubs outside until they have taken several heavy frosts. Then, any time from December through February, they carry the tubs to a warm, dark area, and then, about once a week, they can cut the large, succulent, white shoots. A week later more will be ready. Three large washtubs with about five roots in each one will feed a family for three months.

While only a few gardeners grow poke indoors, many others watch it growing outside, and some find great beauty as the season progresses: deep spring green, early summer white flowers, purple strands of late summer berries, and finally, the fall purple plants. Both birds and farmers are drawn to this drama.

It takes several years for poke seedlings to reach their maximum size, and once they do, the tubers become productive. Around April 20 in the warm areas of eastern Kentucky, as many as eight shoots push up from a single mature poke tuber. Throughout the early spring, the shoots stretch, spread, and grow upward until around June 10, when the first white flowers appear. About three weeks later, the plant, which may be 8 feet tall, is a mass of green leaves and decorated with long stems of tiny, delicate white flowers, each containing five petals that cluster around a green center. Bees pollinate.

Then, in mid-summer, these tiny green centers expand into bright, shiny green berries. They stay green until the first of August, and then as the lower leaves die, the berries and plant stalks turn purple. With each passing week in August, the plants become heavier with berries. On hillsides and road cuts, the plants break down under the weight. Throughout August and into September, the white flowers continue to form and green berries emerge from their centers, but in the late summer purple dominates, green fades, and finally by mid-September the flowers are gone, leaving a plant covered with many long clusters of berries.

A freeze of about 28°F kills poke leaves, but this only lightens the load, and the woody stems continue to support the fruit. After the first frost and during light October and November rains, the purple berries drip purple drops. For several months this purple "rain" causes the soil below to turn purple.

And then the birds come. When the first berries turn purple and continuing through February, large gray mockingbirds visit the plant and eat the berries. Mockingbirds, with their 12-inch wing span and their abusive noise, dash in, eat from odd positions, and dart away, and their interest in the berries remains high through the winter. When snow covers the ground, the birds come back, and, again, they eat with enthusiasm.

By March and April, all that is left of the grand plant is a gray mass of woody stems and a few dried-up and shriveled berries. Yet, still the birds come. Later, when the shoots begin to emerge, the old woody stems lie on the ground and the green of spring hides them from view. The peaceful drama begins again.

When the fire pinks and winter cress are in bloom, the gray, woody stems standing above the new season's growth draw foragers. In a good patch, a mess of poke can be cut in five minutes, but most of the plants are spread out and gathering 20 stems takes a bit longer.

Unfortunately, most of the poke in North America goes to waste even though cutting the edible stems is easy. Gatherers cut the shoots with a sharp knife a little above the ground. If the stem is tough or hollow, it is too old, and they discard it. If the leaves point upward like those at the top of a growing cornstalk, and if the stem is tender, both the shoots and leaves are good to eat, even if the plant is 3 feet tall.

Healthy, fast-growing poke plants will send up shoots that may be as much as 1½ inches across. These thick, solid shoots get tall quickly, but most gatherers prefer using the thinner stems, those that are about ¾ inch across.

After gathering a bunch of poke, foragers remove the dead grass and dry leaves, and in the kitchen they begin cooking. They fill a large pan with enough water to cover the poke, and they bring the water to a boil. Then, they lower the poke into the water, boil it 3 minutes, and pour off the water. The greens are then refrigerated, frozen, or used. While some cooks serve the boiled greens with salt and pepper or even bacon bits, others simmer them with salt pork and onions or fry them with bacon grease. Fried poke is popular. Each bite yields a crunchy, salty outside and a tender, succulent center. Both the preparation process and the results are much like that of fried green tomatoes or battered fried fish.

Poke sallet is a common Appalachian dish of prepared poke that is combined and fried with beaten eggs. Traditional cooks begin by boiling the poke and draining the water. Then, they slice the stems and leaves into a skillet. As the poke dries from frying, most cooks flavor it with lard or bacon grease and add the beaten eggs, continuing to stir and scramble the mixture until the eggs are ready. Finally, they add salt and pepper and serve the sallet with sides of soup beans and cornbread.

The recipe found in Part Two includes cracklings and the variation suggests a poke sallet sandwich. So if you have a hankering for scrambled eggs, fried pork cracklings, and boiled spring poke, the flavor mix here will excite you. Then, several days after you serve the dish to guests, they will still be buzzing with excitement.

Wild Greens: Free for the Pickers

From the Blue Ridge to the Smoky Mountains and in the Cheats and Alleghenies, when low-lying gullies start to warm and grass begins to green, hill country highlanders respond with thoughts about killed chickentoe, poke sallet, and mixed wild greens. With scalding hot bacon grease, they soften and flavor greens, and around the old court house and in new high school gyms, mountaineers talk about "kilt lettuce" and "wilted greens."

Even today, some highlanders regard picking as an alternative to marketing. Shops are a necessity, and green markets as well as supermarkets offer great variety, but for a select few these sources are a second choice to fence rows, empty lots, and stream banks. In old coal camps and out in the country where houses are few, the wild greens of spring pop out of the ground like popcorn fills bags in microwave ovens. When the sky turns blue and temperatures rise, a walk or a drive combined with trained eyes reveals these delicate plants emerging from concrete cracks, around deserted homesteads, and behind outbuildings. On creek banks and hillsides, a wild market in a sea of greens is free for pickers.

These plants are also a tonic for health. Wild herbs help the blood flow, add fiber to the diet, and, as old-timers often recall, they were the essence of spring after a winter of canned turnip greens and boiled pinto beans. Picked on a Saturday morning with children in tow, wild greens are fresh and free of chemicals. Times have changed, but greens have not. Greens attract hobby cooks, fancy chefs, and back-country boys who gather, dig, wash, pound, chop, and fry. Skip the Vietnamese restaurant and Pacific

Rim dim sum. These plants grow wild and free. For a potherb salad recipe that combines many of the following wild greens, see Part Two.

Chickentoe: Also called spring beauty, wild violet, tanglegut, mouse's ear, two-leaf, and fairy spuds, this member of the purslane family is one of the greens of spring. The two common varieties (*Claytonia virginica* and *Claytonia lanceolata*) are widely distributed and grow in moist areas, deep gullies, forest openings, and along roadsides. *Uses:* Serve the leaves and stems fresh as a salad or "killed"—wilted with a hot dressing.

Cresses: This cress, also called dry land cress, winter cress, bitter cress, poor man's cabbage, and yellow rocket (*Barbarea verna* and *Barbarea vulgaris*), is a green that complements market salads or is cooked like turnip and collard greens. A member of the mustard family, it grows up to 2 feet tall and in the warmth of the southern Appalachians is gathered all winter. North of Tennessee it grows in the spring. *Uses:* Serve as part of wilted lettuce salad. Later in the season, chop and boil or boil twice.

Dandelion Greens: From Appalachia to Switzerland, wild food manuals recommend dandelion greens as a savory addition to salad; however, some uninitiated pickers may find them (*Taraxacum officinale*) sour or even bitter. Experienced foragers use young, tender dandelion greens with leaf lettuce, onion blades, and other spring greens in salad, or they cook them as a side dish to accompany the main course. *Uses:* Toss in salads; stir-fry with eggs.

Dock: Also called curled dock, sorrel dock, or spinach dock (*Rumex crispa*), this green is a member of the buckwheat family. The green is robust and healthy. Pick and prepare young leaves in mid to late spring. The plants are big, and with little effort gatherers can fill a grocery bag. *Uses:* Boil. Use as you would spinach, beet, turnip, or mustard greens.

Fiddleheads: Fiddleheads or corkscrew greens resemble the coiled end of a fiddle and are the first growth stage of a fern leaf.

Their color is bright green, and they taste a bit like asparagus and green beans. Texture distinguishes fiddleheads from other vegetables in that the stems are both crunchy and slightly gooey, viscous, or mucilaginous like okra, and when cooked, they add body to soups.

In the spring from Alabama to Vermont, pickers snap fiddleheads from hillsides and creek banks. While ostrich ferns (*Matteucia struthiopteris*) are the most popular, pickers in the central highlands also gather Christmas fern fiddleheads (*Polystichum acrostichoides*) and bracken fern (*Pteridium aquilinium*). Use only young fiddleheads, and avoid any with open fronds or expanding heads. *Uses:* Boil, add to stir-fry. Simmer in soups. Toss with sweet pea or carrot salads.

Lamb's Quarters: This mild-flavored wild green matures with garden peas. The plant grows as fast as or even faster than peas, but while peas die out in June, lamb's quarters stays green and tender most of the summer. Lamb's quarters (*Chenopodium album* and *C. bonus-henrcus*) has been eaten since Neolithic times and came to North America from Europe where in some parts the leaves are still used to prepare alpine soup and green dumplings. *Uses:* Harvest tender leaves and prepare them as you would spinach. Add to mixed potherbs.

Poke: Poke is known by several names, including pokeweed, inkberry, and pigeonberry. This green (*Phytolacca americana*) may be Appalachia's most popular, most available, and most eaten wild potherb. Gatherers eat the shoots when they are young, tender, and crisp; pokeberries, roots, and mature plants are poisonous. When picked, the stems should snap in two, and if they bend and don't break or if they are hollow, the stems are too old. Throughout the month of May, foragers gather the tender shoots and young leaves as they sprout from large underground tubers. Writers who compare poke to asparagus fail to recognize poke's special tenderness, succulent texture, and mild flavor. Poke is boiled 3 to 4 minutes and then the water is discarded. Boiling prepares poke for other uses. *Uses:* Serve boiled, pickled, fried in cornmeal, and stirred or baked in poke sallet. Boil poke stems with spinach, sprinkle them with lemon juice, garnish with hard-boiled eggs.

Purslane: Also called pusley (*Portulaca oleracea*), purslane is a low-growing, ground-hugging succulent. Each year it grows from seed and matures in late spring and summer. In gardens and flower beds, purslane is both prolific and common, and many gardeners pull it as a weed. However, those who eat the fresh leaves find them crisp, tender, greasy, and slightly acidic. Purslane is widespread, growing in the heat of direct sun or in the shade of houses and in both rich and thin sandy soils. In India and Persia, people have eaten boiled purslane for more than 2,000 years. *Uses:* Serve purslane fresh in salads. Euell Gibbons fried it in bacon grease, or he used it cooked to make a casserole with white sauce, eggs, and bread crumbs.

Ramps: Thought of as wild leeks (*Allium tricoccum*) and related to chives, garlic, scallions, and onions, ramps have a strong smell and pungent flavor. They grow in cool, rich, wooded hills and ravines. Gatherers eat both the bulbs and leaves, and they eat them either cooked or raw. When eaten raw, however, the resulting offensive smell is so strong that years ago in the mountains of North Carolina, teachers sometimes dismissed school because of the odor exuding from children. In mountain towns from Georgia to Maryland, communities come together in March and April for ramp suppers and festivals (see the Festivals and Events section at the end of the book). *Uses:* Serve boiled, fried, and with dumplings.

Shepherd's Purse: Also called St. James wort or mother's heart, shepherd's purse is an early spring annual whose roots, leaves, and seeds are eaten. Foragers eat this green (*Capsella bursa-pastoris*) cooked or in salads. In Japan, shepherd's purse is one of the seven most popular spring herbs. The Japanese serve it cooked with rice. *Uses:* Young, tender leaves are added to salads, boiled, or fried. The seeds are ground into meal for baking, and the leaves are sometimes used for tea.

Watercress: Watercress (*Nasturtium officinale*) is a member of the mustard family that grows wild in or near clear slow-moving streams. Its distinct peppery flavor and crisp texture sets it apart as a green or garnish. In the South, this green is available in fresh markets where vendors tie it in bunches and sell it year-round.

Uses: Watercress is used raw in soups, salads, and sandwiches. It pairs well with avocado or feta cheese. Also, use as a substitute for bean sprouts or a garnish with fish.

Wild Game and Fish

In addition to foraging for greens and collecting wild fruit, hunting and fishing have been an element of Appalachian foodways ever since aboriginal Native Americans settled the region some 12,000 years ago. The vast numbers of arrowheads collected near rivers and in hunting areas are evidence of thousands of years of hunting. European explorers learned quickly from Native Americans to hunt and use wild game. When living in the frontier, the fastest and surest way for settlers to meet their high daily caloric requirements was hunting large game. Once Europeans formed small communities, they combined wild and domestic meats in their diets.

In the early period of settlement, starting in the eighteenth century, large game such as buffalo, black bear, elk, white-tailed deer, feral hogs, and, in northern Appalachia, moose, were popular, but even early settlers kept cows for milk and raised hogs for meat. While buffalo were never abundant east of the Mississippi, when they were killed, settlers ate the hump and tongue first.

Frontiersmen took large game in traps and with both rifles and bows and arrows. Trapping or using baited deadfall traps was an important frontier skill. Here the hunter lured the bear with food into a large pit, and when the bear got too close, logs would fall and hold the bear in the pit until the hunter returned. Once the animal was killed, hunters divided the meat, with the tender parts, steaks and hams being most valued. In the case of buffaloes or even elk, the animals were too large to carry, and early hunters left large pieces of their carcasses in the woods. When they killed smaller animals such as white-tailed deer, they used the lower quality parts to make sausage, hamburger, or stew; and they saved the backstrap for frying and grilling.

While large game yielded vast quantities of meat quickly, Appalachians also enjoyed small game and fish, including the bobcat, fox, wild turkey, quail, dove, raccoon, possum, ground hog, rabbit, squirrel, and trout. These small animals survived into the nineteenth and twentieth centuries long after most large game was gone. Once killed, mountaineers used small game to supplement domesticated animals such as chickens, geese, and ducks. In addition, small game added variety to the diet and a break from salt-preserved pork.

Among small game, raccoon has a special allure. Dog-aided coon hunting is a specialty sport popular in the southern mountains from Mississippi to West Virginia. Coon hunting requires good marksmanship, trained hunting dogs, and, of course, the elusive raccoon. Once engaged in the chase, the sport revolves around the fast, clean, and nocturnal raccoon. Some hunters say the raccoon enjoys the hunt as much as the hunter, for this is an animal with character, intelligence, speed, and agility. As evidence of this, a raccoon will swim downstream, run along a fence top, or circle trees. When training dogs to chase coons, hunters often pair young pups with older dogs so they can experience tracking and treeing, as well as the excitement of the hunt. Hunters need from 15 minutes to an entire night to get a coon treed, and treeing a coon may be only the beginning of a hunt that can go on another hour or two. However, if the hunter is lucky, he will "have that coon in the sack" in 20 minutes.

Once the hunter kills a raccoon, he may value the animal for both its meat and skin. The meat has a distinctive sweet flavor, dark color, and smooth texture. In preparing the meat, cooks remove the fat, and they may marinate the meat in buttermilk or salted oil, vinegar, and water. Then, they cook the meat as a fricassee, roast, or stew; or if the critter is young, they fry it in lard or barbecue it on a grill.

The raccoon pelt is the well-known source of coonskin hats, which at some times have made hunting a valuable enterprise. In the 1950s, Fess Parker's portrayal of Davy Crockett had many boys wanting a coonskin cap. What was once a source of moccasins and hats for Native Americans became a symbol of the frontier. In addition to the value of meat and skin, killing raccoons aids farmers and gardeners who want to save their corn and other garden crops from what they call "pesky little critters."

Throughout the history of Appalachia, hunting has been either a necessity or a sport, and today, the mountains are a destination for hunters and fishermen. Fishing in the lakes of the Tennessee Valley Authority and elk viewing tours around Hazard, Kentucky, are both popular. Chefs offer wild game and wild greens. In some restaurants, bear and bison find a place along with chicken and beef, and in others dock with lamb's quarters may replace spinach. Chefs also serve less common meats such as dove and raccoon. For a wild game stew see Part Two.

In addition to wild game, mountaineers have a tradition of catching and preparing trout and bass. The vast, deciduous forests of Appalachia shelter many cold, clear streams, and they in turn support the always-fearful trout that alert hikers may spot in slow-moving pools.

While some people prefer fishing in streams, others enjoy lake fishing. With bait and lures they test their skills fishing for white and black bass, bream, carp, catfish, crappie, perch, pike, sunfish, trout, and even suckers. Some Appalachians use the most modern techniques including palm-sized electronic fish finders that measure fish size and location as well as bottom structures. Other fishermen use more standard techniques such as trolling or casting. Fishermen ply their skills on both public waters that have native or stocked fish and on private pay lakes. Old-timers talk about fishing by the signs of the zodiac and believe that the signs of the moon make a difference; others maintain that when the moon is small and the night dark, the fish bite better. Most fishermen, however, go out when the sun is low, either in the morning or evening.

For those who are not out on the rivers or lakes, mountain retreats often display live trout in large tanks, and for the customers who appreciate this delicacy, they serve the fish fresh from the tanks.

Frying is the preferred method for preparing trout because it allows the cook to watch the fish and, one hopes, not overcook them. For fried trout, you will coat the fish in a flour mixture and fry it in a small amount of oil. The simple flour coating, or *meunière,* develops flavor in the skin while not detracting from the delicacy of the trout.

This discussion of game and fish would not be complete without a comment on what is happening today. Recall that after about 100 years of settlement, Europeans had wiped out the large game including buffalo, bear, and elk. Now, with modern management, large game are coming back.

Starting in 1997 with seven free-ranging wild elk brought to eastern Kentucky from the southern Rocky Mountains, the Kentucky elk restoration program grew to more than 700 elk within three years. By 2003, the Kentucky Department of Fish and Wildlife had documented more than 3,000 elk in the state, and the restoration phase of the program was complete. In 2001, the state conducted the first legal elk hunt in about 150 years. Now, each year the state issues hunting tags, and elk are once again part of the Appalachian diet. The Kentucky program followed similar efforts in the Appalachian region of Tennessee, Maryland, West Virginia, and Pennsylvania. It also followed successful efforts to reestablish wild turkeys, and today, the population of wild turkeys is significant. Black bears have also increased in numbers. Now, not only elk, but also other historic animals have found a niche in the modern Appalachian diet.

Sources

Bradford Angier. *Field Guide to Edible Wild Plants*. Harrisburg, Pennsylvania: Stockpole Books, 1974. This book has wonderful drawings and great descriptions from a trusted author who had almost 50 books in print.

François Couplan. *The Encyclopedia of Edible Plants of North America*. New Canaan, Connecticut: Keats Publishing, Inc., 1998. In almost 600 pages, this book lists about 4,000 edible plants.

Merritt L. Fernald, Alfred C. Kinsey, and Reed C. Rollins. *Edible Wild Plants of Eastern North America*. Mineola, NY: Dover Publications, 1996. This revision has 480 pages and is most valuable for plant uses and identification.

Euell Gibbons. *Stalking the Wild Asparagus*. New York: David McKay Co, Inc., 1987. This is a personal guide with recipes. In print since 1962.

Claire Kowalchik and William H. Hylton, Editors. *Rodale's Illustrated Encyclopedia of Herbs*. Emmaus, Pennsylvania: Rodale Press, 1987. This book includes color pictures and full-page descriptions of more than 140 herbs.

EIGHT

Homeplace Meats

Chicken, Pork, and Lamb

Mountain Farms and the Homeplace

The "old homeplace" is a house, outbuildings, and farm. But this land, which for some families becomes almost sacred, is also a gathering place and is frequently the site of the family's cemetery. As long as the old folks are around, the homeplace is a center for the family and a place for Sunday dinner, with long visits on the front porch. As is often the case, when mountaineers gather at the homeplace, their minds drift off to mamaw and papaw or to age-old homeplace traditions. They enter a unique environment: At one time the place was a food production facility, but now it may have become a repository for family history. For some Appalachians, the old homeplace is acres of land that are passed on from generation to generation, land that cannot be sold outside the family.

As important as the buildings were, so also were the homeplace's geological features. The property's streams, points, hollows, and ridges carried significance. In addition, many farms had logging roads, coal mine openings, and, later, gas wells. Fences—built of wood, stone, and barbed wire—also became important. During the frontier period, livestock roamed wild, but as the population increased, farmers found it necessary to define property lines with some kind of physical boundary. Within farms, fences divided sections so that grazing areas could be controlled. Property lines were important features, often running with a point, creek, or ridge and sometimes being marked by a large poplar, shagbark hickory, or other tree. Family members knew the location of property lines as well as they knew the rooms in their house.

Today, this environment is peaceful, bucolic, and moving, but 50 or 100 years ago, surviving here required hard work. Modern Americans may romanticize a barn raising or hog killing, but the reality of survival and the desire for prosperity required constant toil. Those who lived and worked mountain farms did not have paid holidays, vacations, or delivery trucks. They worked before breakfast, after dinner, and all the hours in between.

Long hours were required because at one time these places were largely self-contained. The homeplace was a collection of buildings and family, with each family member having a job to do. Indeed, families not only dried apples, but they also spun yarn, built rifles, and made candles. They canned, cooked, hunted, and prayed. A review of the *Foxfire* series suggests that the Southern mountaineer had well-honed skills that led to making beautiful fiddles, wooden berry buckets, and pottery of many styles. The *Foxfire* series also documents the making of relatively obscure objects that families used at the homeplace including wooden locks and gourd banjos. On the old homeplace, at least in the first quarter of the twentieth century, farmers made their own tools including dashers, hoes, rakes, and shovels. As one moves back in time, the homeplace can be understood as the basic unit of frontier living.

Not all Appalachian families, not even all rural families, had a homeplace, but those who did may have memories of the spring house, can house, chicken coop, corncrib, smokehouse, outhouse, root cellar, and mule barn. Some places also had potato houses, bee gums, loom houses, and multiple corncribs. The barn was always the biggest structure, with space on the ground floor for mules, horses, steers, wagons, and tack, and space above for straw, fodder, and hay. While the barn was on one hand a romantic place where kids could get lost or tell stories, it was also a place that had fires, sick horses, and swarms of bees.

In addition to barns, spring houses were built to collect cool water, and these structures included shallow basins for keeping foodstuffs cool. Farmers kept crocks of milk, cheese, and butter in the spring house. Somewhere below the water collection point, they built a spigot so that family members could wash their hands or fill jugs. In place of a spring house, some families used the branch (creek) while others built cisterns.

Another storage building, the can house, was used to store canned vegetables, meats, and fruit. This building protected open crocks of pickled corn and relish, sauerkraut, and fermented drinks such as hard cider, beer, and wine. Sometimes the can house was combined with a root cellar, but many times they were separate.

Mountain families not only built a variety of outbuildings, but because of their isolation, many also had a cemetery. While Appalachian churches also had cemeteries, some families buried their dead on a hill above the farm. In some cases, commercial cemeteries were not available, but others built cemeteries because they wanted to have their loved ones close, even in death.

In death, the homeplace was the center of life. When someone died, the word passed to neighbors who came to help with the funeral. Because few rural areas had funeral homes, the women prepared the body for burial, and men dug the grave. Friends brought food, and, on the day of the burial, the homeplace was the place to gather—to pay respects, visit, and eat. But death was not a time to be away from loved ones, so in addition to watching over the body, family members would tell stories, play games, sing, and court.

Today, these family cemeteries draw the family back. Memorial Day weekend is a time to change the flowers, cut the grass, and then gather for a memorial service. Even if much of the mid-twentieth century production—the pigs, corn, and mules—is gone, when family members come, the farm still has apple trees, remnants of a well, and maybe a garden. The farm might even have an old cheese house, sorghum furnace, or blacksmith shop, but these are rare.

Unfortunately, the old homeplace as it existed is disappearing. For 100 years, most families have not needed a blacksmith shop, and for 50 years, or since the arrival of electricity, families have not had to cure hams. They have torn down and burned up their chicken coops, and their root cellars have fallen in and been dozed over. When the family founders die, if no one moves to the house, the homeplace changes quickly.

In recent years, the physical setting of mountain homes has changed dramatically. Modern mountaineers live in houses that line both sides of paved streets. They enjoy city water, concrete driveways, and storm sewers. An occasional mountain valley is home to a few abandoned silos and chimneys without cabins. But unlike the American Southwest where the dry climate helps preserve old structures and create ghost towns, the rainy climate and high humidity of Appalachia cause quick deterioration. The destruction begins only a season or two after the old folks move away: Paths become covered with weeds and vandals take what they want. After a few years, buildings sprout vines, trees fall, and roofs rot. So while the active homeplace is an environment with a culture and history, the abandoned one becomes wild. Over time, even the memories are lost.

Recipes, however, seem to stay with families even after they move off the farm. For a recipe that calls for ingredients that would have been home grown, cook the bacon potato soup in Part Two. Some call it a homeplace potato soup.

The Old Homeplace
Laura M. Lauderdale

I see the times that
marched across your face,
A time stamped so bold.
A time—not forgotten.
A time each person has told.

You seem so neglected,
grown up and old.
But in our hearts and our memory,
your face is bright and bold.

Our memories are different
of things you saw and we've told.
While you alone can tell it all
and watched while it unfolded.

Our hearts, do love you
and your land we cherished so dear
the kids who came before us
and the kids long after us, hold you near.

So once again we came
and wished and told you tales
while you watched in the shadows
and dreamed your dreams as well.

Yardbirds: Homeplace Chickens

On the homeplace, chickens were perhaps the most versatile of the domesticated animals. Families raised them for meat and eggs, and they sold or traded both birds and eggs. This ability to barter or sell chickens and eggs added to the chickens' importance to the lives of families who went to town maybe just twice a month. Like hogs, chickens were well adapted to the mountains in that they ate corn, foraged for food, and lived around the house. Because they lived in the yard, mountaineers called them yardbirds. Also like hogs, chickens could be kept without refrigeration because they were killed just before cooking.

Killing and dressing the chicken were taken for granted as the first step in cooking. Once a decapitated chicken stopped flapping its wings, farm women went on with the task of gutting, scalding, plucking, singeing, and cutting the chicken into pieces. Later, in the kitchen, they prepared a handful of traditional mountain dishes, the most popular of which were chicken simmered with dumplings and chicken fried in lard and served with cream gravy. In addition, fried chicken livers and chicken pieces baked in pie were common. Although not a topic for this cook, cock fighting is another major focus of raising chickens that suggests that animal's versatility. Fighting cocks were a common source of entertainment and another aspect of the symbiotic relationship between chickens and humans.

In North America, this relationship goes back only as far as Christopher Columbus. Because chickens are so adaptable, they easily survived Atlantic crossings. Then, in the eighteenth century, the Scots-Irish, British, Italian, and German settlers brought various breeds of chickens to the mountains, and later in the nineteenth century, Africans, who came to the mountains as slaves, introduced other cooking methods. In the twentieth century when American agricultural experiment stations developed new breeds of chickens, mountain farmers adapted them quickly. This was because chickens, like corn seed or fruit trees, could be shipped by the United States Postal Service. When little chicks arrived at the post office, the postmaster sent word of their arrival or delivered them himself.

Today in the mountains, some who do not garden or farm still keep chickens. The birds can be heard on the streets in small towns, and their early morning cries echo up and down hollows throughout the region. Rural families keep chickens as a hobby, because their family always raised them, and because the various breeds are beautiful. A few chicks purchased in the spring will practically sustain themselves until they become young fryers in early summer. Those who raise them know their breeds and appreciate the flavor of eggs gathered from hens that were raised free to scratch and eat in the yard.

But mountain culture has changed quickly, and today many find it hard to imagine that 50 years ago, the standard rural Appalachian practice when planning a chicken dinner was to go to the yard and catch a young hen. Modern mountain cooks, rather than going to the fattening nook, select chicken from the market meat counter. Then, they drive home with clean, cut-up chicken pieces ready for the skillet, or as in the recipes for Parmesan chicken bites and oven-fried bacon-wrapped chicken thighs in Part Two, a baking sheet or baking pan.

The limited number of chicken recipes in old mountain cookbooks is not an indicator of chicken's importance. For example, in *More Than Moonshine,* Sidney Farr lists only three chicken recipes: chicken and dumplings, country fried chicken, and cream gravy. She makes the gravy in the drippings after frying the chicken. In *Hill Country Cookin' and Memoires,* Ibbie Ledford of east Tennessee offers a recipe for gravediggers' stew. Ledford got the recipe from Minnie Vaughn who lived "down the road a piece" from the cemetery, and when a family was digging a grave, Minnie felt obligated to provide a hearty meal. She made the stew with potatoes and onions as well as home-canned lima beans, corn, and tomatoes. It is most likely that the few chicken recipes found in books indicates that mountaineers knew how to cook chicken, and they did not need written recipes.

In areas where barbecue is popular, chicken is barbecued over coals alongside beef and pork. This is not Southern pit barbecue, but rather what may be called backyard barbecue. Sunday cooks boil the chicken, roast it on a grill, and finally flavor it with sauce. One other important use of chicken that gourmands might prefer to forget is the chicken casserole. In the 1950s when cans of cream soup sold by large corporations became universal binders, chicken became a frequent addition to casseroles baked with broccoli, noodles, or rice. These casseroles go by names such as no-peek, ravishing, Devin, or Mexican, and they were bound together with a can of cream soup.

Mountain Dairy: Milk, Sour Milk, Butter, and Sweet Buttermilk Pie

Just as mountain families raised chickens for meat and eggs, they also kept cows for milk. Prior to electrification, when a cow got too old to produce milk, farmers sold her and bought another. They generally did not eat beef. Milk, however, was an essential food. Mountaineers not only drank fresh milk and made butter, but because it stored better than milk, they treasured buttermilk.

While cows were milked twice a day, when families owned a single cow, buttermilk was made every three or four days. They made butter and buttermilk when they accumulated enough clabbered cream to fill the churn slightly above the halfway mark. Buttermilk, or "sour milk" as it was called, is the thick, acidulous liquid left when clabbered creamy whole milk is churned to make butter. Its acidity aids in baking and storage. Hand churning of milk using a 4- or 5-gallon wooden or crockery churn and dasher could take up to an hour, but eventually, if the temperature was right and the churning constant, the butter came together and the woman lifted it from the churn. What remained was buttermilk, and she took it to the spring house and chilled it. Once chilled, the buttermilk was served for breakfast, lunch, and dinner; used for baking; and, sometimes, taken as a medicinal for fevers and upset stomachs.

Today, buttermilk is a cultured milk product, which means that it is made by combining bacteria and milk to grow a culture. Dairymen make sour cream and yogurt the same way: They add bacteria to milk and allow a culture to grow. The cultures, as well as added heat, thicken the milk and make it less stable. Plain cultured buttermilk is sometimes enhanced with butter granules, cream, cornstarch, salt, and other thickeners. In markets today, nonfat buttermilk is common and is made from skim milk.

Scholars trace the popularity of buttermilk in Appalachia to a similar tradition in England, Scotland, and Ireland. The Irish drink large amounts of fresh milk, sour milk, clotted milk, and buttermilk, and they used milk to make cream, curds, cheese, butter, and buttermilk. In *Simple Cooking,* number 38, John Thorne underlines the importance of milk in Ireland with a quote from the contemporary writer and traveler, John Stevens: "The Irish are the greatest lovers of milk I have ever met. They drink it about twenty different ways, and what is strangest, they love it best when it is sourest." Thorne goes on to talk about how the Irish boiled potatoes in their jackets and ate them with buttermilk. They boiled the potatoes in a giant milk-filled cast-iron pot and served them in a basket. They did this in front of a walk-in fireplace fronted by an equally large hearth. To stay warm, they sat on the hearth, ate potatoes, and passed milk around in a mug. (See the recipe for new potatoes and gravy in Part Two.)

When the Irish migrated to North America, they continued to keep cows and enjoy buttermilk. Today in Appalachia's southern mountains, buttermilk is a drink and an ingredient of great importance. As a drink, buttermilk is tangy, highly flavored, and very nutritious. Like cream, buttermilk is thick and full bodied, and like wine it fills the mouth with a lasting, tart flavor. While mountaineers usually drink buttermilk plain, they sometimes mix it with tomato juice and lemon to make blushing buttermilk.

As a cooking ingredient, buttermilk acts as a leavening agent for cakes, biscuits, pancakes, and cornbread. However, buttermilk is more than a baking ingredient, and in mountain kitchens many cooks stir it into transparent pies, prepare it as a cold soup, and simmer it with sugar and cream to make buttermilk fudge. When they use it to moisten cake batter, buttermilk is a miracle agent that enhances flavor and texture. One cup of buttermilk and ½ teaspoon of baking powder has the leavening strength of about 2 teaspoons of baking powder. Because of its acidity, buttermilk is also used to activate baking soda.

If buttermilk is boiled, stirred vigorously, or salted, it will curdle. In breads or cakes, this curdling does not affect flavor or baking quality; however, in soups, gravies, or stews, curdling buttermilk looks unappetizing. What happens is that particles of protein, also called curds, separate from the other ingredients, so instead of a thick, smooth soup or gravy, you'll have liquid with curds. To avoid curdling, heat buttermilk slowly, stir it slowly, and do not add salt. Acids such as lemon and tomato also cause curdling. In addition, fresh buttermilk curdles less than buttermilk that has been kept for some time. In the buttermilk pie recipe in Part Two, curdling is not a problem because the volume of eggs, sugar, and flour brings the mass together.

For more than 100 years, cooks in the South have been using buttermilk to make custard-like or chess-style pies. In *Southern Food,* John Egerton notes that *Farm and Home Magazine* published a buttermilk pie recipe in 1882. Also called transparent, this group of pies includes pecan pie, sorghum pie, Jefferson Davis pie, and the ever-popular Kentucky bourbon pie. According to Susan G. Purdy in *A Piece of Cake,* these pies are a unique Southern specialty, developed to use the abundant supply of eggs, butter, and sugar.

Buttermilk Pie
Susan L. Helwig

Rosewater
olive oil
pitted dates
the words for each in the language of Homer & Plato
everything belongs to someone else
in this Danforth groceteria
even these words in lines
invented long ago by others
the poem itself, a recipe for thoughts
used again and again
repetitious and not new
I might as well give up on that right from the start
pay homage to Atwood, Ondaatje, Crozier
in the dedication
perhaps the way I'm stirring the ingredients together
is mine alone, like buttermilk pie
found in a hand-written book of my grandmother's
or the trick of separating the eggs
(my mother showed me this)

how to bake it slowly
so important
just the right amount of nutmeg
for success

Pork, Cracklings, and Country Ham

When Scottish and Irish settlers first built cabins in the hollows of eastern Kentucky, they often replaced the mutton of their home-lands with pork. Hogs thrived in the hills, and in the fall they sniffed out the oak and hickory nuts, eating them like candy. Eventually pork became so important that in 1878 the theft of a hog led to the Hatfield-McCoy feud. Before the feud ended, members of both families had been killed, and the governors of Virginia and Kentucky were part of the problem and the solution.

Hogs, in addition to chicken and cows, were common in the late nineteenth century, and an occasional mountaineer is still raising them. In addition to requiring little space, hogs are efficient converters of kitchen scraps, and, when their owners don't have scraps, pigs can forage in the hills.

Once hogs are fat, farmers kill, butcher, and store them. But the task is not easy. "Hog-killing time in the hills is a hard time and a busy time. . . . It means making souse meat and liver mush, turning out sausage, and canning backbones and ribs, rendering lard, and salting down hams and bacon," says John Parris in *Mountain Cooking.*

With frugality being an old obsession as well as a Christian value, mountaineers brag about eating every part of the pig from the ears, to the lips, to the feet. "We eat the whole hog, all but the squeal, and we serve bacon, sausage, and pork chops for breakfast. As for beef, it is not a mountain tradition," says a highlander quoted in Mark Sohn's *Mountain Country Cooking.*

Cracklings are another pork delicacy. Highlanders who know pork know that cracklings are the fibers left after they boil the lard from large pieces of white pork fat. On one of her many television appearances, Julia Child made a different kind of cracklings, duck cracklings. She trimmed the skin from a gigantic Peking duck and then dropped it into a frying pan. Over low to moderate heat, she fried the fat and skin until the fat melted off the skin. She called this process rendering fat (mountaineers use the same term for pork). When the skins were golden brown and crisp, she lifted these duck cracklings from the fat, drained them on paper towels, added salt, and lifted a piece to her mouth. She then smiled with satisfaction and said the cracklings were her favorite duck part. Some mountaineers feel the same way about pork cracklings, which are found in many mountain markets. (For high-quality cracklings, see Poche's Meat Market in the Mail-Order Sources.)

Highlanders distinguish between pork rinds, pork cracklings, and bacon. In the case of pork rinds, cooks use skin. For cracklings, they use fat. For bacon, they use side meat with streaks of lean. In each case, they heat the pork over low heat, melt or render the fat away, and end up with a crunchy delicacy.

Cooks also render fat from pork by boiling pork rind, cracklings, and bacon. They then pour the hot fat into containers, and, when it cools, it turns white and becomes lard. This lard is similar to and as pure as clarified butter. The best lard is leaf lard, the lard from the area around the kidneys.

Traditionally, mountain cooks used lard to make flaky pie crusts and to flavor vegetables. They also used lard when frying green tomatoes, poke, chicken, morels, cornmeal mush, and potatoes. Lard remains so basic to mountain cooking that markets sell it in 25- and 50-pound buckets. They also sell 8-, 4-, 3-, and 2½-pound tubs and 1-pound boxes. Fischer's, Armour, and Field are popular brand names. The print on the buckets is in basic blue, green, and yellow, and the slogans read, "Fine for Pastries," or "No Refrigeration Required." However, being anti-lard is popular these days, but in comparison to butter, lard is slightly more healthy. Tablespoon for tablespoon, lard has one-third the cholesterol and only a few more calories than butter.

In addition to lard, mountaineers crave bacon. Bacon is another pork product with a unique flavor and texture that place it in a class above most other foods. At one time it was an economical pork cut, but today, bacon is a prize. Cut from the sides of the hog and called side meat, streaked lean, or pork flank, bacon has streaks of lean and fat that are cured, smoked, and salted. Butchers sell it in slabs with the rind or sliced without the rind. Most cooks today use medium-thick sliced bacon with 16 to 18 slices per pound.

While mountain cooks might ask butchers for a leg of lamb, they do not ask for a leg of pork. Butchers sell "fresh" hams (uncooked, uncured meat), and home cooks bake them as roasts. Ham, on the other hand, is a fabricated pork product, the end result after processors cure, cook, and pack fresh hams. Processors add salt, smoke, and spice to create a flavor that is so popular markets also sell turkey fabricated in the same way, what butchers label "cured turkey breast."

All over the South, artisan ham producers worked in various settings creating different culinary trophies. The end result was something like the many flavors and varieties of French cheese. Historically, mountaineers cured hams, shoulders, and middlin' meat, but today the focus is on hams.

While the hams in some cultures are wet-cured, Appalachian country hams are dry-cured. To make dry-cured hams, mountaineers salt, season, smoke, and age the meat using neither water nor brine. During curing, salt penetrates to the bone and creates an environment in which bacteria cannot grow. The salting, curing, and summer sweats the hams go through cause them to lose about a third of their weight. Country hams are distinct in their salty, smoky flavor. The meat is firm and velvety in texture, and before it is cooked, it is a deep amber or maroon color.

Because salt was an expensive commodity, particularly during the nineteenth century, some dry-cured hams were prepared with hard-wood ashes instead of salt. In this case, farmers took great care to have clean ashes, and some used only ashes from certain woods such as hickory.

Developing the Flavor of Country Ham

The flavor of country hams is related to a number of factors. First, it depends on what the hog ate. Was it corn, peanuts, acorns, or beechnuts? Did the hogs run in the hills, or did they feed on corn from a trough?

Second, how much salt was used in curing? Less is better, but less requires more skill. In the South, some farmers packed the hams in salt while others covered them with a thin layer. Some others used a combination of sugar and salt. Still others added sorghum syrup, molasses, pepper, saltpeter, and maybe cloves. The use of sweeteners yields what is called sugar-cured ham.

Third, was the meat smoked, and if so, what kind of smoke drifted over the hanging hams? Was it hickory, apple, red oak, sassafras, or walnut, and how long did the smoking last? Smoking was done for a day or two and surely for less than a week. Many farmers did not smoke their meat but stored it in boxes or hung it "green." When they stored the meat boxes, they layered them with sugar, corn, or ashes. Small sealed boxes or wooden barrels protected the meat from invading armies of bugs and rodents.

Fourth, how long did the ham hang? Old-timers talk about a short aging of a year and long aging of two or three years. Longer aging can yield drier ham and a more concentrated flavor, but some of the two- and three-year-old hams got tough and lost both moisture and flavor. In commercial operations today, the process may be completed in as few as 70 days, and the buildings are temperature-controlled and bacteria-free.

Other factors also affect flavor: In what sort of environment did the hams hang? How high was the humidity, what was the temperature, and what dust or microbes floated through the air? What molds grew on the ham? Old-style country hams are a product of the barn's environment.

While mountain curing was commonly done in outbuildings, garages, and smokehouses, the smokehouse has gained public attention, and for some people the building is a symbol of the South. Smokehouses range in size from a building not much bigger than an outhouse to large structures that will hang hundreds of hams and hold up to a dozen iron fire pots with slow-burning, smoldering fires. But 100 years ago when most families cured pork and butchered as few as one or two hogs, farmers used many structures. Today, the small-scale curing tradition that was once as common as milking a cow has made a comeback among hunters who use steel or even stainless steel smokers to cure game.

Farm-based smokehouses were either open or closed structures. When farmers built open buildings with logs or planks that had cracks, they covered the inside walls with screens to keep bugs out. In the case of the closed structures, the walls were solid or logs were chinked, meaning the cracks were filled. Then, to create smoke, ham men built fires in washtubs or fire pots, and to some extent, the smoke stayed inside the "closed" structures.

Regardless of whether the building was open or closed, smokehouses had shelves for salting and rafters for hanging. These structures were like can houses in that they served mountain families as storehouses, symbols of plenty, and hedges against hard times. As storehouses, they held an abundance of hams, sausage, and bacon.

Wherever pork was popular, smokehouses were built, and today Appalachia is famous for country hams. Virginia, West Virginia, Kentucky, Tennessee, the Carolinas, and Georgia are well known for dry-cured, salt-cured, and sugar-cured hams. These hams are flavor miles apart from the canned, water-added, and plastic-wrapped hams. Because country hams are alive and need to breathe, producers pack them in paper and wrap them in cloth. Bring one home and hang it in a cool place. No refrigeration required.

While today's producers identify these hams as Kentucky country, Georgia cured, or Virginia Smithfield, "our" special hams were around long before Hernando de Soto brought 13 pigs to Tampa Bay, Florida, in 1542. Evidence of pork in human diets dates from 5000 BC in countries as far apart as Egypt and China, and curing has been part of human life since man has known hogs and salt.

Like a Cheddar cheese from Cheddar, England, or a Bordeaux wine from the Bordeaux region of France, cured hams are regionally distinct. By law, a Smithfield ham must be made in the city limits of Smithfield, Virginia. In every region, the curing procedure is different, and the end product is named for the town, region, or country. Popular country-style, dry-cured hams are known in China as Yunnan ham, in Czechoslovakia as Prague ham, in France as Bayonne, in Germany as Westphalian, in Spain as Iberian, and in Italy as Parma or proscuitto di Parma.

Southern curing can be better understood by comparing it to the steps followed in the Parma region of Italy. Proscuitto di Parma or proscuitto (an Italian cured ham) is popular in this country. Like mountaineers, the Italians of Parma salt-cure and air-dry their hams. But while mountain farmers generously layer the salt, the Italians use an absolute minimum. Year-long curing is typical in both countries, but in Italy the process is highly regulated, and the use of sugar, spices, and smoke is against the law. Most Southern ham recipes include sugar, and many also use spices and smoke.

In using a minimum of salt, the goal of the Parma ham maker is to preserve the meat without oversalting. If he applies too little salt, the ham will spoil. Adding the required amount of salt is like leaving a brown turkey fig on the tree as long as possible. The

longer the fig hangs, the sweeter it gets, but if it stays too long, it
will spoil. However, just as some farmers pick their figs too early,
some ham makers use too much salt, and in both cases flavor is
sacrificed. In Parma, the ham makers have been skimping on salt
for 2,000 years, first because salt was a highly valued commodity
and second because they live in the northern mountains where
the climate is cool and the meat lasts longer.

In the American South, hams go through what is called "summer sweats." The high heat and humidity of July, August, and September cause the ham to sweat and continue to dry. In Parma,
Italy, the processors begin their curing in high, dry attics and later
move the hams to moist cellars. This extra moisture causes a fermentation to occur. Here in the South, the hogs are killed in the
late fall or early winter and, after a period of salting, the hams are
hung through the dry cold winter. Finally, they are left hanging
through the hot humid summer.

While cured country ham is ready to eat, many mountaineers
cook it before they serve it. Italian proscuitto, however, is always
served in the cured "raw" state. Because Italians use little salt and
slice thin, the ham needs neither soaking nor cooking. In Parma,
Italy, the ham is served as part of an antipasto with several
almost-transparent slices served with bread and white wine.
Nothing else.

Lynne Rossetto Kasper in *The Splendid Table* describes Italian
proscuitto as "rosy red meat with an edging of white fat that tastes
like someone infused the flavors of nuts, cream, ripe fruit and
meat essence into the ham." Another taste and color description
is used by Southerner Sarah Belk in *Around the Southern Table*
when she says that country ham is ". . . mahogany colored . . . and
has a firm texture and a complex salty, smoky, sweet, and spicy flavor." Kasper and Belk, of course, were describing different hams.

Purchase and Use
In mountain markets and throughout the South, buyers must
choose between whole hams and small shrink-wrapped packs.
When buying country ham, regardless of the amount purchased,
buyers must choose from two sources of country ham: the old-
styled artisan hams and commercial quick cures. Many chefs prefer the flavor and variations found in old-style, artisan-cured,
smokehouse-aged, 9- to 12-month-old hams, and Kentucky alone

has more than 20 artisan sources. Throughout the South, butchers, craftsmen, and farmers cure ham in the old way.

Cured hams are not cooked, but neither are they raw. Instead, the salt "cooks" them in the same fashion that it cooks magret, lox, gravlax, seviche, and caviar. Regarding the use of "raw" country ham, Shirley Corriher of Atlanta, author of *Cookwise,* and an authority on food science, says that cured ham is safe to eat. The meat is disease-free, she says, if it was "properly cured and carefully stored," and, therefore, cooking is unnecessary. Understanding that curing is a form of cooking allows many options.

Like a fine wine, aged country ham has become classy, fancy food. At one time, however, country ham was a standard commodity prepared on farms everywhere. Today, mountaineers serve country ham for special occasions, and usually, they fry it. Cooks place ¼-inch-thick slices in a cast-iron skillet and fry them a minute or two on each side. Sometimes they deglaze the drippings with water, coffee, or Pepsi to make the culturally important red-eye gravy. Finally, they serve this breakfast sauce, this ham *au jus,* over the ham with eggs, fried apples, and fried potatoes in the tradition of mountain fare that dates back to the frontier period.

Small amounts of country ham can also be a low-fat substitute for bacon. When making chicken Cordon Bleu, for example, some cooks replace ham or bacon with country ham and enjoy its delicate zing as a counterpoint to the chicken. Others do the same for a club sandwich or hamburger. Like bacon, country ham can be served as a side to eggs and potatoes, and it can be stir-fried with chicken tenders, onions, and bell pepper. Again, the salty, zesty flavor of country ham brings chicken to life. When making a Western omelet or Denver sandwich, cooks slice the ham thin and add diced onions and green pepper. Bouncing from the Midwest to the mid-South, Southern cooks prepare the Kentucky hot brown sandwich with turkey, country ham, tomato, and wedges of toast, and they serve it with a hearty cheese sauce.

In Italian restaurants and today in some Southern kitchens, chefs serve country ham as part of an antipasto plate with cheeses, sausages, olives, and marinated vegetables. They also wrap thin-sliced country ham around fresh figs, honeydew melon, Gala apples, and toasted pecans, serving them with toothpicks as an appetizer or accompaniment to cocktails. Country ham is also served boiled in soups or stirred with sauces. Some cooks simmer country ham with dry beans, and others add chopped pieces to corn chowder and potato cheese soup. This ham also pairs well with cabbage, succotash, and minestrone.

Sliced thin and chopped fresh, country ham is the dominant ingredient in a number of pasta sauces. Cooks add it to Alfredo sauce, and they boil it with heavy cream and Parmesan cheese. In place of sauce, some cooks chop country ham and mix it with pecans, diced sweet onions, fresh peas, and pasta.

Country ham is also a filling for biscuits—just split the biscuits and add thin slices of country ham. Some find this dry and add mustard, mayonnaise, relish, or pickles, or they may fill the biscuits with country ham spread (see the recipe in Part Two) made by moistening ground ham with mayonnaise and mustard.

Not only did mountaineers use pork to make country ham, but they also use it for barbecue. Ribs are particularly luscious: moist, tender, and full-flavored. Mountain cooks have broiled, boiled, baked, grilled, roasted, and barbecued pork ribs, but in the end many come back to a fundamental cooking method: low heat. Slow cooking results in tender ribs, and when the mercury drops outside, some home cooks stay inside and plug in their slow cookers or covered countertop roasters. They toss pinto beans, tomato sauce, tomato paste, vinegar, onion, and hot pepper flakes into the cooker with the ribs. Then, after the ribs cook all day, family members can plate up a robust full-meal indoor barbecue. The country-style pork ribs, barbecue sauce, and bean combination is delightful, soothing, and filling.

Mountain Sheep and Lamb

In the latter part of the nineteenth century, sheep, like pigs and cows, were an always-present Appalachian farm animal. Unlike chickens that were allowed to scratch around and pigs that ran in the hills, sheep were usually fenced. Often, their field on the homeplace was a bit removed from the center of the activity even though they required more care than cows and hogs. Their lambs need assistance, and they are susceptible to foot rot and other diseases. For those who raised them, sheep added quite a bit of work to the routines around the homeplace.

While wool production and making clothing were the primary

reason to raise sheep, some families ate lamb or even mutton. In an article written for the *Asheville Citizen-Times* and republished in *Mountain Cooking,* John Parris documents the use of mutton in southern Appalachian cooking. For the article, Parris interviewed Tennie Cloer, born in 1886, from Murphy, North Carolina. Like many others, Cloer's family raised sheep, and in the fall, when meat was scarce, they killed a wether, or a 2- to 3-year-old neutered male. One of Cloer's childhood memories was that her family "killed two mutton every fall. . . . Everybody used mutton back then. It made for just about the finest eatin' you could set down to." Cloer's family ate the mutton as steaks, chops, roasts, and stew. They served roasted lamb with baked sweet potatoes and lamb chops with green beans. Of her husband, she says, "He was so fond of mutton chops, he would have eat 'em three times a day. . . ." In other areas of Appalachia, lamb is well known as an ingredient in Kentucky burgoo and Brunswick stew. Finally, mutton barbecue is popular in and around Owensboro, Kentucky.

In mountain markets today, particularly in the spring, butchers sell legs of lamb, and chops they cut from the rib, loin, and shoulder. The more tender cuts are rib, loin, and sirloin chops. A rack of lamb, like a beef rib roast, comes from the rib or loin. When sliced, these become lamb chops. Part Two includes directions for grilling lamb chops.

Sources

Broadbent and Smithfield sell cooked country hams. Contact: The Smithfield Companies, P.O. Box 487, Smithfield, VA 23430. Phone: 800-628-2242. Broadbent's B&B Food Products, Inc., 6321 Hopkinsville Road, Cadiz, KY 42211. Phone: 800-841-2202.

John Egerton. *Southern Food: At Home, on the Road, in History.* New York: Alfred A. Knopf, Inc., 1987.

Sidney Saylor Farr. *More Than Moonshine: Appalachian Recipes and Recollections.* Pittsburgh: University of Pittsburgh Press, 1983.

Ibbie Ledford. *Hill Country Cookin' and Memoirs.* Gretna, Louisiana: The Pelican Publishing Co, 1991.

John Parris. *Mountain Cooking.* Asheville, North Carolina: Asheville Citizen-Times Publishing Co, 1978.

Susan G. Purdy. *A Piece of Cake.* New York: Collier Books, 1989.

Mark F. Sohn. *Mountain Country Cooking: A Gathering of the Best Recipes from the Smokies to the Blue Ridge.* New York: St. Martin's Press, 1996.

John Thorne and Matt Lewis Thorne. "The Irish and Potatoes," *Simple Cooking*, Issue 38. Steuben, Maine: John Thorne, April, 1994.

For a list of more than 20 country ham processors in Kentucky, see the *Kentucky Food Products Directory,* published by the Kentucky Department of Agriculture, Division of Market Research, 100 Fair Oaks Lane #252, Frankfort, KY 40601. Phone: 502-564-6571.

NINE

Sweets, Fruit, and Nuts

Apples, Peaches, and Pecans

Mountain Sweets: Honey and Sorghum

Honey is almost as sweet as love and surely as old. Some 4,000 years ago a Sumerian clay tablet described a bridegroom as honey sweet, a bride's caress as more savory than honey, and the wedding bedchamber as honey-filled. In the Old Testament, the Promised Land is flowing with milk and honey. Honey is the oldest sweet used by humans, and it has not changed for 10,000 years.

Years ago, many mountain families either kept bees or knew how to track them. Once they found a bee tree, they cut the tree and robbed the honey. Today, mountain families continue to keep bees, and even those who do not farm or garden may have a stand or two sitting behind their house.

From these stands come the many kinds of Appalachian honey, with the most popular being sourwood, linn, and locust. Beekeepers also collect poplar, wildflower, clover, and buckwheat, with buckwheat being the most distinctive of Appalachian honey. Buckwheat honey is collected in West Virginia and Pennsylvania, while linn honey of the basswood tree is favored in eastern Kentucky. Further south in western North Carolina and northern Georgia, sourwood honey is popular. Generally, these honeys are light in color and mild in flavor. Further north in Pennsylvania and New York, many Appalachians talk fondly about honey from the honey locust tree, and they describe the flavor as rich and full-bodied. Of the various Appalachian honeys, locust is the darkest in color. (For linn and sourwood honey see the Mail-Order Sources.)

As the season progresses, beekeepers rob their hives of honey from the various kinds of flowering plants. For example, in eastern Kentucky they may gather poplar honey from May 10 to 15, linn from June 10 to 15, and then sourwood after June 20. Many say that most good honey is made before July 15, but some beekeepers also boast about the wildflower honey they collect in the fall.

Honey is commonly spread on biscuits or stirred with tea, and it is the outstanding ingredient in ethnic foods such as baklava, lebkuchen, nougat, torrone, halvah, and pasteli. In addition, liqueur manufacturers rely on honey, adding it to Benedictine, Drambuie, and Irish Mist. Years ago in the hot summer when working in the field, Appalachian farmers made a drink they called "switchell." They mixed equal parts of honey and vinegar and then diluted this mixture with water using about a teaspoon per cup of water for a mild drink or twice that amount for something with a bit more flavor. But more important is the fact that before cane sugar from the deep South became widely available, honey and sorghum were the primary sweeteners in central and southern Appalachia. Farther north and starting in the high regions of West Virginia, those who owned a sugar bush made maple syrup or maple sugar.

While some mountaineers called honey long sweetening, they also used sorghum, which, according to *Foxfire 2,* they called short sweetening. This designation may stem from the fact that while sorghum provides an initial burst of flavor, honey is generally more powerful and its sweetness lasts longer on the palate than sorghum's.

Nevertheless, sorghum is very tasty and is the second most popular traditional mountain sweetener. Sweet sorghum is a much-loved sweet syrup made from a large grass plant known as sweet sorghum. Sorghum syrup, like honey, is poured over biscuits and pancakes, and the syrup is also added to breads, cookies, cakes, candy, and savory casseroles.

In Appalachia, as in other parts of the United States, mountaineers made extensive use of sweet sorghum during the second half of the nineteenth and the first part of the twentieth centuries.

After World War II, mountain cooks generally switched from sorghum to sugar, but even today, sorghum, or sorghum molasses as it is known, has a following. It remains popular because of its long history and excellent flavor. The flavor lies somewhere between black strap molasses and light caramel syrup and is far less sweet than honey.

In the various regions of Appalachia, users refer to sorghum syrup as molasses, sorghum molasses, lassies, and sorghums, and they are wary of imitators. Today, many producers label their product as 100 percent pure, sweet sorghum syrup because markets sell many look-alike products made with corn syrup, flavorings, food coloring, and other additives.

Years ago, there would have been no market for imitation sorghum syrups. On even the smallest plots, mountain farmers had enough space to plant sweet sorghum. Half an acre of land yielded from 50 to 100 gallons of syrup, and when sorghum was popular, it was a valuable cash crop. Sorghum and corn are both grasses, and they grow well in the same soils and climate.

Once farmers have selected a variety of sweet sorghum, they plant it, and depending on the variety, it grows to a height of 5 to 15 feet. The stalks are 1 to 2 inches thick. When it matures, growers cut the stalks, strip the leaves, and press the green sap from the stalks into evaporator trays. As moisture evaporates, the sap becomes syrup. In the process of making sorghum syrup, farmers add nothing, and they remove nothing but water. The process for making sugar cane molasses is quite different: During sugar production, manufacturers remove pure white sugar leaving the by-product, molasses. Sugar cane, again unlike corn and sorghum, requires a frost-free environment such as that found in the deep South. (To buy sorghum cane, see the Mail-Order Sources, and to make hot sorghum syrup, see the instructions in Part Two.)

Domestic Fruit and Wild Grapes

While the early settlers could forage for pecan and hickory nuts as well as pawpaws and wild grapes, it was not long until Appalachian families planted fruit trees and enjoyed a harvest of peaches, apples, cherries, and pears. Eventually, their gardens also included blueberries, strawberries, raspberries, and Concord grapes.

Peaches
When European settlers arrived in Appalachia, the native people were growing small red-blushing peaches that Spanish explorers brought here about 200 years earlier. Native Americans from the Deep South to New England cultivated the cling-type peaches, and the fruit became so important that the Natchez Indians of the lower Mississippi Valley named one of the months of the year after the fruit.

As European settlers established themselves in the mountains, they learned from the Native Americans how to grow this peach, and during the early nineteenth century it became not only the most popular fruit tree among settlers but also an early source of income. While 200 years ago a bushel of peaches might sell for only 35 cents, enterprising farm owners increased their value by selling them as brandy, pickles, butter, leather, and even tea. Peach butter was common: Like apple butter, settlers cooked fresh peaches with sugar until enough water evaporated that the smooth mixture was stiff enough to spread. When spread on a sheet in a thin layer and dried, peach butter became peach leather, a candy-like substance settlers rolled, stored, and ate out of hand. Peach leather was also a commercial product that shipped long distances. Even more popular and more profitable was peach brandy that was manufactured in the mountains and sold throughout the east.

The early dominance of peaches is evident today in names that can be seen on old maps. In eastern Kentucky, these include Pikeville's Peach Orchard Hill and the Peach Orchard Coal Mines in Prestonsburg, and two different towns called Peach Orchard in Lawrence County (according to *Kentucky Place Names,* the first Peach Orchard post office closed in 1871 and the second opened ten years later in another part of the county). For a taste of peaches that is styled for a modern kitchen, see the recipe for peach cobbler in Part Two.

Apples
While peaches were dominant early, by the middle of the nineteenth century apples began to replace them as the fruit of first choice. Apples had a longer season, grew under a wider range of climatic conditions, stored more easily, and were used in far more recipes. Modern Appalachian cooks use apples more than any other fruit.

While early Appalachian settlers may have tried to establish familiar European apple varieties using the native American crab apple as a cultivar, it is more likely that apples came to Appalachia during the period that John Chapman, the Massachusetts eccentric known as Johnny Appleseed, traveled west and spread apple varieties. Chapman left his home around 1790 and traveled west planting apple orchards until his death in Fort Wayne, Indiana, in 1845. Once established, apples flourished, and mountain homesteaders developed large orchards throughout Virginia's Blue Ridge as well as the mountains that crossed Kentucky, Tennessee, North Carolina, and Georgia.

Today, tourists enjoy the fall apple harvest as they drive through the region to see the fall foliage. When the leaves change color, civic groups gather at community festivals to make apple butter. Others use a recipe like the one in Part Two to make it at home. Apple butter is a smooth, tangy spread, a sweet, spicy sauce and biscuit topping. In some communities, making apple butter is a decades-long tradition where community groups peel, simmer, and bottle a small part of the apple harvest. From the back of a pickup truck, club members heft bushels of fresh apples into their vendor tents. Over small fires and in giant cauldrons, using wood stirrers with handles that may be 8 feet long, volunteers simmer apples, evaporate water, and make the concentrate they call butter. The boiling takes days, and stirring is continuous. Small groups work around the clock; large groups sit on folding chairs and talk. Later, crowds gather to watch. Then, team members pack the apple butter in pint and quart jars and sell it from tents or tables. Normally, at the apple festivals (see the Festivals and Events section at the end of the book), the demand is great and the supply limited.

At other fall festivals, the same community pride is seen, as groups press sweet sorghum stems and evaporate the green juice, grind and bag dry corn, and offer samples of the summer's honey.

Pears

In addition to apple and peach trees, hill country highlanders grew pears. Pear trees, like apple, apricot, cherry, and plum trees, belong to the rose family, and grow in temperate climates. Even today, many small farms have a number of apple trees, but just an occasional pear tree. Frequently, the pear is a Kieffer. Today's highlanders know Kieffers as old-timey pears, and they flourish here because they are robust and blight-resistant. They thrive in the acidic mountain soil and hot climate. They bear young and are available as semi-dwarfs. In comparison to apple trees, they live longer, and many lingering homesteads are marked by a single Kieffer pear tree growing in a field or near a chimney.

Kieffer pears are hard, hearty, coarse, and gritty. The skins are rough and the centers firm. The fruit is crunchy, juicy, and slightly sweet. These pears lend themselves to poaching, baking, and pear honey, and even though they don't compare to soft-flesh pears, many highlanders enjoy them fresh from the tree. Because they ripen in September and October, mountain farmers refer to Kieffers as late pears. Most farmers pick them while they are hard and keep them in a cool, dark place, but others leave them on the tree to ripen. When ripe, a good Kieffer is sweet and the skin is greenish yellow, but even when they are ripe, Kieffers need more cooking time than the smooth-skinned, soft-flesh pears such as Comice, Bartlett, and Anjou.

Grapes

Another fall fruit is the Concord grape. Like the native American crab apples that farmers grafted with European apples, the Concord grape was the result of an intense breeding program. While European grapes tend to have thin skins, native American grapes are thick-skinned. Botanists call them slipskins; settlers and foragers today call them fox grapes. Two hundred years ago, the wild grapes growing in New England were abundant, beautiful, and sweet-smelling, but they did not taste good, and so some New Englanders stored them in brandy. However, Ephraim Wales Bull of Concord, a friend of Henry David Thoreau, believed he could find a solution to this problem, and he worked hard to create a new grape. After ten years, in 1853, Bull presented a new grape to the Massachusetts Horticultural Society, and he called it a Concord. It did not take long for the new Concords to spread to Appalachia, where mountaineers used them to make wine, juice, and pie.

In southern Appalachia, the wild grapes are muscadines, foxes, possums, and scuppernongs. Scuppernongs are a kind of muscadine, and they taste so sweet that some people compare their jelly to honey. Muscadines grow on tall trees, fence rows, and in cool creek valleys. The grape is common in eastern Tennessee and western North Carolina as well as most other Southern states and even southern Illinois. Unlike most grapes, muscadines, or *Vitis rotundifolia,* grow with just one or two grapes per cluster. Each grape may be an inch across, and the skins are thick. The flavor may suggest Concord, but these are different. The species includes scuppernongs, muscatels, nobles, magnolias, and bullace grapes (see the photo insert).

In the wild, foragers knock muscadines off the vines and pick them off the ground like acorns. In the market, they are the size of cherry tomatoes, and rather than being sold in bunches like other grapes, they are sold loose in boxes. These large, green grapes hold well in a refrigerator, and their flavor is full. Muscadines are used in traditional Southern and mountain kitchens for preserves and wines. Some cooks use them for tea and others make them into pie. Some make juice. And why not? This grape makes a pungent juice, and some modern chefs use it to flavor vinaigrettes.

Mountain Icon: Apple Stack Cakes

Fifty to 100 years ago, long before professionals, hobby cooks, and intellectuals began to value American ethnic foods, mountaineers throughout Appalachia made stack cakes. The cake is not only a specialty of the central Appalachian highlands but also among the regionally distinct American foods. It seems incredible that the recipe for this historic and treasured cake cannot be found in any large-scale, nationally distributed book published before 1980. Until then, the recipe that now seems so vital to Appalachian culture was found only in fund-raiser community cookbooks, donated in hopes of a small profit for not-for-profits. For example, in 1979, Peggy Davis, a Pikeville College anthropology professor, taught a class that published a mimeographed, 39-page booklet of mountain recipes that included five stack cake recipes. More recently, *W-Hollow Cookbook,* published by the Jesse Stuart Foundation, set forth four recipes for stack cake and one for the stack cake filling; and a manuscript prepared by Anna Ellis Bogle of eastern Tennessee for her senior thesis includes recipes for the cake, filling, and glaze. In various forms, the recipes for the stack cake have been published in hundreds of community cookbooks.

Before the recipes made it into cookbooks, these mountain cakes were prepared from recipes written in pencil on pieces of paper that were kept with the Bible, or from directions passed on by word-of-mouth. The cake was popular because five of the essential ingredients—dried apples, lard, sorghum, buttermilk, and eggs—were grown and prepared on the farm, and the others—spices, flour, and baking soda—could be purchased in local markets. Today, mountaineers romanticize this cake because it stands out as one of the region's special creations.

Once the ingredients were combined and the layers baked, cooks stacked them. Why did they stack the layers? Churches own stack chairs and stack tables, and when it comes to pancakes, restaurants offer short or long stacks. Mountaineers enjoy two old-style stacked desserts: stack pies and stack cakes. These desserts are stacked so that they take up less space, fit in a carrying basket, and can be transported to events.

Where Appalachians have migrated, so have old-fashioned stack cakes. Harry and Laura Robie of Berea, studying Appalachians in the state of Washington, once visited Sister Dollyheide of the Western Union Old Regular Baptist Church in Silver Creek, Washington, 25 miles northwest of Mount Saint Helens. Sister Dollyheide shared her recipe for an old-fashioned stack cake, and like so many others, she makes the cake with sorghum, buttermilk, and ginger. Mary Anderson Greene of Myrtle Point, Oregon (originally from Dorton and Shelby Gap, Kentucky) makes a nine- to twelve-layer stack cake for Thanksgiving, and her family knows their roots are Appalachian. When Greene was growing up, she did not know any Christmas fruitcake other than the classic apple stack cake.

Classic stack cakes are comprised of a mildly ginger-flavored cookie-like dough and a sweetened, spiced apple filling. The cake differs from gingerbread in that it is not chewy, and the ginger flavor may be so mild that some people do not even know the recipe includes ginger. The cakes are often made with six to eight layers, are low in fat and sugar, and, usually, the top layer has nothing on it. The cake's many thin layers bring to mind the German-Austrian Dobosch or Dobos torte, a ten-layer sponge cake with a mocha filling and caramel glaze.

While apple stack cakes are unique to this region, within the region they are common fare. Martha Hawkins, who lives on Elkhorn

Creek below Pine Mountain on the Virginia and Kentucky border, likes to eat a piece of stack cake any time of the year, and she eats it for breakfast. Hawkins is following a long tradition; in frontier Appalachia, this cake was also served as an afternoon snack or it was carried in saddlebags for a snack on the trail. But stack cakes are not an everyday treat. As Delphia Elkins, a nonagenarian from Lick Fork Road of Beefhide Creek in Pike County, Kentucky, notes, "it takes time, hard work, and skill to make ten-layer stack cakes, so we usually serve them for special occasions" such as weddings, Thanksgiving, and Christmas. Today, the cake is most often a fall and winter food. "At fall festivals, people run to get stack cakes. You can't buy them in a store," says Martha Hawkins. However, she believes that when cooking was done at home, some cooks prepared it throughout the year for birthdays, family reunions, music festivals, heritage fairs, and Sunday dinners.

The origins of the stack cake recipe are difficult to trace. Some food historians say that James Harrod, the colonist and farmer who founded Harrodsburg in 1774, brought the stack cake to Kentucky from his home in Pennsylvania. While Harrod may have brought the first stack cake to Kentucky, the cake could not have been common until more than 100 years later when flour became readily available. In 1883, The White Lily Foods Company of Knoxville, Tennessee, was established and was an early producer of flour. It was not until this time that biscuits began to replace cornbread, and so it seems logical that the availability of flour allowed stack cake to become more common.

Sidney Saylor Farr advanced another somewhat doubtful origin story in a 1983 *Courier-Journal* interview when she said that "mountain people couldn't afford big, layered wedding cakes. As a substitute, women coming to a wedding each donated layers of cake. . . ." The idea of a cooperative stack cake makes sense when you recall that people helped each other with corn shelling, bean stringing, sorghum processing, and barn raisings; however, it does not make sense that the cake could have been assembled on site and eaten immediately. In *Butter Beans to Blackberries: Recipes from the Southern Garden*, Ronni Lundy notes that the "marriage" of apple filling and cake requires two days to "consummate," and anyone eating this cake on the day it was assembled would wonder "what all the shouting was about." Perhaps those who contributed layers met the day before the wedding and assembled the cake, but it is more logical that this was a washday cake, a cake that pioneers made on Monday and served on Wednesday.

Regardless of its origin, the cake has many names. While the recipe in Part Two is called a dried apple stack cake, other names tell us about the people who made the cakes and include poor man's fruit cake, Confederates old-fashioned stack cake, Appalachian stack cake, Kentucky stack cake, and Kentucky's washday cake. The Little Cowan Primitive Baptist Church of Letcher County, Kentucky, published the recipe as Ruby's Special Stack Cake. Other stack cake names tell us about the ingredients and include the gingerbread stack cake, apple stack cake, apple butter stack cake, applesauce stack cake, and apple cider stack cake. Still other names emphasize the long history of the cake and include pioneer stack cake, old-fashioned stack cake, and old-time stack cake.

Spices: A review of almost 30 stack cake recipes shows that ginger is the most common spice, with about two-thirds of the cakes including the spice. About half of those who make the cake use cinnamon, and other popular spices include cloves, nutmeg, allspice, lemon, and vanilla. Most recipes also call for salt, but many use self-rising flour, which, of course, contains salt. While some cooks refer to the cake as gingerbread, the recipe in Part Two calls for only four teaspoons of spices, including ginger, nutmeg, and cinnamon, and yields a cake that is fully flavored, but mild enough so that the apple and sorghum flavors are evident.

Fillings and Apples: A review of old recipes suggests that the filling for a stack cake is either an afterthought or taken for granted. This is because apple butter, applesauce, apple cider, dried apples, and even peach butter were mountain staples, and every well-stocked can house, pantry, or back porch held a good supply. (While some cooks make stack cakes with peach and blackberry fillings, apple fillings outnumber the others about eight to one.) When cooks use applesauce, they boil it down and add sugar and spices. Some make the apple filling by adding apple cider to dried apples, and others make it with cider butter or cider jelly, an apple cider reduction. (See Sarah Belk, *Around the Southern Table.*) Cooks who make their filling with dried apples, reconstitute, sweeten, and spice the apples.

Selecting the kind of apples to use is a further source of debate. For some cooks, the choice is a question of dried or fresh. Others argue the merits of fresh apple varieties and select from Winesap, Roman Beauty, and McIntosh, always seeking a tart cooking apple. Francis Collier, in a paper published in *Voices from the Hill* (Pikeville College) says that "if you use fresh apples, you must choose fruit that is tart and becomes mushy when cooked. Winesaps are an excellent choice. However, many use dried apples because they give the cake a stronger apple flavor."

Stack Cake Layers and Glazes: The apples become a filling spread between multiple layers of cake. The number of layers varies from a few to 16, but a half-dozen layers is most common (about two-thirds of the recipes in community cookbooks call for six layers.) Regardless of the number of layers, the dough is usually hand-pressed into a cast-iron skillet or rolled and cut and then placed in a skillet. A few cooks use extra buttermilk to make a runny, pancake-like batter they pour into cake pans. The pancake-type stack cake is quickly prepared, but, unfortunately, it feels light and moist, and it does not absorb apple filling as well as cakes that have the consistency of a cookie.

In making the layers, mountain cooks traditionally used their fingers to hand press the stiff dough into a number 10 cast-iron skillet. The technique of pressing the dough into thin layers has been the focus of many stack cake lessons, and some argue that the uneven surface left by fingertips is essential for even absorption of the apple filling. Many, however, use a rolling pin to roll the dough, and this makes the process faster when using the old-style, heavy dough.

Most cooks serve the cake without anything covering the top. However, some cooks brush the top of the cake with egg white, and others dust it with powdered sugar just prior to serving. When the egg white dries, the top shines. Anna Bogle uses the more complex sugar and ginger frosting recipe reproduced in Part Two, which many find satisfying.

Testing the Recipe: Years ago, a focus group tested the dried apple stack cake recipe given with the recipes in this book. Group members were nothing like a panel of county fair judges, but they were carefully critical, saying they liked the cake, or commenting on the number of layers or level of spiciness. One woman, however, made a memorable comment: "This stack cake," she said, "is not like my grandmother's."

Indeed, it was not, and stack cakes are not all the same, and some are not good. Ninety-five-year-old Delphia Elkins has been making stack cakes for more than 75 years, and even she got it wrong at least once. She remembers dumping a two-layer stack cake into the garbage: "The two layers were like thick soggy pancakes and the filling was flavorless canned applesauce." Other stack cakes are almost as bad. Those made with pancake batter or graham crackers are neither old-fashioned nor good. But even these cakes tell us something about the importance of stack cakes: Cooks will take shortcuts to re-create the cake. As Anna Ellis Bogle in *Sitting Down to the Table* states,

Making a stack cake is slow-going, baking the thin layers of buttermilk cake one at a time in an iron skillet, while the dried apples stew down with sugar, cinnamon, cloves, ginger, and nutmeg. A good stack cake baker knows the care needed to make each layer even and thin, and my preferred method is to work the dough with my hands, kneading the sugar-grained mixture and feeling for the right consistency, then gently pressing each layer into the skillet with my fingertips. With the continual contact between my hands and the dough and the methodical nature of the tasks, creating a stack cake is for me a therapeutic process and a good time for thinking. And if, indeed, it is possible to convey a message through food, if a dish can absorb the emotions of its creator, a finished stack cake carries a powerful missive from baker to recipient.

The recipe provided in Part Two will not re-create your grandmother's stack cake, but it will provide the steps and quantities to get you started. This recipe is kitchen-tested, updated, and relatively fast to prepare.

More Than a Memory: Pawpaws

Pawpaws (*Asimina triloba*) are among America's largest native edible fruits, and they are members of the custard-apple family, *Annonaceae*. The fruit resembles other custard-apple family fruits including the pond-apple, cherimoya, custard apple, and sweetsop.

Pawpaws have been compared to bananas, a comparison that is both useful and risky. While bananas are a foreign tropical fruit, pawpaws are a native tropical fruit. Also, in comparison to bananas, pawpaws are softer, sweeter, and more moist. While both fruits have smooth skins and black seeds, pawpaws have about 15 seeds, and the seeds are as big as a nickel and as thick as a bean. Pawpaws are about the thickness of a banana; however, while bananas may be 10 inches long, pawpaws are commonly only about 4 inches long.

Pawpaws played a role in frontier culture, and, through the years, they acquired many names including pawpaw, custard apple, false banana, and Michigan banana. Some food dictionaries refer to the trees as papaws without the first "w," describing the name *pawpaws* as a corruption of *papaws.* To add to the confusion, papayas are also called papaws and pawpaws. Papayas, or *Carica papaya,* however, are members of the *caricaceae* family and look nothing like pawpaws. Pawpaws are peanut-shaped and usually weigh less than half a pound; papayas are pear-shaped and can weigh as much as 20 pounds.

Pawpaws grow on small, understory trees that reach a height of 30 feet. The trees thrive on cool, moist creek banks, wooded areas, and open fields. They are often planted in orchards and around houses, and in these environments, they grow like other fruit trees. They are native to states from Florida and Texas north to Michigan and west to Missouri but are now grown from coast to coast and all over the world. The fruit ripens in August, September, and October. When growing in northern regions, the fruit ripens after fall frosts; however, in warm, southern areas, it ripens long before the first frost.

If there is a late spring frost or below-normal spring rains, the pawpaw crops can be skimpy. Late frosts kill the blooms, and then, when the trees bloom a second time, the fruits are stunted and small. In many years, however, the crop is large, and those who enjoy the fruit easily gather more than they can use.

The flavor of pawpaws is distinct and forceful. The fruit is extremely sweet and highly aromatic, and its texture is soft and creamy-rich and custard-like. Pawpaws are exotic and moist but not juicy, and they lack the tart, sweet-and-sour flavor of other fruit. On the palate, this fruit offers a burst of sweet perfume, a flavor-texture combination that many people find strongly attractive. Others find the fruit too luscious, too delicate, and too flavorful, and may argue that the flavor is overpowering and even cloying.

A few people experience an allergic skin reaction or even stomach cramps when eating pawpaws. The seeds are not edible and contain a depressant.

Even those who love pawpaws find that their flavor varies from fruit to fruit, and not every pawpaw has perfect flavor. Just as it is difficult to find a perfect grape for wine, pawpaw flavor depends on cultural variety, climate, ripeness, seasonal changes, and growing environment.

Historically, Native Americans valued pawpaws, and for more than 12,000 years they consumed the fruit as a fall staple. Then, almost 500 years ago, the pawpaw was sustenance for explorer Hernando de Soto, and about 200 years ago, it may have been responsible for Lewis and Clark's survival. On their return trip from Oregon, the expedition was short on food until they arrived at river bottoms in southern Nebraska and Missouri. It was September, 1806, and Sergeant John Ordway wrote in his journal, ". . . we camped at sunset on the north side of the river at an immense site of papaws, and we gathered some papaws which our party are fond of and are a kind of fruit which abound in these bottoms and are now ripe."

Ripening: It is fortunate that Lewis and Clark arrived at those river bottoms in September because the pawpaw season is short. The fruits fall from the trees before they are ripe, and ripen on the ground or when sealed in plastic. In a moist atmosphere or a sealed bag, they turn from firm to soft. When they get really soft, almost oozy, and the skin turns from green to yellow with black spots, they are ready to eat. At this point, they last only a day or two.

Serving: Pawpaws are often eaten raw as snacks. The easiest way to eat them is to cut open one end and squeeze the pulp and seeds directly onto the tongue. The fruit is also mixed with other cold fruit and eaten with cereal for breakfast or served with mixed fruit for dessert. In a bowl of mixed fruit, the pawpaw adds a distinct dimension. When puréed to make a coulis, it can be served with custards, bread pudding, blintzes, or ice cream.

However, when used as an ingredient, the fruit loses some force of flavor, and is attractive to a broader range of tastes. Pawpaw pulp is cooked in custards, cookies, cakes, pies, and ice cream. Heat alters the delicate flavor, making it mild; and when baked in cakes, pawpaws lose much of their flavor.

In response to their wonderful flavor, high-end restaurants have been featuring pawpaws for many years. At the Oak Room in Louisville's Seelbach Hilton Hotel, the menu has included pawpaw and bananas Foster. The dessert menu at Charlie Trotter's in Chicago has included a pawpaw coulis as a sauce for ice cream.

In developing pawpaw recipes almost 30 years ago for her book, *The Wild Flavor,* Marilyn Kluger offered three guidelines. First, she suggests that pawpaws are ideal in combination with desserts that have a custard base. Second, she uses pawpaws in recipes that call for bananas. And third, the best of the three, she suggests eating them raw. The pulp of a ripe pawpaw is at its peak when it is pressed from the skin and eaten. With these rules in mind, Kluger offers recipes for pawpaw chiffon pie, pawpaw cream pie, and pawpaw custard ice cream.

Agronomists at Kentucky State University grow almost 50 varieties of pawpaws for use in the university's applied pawpaw research program. The Kentucky State University web site lists about 25 recipes and the university works with the Pawpaw Foundation, also in Frankfort, Kentucky. In studying pawpaws, nutritionists have found them to have more vitamins, minerals, and amino acids than apples, peaches, or grapes. Pawpaws compare well in food value to citrus fruits like oranges and are good sources of potassium. They also contain significant amounts of riboflavin, niacin, calcium, phosphorus, and zinc.

Storage and Preparation: Once ripe, whole pawpaws can be held in the refrigerator for several days or even a week. If the fruit is not fully ripe, it will last several weeks in the refrigerator, and then it can be brought to room temperature to ripen. Finally, pawpaws can be frozen whole for several months, or when the pulp is separated from the seeds and skin, the pulp can be frozen for up to a year.

Pawpaws have many seeds, and the skin tastes sharp or bitter. The easiest way to remove the seeds and skin is to cut one end off the fruit and press out the pulpy center. Then, some cooks press the pulp through a food mill, leaving the seeds behind. Some cooks also process both the skin and seeds through a food mill. Others remove the seeds by hand. It's a mushy mess, but it works.

When milk, eggs, and sugar are whipped together and baked slowly, they become a sweet custard. In the recipe for pawpaw custard in Part Two, the milk is replaced with cream, pawpaw purée is added, and what was a light custard becomes rich. With the addition of pawpaw pulp, the custard has a full, almost hefty texture. For a pawpaw mousse, the pulp can be stirred into whipped heavy cream, and for a wonderful pawpaw breakfast treat, pawpaw pulp is added to other fruits and served over cold cereal.

Sweet in flavor, subject of scorn, focus of research—many know this fruit by the camp song:

> Where, oh, where, oh where is Susie?
> Where, oh, where, oh where is Susie?
> Where, oh, where, oh where is Susie?
> —Way down yonder in the pawpaw patch.
>
> Come on boys, and let's go find her
> Come on boys, and let's go find her
> Come on boys, and let's go find her
> —Way down yonder in the pawpaw patch.
>
> Pickin' up pawpaws, 'n puttin' 'em in a basket
> Pickin' up pawpaws, 'n puttin' 'em in a basket
> Pickin' up pawpaws, 'n puttin' 'em in a basket
> —Way down yonder in the pawpaw patch.

However, others know it by poet James Whitcomb Riley's verse recalling his boyhood in the "Up and Down Old Brandywine":

> And sich pop-paws!—Lumps o' raw
> Gold and Green,—jes' oozy th'ough
> With ripe yaller—like you've saw
> Custard-pie with no crust to.

And finally, some know the fruit by the names of towns or creeks such as Pawpaw Creek in Indiana and Pawpaw, West Virginia; Pawpaw, Indiana; and Pawpaw, Kentucky.

Forest Nuts: Walnuts, Butternuts, and Pecans

The mountains of Appalachia have within them long ridges that shade deep valleys. They also enjoy high plateaus edged by bold rocky escarpments, bald mountaintops that rise from rolling highland bogs, and glades that offer sweeping views. From this ancient topography, plants and animals have evolved for 200 million years, or longer than any other American forest. Settlers arriving from Europe did not know that they were in the largest, most diverse, and possibly oldest temperate deciduous forest in the world. These factors resulted in a great abundance of edible wild plants and animals.

Specifically, these broadleaf forests were home to many edible nuts. Today and for the last 12,000 years, a ready supply of wild and domesticated nuts has added diversity to Appalachian cooking. Nut-flavored pies, cakes, and cookies are as much a part of Appalachian culture as are the walks in the woods.

In the fall and through the Christmas season, markets are loaded with nuts, and consumers are using them in quantity. Some buy hickories, walnuts, and pecans to make the apple crisp recipe offered in Part Two.

Nutting-Time
Effie Waller Smith

When the nights have lengthened,
And the days have shorter grown;
When the birds have flown southward
To a milder, warmer zone;

When the night and mornings have
Grown frosty, sharp and cold;
When leaves have changed their color
From green to red and gold;

When apple trees are burdened
With delicious apples bright;
When the crescent harvest moon
Shines all through the night,

Then to hunt and gather nuts,
What fun and what delight!
And store them away to eat
By winter fires bright.

Hickory nuts and walnuts,
Hazelnuts and chestnuts brown;
Butternuts and chinquapins,
Listen at 'em patter down!

Effie Waller Smith was born in Pikeville, Kentucky, in 1879, and died in Wisconsin in 1960. She was the daughter of former slaves, and she is credited with three books of poetry: *Songs of the Months,* 1904; *Rhymes from the Cumberland,* 1909; and *Rosemary and Pansies,* 1909. "Nutting-Time" appears in *Songs of the Months.* In 1991, the Oxford University Press published *The Collected Works of Effie Waller Smith* as part of The Schomburg Library of Nineteenth-Century Black Women Writers, Henry Louis Gates, Jr., General Editor.

Nuts that are popular in Appalachia include:

Almonds: Almonds are not native to Appalachia, but they have become popular, and today mountain cooks, like cooks across America, use them in candies, cookies, and cakes. They are used to make almond bark, oil, meal, and milk. After peanuts, almonds are America's favorite nut, and most of them are grown in California.

Beechnuts: The American beech tree produces the beechnut used in cooking. The tree is also called the "lovers tree" because young people carve their initials on the smooth, gray bark. Beechnut trees are part of the beech family, a family with about 100 species native to North America, including the chestnuts, oaks, chinquapins, and tanoaks. Mountaineers eat beechnuts raw or cooked and use them in any recipe that calls for pecans. They are especially good when substituted for pecans in pecan pie.

Black Walnuts: The ever-popular black walnuts grow in the wild from New England across the northern states to Minnesota and south from Texas to Florida. In the mountains, the trees prefer cold, damp valleys, but they also grow in the open. The fruit is almost round, and has a green husk and a strong, corrugated nut shell. Black walnut trees produce a sharp, strong-flavored, and oily nut that is popular in pies, cakes, cookies, fudge, and cake frostings. Of the nuts on this list, black walnuts may be the most typically Appalachian. (Two recipes in Part Two call for black walnuts: the fresh apple cake and the hot vinaigrette with black walnuts.)

Butternuts: Closely related to black walnuts but growing farther north, butternuts are also called oilnuts and walnuts. During the fall and early winter, hill country highlanders use this rich, flavorful, and oily nut in cakes and cookies; however because of the high oil content it does not store well.

Cashews: Cashews are a soft, butter-flavored, kidney-shaped nut. Here in the mountains, cashews are a popular snack food and are sold at quick markets and service stations. Large containers are given as gifts at Christmas. While some members of the cashew family are native to North America, the *Anacardium occidentale,* the popular nut tree, is native to South America and grown commercially in the tropics.

Chestnuts: Chestnuts are a large, prolific nut tree that grows around the world, and prior to an ecological catastrophe that occurred in the first quarter of the twentieth century, the American chestnut flourished throughout the Appalachian Mountains. It has been said that the tree grew so densely that a squirrel could travel its branches from New York to Georgia. Now, over 80 years after the blight killed the American variety, Chinese chestnuts flourish and nuts are once again available for use in soups, purées, and stuffings.

Chinquapins: Chinquapins are a shrubby chestnut-related tree that flourishes in Appalachia. Usually an understory growth, the tree yields a small, edible nut. The nuts resemble chestnuts but are sweeter. However, because of their small size and difficulty of shelling, few, if any, mountaineers take the time to collect them.

Hazelnuts: Also called filberts, hazelnuts grow in Appalachia on an understory bush, but the bushes are not productive and their use in traditional cooking is limited. The hazelnuts seen in mountain stores around Christmas are shipped from Oregon, California, or the Middle East. The nuts are used whole, chopped, ground, and even as flour.

Hickory Nuts: Hickory nuts, most of which are edible, grow on large, deciduous trees. Hickories are part of the walnut family, and among the hickories are 20 or more varieties, many of which grow in the Appalachian region. Hickory nuts are prized by Appalachian cooks as they include pecans, mockernuts, shagbarks, bitternuts, pignuts, and black hickory nuts.

Peanuts: While peanuts are a legume and not a nut, they belong on this list because cooks use them like nuts, adding them to cookies, cakes, and pies. This "nut" flowers above the ground on an annual plant, but then the flowers bend over and the seed grows in the ground. Other names include earth nuts, ground-nuts, and goober peas.

Pecans: Pecan trees are pecan hickories and a member of the walnut family. This soft, oily, oval, smooth-shelled, native American nut is by far the most used Appalachian nut. Pecan pieces are found in cheese balls, cookies, cakes, pies, dressings, and gravy. The nuts are also served candied, salted, toasted, and spiced.

Walnuts: The walnut family includes walnuts and hickories. Unlike black walnuts, English or Persian walnuts are not native to the Appalachian Mountains, and in addition, mountain cooks do not use them very often.

Yellow Walnuts: Another name for hickory nuts.

A Nut-based Snack: Peanuts and Cola: Some mountaineers and others from the Midwest and throughout the South engage in the widespread practice of combining peanuts and cola. Since colas were first marketed, combining salted peanuts with pop has been a common practice among both adults and children. Like salting beer or dropping ice cream into Cokes to make Coke floats, mountaineers pour peanuts into pop: The cola fizzes and the salt dissolves. The peanuts float, and then as they drink the cola, they munch on the peanuts. It's a bit like drinking a Coke with salty, flavored potato chips.

An Appalachian who documented this practice is Linda Scott DeRosier. In her book, *Creeker*, DeRosier talks about how in the 1950s her parents made her eat in the school cafeteria, but she would have preferred to walk over to Walter Pack's store "where all the cool kids drank Pepsis with peanuts poured in them. . . ." While DeRosier was stuck at school picking at the pinto beans and cornbread her mom fixed, she probably found herself envying her classmates who were buying peanuts, Pepsi, Nabs cheese crackers, and Moon Pies at Pack's.

School lunch periods weren't the only opportunity for enjoying peanuts and Pepsi. The mail delivery at Leonie Wallen's store 8 miles east of Paintsville, Kentucky offered a second chance to enjoy this treat. Once the mail was sorted, someone had to go to the store, and just maybe, they would buy an RC and fill it with a bag of peanuts. This happened around ten o'clock, and the combination of neighbors gathering, mail from a faraway friend, and a store-bought snack added pleasure to the day. When the morning chores were done and people were waiting for the mid-day dinner, it was a joy to sit in front of the store on benches or pop cases and enjoy a snack of peanuts and pop.

Colleagues in the public affairs office of Pikeville (Kentucky) College discussing the practice not long ago exhibited strong opinions on the subject. Judy, stopping to chat on her way to the copier, opined, "It *has* to be RC." And from behind the desk another said, "No, I pour peanuts into Pepsi." Sara Dunne of Middle, Tennessee, claimed her Louisiana-born father was a strong advocate of peanuts in Coke: "He drank the Coke, which fizzed like crazy. Then he slid the peanuts out of the bottle and into his mouth."

Just as there is no agreement on what kind of cola is best, the kind of peanut to use is also subject to debate. Today's snackers choose from salted peanuts, dry-roasted peanuts, boiled peanuts, or oil-fried peanuts. Some argue for Spanish peanuts, and some even add cashews to their Pepsi. To get maximum enjoyment from the practice, some people look for old-style long-neck pop bottles and peanuts in small bags.

The origins of the tradition are unclear. In eastern Kentucky, some relate the practice to coal mining. Working underground, they say, miners get dehydrated and need the energy from peanuts and the liquid from cola drinks. In the South, factory workers associate the tradition with vending machines. On a break from the job, workers drop coins into a machine; one machine is for pop and another for peanuts. Years ago, the food machines stood side by side and held long, narrow cellophane tubes of Tom's 5-cent peanuts and bottles of RC Cola. In Columbus, Georgia, a mill town, the RC Cola factory was close to Tom's, the peanut roaster. Certainly, the residents of Columbus, loyal to their town and factories, would argue that Tom's peanuts must be dropped into RC Cola (see sources, John T. Edge). Please, they would say, no Pepsi or Coke. For them it's peanuts and RC Cola.

Sources

Anna Ellis Bogle. *Sitting Down to the Table: A Collective Memoir of Appalachian Food.* Amherst, Massachusetts: Self-published thesis, Hampshire College, 2000.

Maurice Brooks. *The Appalachians.* Boston: Houghton Mifflin, 1965.

George Constantz. *Hollows, Peepers, Highlanders: An Appalachian Mountain Ecology.* Missoula, Montana: Mountain Press Publishing Co., 1994.

Alan Davidson. *The Oxford Companion to Food.* Oxford: Oxford University Press, 1999.

Linda Scott DeRosier. *Creeker: A Woman's Journey.* Lexington, Kentucky: The University Press of Kentucky, 1999.

John T. Edge, Director, Southern Foodways Alliance. Email dated Dec. 5, 2000.

Henry Louis Gates, Jr., Editor. *The Collected Works of Effie Waller Smith.* New York: Oxford University Press, 1991.

Marilyn Kluger. *The Wild Flavor.* New York: Henry Holt and Co, 1973. In 15 pages of recipes and discussion, this is by far the most comprehensive source on pawpaws, other than the Kentucky State University web site, *www. pawpaw.kysu.edu/pawpaw.*

National Sweet Sorghum Producers and Processors Association. *Sorghum Treasures.* Audubon, Iowa, Jumbo Jack's Cookbooks, 1991.

Robert M. Rennick. *Kentucky Place Names.* Lexington, Kentucky: The University Press of Kentucky, 1984.

Jesse Stuart Foundation. *W-Hollow Cookbook.* Ashland, Kentucky, 1990.

TEN

Sweet Endings

Pies, Cakes, and Candy

Pies of Every Description

When large numbers of hill folk grew what they ate, cut timber with axes, crossed rivers in boats, and mined coal by hand, they ate pies for breakfast, lunch, and supper. Even today, the cooks of the central and southern Appalachian Mountains make twice as many pies as cakes. They serve these pies sweet or savory, hot or cold, thick or thin, light or heavy, single or double crust. Some pies are distinct. Stack pies are thin, turnovers are small, and upside-down pies have fruit on top. Rather than being a passport to marriage, as they were years ago, today pies are a standard for celebration, an occasional treat, and a cook's glory.

And mountain cooks make just about every kind of pie imaginable. Blueberry, apple, peach, pecan, Concord grape, and coconut cream are very popular, as are rhubarb, chocolate, banana, and custard pies. Pies such as lemon slice, sweet potato, pawpaw, and pumpkin announce their contents in their names, and others such as shoofly, derby, million dollar, affinity, chess, mincemeat, Mississippi mud, and transparent, test our imaginations. As you might think, turtle, grasshopper, poor man's, and mother's pies do not contain turtles, grasshoppers, poor men, or mothers. But other pies include their namesakes: dried apple, vinegar, and pinto bean.

Mountain cooks identify light pies with names such as angel, elegant, heavenly, luscious, and chiffon. For light toppings, nothing is lighter than a mile-high meringue. Other toppings include whipped cream, streusel, cinnamon-sugar, bread crumbs, and nuts. In northern Appalachia, many cooks prepare vinegar, oatmeal, and raisin pie, while in the southern region grape, sweet potato, pawpaw, and buttermilk pies are popular.

Inspired by far-off and perhaps exotic places, mountain cooks prepare Hawaiian, Parisian, and California pies. Closer to home, mountaineers bake two chocolate pies: Mississippi mud and Tar Heel (North Carolina) pie. Cooks remember politicians with Washington, Tyler, and Jeff Davis pies. Brand names that make their way into pie vocabulary include Ritz, Milky Way, and Toll House.

Apple pies are so common and varied in Appalachia that they become a category that includes Dutch apple, dried apple, apple stack, apple custard, apple sorghum, and double crust apple. In southern Appalachia, cooks also prepare half-moon or fried apple pies. They fry these single-serving apple turnovers in lard and eat them out of hand.

To prepare the transparent pies of southern Appalachia and the shoofly pies of the northern region, cooks stir an egg-and-sugar-based filling and bake the mixture in a crust. These stir-pour-and-bake pies are so sweet they are sometimes called confections. Many of the pies listed here fit into this category, but buttermilk, molasses, and chess pies stand out. The chocolate chip pecan pie recipe in Part Two also fits in this category.

Pecan pies are Southern but not particularly old. Cooks have been making them for only about 60 years, and despite their relatively recent appearance, chefs from around the world consider pecan pie to be a typically Southern dessert. The addition of chocolate chips to pecan pie adds a contrasting nuance that delights. The filling is sweet, but the crust, nuts, and chips moderate the flavor.

Cake History: Native American and Ethnic Traditions

In the long period before Europeans brought wheat to North America, Indians used corn and acorns to prepare a variety of breads. These breads were not cake in the manner of modern cakes, but rather they included a variety of solid or formless preparations such as Inca *mote,* which is corn boiled in water, and breads containing chestnuts and sweet potatoes. Lesser bread ingredients were beans, hazelnuts, and pumpkin. On the California coast, the Chumash Indians ground acorns into meal and used it to thicken mush. In *American Indian Cooking Before 1500,* Mary Gunderson presents a recipe for acorn cake made with acorn meal. Sophie D. Coe, writing in *America's First Cuisines,* says that the Mayans made bread with three tubers: manioc, macal, and jícama.

While the early settlers learned to make some of the native peoples' cakes, the cakes popular on the Appalachian frontier included dried apple stack cakes, scripture cakes, gingerbread cakes, and pound cakes. Later, in the nineteenth century, cakes such as applesauce cakes, chiffon cakes, upside-down cakes, funnel cakes, and pumpkin rolls became popular. Of particular importance and popularity was the angel food cake.

Frontier women made gingerbread and stack cakes without the use of measures or temperature control, but with time, science-oriented techniques would alter the nature of cakes. Fannie Farmer, author of *The Boston Cooking-School Cook Book,* is known as the "mother of level measurements." Prior to her writing, recipes might call for a gill of liquid or an amount of butter the size of a walnut. Farmer developed recipes at a time in history, starting with her first book in 1896, when new technology brought oven thermometers, thermostats, measuring cups, and scales to home kitchens. These tools ushered in a new level of sophistication for home baking, and Farmer's cooking school was on the forefront of history.

These new baking methods gave rise to a new awareness of cakes, and baking became an art that was part of the region's social fabric. Fifty to 100 years ago, box suppers, cakewalks, and ice cream socials encouraged home baking. The ability to bake a fine cake was a prized and socially respected skill. Hog killings and bean stringings were essential, and the baking of biscuits and cornbread was a daily chore, but in frontier America cake baking was for special events. Appalachian communities still come together for celebrations that encourage both ordinary and fancy cakes.

The Fannie Farmer kitchen was not the only source of new cakes. Many common homemade cakes originated in commercial test kitchens, and some of Appalachia's favorite cakes from the 1920s through the 1970s were inspired by the manufacturers of leavening agents, flour, and chocolate. Eagle Brand condensed milk, Jell-O, and 7-Up are cake ingredients because their manufacturers created recipes. The *Hershey's 1934 Cookbook* remains in print. The red velvet, prune, fresh apple, and angel food cakes that were so popular in Appalachian kitchens were quite likely adapted from recipes printed on a manufacturer's label. However, as these recipes were published and republished in community cookbooks, they took on lives of their own. Cooks added ingredients, combined steps, and changed names.

Today, mountain cooks bake all of the above cakes as well as egg (sponge) cakes and butter cakes, quick baking-powder cakes and slow-rising yeast cakes. They enjoy fried cakes and icebox cakes as well as big wedding cakes and small cup cakes and petit fours. The no-cook icebox and mousse cakes are mostly pudding. Box cakes are yellow, white, and German chocolate. Mountaineers make Baby Ruth, Butterfinger, and Milky Way cakes. Cheesecakes are either baked in an oven or chilled in an icebox and have only a touch of flour. Deep fat-fried cakes include elephant ears, funnel cakes, crullers, and doughnuts. In the northern reaches of the Appalachian Mountains in Nova Scotia and Prince Edward Island, the popular cakes are lemon rolls and oat cakes.

In addition to these common cakes, many ethnic groups continue to bake their special cakes. Appalachian Germans make *kuchen* (cakes made with yeast) and *torten* (cakes made with nuts or crumbs instead of flour). Polish-Appalachian cooks pride themselves in baking *babka* cakes, an Easter cake made with chocolate pieces and raisins or cheese. From the Scots, Irish, and English, some Appalachians have come to know Black bun, Scotch bun, or Dundee cakes. English-Appalachians flavor these fruitcakes with ginger and fill them with dried fruits, candied peel, and nuts. Sometimes they soak them in liqueurs. Third-generation Appalachian-Swiss make *berner biberli,* or yeast-raised jelly donuts (see the *Encyclopedia of Appalachia*). Italians brought to America and Appalachia their well-known *panettone* or yeast Christmas bread and their cookies or Italian *biscotti*.

Through most of this history, Appalachian cooks have prepared two opposite types of cake: heavy cakes made with shortening and light cakes made without shortening. For example, the angel food cake is a light sponge cake. Made without shortening or egg yolks, it has no fat. Pound cakes and black walnut cakes on the other hand are made with butter and are among the popular heavy cakes.

Pound Cakes: Smooth and Full

The pound cake enjoys a long history and great popularity. Pound cakes engage the senses and offer substantial taste, smooth texture, and high energy. The cake is at one time the cake of athletes, gourmands, and Appalachians. Its name reflects its recipe: Early pound cakes were made with one pound of eggs, butter, sugar, and flour. The French call it *quatre quarts,* or four quarters, meaning a quarter pound of each ingredient. Today, the pound cake is among the important cakes of Appalachia, and there are many popular variations. These include pound cakes made with heavy cream, black walnuts, lemon juice, mixed spices, and dried fruits. The cakes are frosted and glazed and baked as loaves or in Bundt pans.

Why this cake of French, English, Scottish, and German origin has remained so popular in the mountains is hard to say, but the cake is indeed a favorite. *The Foxfire Book of Appalachian Cookery* lists three groups of cakes: pound, plain, and other. Another Appalachian cookbook, Lyn Kellner's *The Taste of Appalachia,* includes only one cake, a pound cake. While the pound cake is Appalachian, it is also ubiquitous across the United States, and it enjoys a history of its own.

A possible original source of these recipes is the pound cake recipe in *The Art of Cookery Made Plain and Easy* by Hanna Glasse and dated 1747. This book was the most popular English cookbook of the eighteenth century; it remained in print for about 75 years, and recently it was reprinted. The Glasse recipe tells us something about the history of pound cakes. First, she instructs us to mix the cake in a clay pot. Then, her directions call for one pound each of butter, sugar, and flour, and 12 eggs. Glasse's cake is a "mixing cake," and as the recipe instructs, Glasse beats it by hand for one hour. A long beating time lightens the cake as air is forced into the batter. Finally, as an alternative, the recipe suggests adding a pound of currants.

Slowly now, try to follow her recipe:

Take a Pound of Butter, beat it in an earthen Pan, with your Hand one Way, till it is like a fine thick Cream; then have ready twelve Eggs, but half the Whites, beat them well and beat them up with the Butter, a Pound of Flour beat in it and a Pound of Sugar and a few Carraways; beat it all well together for an Hour with your Hand or a great wooden Spoon. Butter a Pan and put it in and bake it an Hour in a quick Oven. For Change, you may put in a Pound of Currants clean wash'd and pick'd.

As time passed, the pound cake progressed, and about 75 years later, in 1824, Mary Randolph's *The Virginia House-wife* instructed cooks to "Wash the salt from a pound of butter . . . add grated lemon peel, a nutmeg, and a gill of brandy." She goes on to say, "This cake makes an excellent pudding if baked in a large mould, and eaten with sugar and wine."

In 1871, *Mrs. Porter's New Southern Cookery Book and Companion for Frugal and Economical Housekeepers; Containing Carefully Prepared and Practically Tested Recipes for all Kinds of Plain and Fancy Cooking* offered six pound cake recipes, including a rice pound cake, an imitation pound cake, and the more conventional citron pound cake. Then in 1970 in Volume Two of *Mastering the Art of French Cooking,* Julia Child and Simone Beck encouraged the use of an electric mixer in place of the hour of hand beating suggested by Hanna Glasse. Child and Beck say, "Of the several methods for making a pound cake, we find by far the best one results from beating the eggs and sugar in an electric mixer until they double in volume. . . ." Finally, and again suggesting the Southern love of the pound cake, Jean Anderson in *The Grass Roots Cookbook* of 1977 includes three pound cake recipes. She offers a black walnut pound cake from Maryland's Eastern Shore, a blue ribbon pound cake from Rockingham County, North Carolina, and finally a brown sugar poundcake [sic] with walnut glaze from Marengo County, Alabama.

Much like those in the old cookbooks, the pound cake recipe in Part Two produces a butter cake. Flavor oozes from the combination of vanilla, butter, and buttermilk. The cake body is wonderfully moist and sweet while the edges yield crunch and chew. The use of buttermilk gives the cake its Southern pedigree.

Scripture Cake: Another Butter Cake

Another cake that could also be called a pound cake is the scripture cake. This cake is well known because its creators, their names lost long ago, list each ingredient as a verse in the King James Version of the Bible. Today, Bible school teachers use the recipe as a trivia game, with the goal being to list the cake's ingredients by reading the Bible verse. The challenge comes not only from knowing the Bible verse, but also because many verses include more than one ingredient.

Often compared to fruitcake, this subtle, fruity scripture cake excites cooks from Georgia to Iowa to Vermont. The cake has a long history. In 1809, Dolly Madison, the First Lady of President James Madison, made the cake. Cooks from the Southern Bible Belt think of the cake as their invention, while others associate it with Maryland's Eastern Shore, and research shows that scripture cakes are common in the British Isles. One recipe posted on the Internet is from Ireland and dated 1788.

When served, the cake is slightly spicy, a bit sweet, and soft-textured. The inclusion of dried fruit and almonds distinguishes the cake. To add flavor and moisture, some cooks wrap the cakes in brandy-soaked cloths while others increase the spices. When the cake is frozen, it slices clean and straight. In place of figs, the cake can be made with dried apricots or dates. As to the half teaspoon of salt, it adds a Bible verse, but not much flavor. See the recipe in Part Two, and then relate each ingredient to one of the verses below.

I Kings 4:22, "And Solomon's provision for one day was 30 measures of fine flour."

Amos 4:5, "And offer a sacrifice of thanksgiving with leaven [baking powder]."

Exodus 30:23, "Take thou also unto thee principal spices, pure myrrh five hundred shekels, and of sweet cinnamon half so much, even two hundred and fifty shekels, and of sweet calamus two hundred and fifty shekels. . . ."

II Chronicles 9:9, "And she gave the king an hundred and twenty talents of gold, and of spices great abundance, and precious stones: neither was there any such spice as the queen of Sheba gave king Solomon."

Leviticus 2:13, "With all thine offerings thou shalt offer salt." Also, Mark 9:50, "Salt is good."

Nahum 3:12, "All thy strong holds shall be like fig trees with the first-ripe figs."

I Samuel 30:12, "And they gave him . . . two clusters of raisins: and when he had eaten, his spirit came again to him: for he had eaten no bread, nor drunk any water, three days and three nights."

Numbers 17:8, "And it came to pass, that on the morrow Moses went into the tabernacle of witness; and, behold, the rod of Aaron for the house of Levi was budded, and brought forth buds, and bloomed blossoms, and yielded almonds."

Judges 5:25, "She brought forth butter in a lordly dish."

Jeremiah 6:20, "To what purpose cometh there to me incense from Sheba, and the sweet cane [sugar] from a far country? Your burnt offerings are not acceptable, nor your sacrifices sweet unto me."

Isaiah 10:14, "And my hand hath found as a nest the riches of the people: and as one gathereth eggs that are left, have I gathered all the earth; and there was none that moved the wing, or opened the mouth, or peeped."

Exodus 16:31, "And the house of Israel called the name thereof Manna: and it was like coriander seed, white; and the taste of it was like wafers made with honey."

Judges 4:19, "And she opened a bottle of milk, and gave him drink."

Bourbon Balls, Peanut Brittle, Sea Foam, and Toffee

During the Christmas season and at fall fairs, school reunions, and family celebrations, many mountaineers serve homemade candy:

chocolate, vanilla, peanut butter, cream, and caramel. Making candy is a common practice, and frequently it brings different generations together. Grown women make candy with their mothers while young children go to their grandmothers. Men and women both old and young work for weeks before Christmas making candy. Boiled. Cut. Stacked. Piled and covered. Usually, the older cook teaches the younger one, but sometimes the roles are reversed. Candy making is an annual affair, and in Appalachia cooks know that it has to be done during the dry winter months. The heavy humidity of summer melts sugar.

Starting around December 15, homemakers complain about not having their Christmas candy ready, and they struggle to find time to make it. Eventually, however, they make the candy and when family and friends gather to celebrate the season, Junior will pass a tray with five, seven, or ten different kinds of candy. Making candy in the mountains is either a family tradition or a social event. Women's clubs, church auxiliaries, and youth organizations such as Boy Scouts make candy to sell or to serve at parties.

When the groups set up sale tables or gather for a party, they have a variety of candies, but certain ones dominate. An informal survey of 20 recent Appalachian cookbooks that include recipes for candy (five others did not include candy) resulted in 200 candy recipes or about 20 recipes per book. Most of the books were community cookbooks, but books from major publishers were also included. Of the 200 recipes, 30 were for fudge. "Fudge" is chocolate fudge and that includes varieties such as million dollar, black walnut, quick, 15-minute, marshmallow cream, and cocoa. The second most popular candy is peanut butter fudge, with 20 recipes, and in third place is peanut brittle, with 11 recipes. Chocolate peanut butter fudge was included seven times as were cream pull candy and molasses taffy.

Authors such as Joe Dabney, John Parris, and Sidney Farr in presenting traditional Appalachian cooking offered recipes such as molasses taffy, vinegar taffy, and sorghum molasses candy. Farr also presented birch and black walnut candies. These recipes are in contrast to those found in community cookbooks. Some committees load their books with recipes for chocolate fudge, peanut butter fudge, peanut brittle, and other favorite candies including bourbon balls, popcorn balls, caramel corn, potato candy, divinity, rocky road, pecan pralines, cream pull candy,

peanut butter rolls (also called potato candy or pinwheels), cara-
mels, fondant, sea foam, toffee, turtles, and mint patties. Each of
these recipes appeared in two or more cookbooks. Other recipes
that appeared only once were broken glass, chocolate pull candy,
sour cream candy, spiced nuts, rum balls, and stiffjack candy,
which is a vinegar taffy. The books in this survey included four
date candies: date nut rolls, date balls, date nut fudges, and date
loaves. Coconut candies are called bonbons and mounds.

The candy recipes for peanut brittle, bourbon balls, and cream
praline fudge in Part Two produce large batches, but perhaps not
large enough for some purposes. In the mountains when cooks
take these candies to an event, they like to load their platters and
to do so they may double or triple these quantities. Bourbon balls
are typical. A tiny treat. A large recipe. An ultimate ending. This
candy is soft, and it melts quickly in your mouth. As it melts, you'll
get a tinge of chocolate and a burst of bourbon. These bourbon
balls are soft-centered, chocolate-coated, and liqueur-flavored.

Bourbon balls, also called chocolate rum balls, brandy balls,
bourbon creams, nut balls, and candy bonbons are names that
have been around since about 1940, or perhaps sometime after
Prohibition. In these 60-plus years, mountain cooks have developed three kinds of bourbon balls. First, cooks make them with
corn syrup and vanilla wafer crumbs, and second, like the recipe
in Part Two, they make them with butter cream centers. Finally,
some cooks make bourbon balls with fondant centers. The cream
praline fudge recipe in Part Two yields squares of pecan cream
fudge rather than round praline candies that are dropped by
spoonfuls onto waxed paper. Mountain cooks sometimes call it
white fudge or penuche.

Sources

Jean Anderson. *The Grass Roots Cookbook*. New York: The New York Times
    Book Co., Inc., 1977.
Sarah Belk. *Around the Southern Table: Innovative Recipes Celebrating 300
    Years of Eating and Drinking*. New York: Simon and Schuster, 1991.
Julia Child and Simone Beck. *Mastering the Art of French Cooking*, New York:
    Alfred A. Knopf, 1961.
Sophie D. Coe. *America's First Cuisines*. Austin: The University of Texas Press,
    1994.

Shirley Corriher. *Cookwise: The Hows and Whys of Successful Cooking.* New York: William Morrow and Co., 1997.

Joseph E. Dabney. *Smokehouse Ham, Spoon Bread, & Scuppernong Wine: The Folklore and Art of Southern Appalachian Cooking.* Nashville, Tennessee: Cumberland House, 1998.

Alan Davidson, *The Oxford Companion to Food.* Oxford University Press, 1999.

Fannie Merritt Farmer. *The Boston Cooking-School Cook Book,* The Eighth Edition, revised by Wilma Lord Perkins. Boston: Little, Brown and Company, 1947.

Sidney Saylor Farr. *More Than Moonshine: Appalachian Recipes and Recollections.* Pittsburgh: University of Pittsburgh Press, 1983.

Hannah Glasse. *The Art of Cookery Made Plain and Easy,* First Edition. London: Mrs. Ashburn's China Shop, at Fleet and Dish, 1747. Facsimile Edition: Totnes, Devon: Prospect Books, 1995.

Mary Gunderson. *American Indian Cooking Before 1500: Exploring History Through Simple Recipes.* Mankato, Minnesota: Capstone Press, 2001.

Jean Haskell and Rudy Abramson, Editors. *The Encyclopedia of Appalachia.* Knoxville, Tennessee: The University of Tennessee Press, in press, 2006.

Lynne Rossetto Kasper. *The Splendid Table.* New York: William Morrow and Co, 1992.

Lynda W. Kellner. *The Taste of Appalachia: A Collection of Traditional Recipes Still in Use Today.* Boone, North Carolina: Simmer Pot Press, 1987.

Ronni Lundy. *Butter Beans to Blackberries: Recipes from the Southern Garden.* New York: North Point Press, 1999.

Linda Garland Page and Eliot Wigginton, Editors. *Foxfire Book of Appalachian Cookery, The Regional Memorabilia and Recipes.* Garden City, New York: Doubleday, Anchor Books, 1984.

John Parris. *Mountain Cooking.* Asheville, North Carolina: Asheville Citizen-Times Publishing Co, 1978.

Mrs. M.E. Porter. *Mrs. Porter's New Southern Cookery Book and Companion for Frugal and Economical Housekeepers.* Philadelphia: John E. Potter and Company, 1871.

Susan G. Purdy. *A Piece of Cake.* New York: Collier Books, 1989.

Mary Randolph. *The Virginia House-Wife.* Washington, D.C.: Davis and Force, 1824. Facsimile Edition: Columbia, South Carolina: University of South Carolina Press, 1984.

While they do not sell scripture cakes, Sunnyland Farms listed in the Mail-Order Sources offers an excellent selection of Southern pound cakes. To order bourbon balls, see Ruth Hunt Candies in the Mail-Order Sources.

Apples. While peaches were planted during the early frontier period, once Johnny Appleseed passed across the country during the early eighteenth century, apples tended to replace peaches, and mountain farmers began making more fried apple pies, apple butter, and dried apples. Many old-style apples such as these are still available during the fall. See Chapter 9.

Kieffer Pears. Highlanders know Kieffers as old-timey pears, and the pears flourish because they are robust and blight-resistant. While many use them cooked, eaten raw the pears are a true culinary sensation. The fruit is crunchy, juicy, and slightly sweet. Kieffer pears are also hard, hearty, coarse, and gritty. The skins are rough and the centers firm. See Chapter 9.

Cast-Iron Cookware. Cast-iron cookware continues to be prized by cooks and chefs because it distributes heat evenly, quick-seals meats, and slow-cooks stews. In country kitchens, the highly durable cast-iron skillet is the pan of choice for cornbread and biscuits, but as shown above mountaineers also bake cornbread as sticks, muffins, and wedges. See Chapter 6.

Cast-Iron Skillets. The skillet is the most common cast-iron utensil. This heavy frying pan is available in sizes that range from a few inches to a few feet across. Typical diameters are 6, 8, 10, and 14 inches, but iron foundries numbered skillets so that, for example, a number 6 measures 9 inches across and an 8 is 10½ inches. See Chapter 6.

Muscadines. In southern Appalachia, wild grapes are muscadines, foxes, possums, and scuppernongs. Scuppernongs are a kind of muscadine, and they taste so sweet that some people compare their jelly to honey. Muscadines grow on tall trees, fence rows, and in cool creek valleys and are used for juice, wine, and pie. See Chapter 9.

Pawpaws. Pawpaws grow on small understory trees that reach a height of 30 feet. The trees thrive on cool moist creek banks, wooded areas, and open fields. They are often planted in orchards and around houses. The tropical-style fruit is sweet and highly perfumed. See Chapter 9.

Morels. This wild mushroom, or dry land fish, is prized in Appalachia. Some mountain cooks use them in soups, sauces, and stuffing, while others like them in omelets, canapés, turnovers, soufflés, spring rolls, enchiladas, and lasagna. Fried like fish, morels are especially tasty. See Chapter 7.

Cushaw Squash. For 9,000 years, Native Americans have grown and eaten cushaw squash. The long vines thrive in southern Appalachia's hot humid summers, and in the fall, the yield is bountiful, with each squash weighing 20 or more pounds. Here, the squash is shown at a farmer's market. See Chapter 3.

Shucky Beans: Also called shuck beans and leather britches, these beans are mature dried green beans. Here, the beans are still green, but when they dry, they turn brown and will be stored for winter use. Mountaineers prize shuck beans for their concentrated flavor. See Chapter 3.

Tomatoes and Peppers. Garden vegetables are the backbone of traditional Appalachian cooking, and during the summer farmers produce buckets of green peppers, banana peppers, and cherry tomatoes. See Chapter 3.

Chickentoe. Common wild spring greens include chickentoe, dandelions, dock, fiddleheads, purslane, ramps, shepherd's purse, and watercress. Also called spring beauty, tanglegut, mouse's ear, and two-leaf, chickentoe is served mixed in salad and fresh or killed. See Chapter 7.

Poke and Poke Sallet. This photo shows poke leaves and a poke stem. Poke comes into season when dogwoods and wild iris bloom. Here, the poke was boiled and then fried with eggs and, finally, placed between slices of bread to make a poke sallet sandwich. See Chapter 7.

Sausage Gravy. While folks all over the United States serve biscuits and gravy for breakfast, here in eastern Kentucky we call it sausage gravy, breakfast gravy, morning gravy, white gravy, and soppy. The selection of mild, medium, or hot pork sausage as well as the amount of added salt and pepper determine the flavor. See the recipe in the Sauces section.

Fried Trout with a Baked Potato. Most markets sell fresh trout, and usually they are farm-raised. At home, many cooks coat them with salted flour and fry them in a touch of oil and maybe some butter. Some then serve the trout with a baked potato and steamed fresh vegetables. See the recipe in the Meat and Fish section.

Deviled Eggs. Stuffed or deviled, hard-cooked eggs are wildly popular, and no mountain dinner is complete without them. Markets sell the deviled egg trays pictured here, and many cooks make deviled eggs with mayonnaise, mustard, salt, and pepper. Others add chili powder, dill, and capers. See the recipe in the Salads and Soups section.

Biscuits. Before being baked, these biscuits were sprinkled with flour and placed edge-to-edge in a cast-iron skillet. When cooked, the tops were broiled, and then the biscuits were placed in a wooden basket for serving at breakfast with pork sausage, fresh tomatoes, fried potatoes, white gravy, and eggs. See the recipe in the Breads section.

Cabbage Rolls. Cabbage rolls are at once the special food of Lebanese, Russian, Polish, and German people; they are a traditional preparation of Jewish, Catholic, and Protestant families; and they are Appalachian. Mountain cooks make this main dish with a rice and ground meat filling similar to that made to stuff peppers. Cabbage rolls are a full meal casserole, and a take-to-the-church classic. See the recipe in the Main Dishes section.

Green Beans. Green beans cooked with bacon are a dominant Appalachian vegetable. Some forget that what was once a Native American food includes tiny French *haricots verts,* shuck beans, and shelly beans as well as different green bean preparations such as three-bean salad. See the recipe in the Vegetables section.

Ham and Sweet Potato Casserole. Sweet potatoes, ham, and casseroles go together like summer and baseball. When cooks mash sweet potatoes and add other ingredients such as crushed pineapple, orange juice, and brown sugar the result is moist, smooth, and sweet. See the recipe in the Starchy Vegetables section.

Indoor Pork Barbecue. With this recipe, the cook doesn't grill, roast, or bake. He or she just shops for ribs and dusts off the slow cooker. After the ribs cook all day, the aroma of saucy beans and pork barbecue will fill the house. Served on a roll with broccoli and corn on the side, the dish makes a robust, full meal. See the recipe in the Meats and Fish section.

Chow Chow, Cornbread, and Soup Beans. Mountaineers often serve pinto beans with boiled greens, but this photo suggests cornbread and chow chow. Chow chow is a mixed vegetable relish made with cabbage, onions, green beans, and corn and colored with turmeric. A recipe for chow chow appears in the Vegetables section.

Oven-Fried Chicken Thighs. Wrapping chicken thighs with bacon melds the tastes of two barnyard animals to yield great flavor: The chicken absorbs some fat as well as a bit of the salty, smoky tang that is characteristic of bacon. See the recipe in the Meats and Fish section.

Skillet-Fried Potatoes. Shown with scrambled eggs, fried potatoes are fine, fancy, delicate, hearty daily fare. Taste the salt, bite into the crisp outside shell, and feel the moist centers. Caramelized onions add contrast. Serve for breakfast with orange juice and gravy. See the recipe in the Starchy Vegetables section.

Buttermilk Pie. Since the 1880s Southern cooks have been making buttermilk pie. Some top it with meringue while others sprinkle it with cinnamon or nutmeg, but always this recipe calls for eggs, sugar, and buttermilk. See the recipe in the Pies and Cakes section.

Scripture Cake. This cake is well known because its creators list each ingredient as a verse in the Bible. The recipe may have originated in Ireland in the 1780s, and, today, Bible school teachers use it as a trivia game with the goal being to list the cake's ingredients by reading the Bible verse. See the recipe in the Pies and Cakes section.

Sweet Potato Pie. In comparison to squash or pumpkin pie, this mix of puréed sweet potato is more substantial, and the sweet potato yields a fuller, more complete, more dense, and even richer taste. The filling is like custard in that milk and eggs give it body. After adding a dollop of whipped cream, each piece was decorated with a bit of left-over sweet potato. See the recipe in the Pies and Cakes section.

Fresh Apple Cake. This brownie-like cake is chewy, moist, and black-walnut flavored. Fresh from the oven, the cakes are crunchy on the outside and moist on the inside. Like prunce cakes, carrot cakes, and pumpkin cakes, apple cake recipes call for either oil or margarine.

Apple Crisp. Mountain cooks bake this sweet apple and oat mixture in a tin, and it comes from the oven much like a pie filling. Some call it apple betty. Historically, cooks prepared these crisps by layering sugar, spiced fruit, nuts, and buttered bread crumbs. Here it is served with vanilla ice cream. See the recipe in the Pies and Cakes section.

Stack Cakes. At fall festivals, customers line up to buy stack cakes, but you might make one at home. This slice of cake has eleven layers and was made from scratch using flour, sorghum, dried apples, and four spices. Notice the ginger glaze that dripped down the side of the cake. See the recipe in the Pies and Cakes section.

Bourbon Balls and Peanut Brittle. These two candies shown on Autumn Leaf Jewel Tea dishes include nuts and sugar. Bourbon balls are also called chocolate bourbon creams, nut balls, and candy bonbons, and they have been made since about 1940. See the recipe in the Desserts and Candy section.

Moonshine. Made with corn, moonshine is either a living link to a proud past, or what the term suggests: illegal, home brewed, distilled corn whiskey. Practically all foodstuffs, but most notably vegetables, fruit, and grain, can be fermented and made into spirits—the magical mountain dew or white lightning. See Chapter 6.

Canned Green Beans, Baby Sweet Corn, and Tomato Juice. From left to right this photo shows canned green beans, honey, pickled baby sweet corn, mixed vegetables, and tomato juice. Chow chow is shown in front, and note that the tomato juice is separated into juice and tomato water. Some mountaineers serve tomato water as a delicacy. See Chapter 3.

PART TWO

Appalachian Food

Recipes

To keep Appalachia's culinary tradition alive, the region's foods have to be cooked, and while the following recipes could easily be used in the context of living history reenactments, their new life starts in the modern home kitchen, where fresh ingredients and healthy foods are paramount.

Some scholar-historians might prefer to include ingredients, recipes, and techniques that were used in the past, but are, by today's standards, obscure. For example, it is true that long ago home cooks started with a whole pork liver or ten dozen ears of corn, and they added lard to every ingredient that passed over their stoves. But to repeat these old recipes does not serve the present. Appalachian culture is yeasty and in flux. The recipes that follow don't call for hearth cooking or hog killing, but instead for stovetop cooking, oven-baking, or microwaving. The cooking steps assume stand-alone mixers, food processors, cooling racks, and whisks. Hearth cooking is the subject of another book.

However, being cookable is not enough—the food must also be enjoyable. This selection of Appalachian-style recipes will compete with McDonald's hamburgers and Subway sandwiches. They not only have a place in schools and at home, but they also have the flavor components to be enjoyed by everyone every day.

Even now, Appalachia has large numbers of home cooks, and indeed, many of them cook daily. The following recipes are an attempt to capture a few of their favorites. Unfortunately, space would allow the inclusion of only a tiny fraction of the many hundreds that are widely popular.

Pies & Cakes   257

Desserts, Candy, and Tea   271

Breads

Baking Powder Biscuits

Biscuits can be eaten with peanut butter and jelly, but in traditional mountain kitchens they are covered with gravy, spread with butter and honey, or split open for a sausage or ham filling. For a traditional dinner, serve biscuits with Southern fried chicken and coleslaw or chicken-fried steak; or for a country breakfast, offer biscuits with hot sorghum molasses, fried apples, fried potatoes, pork chops, sliced fresh tomato, and gravy.

PREPARATION TIME: 10 minutes
START TO FINISH: 25 minutes
YIELD: 8 to 12 biscuits depending
   on the size of the cutter

2 cups all-purpose flour
1 tablespoon baking powder
1 teaspoon salt
⅓ cup (5 tablespoons plus 1
   teaspoon) lard or shortening
¾ cup milk

Step 1   Move the oven rack to the lowest third of the oven and preheat the oven to 450°F.

Step 2   In a large bowl, mix together the flour, baking powder, and salt. Use a pastry blender to cut the lard or shortening into the dry ingredients until the pieces are about the size of rice grains. Lightly stir in the milk, adding more if the dough does not come together.

Step 3   Form the dough into a ball and dump it onto a floured surface. Pat the dough to a ¾-inch thickness. Cut biscuits with a 2- to 3-inch round biscuit cutter, and place them about an inch apart on a large cookie sheet or jellyroll pan. Gather the scraps and repeat until all the dough is used. Bake 10 to 14 minutes or until brown on the bottom. If the tops are white, broil until brown, about 1 minute.

Healthy Alternative: In place of the shortening or lard, use canola oil. Cut the salt to ½ teaspoon.

Variations: Add pecans, black walnuts, or pitted kalamata olives. Flavor with rosemary, garlic, lemon zest, or parsley. Enjoy a Southwest biscuit by adding cooked black beans, kernel corn, and diced jalapeño peppers.

Sweet Potato Biscuits

Classic mountain. Country to the core. Sweet potato biscuits. The recipe is simple and if you do as most mountain cooks and use self-rising flour, you can make these biscuits with three ingredients: butter, 1 cup of sweet potato casserole, and self-rising flour. The biscuit is a showstopper, a flag-raising treasure, and a topic of conversation. Serve them with fresh butter and linn (basswood) or sourwood honey for breakfast, lunch, or supper. They are especially good with Sunday dinner during the fall and winter.

You can make them with 1 cup of leftover sweet potato casserole from the recipe in the Starchy Vegetables section or use the recipe below. The casserole provides sweetened, spiced, and puréed sweet potatoes that make the biscuits heavy, moist, and rust-colored.

PREPARATION TIME: 15 minutes when
    using leftover casserole
PREPARATION TIME: 45 minutes if
    using fresh sweet potatoes
START TO FINISH: 30 minutes when
    using leftover casserole
YIELD: 8 biscuits

For the sweet potato casserole:
1 cup cooked mashed sweet
   potatoes
1 tablespoon brown sugar
1 tablespoon butter
½ teaspoon salt
¼ teaspoon nutmeg
¼ teaspoon cinnamon

For the biscuits:
3 tablespoons butter plus ¼ cup
   butter
1 cup all-purpose flour
2 teaspoons baking powder
1½ teaspoons salt
1 cup sweet potato casserole

Step 1 If preparing the sweet potato casserole, combine the mashed sweet potatoes, brown sugar, butter, salt, nutmeg, and cinnamon.

Step 2 Preheat the oven to 400°F and melt 3 tablespoons of butter in an 8×8-inch baking tin.

Step 3 Mix the flour, baking powder, and salt. Using a pastry blender, cut the ¼ cup butter and then the sweet potato into the flour mixture. On a floured surface, knead the dough. Pat out to ½- to ¾-inch thickness and cut into 2-inch round biscuits. Place the biscuits in the baking pan with the butter.

Step 4 Bake 12 to 15 minutes or until brown on the edges. To check for doneness, break a biscuit open and see that the dough is cooked in the center—not wet and doughy. Broil 1 minute to brown the tops.

Healthy Alternatives: Omit the 3 tablespoons of butter from the pan. Dust the pan or the bottom of the biscuits with flour. If you are concerned about saturated fats, replace the ¼ cup butter with canola oil. Cut the salt.

BREADS

Simple Cornbread

Because it is made in a skillet, this cornbread should be cut into wedges. It is delicious served with soup beans or fried cabbage and a thick slice of sweet onion. Mountain people also crumble it into a bowl and pour buttermilk or pot likker over it. Note that this healthy recipe contains neither oil nor eggs, and the buttermilk is fat-free. In addition, you can spray the skillet with a thin coating of nonstick cooking spray instead of using grease or lard.

PREPARATION TIME: 10 minutes
START TO FINISH: 35 minutes
YIELD: 4 to 6 servings

2 tablespoons bacon grease or lard
1½ cups self-rising cornmeal mix,
   see Recipe Note
1½ cups buttermilk
½ teaspoon salt

Step 1 Drop the grease into a number 8 (10-inch) cast-iron skillet, and using a rack in the lower third of the oven, slide the pan into the oven. Preheat both the oven and the skillet to 450°F.

Step 2 As the skillet gets hot, measure the cornmeal mix into a large bowl and stir in the buttermilk and salt. Scrape the batter into the hot skillet.

Step 3 Slide the skillet into the oven and bake for about 20 minutes, or until brown on the bottom and edges. If the top is too pale, brown it under the broiler for about 1 minute.

Recipe Note: You may replace the self-rising cornmeal mix with 1 cup cornmeal, ½ cup all-purpose flour, 1½ teaspoons baking powder, and 1 teaspoon salt.

Variation: Quick Kernel Cornbread. To the above batter add 1 cup whole kernel corn. Bake 25 minutes.

Mountain Country Cornbread

You can bake this cornbread in the oven, or fry it on top of the stove. When frying, divide the recipe between two skillets so it won't be too thick. Using eight ingredients, this recipe is moderate in difficulty; however, it can be simplified by omitting the stone-ground cornmeal. Crumble this bread into soup beans, or serve it as a side to soup beans, turnip greens, fried potatoes, wilted lettuce, and buttermilk.

PREPARATION TIME: 20 minutes
START TO FINISH: 50 minutes
YIELD: 10 servings

2 tablespoons bacon grease or lard
   or a thin coat of nonstick
   cooking spray
1 ½ cups self-rising cornmeal mix,
   see Recipe Note
½ cup bread flour
6 tablespoons stone-ground
   cornmeal, divided
1 teaspoon salt
½ teaspoon baking powder
2 large eggs
2 cups buttermilk

Step 1 Grease the bottom of a heavy 12-inch cast-iron skillet with bacon grease, lard, or cooking spray, place it on the top rack of the oven, and preheat the oven to 450°F. While you prepare the batter, heat the skillet in the oven.

Step 2 Combine the dry ingredients in a large bowl and make a well in the center. Add the eggs and then beat them with a fork or whisk. Pour in the buttermilk and stir until mixed.

Step 3 Remove the skillet from the oven and sprinkle the bottom with 1 tablespoon stone-ground cornmeal. Pour the batter into the skillet and sprinkle the top with the remaining cornmeal. Bake until the pone pulls away from the edge of the pan, the edges are a deep brown, and a toothpick inserted into the center comes out clean, or about 30 minutes. If the top is too pale, brown it under the broiler for about 1 minute.

Step 4 Remove the cornbread from the oven and turn it out of the skillet onto a wire rack. Cool 2 minutes. Flip it back onto a cutting surface, cut into wedges like a pie, and serve.

Recipe Note: You may replace the self-rising cornmeal mix with 1 cup cornmeal, ½ cup all-purpose flour, 1½ teaspoons baking powder, and 1 teaspoon salt.

Healthy Alternative: If you use cooking spray, the only sources of fat and cholesterol in this recipe are the two egg yolks, and for an even more robust crumb, you may omit them, using only the egg white.

Variations: Corn Sticks or Corn Muffins. Pour the batter into a muffin pan or cornstick mold, and bake until the edges are deep brown, the top is golden or even spotted with brown, and a toothpick inserted into the center comes out clean. Allow 20 to 30 minutes.

Crackling Cornbread. To the above recipe add 1¼ cups cracklings. Bake as muffins, sticks, or a pone, and adjust the baking time according to your pan.

Jalapeño Cornbread

Serve this cornbread in the winter with soup beans, pinto bean chili, or winter vegetable soup. For another mountain meal, serve this bread with fried potatoes, cold sliced tomatoes, and crisp bacon. When chopping the jalapeño peppers, wear rubber gloves to keep the heat from the pepper juices off your fingers and out of your mouth. However, don't be scared away from the peppers because once you cook them, they lose heat.

PREPARATION TIME: 25 minutes
START TO FINISH: 60 minutes
YIELD: 8 servings

2 tablespoons bacon grease or lard
   or nonstick cooking spray
1 cup self-rising cornmeal mix

1 large egg
1 cup buttermilk
½ cup diced onion
½ cup diced bell pepper, any
  color
2 jalapeño peppers
1 cup (4 ounces) grated sharp
  Cheddar cheese

Step 1 Grease a 10-inch cast-iron skillet, slide it into a cold oven, and preheat both the skillet and the oven to 400°F.

Step 2 Mince 1 jalapeño pepper. Pour the cornmeal mix into a large bowl and, using a fork or wire whisk, form a well in the center. Drop the egg into the well and beat it. Stir in the buttermilk and then the onion, bell pepper, minced jalapeño pepper, and cheese. The batter should be stiff.

Step 3 Scrape the batter into the skillet and smooth the top with a spoon. For garnish, slice the second jalapeño pepper into 8 slices and place the slices in a circle on the batter. Bake for about 30 minutes or until the crust browns and the pone shrinks a bit from the pan's edge. If the top is too pale, brown it under the broiler for about 1 minute. Remove the cornbread from the oven, turn onto a cooling rack, and let cool 5 minutes before cutting into 8 wedges.

Recipe Note: You may replace the self-rising cornmeal mix with ⅔ cup plus 1 tablespoon cornmeal, ⅓ cup plus 1 tablespoon all-purpose flour, 1 teaspoon baking powder, and ½ teaspoon salt

Healthy Alternative: Omit the egg and reduce the cheese to 2 ounces, or use low-fat cheese.

Sauces

Tomato Gravy

This recipe produces gravy that resembles a thick cream of tomato soup. Tomato juice is the primary ingredient, and with only four other ingredients, this boiled sauce is easy to prepare. Tomato gravy has countless uses. Serve it for breakfast or dinner over hot biscuits. Pour it over fried green tomatoes or fresh, ripe, sliced tomatoes and garnish with basil leaves. And for a wonderful hot lunch, try a tomato gravy sandwich. Layer slices of toast with sliced fresh tomatoes, meat loaf, and mashed potatoes. Moisten the filling with tomato gravy and serve as an open-faced or closed sandwich, garnished with chopped country ham. A light side salad and sweet tea completes the meal.

PREPARATION TIME: 15 minutes
START TO FINISH: 15 minutes
YIELD: 2 cups or 4 servings

3 tablespoons butter
3 tablespoons all-purpose flour
1 ½ cups tomato juice
½ cup heavy cream, milk, or skim
   milk
½ teaspoon salt

Step 1 In a small saucepan over medium heat melt the butter and whisk in the flour. Stir constantly until butter and flour mixture begins to bubble. Cook 1 minute.

Step 2 Add the tomato juice, cream, and salt, mix well. Bring the mixture to a boil, reduce the heat, and simmer 1 minute, or until the sauce is the consistency of a thick soup. Adjust the flavor with additional salt.

Healthy Alternative: To omit the butter, stir instant, quick-mixing sauce and gravy flour into the cream or juice.

Variations: For additional tomato flavor, add 1 tablespoon of tomato paste.

Green Pepper Tomato Gravy. To the above add 1 cup diced green bell peppers.

White Sausage Gravy

The sausage gravy that follows is prize-winning, but not unique. Cooks prepare the gravy in the grease and drippings left from frying sausage. At breakfast, they split a biscuit and cover it with gravy, or they serve the gravy beside sunnyside-up fried eggs, and mountaineers can mix the eggs with the gravy as they eat them. The gravy is also a wonderful accompaniment for sausage, pork chops, morels, fried potatoes, fried apples, or spooned over batter-fried meats such as chicken, liver, pork, and beef.

To keep the gravy white, don't brown the flour, and use white ground pepper. Keep in mind that your selection of mild, medium, or hot sausage as well as the amount of pepper added determines the level of heat in the gravy.

PREPARATION TIME: 15 minutes
START TO FINISH: 25 minutes
YIELD: 4 servings

¼ pound pork sausage
¼ cup all-purpose flour
2 cups milk
½ teaspoon salt
½ teaspoon pepper

Step 1 In a large cast-iron skillet over medium heat, fry the sausage, breaking it into small pieces. When the sausage is no longer pink, add the flour. Stir to moisten. The grease from the sausage must absorb all the flour. Add oil if the flour remains dry.

Step 2 Whisk in the milk, salt, and pepper. When the milk boils, reduce the heat and simmer 1 minute or until the mixture is as thick as pancake batter.

Step 3 If the gravy is not thick, continue to cook over low heat 5 to 15 minutes, stirring every few minutes. Remove from the heat and reheat before serving. If the gravy gets too thick—you do not want a gooey blob—add milk, water, or heavy cream.

Blue Cheese Dressing

We see it on salad bars, buy it from our grocer, and hear our waitresses announce it as a choice for dinner salads. Blue cheese dressing is a popular commercial dressing, but when made at home, it has an edge of distinction that mountain cooks achieve by using chunks of blue cheese and real mayonnaise. Your guests will be impressed when you carry the dressing to the table in a gravy boat, and ladle it over green salads. You can also serve it over a steak or with a slice of prime rib and a baked potato.

For this recipe, break large chunks of blue cheese from a wedge and then crumble some of the chunks and leave some of them whole.

PREPARATION TIME: 15 minutes
START TO FINISH: 15 minutes
YIELD: 4 servings

2 ounces blue cheese
⅓ cup mayonnaise
⅓ cup sour cream
2 tablespoons milk
½ teaspoon Worcestershire sauce
¼ teaspoon salt

Step 1 Crumble the blue cheese, leaving some large pieces, about ½-inch in size. Set aside.

Step 2 In a medium-sized bowl, combine the mayonnaise, sour cream, milk, Worcestershire sauce, and salt. Stir in the blue cheese.

Step 3 Refrigerate until serving. If the dressing gets thick, loosen it with additional milk.

Healthy Alternative: Replace the mayonnaise and the sour cream with fat-free mayonnaise and fat-free sour cream.

Hot Sorghum Syrup

Let the syrup run to the plate. Sop it up. Enjoy the thick foamy sweetness of 100% pure sweet sorghum syrup. In comparison to other sorghum, foamed sorghum is fuller, less sharp, and almost creamy. This effect is achieved when sorghum is mixed with baking soda and brought to a boil. Volume may increase six times, and when it settles down, foam remains. Served hot the syrup can be poured over pancakes; served cold it can substitute for a frosting. Breakfast cooks serve hot sorghum syrup over hot biscuits while dinner cooks sometimes serve it over fried chicken. Combine the syrup with baked winter squash, or for an ultimate treat, split a fresh crusty biscuit in half, add pats of real butter, and then pour hot, foamed syrup over the top.

> PREPARATION TIME: 5 minutes
> START TO FINISH: 5 minutes
> YIELD: 1 1/2 or 6 servings
>
> 1/2 cup 100% pure sweet sorghum
> 1/8 teaspoon baking soda

Step 1 Pour the sorghum into a 4-cup microwavable bowl. Sprinkle the soda one pinch at a time evenly over the top. Stir to mix.

Step 2 Microwave on high for about 1 1/2 minutes, or until the sorghum foams. Stir to mix the sorghum with the foam and serve immediately or let it cool a little. If it gets too cold, microwave again and stir.

SAUCES

Oven Apple Butter

Apple butter is delicious warm or cold on gingerbread or graham crackers. It can be spread on biscuits, toast, pancakes, waffles, muffins, sweet potatoes, bean cakes, roast pork, pork chops, sugar cookies, or ice cream.

This master recipe yields a slightly sweet, but mild-flavored butter; the spiced apple butter variation has a more intense, candy-like flavor. Mountain cooks might also add sorghum and fresh ginger root to their apple butter. Whatever the ingredients, home cooks thicken the apple purée on top of the stove, in a slow cooker, or in the oven until it takes on a butter-like spreadability.

PREPARATION TIME: 35 minutes
START TO FINISH: 6 hours
YIELD: 4 cups

8 tart apples
1 cup apple juice
1 cup sugar
1 teaspoon cinnamon

Step 1 Wash, peel, core, and cube the apples to make about 10 cups.

Step 2 Pour the apples and apple juice into a large saucepan or pressure cooker and cook until soft (about 10 minutes in a pressure cooker or 30 minutes in a saucepan). Stir to make applesauce. Blend in the sugar and cinnamon.

Step 3 Pour the sauce into a china crock, glass casserole, or stainless steel roasting pan, and bake at 275°F, until the apple butter is thick and not watery, or 4 to 5 hours. Stir every hour or two. The finished butter should hold peaks and spread with a knife.

Step 4 Refrigerate or pour into pint jars and seal.

Variation: Spiced Apple Butter. Increase the cinnamon to 2 teaspoons, and add ½ teaspoon of ground cloves and ¼ teaspoon of allspice.

Chocolate Gravy

As badly as itinerant preachers need converts, you need to taste this gravy. Break a biscuit open, spread it with butter, and lay the two halves on a breakfast plate. Ladle the chocolate gravy over the biscuit, and eat with a knife and fork. Chocolate gravy is low-cost, fat-free, and easy to prepare. It is thick, smooth, and chocolaty.

This gravy, once served by isolated highlander families as a treat for children, is now a treat for adults. Unfortunately, children don't know it. They don't see it advertised on TV, and they can't buy it at McDonald's. None of this, however, lessens the fact that chocolate gravy is a mountain venue for serving chocolate at breakfast. If at first the name lacks appeal, keep in mind that the taste and texture are true to chocolate.

PREPARATION TIME: 10 minutes
START TO FINISH: 10 minutes
YIELD: 5 servings

½ cup sugar
¼ cup all-purpose flour
¼ cup cocoa
2 cups milk
1 teaspoon vanilla

Step 1 Over a cool surface and in a medium saucepan, fully mix the dry ingredients: sugar, flour, and cocoa. Whisk until the lumps of flour and cocoa are gone. Gradually stir in the milk.

Step 2 Then, place the saucepan over moderate heat and bring the mixture to a boil. Reduce the heat and simmer for about 1 minute, stirring continuously. When the sauce is as thick as pancake batter or brown gravy, stir in the vanilla. Serve hot.

Salads & Soups

Deviled Eggs

No mountain dinner is complete without deviled eggs. At dinner on the grounds, they may be plucked away before the blessing is given, and at Thanksgiving dinners, even small families often serve two platters. Local markets sell deviled egg trays, and unlike yeast dinner rolls, which few cooks prepare at home, many cooks make deviled eggs.

Normally mountain cooks prepare deviled eggs in the American tradition flavoring the yolks with mayonnaise, mustard, salt, and pepper. However, like the cooks all across North America, mountain cooks experiment with other flavors. For a Mexican flavor they add chili powder and coriander. To conjure up the Pacific Northwest, they'll add chopped salmon, dill, and capers. To be truly Southern, they add country ham, and for a French-style egg, they stir some Roquefort cheese, Cognac, and sour cream into the yolk filling. Consider the following recipe, but please note that if the pickle juice is not salty, the recipe will need ½ teaspoon salt.

PREPARATION TIME: 20 minutes
START TO FINISH: 1 hour 30 minutes
YIELD: 24 halves or 12 servings

12 large eggs
¼ cup mayonnaise
2 tablespoons pickle or green-olive
    juice
2 tablespoons yellow mustard

½ teaspoon ground white pepper
¼ teaspoon turmeric

Step 1 Boil the eggs 10 minutes. Run them under cold water and remove the shells. Refrigerate until cool, or about an hour.

Step 2 Cut each egg in half lengthwise, remove the yolks, and drop them into a mixing bowl. Using a fork, thoroughly mash the remaining ingredients into the yolks with a fork. The filling should be the consistency of mashed potatoes.

Step 3 With either a spoon or a pastry tube with a rosette tip, press the filling into the 24 egg white cups. If desired, garnish with paprika and then half a green olive. Cover and chill.

Potherb Salad with Hot Vinaigrette

This wild greens salad is an exhibit for the bounty of spring and foragers' talent. Use any salad dressing, but the hot vinaigrette with black walnuts suggests 1980s style gourmet country cooking. Washed, spun dry, and sealed in plastic with a dry paper towel, greens will last a week or more in the refrigerator. (For a discussion of 11 wild greens, see Chapter 7.)

Garnished with egg slices and tomato and served with a bagel, toast, or crackers, this salad makes a complete lunch. For a traditional mountain treat, serve with spicy tomato aspic, deviled eggs, and buttermilk cornbread.

PREPARATION TIME: 2 to 3 hours,
   includes gathering the greens
START TO FINISH: same
YIELD: 3 servings

*Depending on the season use
   four of the following:*
1 cup chickentoe
1 cup shepherd's purse
1 cup young dock leaves cut into
   thin strips
1 cup dandelion greens

1 cup watercress
1 cup purslane
1 cup small tender lamb's quarters
 leaves

Select one of the following:
¼ cup ramps, chopped fine
½ cup blue violets
¼ cup wild onion, minced
½ cup pepper grass

For the hot vinaigrette:
3 strips (3 ounces) bacon
2 tablespoons vinegar
2 tablespoons water
1 tablespoon sugar
½ teaspoon salt
¼ teaspoon pepper
¼ cup black walnuts

Step 1 Wash the potherbs two or three times, or until every speck of dirt is gone. Using a lettuce spinner, spin the greens dry. Mix, place in a large, heat-safe bowl, and refrigerate.

Step 2 Fry the bacon over medium heat until crisp, lift it from the pan. Drain, cool, crumble, and set aside. Reserve the bacon grease in the frying pan. Cool.

Step 3 Whisk the vinegar, water, sugar, salt, and pepper into the bacon grease. Careful now: If the grease is too hot, the vinegar and water will go wild with their bubbling, steaming, splatter, and sizzle. Bring to a boil. Add the walnuts and bacon. Let the dressing simmer a moment, then pour over the greens and toss. Serve immediately.

Appalachian Fusion: For a Swiss potherb salad, serve over a ladle of hot cheese sauce and oven-fried potatoes.

Killed Lettuce

While most people make this salad with just three ingredients (hot bacon grease, lettuce, and green onions), some cooks use as many as 12 ingredients. The recipe below lends itself to many variations. To the lettuce some add radishes, endive, or scallions. Common dressing additions are vinegar, salt, pepper, garlic, sugar, water, and dry mustard. Some make the salad with lettuce only and others add fried onions or onion blades. Others refer only to the dressing and call it hot salad dressing or bacon dressing. For a traditional mountain meal, serve killed or wilted lettuce as a side to soup beans, cornbread, fried potatoes, and a glass of cold buttermilk.

Leaf lettuce is light and thin. Two varieties are often used: oak leaf and black seeded Simpson. If a heavier, more robust lettuce is selected, it will not wilt as easily.

PREPARATION TIME: 20 minutes
START TO FINISH: 20 minutes
YIELD: 4 to 6 servings

8 strips (½ pound) bacon or ½
    pound middling meat, sliced
1 large mess (2 quarts) leaf lettuce,
    washed, torn into pieces, and
    dried
2 bunches (2 cups chopped) green
    onions

Step 1   Using a large skillet, fry the bacon over medium heat until crisp. Lift the bacon from the pan, and drain, cool, chop, and set aside. Hold the bacon grease in the frying pan.

Step 2   At serving time, heat the bacon fat until it smokes, pour it over greens, toss the salad, and sprinkle the crumbled bacon on top.

Variations: Wilted Lettuce with Hot Vinaigrette. Whisk ¼ cup vinegar, 3 tablespoons water, 2 teaspoons sugar, 1 teaspoon salt, and ½ teaspoon pepper into the bacon grease in the frying pan. Proceed as directed above. For another variation, add ½ cup heavy cream and/or ½ cup black walnut pieces.

Composed Salad: For a chef-like presentation, as well as a complete meal, serve on warmed plates with hard-boiled eggs, sectioned tomatoes, and sliced mushrooms. Offer salt and pepper and maybe saltine crackers.

Coleslaw

Coleslaw is picnic, sandwich, barbecue, and buffet food. Mountain cooks serve slaw as a salad, as a side dish for fried fish and chicken, and also as a relish on hot dogs or hamburgers. This modern adaptation of an old mountain staple produces a cold, crunchy salad that is almost neutral in flavor. The recipe is from the 1970s, and it's not creamy, salty, or sweet.

PREPARATION TIME: 15 minutes
START TO FINISH: 15 minutes
YIELD: 6 servings.

½ of a small cabbage
¼ cup mayonnaise
¼ cup Italian dressing
½ teaspoon dry dill weed

Step 1 Shred or grate the raw cabbage to equal 4 to 5 cups. Stir in the mayonnaise, dressing, and dill, scrape into a serving bowl, and garnish with fresh dill weed and green olives. Refrigerate until ready to serve. For more flavor, add a tablespoon of sugar and a teaspoon of salt.

Healthy Alternative: Use low-fat or fat-free mayonnaise and a mild vinegar salad dressing.

Cornbread Salad

Mountaineers make bread pudding with leftover biscuits, they crumble cornbread into buttermilk, and they stir large croutons into Caesar salads. They also use cornbread to stuff the turkey and thicken soup beans. Now, at least since the early 1990s, the same country cooks have been making a tossed cornbread salad. The results are amazing.

Cornbread salad engages the mountain passion for cornbread, bacon, and tomatoes, and if the salad were not so new, many would think of it as traditional mountain fare. This recipe can be adapted to a low-fat version that is both low-calorie and cool-tasting, and then with the addition of salt, full-flavored. Serve either version as a side dish to a Sunday dinner of fried chicken and hot biscuits.

Note that crumbly, cake-style cornbread will turn to mush in this salad. The preparation time below includes baking the cornbread, frying the bacon, chopping the vegetables, and mixing the salad.

PREPARATION TIME: 45 minutes
START TO FINISH: 4 to 5 hours
YIELD: 12 servings

½ pone (5 cups diced) simple
  cornbread (see page 184)
1 pound bacon
3 cups diced tomatoes
2 cups green, red, or yellow bell
  pepper
1 cup diced onion
2 cups mayonnaise
2 cups shredded Cheddar cheese

Step 1 A day or at least 3 hours ahead, bake the cornbread and fry the bacon over medium heat until crisp. Drain the bacon. Chill the cornbread. Chop and refrigerate the tomatoes, peppers, and onion.

Step 2 Two hours before serving, prepare the salad. Chop the cornbread and bacon into ½- to ¾-inch pieces. Mix the ingredients: cornbread, half of the bacon, tomatoes, peppers, onions, mayonnaise, and cheese. Pour the salad into a serving bowl and spread the remaining bacon on top. Refrigerate.

Healthy Alternatives: To make a low-calorie, low-fat dressing, reduce the amount of bacon to ½ pound; replace the 2 cups mayonnaise with 2 cups nonfat sour cream; and replace the 2 cups Cheddar cheese with 2 cups nonfat, small curd cottage cheese. To enhance the flavors, add 1 tablespoon salt or flavored salt such as lemon pepper, garlic salt, or seasoned salt.

Appalachian Pork Salad

When served with crusty dinner rolls, hot biscuits, cheese biscuits, or wedges of cornbread, this warm salad is a complete meal (allow about 4 ounces of pork per serving). A smaller portion makes a good first course for a festive dinner. Be sure to serve the salad before the meats cool.

PREPARATION TIME: 40 minutes
START TO FINISH: 1 hour
YIELD: 4 to 6 servings

3 large eggs
1 head (1 to 1½ pounds) leafy
    lettuce such as Bibb or Boston
1 large tomato
3 strips (3 ounces) bacon
½ cup vinaigrette dressing
½ cup toasted pecans
6 ounces thin-sliced country ham,
    cut into 1-inch strips
6 ounces Canadian bacon, cut into
    1-inch strips

Step 1 Hard-boil, chill, and quarter the eggs.

Step 2 Wash, tear, and dry the lettuce. Cut the tomato into wedges.

Step 3 In a large skillet, fry the bacon over medium heat until crisp, or about 8 minutes. Drain the bacon on paper towels and reserve it to place across the top of the salad with the other meats.

Step 4 Toss the lettuce with the dressing, arrange it on a large platter, and sprinkle the pecan pieces on top. Garnish with hard-boiled eggs and sections of tomato.

Step 5 To the hot bacon grease, add the country ham and Canadian bacon. After the meats are heated through, drain them briefly on paper towels, then, while they are still hot, arrange them on the salad. Serve immediately.

Winter Vegetable Soup

You can serve this soup when it is cooked, but it tastes better the second day. Serve with crackers, buttermilk cornbread, or Sally Lunns, and make sure salt and pepper and bowls of hot chilies and diced sweet onion are on the table so guests can season the soup to their own tastes. (For a discussion of mountain soups, see Chapter 5.)

PREPARATION TIME: 40 minutes
START TO FINISH: 2½ hours
YIELD: 24 cups or 12 servings

2 pounds stewing beef, cut to ½- or ¼-inch pieces
1 quart water
1 quart tomato juice
4 carrots (2 cups) sliced ⅛-inch thick
4 stalks celery (2 cups) sliced ¼-inch thick
12 ounces or 1 large diced (½-inch cubes) potato
½ medium head or 4 cups sliced and chopped cabbage
1 large onion or 2 cups diced
2 cups green beans, cut into 2-inch lengths
1 (28-ounce) can whole tomatoes with the juice
½ cup beef bouillon grains
1 teaspoon hot red pepper sauce
1½ cups whole kernel corn
1 red bell pepper, seeded and chopped
1 green bell pepper, seeded and chopped

Step 1   Brown the beef on all sides in an 8- to 10-quart stock pot, about 10 minutes. Add the water and simmer for 1 hour. Cool and skim the fat from the top.

Step 2   Return the beef to the heat, add the tomato juice, carrots, celery, potato, and cabbage, and simmer for about 20 minutes. Add the onion and beans and simmer another 20 minutes. Add the whole tomatoes, beef bouillon, hot sauce, and corn. Bring this to a boil, and finally, add the chopped red and green peppers. Adjust the flavor with hot sauce, salt, and pepper. The soup has little broth, and if served quickly, the red and green peppers will be crunchy.

Butternut Squash and Potato Soup

This soup is popular with children and adults alike. Thoughtful cooks make it with various squashes including cushaw, acorn, and pumpkin, but butternut is the most popular. At a large gathering or buffet, you can serve it in insulated hot beverage cups and drink from the cup. For a light lunch, serve with buttered French bread or soft dinner rolls. At a dinner party, serve in cream soup bowls with crackers as a first course, and garnish with ribbons of sour cream or cubes of savory flan. You might like the spicy variation given below, but many prefer the gentle flavors of pure pumpkin, chicken, salt, and cream. With six ingredients and a food processor, this recipe is moderately difficult to prepare.

> PREPARATION TIME: 25 minutes
> START TO FINISH: 70 minutes
> YIELD: 6 servings
>
> 1½ cups water
> 5 cups fresh butternut squash (1 medium squash, about 1½ pounds)
> 1 medium potato (about 8 ounces)
> 1½ cups chicken broth
> 1 teaspoon salt
> ⅓ cup heavy cream

Step 1 In a large saucepan, braise the whole squash and potato in the water until tender (about 40 minutes). Add water as needed to maintain 1½ cups. You can also pressure cook the squash and potato for 15 minutes after the pressure is up. Cool.

Step 2 Peel the squash and potato, chop into large pieces, and, after removing the seeds from the squash, place in the bowl of a food processor. Combine the 1½ cups water with the chicken broth. Pour half the water and broth mixture and the salt over the squash and potato and process until smooth.

Step 3 Return the purée to the saucepan, reheat, and adjust the thickness of the soup with some of the remaining water/broth mixture. The soup should be thicker than cream but not as thick as pancake batter. Before serving stir in the cream and reheat.

Variation: Spiced Butternut Squash and Potato Soup. To the above recipe, add 1 teaspoon cinnamon, ½ teaspoon nutmeg, and ¼ teaspoon allspice to the ingredients in the food processor.

Bacon Potato Soup

This old homeplace recipe yields a rich, full-flavored, bacon-garnished, main-dish potato soup, a hearty mountain dish. The puréed vegetables provide the thickening and the cream the richness.

The results are heavenly. Add a ham and cheese sandwich, and you have a satisfying meal. Note that the bacon and ham provide the needed salt.

PREPARATION TIME: 20 minutes
START TO FINISH: 40 minutes
YIELD: 4 cups, 6 servings

3 cups diced potatoes (2 small
   potatoes, about 1 pound)
2 stalks celery
1 medium onion
2 strips (2 ounces) bacon

SALADS
& SOUPS

1 ½ cups chicken broth
6 ounces cooked ham, diced
½ cup heavy cream (optional)

Step 1 Wash the potatoes and remove spots and blemishes. For this soup, the potatoes can be used with or without the peel. Cut into ¾-inch pieces to equal about 3 cups. Wash and cube the celery and onion to equal about ¾ cup of each.

Step 2 In a large saucepan, fry the bacon until crisp. Remove the bacon and, when cool, crumble and set aside. Add the chicken broth to the bacon grease in the saucepan and bring it to a boil. Add the potatoes and celery, and simmer 15 minutes. Add the onion and simmer an additional 5 minutes, or until the potatoes, celery, and onion are tender.

Step 3 Using a food processor or blender, process three-fourths of the potatoes, celery, and onions until smooth. If the vegetables get too thick to process, add broth and continue to process until smooth.

Step 4 Return this purée to the saucepan with the reserved vegetables and broth and stir. At this point the soup should be the thickness of a cream soup.

Step 5 Stir in the ham, bring to a boil, then reduce the heat. When the soup reaches a simmer, stir in the cream. Do not boil. Serve garnished with the crumbled bacon.

Vegetables

Green Beans with Bacon

The first Kentucky cookbook, *The Kentucky Housewife,* by Lettice Bryan, offers recipes for stewed green beans, French beans, and common snap or bunch beans. The directions in this recipe are quite similar to directions given by Bryan more than 160 years ago, ". . . gather common beans in the morning; pick young and tender; draw off the strings; soak in fresh water; add bacon and salt; and boil until tender." In the tradition of Lettice Bryan, mountain cooks prepare the recipe with a popular summer bean, the white half-runner.

Notice that it takes 40 minutes to break and string the beans and fry the bacon. Then, an additional 25 minutes are required to cook the beans. This is relatively quick; many recipes call for 45 minutes of cooking. This slow process is the traditional Appalachian style, and it contrasts dramatically from the 10 minutes it takes to prepare a package of frozen French cut beans. The results, too, are dramatically different. Served with sweet white onions, sliced garden-ripened tomatoes, fried cornbread, and a glass of buttermilk, the dish can be a meal in itself.

PREPARATION TIME: 35 minutes
START TO FINISH: 60 minutes
YIELD: 8 servings

2 strips (2 ounces) bacon, cut into
    ¼-inch pieces
2 pounds white half-runner beans
    or pole beans

1 cup (1 medium) onion (optional)
½ cup water
1 teaspoon salt
¼ teaspoon ground black pepper

Step 1 Break, string, and remove the ends from fresh beans. If using, dice the onion.

Step 2 Fry the bacon in a large covered saucepan and then remove it to drain on a paper towel. Dump the beans, optional onion, water, salt, and pepper into the saucepan with the bacon grease. Bring to a boil and reduce the heat to a simmer.

Step 3 Braise covered until the beans are tender, about 25 minutes. Add water if necessary, but when the beans are ready, most of the water should have evaporated. Stir and serve.

Healthy Alternative: Omit the bacon, but you'll miss out on that touch of pork that is the trademark of mountain cooking.

Green Beans with Hot Black Walnut Vinaigrette

Traditional mountaineers flavored most vegetables with pork or lard, and they usually cooked their beans with bacon grease, fat back, or salt pork. In this recipe, steamed beans are combined with bacon, bacon grease, and a nutty vinaigrette. For convenience, prepare the beans and dressing ahead and reheat them at serving time. Serve the beans with roast turkey, pork, or beef, or with sautéed trout. Order black walnuts from Sunnyland Farms. See the Mail-Order Sources.

PREPARATION TIME: 30 minutes
START TO FINISH: 45 minutes
YIELD: 6 servings

1½ pounds white half-runners, fall
    greasies, or any fresh green bean
8 strips (½ pound) bacon
¼ cup vinegar
3 tablespoons water

2 teaspoons sugar
1 teaspoon salt
½ teaspoon ground black pepper
½ cup black walnut pieces

Step 1 Wash, break, and string the green beans. Remove the tips and ends.

Step 2 Steam the green beans until tender, 8 to 12 minutes, depending on size. As the beans steam, fry the bacon in a large frying pan. Lift the bacon from the pan and drain on paper towels. To the bacon drippings in the frying pan, add the vinegar, water, sugar, salt, and pepper. Bring to a boil and stir.

Step 3 Crumble the bacon and mince or grate half the nuts. Add half of the bacon and half of the nuts to the dressing. Add the green beans to the pan. Bring to a boil. Stir. Pour into a serving bowl and toss. Garnish with the reserved bacon and nuts.

Shuck Beans

While it takes a long time to grow, string, and dry beans, preparing a pot of cooked shuck beans is as simple as soaking and boiling. In addition, beans used to be dried for winter as an essential food, but today traditional cooks crave their intense flavor. The pot likker (liquor) is a full-flavored sauce for the beans. Serve the beans with pork chops, cornbread, sliced raw onions, and buttermilk. Order shuck beans from Floyd Skean's Marathon in the Mail-Order Sources. (For a discussion of shuck beans, see Chapter 3; dry beans are discussed in Chapter 5.)

PREPARATION TIME: 15 minutes
START TO FINISH: 14 to 18 hours
YIELD: 4 to 6 servings

3 to 4 cups dried green (shuck)
    beans
4 ounces salt pork

½ teaspoon salt
⅛ teaspoon pepper
water

Step 1 Wash the beans and discard any that are black or look bad. Cover them with water, soak overnight or about 12 hours, and then drain.

Step 2 Remove the rind from the salt pork, discard it, and dice what remains. Fry the diced salt pork in the bottom of a medium-size saucepan until brown. Add the beans, salt, and pepper. Cover with water and simmer covered over low heat 2 to 6 hours, adding water as needed. Cooking time depends on the size, maturity, and variety of the beans.

Step 3 When the beans are tender (mash a bean seed to check), remove the lid, raise the heat to medium, and continue to cook, reducing the broth until it thickens.

Boiled Fall Greens

For heightened flavor and sweetness, pick turnip, collard, rape, and kale greens after the first frost. The tedious part of fixing greens is washing and stripping the leaves. Because greens give off water as they are cooked, it is important not to use more water than recommended in the recipe.

Cook the greens until the thickest veins or stems are tender, the mass cuts with the side of a fork, the leaves are mush, and the pot likker (the broth) is fully flavored. Cooking time depends on how cold it has been; greens that have withstood hard freezes cook relatively quickly. Greens can be cooked in a pressure cooker, taking about 25 minutes after the pressure comes up.

For this recipe, use a single green or a combination of two or more. In place of the country ham, use a smoked ham hock or 6 ounces of salt pork. When cooked, these greens are easily stored in the refrigerator or freezer and reheated in a microwave oven. Serve the ham, greens, and pot likker in a soup plate with a side of cornbread, or offer the greens as a side to soup beans and offer vinegar. These go well with beer, hard cider, or a glass of buttermilk.

PREPARATION TIME: 30 minutes
START TO FINISH: 2 hours
YIELD: 4 servings

1 ½ pounds fresh turnip, collard,
   rape, or kale greens
2 cups water
8 ounces country ham pieces or
   scraps, sliced thin

Step 1 Leaf by leaf, wash the greens, and remove the thick stems. Wash again in a sink full of cold water. With the stems removed, you'll have about 1 ¼ pounds of greens. Gather the leaves into small bunches, and, using a chef's knife, slice them into ½-inch-wide strips.

Step 2 Place the greens, water, and ham in a covered saucepan, bring to a boil. Reduce the heat, and simmer for 1 ½ hours. Add water as needed to maintain at least 1 ½ cups of liquid.

Step 3 For a smoother texture and easier eating, process half the greens in a food processor until the pieces are the size of a kernel of corn, combine the processed greens with the sliced greens, and then serve.

Variation: Greens with Pot Likker. To the above, add 2 cups water. Serve the greens in soup bowls, crumble cornbread over the greens, and add about ¾ cup of the broth or pot likker to each serving.

Fried Dry Land Fish with Spring Onions

Green onions and morels come into season at the same time, and as a result, they may end up in the same skillet. Coated with cornmeal mix and fried in lard, the results are crisp and flavorful. Note, however, that, like fried green tomatoes, the crisp exterior of fried morels and onions will soften and even get soggy if they sit too long. Serve them as a side dish with boiled new potatoes, cream gravy, and country fried steak, or for breakfast with bacon, scrambled eggs, and cornbread. This recipe, with five ingredients and one cooking step, is easy to prepare. For a discussion of morels, see Chapter 7.

PREPARATION TIME: 20 minutes
START TO FINISH: 20 minutes
YIELD: 4 servings

½ cup self-rising cornmeal mix
   (or use 6 tablespoons cornmeal,
   3 tablespoons all-purpose flour,
   ½ teaspoon salt)
1½ teaspoons salt
1½ cups morels, cut into bite-
   sized pieces
1½ cups green onion slices
¼ cup lard or shortening

Step 1 Combine the cornmeal mix and salt and pour over the morels and onions. Stir to coat.

Step 2 Drop half of the lard or shortening into a large, cast-iron skillet and heat it on medium-high heat until it starts to smoke or reaches 325°F to 350°F. If the lard smokes badly, set the pan off the heat and lower the setting.

Step 3 Lift the onions and morels from the cornmeal mix and ease them into the skillet. Fry until golden brown or about 3 minutes on each side, adding the remaining lard as needed. The onions will blacken in spots, but other parts remain green.

Step 4 Drain on paper towels and serve immediately.

Healthy Alternative: The results are not the same, but you can substitute safflower oil for lard. Adding the safflower oil 1 tablespoon at a time, you may find that you can fry the entire recipe with 1, 2, or 3 tablespoons of oil.

Variations: As an appetizer, fry the mushrooms at tableside and serve them with pickled beans, pickled beets, and angel biscuits.

Appalachian Fusion: Serve with steamed broccoli, risotto, barley, or soba noodles.

Fancy Poke Sallet

To understand this recipe, compare it to a baked omelet, Italian frittata, or quiche. You might replace the cracklings with bacon pieces or fried salt pork. Serve it as you would an omelet. You can also serve it with cornmeal gravy and sides of soup beans and cornbread. Poke sallet also enhances pork chops, country ham, and baked sweet potato, and is complemented by coffee, tea, or buttermilk. (For a perspective on poke, a wild green, see Chapter 7.)

PREPARATION TIME: 25 minutes
START TO FINISH: 1 hour
YIELD: 8 servings

1 pound tender fresh poke stems
  with young leaves
2 tablespoons lard or bacon grease
6 large eggs
½ cup milk
1 teaspoon salt
½ teaspoon pepper
¼ cup pork cracklings (optional)
1 cup (4 ounces) grated sharp
  Cheddar cheese

Step 1 Preheat the oven to 300°F. Bring a large pot of water to a boil, add the poke, and boil 4 minutes. Drain, run under cold water, and cut into half-inch-long pieces. This should equal 3 cups of poke.

Step 2 Heat the lard in a 10-inch cast-iron skillet and add the poke. Fry on low heat for 4 minutes or until any excess liquid is gone.

Step 3 As the poke simmers, break the eggs into a bowl and whisk in the milk, salt, and pepper.

Step 4 Layer the cracklings and then the cheese over the greens in the skillet. Pour the egg mixture on top, slide the skillet into the oven, and bake 30 to 35 minutes or until the egg is firm on top and cooked through.

VEGETABLES

Healthy Alternatives: Add 4 ounces fresh spinach leaves. Replace the lard with canola oil. Omit three of the egg yolks or use an egg substitute. Use a reduced-fat cheese or replace the cheese with a package of dry ranch salad dressing spices.

Variations: Garnish with blue violets or serve with dry toast and a green salad mixed with fresh flowers such as violets and pansies.

Poke Sallet Sandwich: For lunch, warm the poke sallet and place it on a slice of bread. Spread with mayonnaise and mustard and top with another slice of bread.

Appalachian Fusion: Serve with a slice of cheese pizza, a citrus fruit salad, or a Maryland crab cake.

Fried Apples

During the Industrial Period and through the 1970s, many mountaineers prepared fried apples every day. They can be served warm for breakfast with pork chops, country ham, sausage, gravy, grits, eggs, biscuits, and hot sorghum. They make a delicious side dish or a vegetable to a lunch of pork, ham, or fried chicken. Topped with whipped cream and a maraschino cherry, they are a light seasonal supper dessert. In the mountains, fried apples may be served as a sweet breakfast fruit, a lunch-plate vegetable, and a dinner side dish.

The following recipe may be prepared in a skillet on top of the stove or in a microwave oven. The microwave oven is fast, preserves the apples' light color, yields great apple flavor, and produces extra syrup. With five ingredients and one cooking step, this recipe is easy to prepare. For good texture, use half Granny Smith or Golden Delicious and half Rome Beauty apples.

PREPARATION TIME: 15 minutes
START TO FINISH: 25 minutes
YIELD: 8 servings

6 cups (4 large) apples
1 cup sugar
2 tablespoons cornstarch
½ teaspoon cinnamon

¼ cup water
2 tablespoons lard or bacon grease
   (optional)

Step 1 Wash, peel, quarter, core, and section the apples. In a small bowl, mix the dry ingredients: sugar, cornstarch, and cinnamon, stirring until the cornstarch is fully incorporated and free of lumps.

Step 2 Transfer the apples to a skillet and stir in the dry ingredients. If using, add the lard or bacon grease. Add ¼ cup water, cover the pan, bring to a boil, then reduce the heat and simmer 5 minutes. Stir and cook, uncovered, another 4 minutes, or until the apples are soft through to the center or fork tender.

Step 3 If using a microwave, omit the water and microwave the other ingredients, covered, on high for 5 minutes, or until the sugar is melted, then stir.

Variations: Sprinkle with black walnut pieces. Serve as a side to yogurt, grits, or muesli. Serve as a Napoleon in layers alternating vanilla wafers softened with Calvados, fried apples, dried, minced apples, diced fresh apple, and rounds of fried Parmesan cheese.

Appalachian Fusion: Serve as a side to lox, sliced onions, gherkins, and bagels. Serve with lamb chops (in place of mint jelly) and an eggplant casserole. Serve with baked orange roughy, sticky rice, wasabi, and creamed spinach.

Puréed Butternut Squash

With a glass of red wine or buttermilk or a cup of coffee, this dish is a delicious accompaniment to a dinner of crispy fried potatoes, lamb chops, and raw sliced sweet onion.

PREPARATION TIME: 15 minutes
START TO FINISH: 35 minutes
YIELD: 6 servings

3 to 4 pounds fresh butternut
  squash
4 tablespoons (2 ounces) butter or
  ¼ cup heavy cream
½ teaspoon salt
¼ teaspoon cinnamon
1 pinch nutmeg

Step 1 Cut the squash into pieces, remove the seeds, and boil or steam for about 20 minutes, or until tender. If using a pressure cooker, cook the squash for 10 minutes after the pressure is up. Cool and remove the peeling.

Step 2 Use a masher, mixer, or food processor to mash or purée the squash. To 4 cups puréed squash, add the butter or cream, salt, cinnamon, and nutmeg. Reheat and serve.

Step 3 If, after adding the cream, the purée is too runny, add a tablespoon of a quick-mixing sauce and gravy flour, bring to a boil, and simmer one minute.

Cushaw Casserole

This casserole is a simple, nutritious, and delicious dish of sweetened squash. The squash flavor is true and the fiber brings health to the digestive tract. Here, the squash is sweetened with brown sugar, but mountain cooks also use other sweeteners including sorghum syrup, molasses, maple syrup, honey, brown sugar twin, or even granulated sugar. Serve this casserole with biscuits, country ham, fried chicken, green beans, and black-eyed peas. Its golden color also makes it the perfect contrast to a dinner of country ham, boiled creases, and biscuits. (For a discussion of cushaw squash, see Chapter 3.)

PREPARATION TIME: 20 minutes
START TO FINISH: 1 hour 20 minutes
YIELD: 15 servings

4 pounds fresh cushaw squash
2 cups water

1 cup brown sugar
2 teaspoons salt

Step 1 Halve the cushaw, remove the seeds, and cut the squash into 1-inch-thick pieces. Place it in a large saucepan, add the water, cover the pan, and braise until tender, about 30 minutes (check the squash by pressing a fork to the center; it should be as soft as boiled potatoes). If using a pressure cooker, cook the squash for 15 minutes after the pressure is up. Remove from the heat, and cool the squash.

Step 2 Heat the oven to 350°F. Pull or cut the skin from the squash. Pack the squash into a 13×9×2-inch oven-to-table casserole dish, pressing it flat with the tines of a fork. Stir the sugar and salt together and then sprinkle the mixture over the squash.

Step 3 Bake until the sugar melts and the squash is piping hot, about 30 minutes.

Appalachian Fusion: Tex-Mex Squash Casserole. Omit the sugar. Combine and sprinkle over the top the salt, ½ cup diced hot banana peppers, and 2 tablespoons of hot Mexican-style chili powder.

Broccoli Casserole

Serve this casserole with boiled new potatoes, pickled beets, and Southern fried chicken. For added flavor and gusto, double the Cheddar cheese. (For a detailed discussion of this casserole, see Chapter 4.)

PREPARATION TIME: 20 minutes
START TO FINISH: 60 minutes
YIELD: 10 servings

1 cup cracker crumbs
¼ cup melted butter, divided
2 bunches fresh broccoli
3 tablespoons all-purpose flour
2 cups milk

VEGETABLES

> 1 cup (4 ounces) grated sharp
>   Cheddar cheese
> ½ teaspoon salt
> ¼ teaspoon ground black pepper

Step 1   Preheat the oven to 350°F and grease a 2-quart (10×6×2-inch) casserole dish. Combine the cracker crumbs and half of the butter and set aside.

Step 2   Wash the broccoli and cut into ¾-inch florets to equal 8 cups. Braise or steam the broccoli until tender, about 4 minutes. Drain.

Step 3   In a medium saucepan over medium heat, stir the other half of the butter into the flour. Whisk in the milk, bring to a boil, and cook one minute. Remove from the heat and stir in the Cheddar cheese, salt, and pepper.

Step 4   Spread the broccoli into the casserole dish and pour on the cheese sauce. Stir until mixed. Spread the cracker crumb mixture on the top and bake until the casserole bubbles in the center, forms a mass, and browns on the edges, about 40 minutes.

Fried Ramps

To extend the ramp season, many cooks boil and freeze the ramps because when parboiled and then frozen, ramps keep their flavor. Use frozen or fresh ramps for this recipe. (The Cherry River Food Land in Richwood, West Virginia, sells fresh ramps through the mail from February through April. See the Mail-Order Sources.) Serve the ramps with Southern fried chicken, fried potatoes, fried chicken livers, scrambled eggs, waffles, or fried green tomatoes.

> PREPARATION TIME: 20 minutes
> START TO FINISH: 20 minutes
> YIELD: 4 servings

> 4 cups (8 ounces) fresh ramps
> 3 strips (3 ounces) bacon, cut in
>   tiny strips
> ½ teaspoon salt

Step 1 To prepare the ramps, cut off the root and remove the old outside leaf. Wash. Use the ramps whole or cut them into small lengths.

Step 2 Fry the bacon and, when crisp, add the ramps. Fry on low heat, covered, until tender, about 6 minutes. Uncover and fry an additional 2 minutes. Sprinkle with salt.

Healthy Alternative: Boil the ramps until tender and then fry with 1 tablespoon safflower oil.

Appalachian Fusion: Use as a garnish for white bean soup, grits, rice, couscous, or mashed potatoes. Use as a filling for butterflied chicken breasts, Chinese dumplings, or crab cakes. Bake in a custard, and serve the custard in cubes with spring lamb or as a topping for chicken consommé. Combine with winter pears and hot peppers to make spiced spring preserves.

Chow Chow

Typically, pickles and relish develop over time. For example, making 14-day pickles requires 14 days. This recipe is a quick overnight chow chow. The flavorings are based on using 4 cups of raw vegetables. Less vinegar and salt are used than called for in traditional recipes, resulting in a mild relish that can be served immediately after cooking. This small quantity is easy to prepare while at the same time authentic in terms of ingredients and flavor. You can serve chow chow hot or cold as a condiment, garnish, or vegetable. Spread it over hamburgers, crackers, or lettuce salads. Or offer it with soup beans, cornbread, and buttermilk. (For further discussion of pickling and chow chow, see Chapter 3.)

PREPARATION TIME: 30 minutes
START TO FINISH: 7 to 24 hours
YIELD: 3 cups, 12 servings

1 cup cabbage or 1 green tomato
1 red bell pepper
1 medium onion
1 small cucumber
1 tablespoon salt

¼ cup sugar
1 teaspoon ground mustard
½ teaspoon turmeric
⅓ cup white vinegar
⅓ cup water

Step 1 Chop, grate, or dice the cabbage or tomato, pepper, onion, and cucumber. Combine. Measure 4 cups of raw vegetables into a bowl. Mix with the salt. Cover and let stand most of the day or overnight.

Step 2 Drain the vegetables and rinse off most of the salt. Transfer to a saucepan and stir in the sugar, mustard, turmeric, and vinegar. Simmer over low heat 15 minutes.

Spiced Pickled Beets

These beets can be served hot or cold as a vegetable, condiment, or snack. Enjoy chilled pickled beets with cold cuts or as part of a composed salad. Pair warm beets with soup beans or Brunswick stew.

PREPARATION TIME: 15 minutes
START TO FINISH: 1¼ hours
YIELD: 4 servings

1½ pounds fresh or 2 cups
    prepared beets
1 cup beet juice or water
¼ cup cider vinegar
¼ cup sugar
½ teaspoon salt

Step 1 When using fresh beets, remove the tops and wash the tubers. Preheat the oven to 350°F and bake young beets 30 minutes or older ones 1 hour. Cool, pull off the skins, and chop, slice, or leave the beets whole.

Step 2 In a glass or stainless steel saucepan, bring the beet juice or water, vinegar, sugar, and salt to a boil. Add the prepared beets, and return to a boil. Remove from the stove.

Step 3 Pack hot beets into hot canning jars, cover with boiling syrup, cap the jars, and boil 30 minutes in a water bath. Alternatively, place the beets in plastic containers, cover them with the syrup, and freeze.

Starchy Vegetables

Custard Corn Pudding

The miracle of this recipe is the simplicity of the custard, and because it is a true custard, most cooks bake it in a water bath. The
slow, even heat of the water bath keeps the egg from getting too
hot and curdling. For this pudding use either cream-style or
whole-kernel corn. Note, however, that commercially prepared
canned cream-style corn is often too creamy and too saucy. It may
also be high in salt, sugar, water, and cornstarch, and unfortunately,
it may not contain much corn.

Serve the corn pudding as you would any savory corn or other
starchy dish. It is a wonderful accompaniment to fried catfish and
hush puppies or fried pork chops and steamed green beans. (For
a discussion of corn, see Chapter 6.)

PREPARATION TIME: 20 minutes
START TO FINISH: 1 hour 20 minutes
YIELD: 8 servings

4 large ears fresh corn
2 large eggs
1 cup milk
1 teaspoon salt

Step 1 Preheat the oven to 300°F. To prepare a water bath, boil a
pot of water. Select a 1-quart casserole and a second oven-
proof container into which the casserole will fit. Prepare
the corn as directed above to equal 2 cups, and spread it
into the bottom of the casserole.

Step 2 In a small mixing bowl beat the two eggs. Add and combine the milk and salt. Pour this mixture over the corn.

Step 3 Set this in the larger oven-proof container, and add 1½ inches of boiling water to the larger container. Bake until the center is set and a toothpick inserted near the center comes out clean, or about 1 hour. If at any time the water bath starts to bubble, reduce the oven temperature.

Healthy Alternative: Use skim milk and omit one egg yolk. Add about 10 minutes to the baking time.

Succotash

Succotash can be served as a vegetable or starch. Mountain cooks might offer it with fried chicken, hot rolls, and steamed carrots. To the following ingredients, some cooks add cooked chopped bacon, chopped tomatoes, or chopped red bell pepper. Do not use cream-style corn, and if using canned corn and beans, drain the liquid.

PREPARATION TIME: 10 minutes
START TO FINISH: 15 minutes
YIELD: 4 servings

1½ cups cooked corn
1 cup cooked lima beans
2 tablespoons butter
1 teaspoon salt
½ teaspoon pepper

Step 1 Mix ingredients and heat in a microwave oven or double boiler. Serve hot.

Corn Relish

Prepare this relish with fresh, canned, or frozen sweet corn. Adjust the amount of vinegar and sugar to your taste. During the winter and spring, use frozen corn. Adding the bell pepper at the end keeps it green and pretty.

Serve the relish hot or cold. It can be an accompaniment to a festive dinner or to everyday foods such as a hamburger, ham sandwich, soup beans, shucky beans, home-fried potatoes, potato salad, or fried chicken.

With seven ingredients and one cooking step, this recipe is moderately difficult to prepare. To simplify traditional formulas, the cabbage is omitted.

PREPARATION TIME: 15 minutes
START TO FINISH: 15 minutes
YIELD: 1¼ cups or 5 servings

1¼ cups yellow whole kernel corn
¼ cup diced onion
¼ cup diced green sweet bell
   pepper
⅓ cup white vinegar
½ cup sugar
¼ teaspoon dry mustard
¼ teaspoon turmeric

Step 1   Cut corn from 2 to 3 ears to equal 1¼ cups. Do not cream the corn; whole kernels are desirable. Chop the onion and peppers into pieces the size of a kernel of corn and mix with the corn.

Step 2   In a small saucepan over medium heat bring the vinegar, sugar, mustard, and turmeric to a boil. Add the corn and onion, return to a boil, reduce the heat, and simmer 3 minutes. Remove from the heat and stir in the bell pepper.

Soup Beans

For a traditional dinner, serve soup beans with buttermilk, cornbread, slices of sweet onions, stalks of green onions, and wilted lettuce. Hill folk also serve soup beans with winter foods such as fried potatoes, boiled greens, sauerkraut or kraut and wieners, relish, and pickles. In this easy-to-prepare, traditional, three-ingredient recipe, beans are boiled with salt pork or smoked ham hocks. Once the beans are cooked, most highlanders remove the pork and serve it as a side dish. While some mountaineers serve soup bean broth as thin as pot likker to be sopped up with crumbled cornbread, others serve it as a thick sauce. (For a discussion of soup beans, see Chapter 5.)

PREPARATION TIME: 10 minutes
START TO FINISH: 20 to 24 hours
YIELD: 10 to 12 servings

1 pound dried pinto beans, washed
  and picked over for pebbles
7 cups water
8 ounces salt pork or 2 smoked
  ham hocks to equal about 1
  pound

Step 1 Soak the beans in the 7 cups of water overnight. Use a glass or china container and do not drain.

Step 2 Place the beans and all the water in a saucepan and add the pork. Simmer covered for 6 to 8 hours. Add water as needed to keep the beans covered. When cooked, the beans hold their shape but are soft throughout. Remove the pork and serve it as a side dish.

Step 3 If desired, thicken the broth by boiling it down and mashing in some cooked beans, or purée a cup of the beans in a food processor and return the purée to the soup.

Healthy Alternative: Replace the pork with ¼ cup safflower oil; add 1 tablespoon of salt and ½ teaspoon pepper, or offer them at the table.

Variations: Add diced soft vegetables such as onions, tomatoes, and bell peppers at the end of the cooking time. These vegetables add contrast and complementary texture to cooked beans, but they cook quickly, and if they turn to mush, their appearance and texture are lost. In addition, the acid of tomatoes slows the cooking time.

You can use a pressure cooker to cut the cooking time in half.

Pinto Bean Chili

By adding ground beef, as suggested, this vegetarian dish becomes a hearty main dish. Spruce it up further by adding a topping such as sour cream, grated Cheddar cheese, diced onions,
chopped green onions, or unsalted cashews. Serve it in large
bowls with a side of cornbread, or serve it with wilted lettuce and
spring onions, hot peppers, and a glass of buttermilk.

PREPARATION TIME: 25 minutes
START TO FINISH: 15 hours
YIELD: 14 cups or 9 hearty servings

1 pound (2 cups) dry pinto beans
7 cups water
6 ounces tomato paste
3 cups diced onions
4 cloves minced garlic
3 tablespoons hot chili powder
1 ½ tablespoons salt
2 teaspoons ground cumin
3 cups diced green peppers
3 cups diced fresh tomatoes
Optional: 1 pound ground beef

Step 1 Pick over the beans for foreign matter and rinse them in
cold water until the water is clear. Soak overnight in 7
cups of water. Wash and dice the vegetables: onions,
green peppers, and tomatoes.

Step 2 Pour the beans (6 cups soaked beans) and water into a 6-
quart saucepan. Stir in the tomato paste, and add 2 cups of
the onions, the garlic, chili powder, salt, and cumin. Stir
until mixed. Simmer, covered, on low heat for 3 hours,
adding water as needed to keep the beans covered.

Step 3 Stir in the peppers, tomatoes, and remaining onions, and
simmer an additional 10 minutes. Optional: Add 1 pound
of browned and drained ground beef.

STARCHY VEGETABLES

Bean Patties

Cooks prepare these cakes with or without egg, onion, or flour. Most fry them in lard, and all are careful to cook them through to the center. The patties can be served as a side dish in place of beans, pasta, potatoes, or corn, or alone as a snack.

PREPARATION TIME: 35 minutes
START TO FINISH: 35 minutes
YIELD: 5 servings

3⅓ cups cooked pinto beans,
   divided
4 tablespoons vegetable oil or
   bacon drippings, divided
1 cup diced onion
1 teaspoon salt
½ teaspoon pepper
2 large eggs, beaten
½ cup all-purpose flour

Step 1 Prepare one recipe of soup beans (see above) and reserve 3⅓ cups of cooked beans, or purchase two 16-ounce cans of pinto beans. If using canned beans, wash and drain the beans, and lightly pat them dry.

Step 2 Heat 1 tablespoon of oil in a large cast-iron skillet, and fry the onions until they soften. Lift out the onions and set aside.

Step 3 Pour 1⅓ cups of beans into a bowl, and add the salt and pepper. Using a potato masher or a fork, mash until smooth. Stir in the remaining whole beans and the cooked onions.

Step 4 Form ten patties. If they are too soft to hold their shape, add some flour. Dip the patties in the beaten egg, first on one side and then on the other, then dredge both sides in the flour. Fry the patties over medium heat, adding oil a tablespoon at a time as needed, until crisp and nicely browned, about 3 minutes on each side. Then lift the patties onto a paper towel or cooling rack.

Variations: To a plate of bean patties, add garnishes of sour cream, spicy mustard, chow chow, fried onions, apple chutney,

STARCHY
VEGETABLES

onion relish, fried green tomatoes, or green tomato pickles. Decorate with chives, sweet raw onions, fresh apple slices, or cilantro.

Fried Potatoes

For mountaineers, fried potatoes are fine daily fare. Memory food. Home food. Essential food. Good food. Taste the salt, bite into the crisp outside shell, and feel the soft, moist centers.

> PREPARATION TIME: 10 minutes
> START TO FINISH: 30 to 40 minutes
> YIELD: 3 servings

3 cups cubed, firm, new potatoes
About 4 tablespoons shortening or
  oil
1 cup diced onions (optional)
1 teaspoon salt

Step 1 Wash the potatoes, remove any brown spots, and cube. Fried potatoes are made with fine-diced (¼-inch), medium-chopped (½-inch), or coarsely-cubed (¾-inch) potatoes. With larger cubes, more potatoes will fit in a single layer in the skillet and require additional cooking time.

Step 2 Over low-medium heat melt 2 tablespoons of the shortening or oil in a large, heavy-bottomed or cast-iron frying pan with a cover and add the potatoes. Do not crowd the pan. Cook covered 10 to 15 minutes.

Step 3 Turn the potatoes, and add the onions, if using. Add another tablespoon shortening. Raise the heat to medium, and cook uncovered another 10 to 15 minutes, turning the potatoes every 5 minutes or until they have browned on all sides and are soft in the center. Add the final tablespoon of shortening, let it sizzle, and sprinkle with the salt.

Variation: Allegheny Home Fries. Home fries are steam-fried potatoes. To make home fries, double or triple the above recipe (or reduce the size of the pan), and layer sliced potatoes and onions in a frying pan. Use a large proportion of sliced, not diced, onions. Cook covered over low heat for 30 minutes, turning after 15 minutes. Then, fry uncovered an additional 15 minutes. Due to low heat and layers of potatoes in the pan, these "fries" will be steamed, soft, and slightly fried. Yield: 6 servings.

Fancy Potato Casserole

To prepare the dish gather ten ingredients, prepare a white sauce, and oven bake the casserole. For a crusty (*au gratin*) surface, add the topping. Serve with baked ham, pork barbecue, or ground venison steaks.

PREPARATION TIME: 25 minutes
START TO FINISH: 1 hour 10 minutes
YIELD: 12 servings

For the béchamel sauce and casserole:
6 tablespoons butter
⅓ cup all-purpose flour
3 cups milk
4 ounces Velveeta or cream
    cheese, sliced
¼ cup Parmesan cheese
2 tablespoons chicken bouillon
    grains
½ teaspoon ground black pepper
6 cups washed and thinly sliced
    new potatoes
2 cups sliced fresh mushrooms

For the topping:
½ cup cracker crumbs (10
    crushed saltine crackers)
¼ cup grated Parmesan cheese
2 tablespoons melted butter

Step 1 Preheat the oven to 350°F, and select a 13×9×2-inch casserole dish. Melt the butter in a medium saucepan. Stir in the flour, add the milk, and cook 1 minute. Remove from the heat and stir in the Velveeta and Parmesan cheese, bouillon, and pepper.

STARCHY VEGETABLES

Step 2 Layer the potatoes, mushrooms, and sauce in the casserole dish. Smooth the top with the back of a spoon. Bake for 30 minutes.

Step 3 *To prepare the topping,* mix the crumbs, cheese, and butter. Sprinkle this mixture over the casserole, and return it to the oven until the potatoes are tender or about 15 additional minutes. If the topping has not browned, broil it to brown or about 1 minute. Let stand 5 minutes before serving.

Healthy Alternative: To lighten the sauce, use skim milk, half the butter, and no cheese.

Variations: After layering the potatoes, mushrooms, and sauce, add a layer of catfish, pork chops, or link sausage.

Appalachian Fusion: Serve with deep-fried shrimp, crab cakes, smoked Alaskan salmon, or Albacore tuna sashimi.

New Potatoes and Gravy

This potato dish is boiled in one pot. Using the potato water and five other ingredients, you make a gravy by stirring flour with milk and adding butter, salt, and pepper. The dish might complete a meal of meatloaf, greens, and cornbread.

PREPARATION TIME: 20 minutes
START TO FINISH: 40 minutes
YIELD: 8 servings

3 pounds new potatoes, washed,
    bad spots removed, and cut into
    1-inch pieces
water to cover the potatoes
2 teaspoons salt
⅔ cup flour
⅔ cup milk
¼ cup (½ stick) butter (optional)
1 teaspoon pepper

Step 1 Drop the prepared potatoes into a saucepan and add water to cover them. Add the salt. Bring to a boil, reduce the heat, and simmer about 20 minutes, or until the potatoes are almost tender. To check for doneness, remove one potato from the pot and cut it in half. The center can be firm but not hard.

Step 2 As the potatoes simmer, pour the flour into a medium-size bowl. Make a cold roux by slowly pouring the milk into the center of the flour and whisk together. Do not pour the milk in all at once. At first, with a small amount of milk, the flour will ball up and get sticky, but then, as you add milk, it will soften until it reaches the consistency of pancake batter. Now mix about half of the water from the potatoes into the cold roux.

Step 3 With the potatoes still simmering, if using, add the butter and pepper, and then slowly pour the roux into the pot. Add just enough of the roux to thicken the water to the consistency of gravy. If the gravy is too thin, add more roux; if it gets too thick, add milk or water. The gravy should be the consistency of pancake batter.

Variations: Add diced mushrooms, peas, chicken bouillon grains, or fried onions. Consider adding capers, dried blueberries, or black walnuts.

Sweet Potato Casserole

For a discussion of sweet potatoes, see Chapter 5.

PREPARATION TIME: 30 minutes
START TO FINISH: 1½ hours
YIELD: 8 servings

3 large (3 pounds) sweet potatoes
  (4 cups mashed)
¼ cup brown sugar
¼ cup butter
1 teaspoon salt
½ teaspoon mace or nutmeg

½ teaspoon cinnamon
1 cup miniature marshmallows

Step 1 To prepare the potatoes, wash, remove the bad spots, quarter, cover with water, simmer (20 minutes or until tender), drain, and peel.

Step 2 Preheat the oven to 350°F. If the potatoes are soft and moist, stir them up. If they seem to be firm and dry, purée them in a food processor.

Step 3 To 4 cups of mashed sweet potato add the sugar, butter, salt, mace, and cinnamon, and mix well. Scrape into a medium-size casserole dish and bake 25 minutes. Remove from the oven, spread the marshmallows over the top, and broil about 1 minute or until the marshmallows puff up and brown.

Sweet Potatoes and Apples

This recipe is forgiving, and it calls for just six ingredients. It is delicious served with pork barbecue, fried catfish, baked turkey, or any other main dish. In step 3 below, it is amazing how easily the cornstarch absorbs the water. (For a discussion of this recipe, see Chapter 5.)

PREPARATION TIME: 15 minutes
START TO FINISH: 35 minutes
YIELD: 4 servings

1 large (2 cups) peeled and cubed
    sweet potato
½ cup water
2 (2½ cups) peeled and cubed
    cooking apples
¼ cup brown sugar
1½ teaspoons cornstarch
1 tablespoon water

Step 1 In a large, covered saucepan, bring the sweet potatoes and water to a boil. Reduce the heat, cover, and simmer for 15 to 20 minutes, or until the potatoes are soft. Add water as needed to maintain ⅛ inch of water across the bottom of the pan. When the potatoes are soft, add the apples and simmer 3 minutes or until slightly cooked but not soft.

Step 2 As the apples simmer, mix the sugar and cornstarch in a small bowl until smooth. Stir in the 1 tablespoon water.

Step 3 Pour the cornstarch mixture into the saucepan, stir, and bring to a boil. Simmer 1 minute.

Fancy Cheese Grits Casserole

In this two-step process you enrich grits with eggs and cheese, and then bake the mixture in a casserole. As you whisk in the chunks of butter, the grated cheese, and the three eggs, you can almost see flavor emerging from the pan. Once the cheese and butter have melted away, take a taste, enjoy the flavor, and check for salt. Cherish this combination of corn and cheese.

Serve the casserole hot for breakfast or brunch or in place of potatoes with any seafood or main dish. With seven ingredients and two cooking steps—first boil and then bake—this recipe is moderately difficult to prepare.

PREPARATION TIME: 15 minutes
START TO FINISH: 45 minutes
YIELD: 6 servings

1 ½ cups milk
1 ½ cups water
¾ cup quick-cooking grits
1 teaspoon salt
½ stick (4 tablespoons) butter
3 large eggs, beaten
1 ½ cups (6 ounces) grated
   Cheddar cheese, divided

Step 1 Preheat the oven to 375°F and grease a 1 ½- to 2-quart casserole dish.

Step 2 Using a medium saucepan, bring the milk and water to a boil. Slowly stir in the grits and salt and reduce the heat to

STARCHY VEGETABLES

medium-low. When the grits absorb the liquid and have the texture of applesauce, stir in the butter, eggs, and 1 cup of cheese, stirring until fully melted and mixed. Adjust the salt. (The amount needed depends on the salt in the cheese.)

Step 3 Scrape the mixture into the prepared casserole dish and bake until the center becomes firm and puffs up, 25 to 30 minutes.

Step 4 Remove from the oven and garnish with ½ cup cheese. The cheese will melt from the heat of the dish.

Main Dishes

Saucy Macaroni and Cheese

To make this dish, you will boil the macaroni, prepare a white sauce, add cheese to make a Mornay sauce, combine, and then bake the casserole. For a hearty main dish, include the diced ham; for a side dish omit it. The recipe results in a dish of quality and a casserole worthy of the label, fine home dining. It can be served as a main dish or as a side dish with broiled trout, and spinach strawberry salad or green beans.

PREPARATION TIME: 25 minutes
START TO FINISH: 55 minutes
YIELD: 12 servings

For the macaroni:
12 ounces (3½ cups) macaroni

For the cheese sauce:
6 tablespoons butter
6 tablespoons all-purpose flour
1 teaspoon salt (omit salt if using ham)
1 teaspoon pepper
3 cups milk
3 cups (12 ounces) grated Cheddar cheese
¾ cup heavy cream

For the casserole:
1 pound diced cooked ham
   (optional)
½ cup grated Parmesan cheese

Step 1 Preheat the oven to 450°F and grease a 13×9×2-inch casserole dish.

Step 2 Boil three quarts of water, add the macaroni, and boil for about 7 minutes or as directed on the package. Rinse under hot water.

Prepare the cheese sauce:

Step 1 As the macaroni cooks in one pan, melt the butter and stir in the flour, salt, and pepper in another. When you have fully mixed the butter and flour, add the milk and bring to a boil. Reduce the heat, and simmer 1 minute. Remove from heat and stir in the cheese and cream.

Step 2 Stir in the ham, if using, and add the cooked macaroni. Pour the mixture into the prepared baking dish and sprinkle with the Parmesan cheese. Bake until the mixture bubbles in the center and browns on top or about 30 minutes. If needed, broil the top.

Healthy Alternative: Omit the cream. Use low-fat cheese and skim milk. Omit the butter and use instant, quick-mixing sauce and gravy flour.

Soup Beans: U.S. Senate Bean Soup

In the 1950s and 1960s, chefs at the Rayburn Senate Office Building in Washington, D.C., made this alternative and slightly more complex soup bean recipe. It calls for nine ingredients, overnight soaking, and slow cooking. Here, the word *simmer* means bubble slowly. If the slow cooker is set too low, the broth will not bubble and, after about 8 hours, the soup will be too thin. If the soup bubbles too fast and the beans start to dry, add water. When cooked, the beans hold their shape but are soft throughout, and the pork is almost falling apart. The prepared soup beans will be as thick as a cream soup or chowder.

MAIN
DISHES

To serve, garnish the soup beans with sour cream and diced onion, then offer guests a raw vegetable plate and Mexican-style or buttermilk cornbread. Traditional Appalachians would serve soup beans with a choice of popular winter foods such as fried potatoes, boiled greens, sauerkraut, kraut slaw, and chow chow or pickles.

PREPARATION TIME: 20 minutes
START TO FINISH: 20 to 24 hours
YIELD: 10 servings

1 pound dried pinto beans, washed
   and picked over for pebbles
9 cups water
8 ounces salt pork or 2 smoked
   ham hocks to equal about 1
   pound
1 cup grated raw potato
¼ cup barley (optional)
2 teaspoons garlic powder
1 teaspoon salt
1 teaspoon pepper
2 cups diced onion

Step 1 Soak the beans in the water overnight in a glass or china container. Do not drain.

Step 2 Place the beans, water, pork, potato, barley (if using), garlic powder, salt, and pepper in a slow cooker or saucepan and simmer covered for 6 to 12 hours. If the beans get too thick and start to dry, add water.

Step 3 Stir in the onions and serve.

Healthy Alternatives: Replace the pork with ¼ cup safflower or canola oil; add ½ teaspoon pepper and 1 tablespoon salt, or offer them at the table.

Stuffed Bell Peppers

In place of the beef or turkey, some mountain cooks prepare stuffed peppers with ground pork or chopped pork chops. Serve the peppers with a green salad, baked potato, baked squash, or sweet potato casserole.

PREPARATION TIME: 40 minutes
START TO FINISH: 1 hour 50 minutes
YIELD: 8 servings

1 cup rice
1 teaspoon salt
8 medium green, red, or yellow
   sweet bell peppers
4 cups spaghetti sauce
1½ pounds ground beef or turkey
10 ounces frozen carrots and peas
1 cup diced bell pepper
1 teaspoon salt
1 teaspoon pepper
½ cup grated cheese

Step 1 Prepare the rice with 1 teaspoon of salt according to the package directions.

Step 2 Cut off the tops of the peppers, discard the stems, and cut thin slices off the bottoms so the peppers can stand upright. Dice the removed parts. Remove the seeds and membranes from inside the peppers and discard.

Step 3 Preheat the oven to 350°F. Pour the spaghetti sauce into a 13×9×2-inch casserole dish.

Step 4 Combine the ground meat, vegetables, diced pepper, salt, pepper, and cooked rice. Stuff the mixture into the peppers and stand them up in the casserole. Cover with aluminum foil, and bake for 1 hour and 10 minutes. Remove the foil, sprinkle with cheese, and serve.

Stuffed Cabbage Rolls

As they do stuffed peppers, mountain cooks make these cabbage rolls with a ground meat filling. The dish is a full meal, casserole, and take-to-the-church classic.

PREPARATION TIME: 50 minutes
START TO FINISH: 2 hours
YIELD: 12 servings

1 large (3 pound) cabbage
filling for stuffed peppers (see
    above)

Step 1 Using a thin paring knife, cut the stem from the bottom of the cabbage, making a cone-shaped opening almost to the center of the cabbage. Then, using a pot large enough to hold the cabbage, cover it with water and boil 5 minutes.

Step 2 Cool, and carefully remove the limp outer leaves. If you don't have 12 limp leaves, return what remains of the cabbage to the boiling water and repeat. Using a scissors, remove the ribs from 12 leaves. Chop the remaining cabbage and spread it in the bottom of a 13×9×2-inch casserole dish. Cover with the spaghetti sauce.

Step 3 Divide the ground meat mixture into 12 parts and form each into a ball. Place a ball in the center of each cabbage leaf, and fold in the sides and roll to enclose the filling. Pack the cabbage rolls, flap side down, into the casserole. Cover with foil and bake for 1 hour and 10 minutes.

Wild Game Stew

Mountaineers prepare stew with a variety of meats including beef, lamb, deer (venison), bear, elk, wild hogs, and buffalo (bison). Serve this stew for dinner with a green salad, cornbread, or hot dinner rolls, and sweet tea, water, or milk. To order bison from TheBuffaloguys.com or venison from the Broken Arrow Ranch, see the Mail-Order Sources. For a discussion of wild game, see Chapter 7.

PREPARATION TIME: 20 minutes
START TO FINISH: 1 hour 50 minutes
YIELD: 4 servings

For the stew:
1½ pounds venison, cut into ½-
  inch size pieces
3 cups water
1 pound cubed potatoes
½ pound carrots, scraped and cut
  in ¾-inch lengths
½ pounds turnips, peeled,
  quartered, and cut into 1-inch
  pieces
1½ teaspoons salt
¼ teaspoon pepper

For the gravy:
¼ cup plus 1 teaspoon all-purpose
  flour
¼ cup water

Step 1   Over medium-high heat, brown the meat in the bottom of a large saucepan. Add the water and bring to a boil. Reduce the heat, cover the saucepan, and simmer the venison for 1 hour. Add the potatoes, carrots, turnips, salt, and pepper. Simmer, covered, until the vegetables are tender, about 20 minutes.

Step 2   Prepare the gravy. At this point you should have about 2½ cups of broth. If needed, add water to equal that amount. Pour the flour into a small bowl and slowly whisk in the ¼ cup water. Mix until smooth. Dribble this roux into the stew, mix well, stir to the bottom, and bring the stew to a boil. Boil 1 minute. The gravy should be as thick as heavy cream or, if you prefer, as thick as pancake batter. If it is too thin, add additional cold roux and boil again; if it is too thick, add water.

Irish Stew

Irish stew is often served in soup plates or soup bowls with Irish dumplings, a soda-leavened dumpling that is cooked on top of the stew just before serving. Other accompaniments are soda bread, hard rolls, toast, and red cabbage or pickled red cabbage. (For a discussion of potatoes and Irish stew, see Chapter 5.)

PREPARATION TIME: 20 minutes
START TO FINISH: 1 hour 50 minutes
YIELD: 6 servings

2 medium (1 ½ pounds) peeled
    potatoes
1 medium (½ pound) diced onion,
    divided
1 pound peeled carrots, cut into 1-
    inch lengths
1 ½ pounds lamb or beef stew cut
    into ½- to 1-inch cubes, fat
    removed
1 tablespoon parsley flakes
2 tablespoons salt
½ teaspoon pepper
water

Step 1 Place the lamb in a large saucepan, almost cover with water, and simmer 30 minutes.

Step 2 Dice half of the potatoes to the same size you diced the stew meat and cut the other half into large pieces. Do the same for the onions. Add the potatoes, carrots, large pieces of onion, parsley, salt, and pepper. Simmer covered for about 1 hour maintaining about 1 inch of broth in the bottom of the pan.

Step 3 Add the small pieces of onion. Adjust the flavoring with additional salt and pepper.

Variations: For garnish, top the stew with pomegranates, toasted walnuts, yogurt, or fresh mint. Flavor the stew with hot pepper sauce, turmeric, cinnamon, or garlic. Cook the stew with leeks, peas, celery, tomatoes, or chestnuts. Boil in Guinness.

MAIN
DISHES

Dutch Oven Chicken Dinner with Gravy

This stovetop-baked chicken combines some favorite Appalachian ingredients including salt pork, chicken, carrots, onions, and potatoes. It is similar to a French dish called *Poulet en Cocotte* or chicken in a casserole. The recipe calls for 14 ingredients and results in a complete dinner. Serve with dinner rolls or French bread, and red wine. For a real feast, offer broiled tomatoes, mashed sweet potatoes, and green beans as side dishes.

You can prepare this dish in any covered roaster or casserole, but cast-iron Dutch ovens and chicken fryers (see Chapter 6) are ideal. Keep the cooked chicken and vegetables warm in the oven while you prepare the gravy.

PREPARATION TIME: 30 minutes
START TO FINISH: 2 to 2½ hours
YIELD: 4 to 5 servings

For the chicken and vegetables:
4 ounces salt pork
1 (3- to 4-pound) whole chicken
1 tablespoon butter
4 carrots, diced
1 potato, diced
2 stalks celery, diced
¼ cup parsley
2 cloves garlic, minced
1 teaspoon dried leaf thyme
3 bay leaves
1 cup diced onions

For the gravy:
1 cup water or white wine
1 clove minced garlic
1 teaspoon salt
1 cup sour cream

Step 1 Select a large Dutch oven or covered roasting pan. If the salt pork has a rind, cut it off and set aside. Dice the salt pork and fry it in the Dutch oven on high until it is brown, or for 1 minute. Pour off half the fat.

Step 2 Wash and dry the chicken. Set the giblets aside. Tie or truss the chicken. Add the butter to the Dutch oven and then brown the chicken on all sides. This takes about 10 minutes. Place the rind of the salt pork (optional) on the chicken, cover the Dutch oven, and simmer over low heat for 30 minutes.

Step 3 While the chicken cooks, wash, dice, and combine the giblets, carrots, potatoes, and celery. Stir in the parsley, garlic, thyme, and bay leaves. Cover and set aside.

Step 4 Remove the chicken from the pot and add the vegetable mixture. Stir. Push the vegetables aside to make a spot in the center for the chicken. Return the chicken to the pot. Reduce the heat to low, and simmer covered an additional 30 to 60 minutes, or until the juices run clear and the chicken reaches an internal temperature of 165°F.

Step 5 Remove the chicken from the Dutch oven, place it on a large serving platter, and remove the trussing string. Stir the diced onions into the vegetables and spoon the vegetable mixture around the chicken. Cover with aluminum foil and keep warm in the oven while the gravy is being prepared.

Step 6 To make gravy, add the water or wine, garlic, and salt to the Dutch oven, boil 5 minutes, separate and discard the fat, stir in the sour cream, and serve.

MAIN DISHES

Meats & Fish

Fried Trout

For a crisp coating, fry the fish immediately before serving, and for a chef-like effect, fry it tableside and serve it from the skillet. Garnish with wedges of lemon and parsley or other fresh greens. Serve with tomato aspic or cucumber salad. Or match the trout with fried mush, boiled new potatoes, sweet potato biscuits, or fried cabbage.

PREPARATION TIME: 20 minutes
START TO FINISH: 20 minutes
YIELD: 4 servings

¾ cup flour
1 tablespoon salt
1 tablespoon dry parsley
4 (10-ounce) brook or rainbow
    trout, cleaned with heads intact
    or removed
2 tablespoons oil
2 tablespoons butter

Step 1 Shake the flour, salt, and parsley in a large bag. Add the fish and shake or roll the bag until the fish is fully coated with the mixture. One at a time, lift the fish from the bag and allow the excess flour to fall back into the bag. Set the fish aside and prepare the skillet.

Step 2 In a very large skillet over medium heat, heat half the oil and half the butter. When the butter-oil mixture foams, add the fish and fry several minutes on each side, adding the remaining oil and butter after turning the fish. The trout is cooked when it pulls from the bone at the thickest point, the mid-section, or when an instant-read thermometer reaches 130°F. Lift to serving platter.

Appalachian Fusion: The neutrality of trout allows you to pair it with many flavors. For an Appalachian/Malaysian combination, serve the trout with coconut rice and string beans sautéed with spicy shrimp sauce.

Parmesan Chicken Bites

This dish can be served hot, at room temperature, or cold. Pass trays of the bites with toothpicks as a party appetizer, or add them to a Caesar salad. You can prepare the seasoned flour mix from the recipe below or use a seasoned coating mix such as Shake 'n Bake, Golden Dipt, French's Roasting Bag, or Kentucky Kernel Seasoned Flour. Note that the chicken pieces must be brought to room temperature because if the chicken is too cold, the butter will get hard before it coats the chicken. (For a general discussion of mountain chicken recipes, see Chapter 8.)

PREPARATION TIME: 30 minutes
START TO FINISH: 1 hour and 40
  minutes
YIELD: 8 servings or appetizers for 15

3 pounds boneless chicken,
  breasts or tenders
¾ cup seasoned flour mix
  (combine ¾ cup flour, 3
  tablespoons salt, 2 teaspoons
  pepper, 1 teaspoon cumin, and
  ¼ teaspoon red (cayenne)
  pepper)
¾ cup grated Parmesan cheese

MEATS
AND FISH

3 tablespoons mixed dry herbs
½ cup melted butter

Step 1 An hour before preparing the dish, remove the chicken from the refrigerator, wash it, cut it into 1½-inch pieces, and let it come to room temperature. Move the oven racks to the upper levels and preheat the oven to 400°F.

Step 2 In a large bowl, combine the flour, cheese, and herbs. In a second large bowl, toss the chicken with the butter. One-third at a time, lift the chicken pieces into the dry mixture and stir them together, tossing like a salad.

Step 3 Spread the coated chicken on two 17×11×1-inch nonstick jelly roll sheets, separate the pieces, and bake until cooked to the center or 170°F. To test for doneness, cut a large piece of the chicken in half to see whether the center is uniformly tan in color with no pink or red. This takes about 9 minutes.

Oven-Fried Bacon-Wrapped Chicken Thighs

Wrapping chicken thighs with bacon melds two barnyard animals to yield a great flavor: The chicken absorbs some fat as well as a bit of the salty, smoky tang that is characteristic of bacon. Garnish the chicken with parsley or any spring or fall greens, and serve it with cold salads and oven-fried potatoes.

The two tablespoons of salt in this recipe are not a misprint. This chicken coating will be less salty than those prepared from a box or the chicken purchased at a fast-food restaurants. In addition, some of the cornmeal coating is left in the bag. Note also that softened bacon bends, stretches, and sticks around the chicken, while cold bacon is a bit firm and difficult to handle.

PREPARATION TIME: 20 minutes
START TO FINISH: 1 hour 25 minutes
YIELD: 8 servings

MEATS
AND FISH

1 strip bacon for each piece of
    chicken
4 pounds skinless chicken thighs
    or about 10 thighs
toothpicks
1 cup cornmeal
2 tablespoons salt
1 teaspoon paprika
1 teaspoon pepper

Step 1 Bring the bacon to room temperature, or using 30-second bursts of heat, warm it in a microwave oven. Preheat the oven to 350°F. Wash the chicken and pat it dry. Select a roasting pan with an inside rack.

Step 2 Wrap each piece of chicken with a strip of bacon, and secure the bacon with a toothpick or two. In a large bag, mix the cornmeal, salt, paprika, and pepper. Several pieces at a time, add the chicken, seal the bag, and roll it on the table to coat.

Step 3 Place the chicken on the baking rack in the roasting pan, and bake until brown on the outside and cooked to the center. The juices will run clear, the internal temperature should reach 170°F, and time elapsed will be 55 to 65 minutes.

Mountain Dumplings: Slick Runners

In addition to chicken, these dumplings are combined with greens, tomatoes, rhubarb, and beans. After mixing the dough, the dumplings are formed, cut, and boiled; when they are ready, the broth is thickened to make gruel. See Chapter 5 for comments on dumplings.

PREPARATION TIME: 30 minutes
START TO FINISH: 1 to 1½ hours
YIELD: 6 to 8 servings

2¼ cups all-purpose flour, divided
1 teaspoon salt

¼ cup melted chicken fat or
  shortening
½ cup chicken stock, pot likker, or
  water

Step 1 Combine 2 cups of the flour with the salt and stir in the shortening. Add the stock and mix until you have a stiff dough. Knead for 30 strokes or until stiff.

Step 2 Working on a floured surface and using a rolling pin, roll the dough to a thickness of ⅛ to ¼ inch, as if making a piecrust. Use a pizza cutter to cut 1-inch by 2-inch strips. Dry the surface of the dumplings by sprinkling them with a bit of the extra flour.

Step 3 Slip the dumplings, one at a time, into a large pot of simmering broth. Stir to keep the dumplings separated. Cover, reduce the heat, and simmer for 15 minutes.

Step 4 Remove from the heat, cover the pan, and cool 30 to 60 minutes. This resting time helps to thicken the gruel and tenderize the dumplings. Reheat before serving.

Tenderizing the Dumplings: The longer these dumplings sit after you cook them, the more tender they will be, and they will hold for several days. If the recipe is richer (more shortening), the dumplings will fall apart as they cook. The goal is to balance dumpling richness with soaking time.

Chicken and Dumplings

To make the complete chicken and dumpling recipe, follow three steps. First, cook the chicken and remove the cooked meat from the bones. Second, prepare and cook the dumplings. Finally, thicken the gruel. Because the recipe makes extra gruel, serve the dumplings and gruel in soup bowls, or pour off most of the gruel and serve it as gravy or use later as a soup base. Classic side dishes with chicken and dumplings are hot rolls, green beans, and mashed potatoes. Mountain cooks also serve the dish with macaroni and cheese, scalloped turnips, and sweet potato casserole. (For a discussion of this classic mountain dish, see Chapter 8.)

PREPARATION TIME: 45 minutes
START TO FINISH: 2¾ hours
YIELD: 6 servings

For the chicken and gruel:
7 cups water
1 (3- to 4-pound) chicken cut into
    pieces
1 tablespoon chicken bouillon
    grains
1 teaspoon salt
½ teaspoon pepper

For the dumplings:
1 recipe slick dumplings (see
    above)

To thicken the gruel:
½ cup all-purpose flour
½ cup water

Step 1   Several hours or the day before cooking the dumplings, combine the water, chicken, bouillon, salt, and pepper in a large saucepan, and simmer 40 minutes or until the chicken is cooked. Cover and refrigerate.

Step 2   When the chicken and broth has completely cooled, remove and discard the fat from the top of the gruel. Take the chicken out of the gruel and separate and discard the bones and skin. Set the chicken aside and cover.

Step 3   Bring the gruel back to a low boil and prepare the slick dumplings (see the recipe above).

Step 4   In a small bowl, prepare a cold roux by slowly whisking the ½ cup water into the ½ cup flour. One-third at a time, pour this cold roux into the simmering dumplings. Return the prepared chicken to the pot, bring to a boil, and remove from the heat.

MEATS
AND FISH

Fried Chicken

Breaded fried chicken becomes Southern fried chicken when it is covered with chicken cream gravy. It's a symbiotic relationship—one is not complete without the other. The dish is so popular that mountaineer cooks copy the recipe using beef and call it country fried steak. In the summer, mountaineers serve fried chicken with a platter of chilled watermelon, cantaloupe, strawberries, and grapes. Or, they might cover the fried chicken with chicken cream gravy and round out the meal with mashed potatoes, biscuits, and a garden salad.

Bacon grease adds flavor to the chicken, and buttermilk, as opposed to milk, adds flavor and texture to the coating. Serve the bacon over the chicken or on a salad.

PREPARATION TIME: 30 minutes
START TO FINISH: 1½ hours
YIELD: 4 servings

For the fried chicken:
2 pounds chicken parts, light or
    dark meat
8 ounces bacon
about ½ cup lard, bacon
    drippings, or canola oil

For the buttermilk batter:
⅔ cup self-rising cornmeal mix
1 tablespoon paprika
1 teaspoon salt
½ teaspoon pepper
¼ cup buttermilk
1 egg

Step 1   Fry the bacon in a large cast-iron skillet and set it aside. Add oil to the pan until you have about ¼ inch and heat it to 365°F, until the oil just begins to smoke, or when a drop of water pops back after you drop it into the pan.

Step 2   As the oil gets hot, wash and dry the chicken. In the bottom of a large bag, mix the cornmeal, paprika, salt, and pepper. In a small bowl whisk together the buttermilk and egg. Dip the chicken pieces in the milk and egg mixture. Lay the chicken onto the bottom of the bag, fold the bag closed, and roll or shake until coated.

Step 3 Slowly ease the chicken into the skillet and brown it on all sides, cooking uncovered 10 to 15 minutes. Reduce the heat to medium and simmer uncovered an additional 20 to 30 minutes, turning at the half-way point. The chicken is cooked when the juices run clear or it reaches an internal temperature of 170°F. Drain the chicken on paper towels.

Healthy Alternatives: Fry the chicken in canola or vegetable oil and omit the bacon. Do not use saturated fats such as lard, bacon grease, or butter. To further reduce fat, use skinless chicken.

Chicken Cream Gravy

One hundred years ago mountain cooks prepared fricasséed chicken by browning flour-dredged chicken pieces in lard, covering them with water, and simmering until tender. They removed the chicken from the pot and added flour and perhaps cream to create cream gravy, which they served over the chicken.

Chicken cream gravy should be the thickness of pancake batter, not a heavy blob of goo. Pour it into a gravy boat and serve it over fried chicken, sliced turkey, mashed potatoes, or cornbread dressing. To prepare the gravy without frying chicken, start by melting 3 tablespoons of butter.

PREPARATION TIME: 12 minutes
START TO FINISH: 12 minutes
YIELD: 5 servings

¼ cup all-purpose flour
2 cups milk
1 tablespoon chicken bouillon
   grains
¾ teaspoon pepper
½ teaspoon salt

Step 1 When preparing this gravy after making fried chicken, pour all but 2 to 3 tablespoons of the oil from the frying pan and keep the other drippings in the pan. Stir in the flour, and cook until beige or light brown. Whisk in the milk, bouillon, pepper, and salt; bring to a boil; reduce the heat; and simmer 1 minute.

Fried Bacon

Mountaineers prepare bacon for breakfast using a cast-iron skillet or other frying pan to melt (render) the fat from the strips of side meat and in the process they create a crisp, smoky delicacy. Bacon is also called streaked lean or pork flank. Meat packers cure, smoke, and salt it while cooks prize it as a flavoring for vegetables, meats, and baked goods. Bacon is the natural accompaniment for a breakfast with eggs, fried potatoes, and pancakes or waffles, and a bacon, lettuce, and tomato sandwich is a classic lunch nationwide. Bacon is also an ingredient in many recipes including green beans, wilted lettuce, poke, cornbread salad, and bacon cornbread.

PREPARATION TIME: 10 minutes
START TO FINISH: 15 minutes
YIELD: 4 servings
12 ounces bacon

Step 1 Let the bacon come to room temperature or warm slightly in the microwave oven. At about 60°F the strips pull apart easily.

Step 2 Spread the slices across the bottom of a cold skillet and over medium or low-medium heat fry them, turning with tongs or a sharply pointed fork after about 4 minutes. Fry another 3 minutes. As the bacon cooks, reduce the heat to prevent burning. When bacon is almost ready, it cooks quickly. Careful now, it can easily get too crisp or too dark.

Step 3 When the bacon is crisp and brown, lift each strip onto paper towels to drain and cool.

MEATS AND FISH

Ham Biscuits and Country Ham Spread

Country hams spread has myriad uses: Spread it on any small split biscuits and serve for breakfast with scrambled eggs and fruit salad. Or serve it on a party buffet or as an appetizer. If the spread is too salty, add more mayonnaise or even cream cheese. (For a discussion of country ham, see Chapter 8.)

PREPARATION TIME: 10 minutes
START TO FINISH: 10 minutes
YIELD: 1 cup, or filling for 24 small
    biscuits

8 ounces thin-sliced cut-up
    country ham
¼ cup mayonnaise
¼ cup mustard

Step 1 Place country ham in a food processor, process until pieces are the size of a grain of rice, and then mix in the mayonnaise and mustard. The mixture should spread with a knife, but if it is too thick or too salty, add more mayonnaise and mustard.

Country-Style Barbecued Ribs

For an Appalachian taste of heaven on earth, serve these ribs with onion-enhanced jalapeño cornbread, creamy coleslaw, and sweetened iced tea. Or make a hot sandwich by stripping the meat from the bones, piling it on both halves of a split Kaiser roll, and ladling the sauce on top. Serve coleslaw on the side and accompany with cold beer or a carbonated soft drink. You might also take Julia Child's advice in *The Way to Cook* and serve the ribs with ratatouille, lentils, or a green salad, or follow Irma Rombauer's suggestion in the *Joy of Cooking* and serve sauerkraut as a side dish. (For a discussion of pork, see Chapter 8.)

PREPARATION TIME: 15 minutes
START TO FINISH: 5 to 9 hours
YIELD: 6 servings

MEATS
AND FISH

1 (15-ounce) can tomato sauce
1 (6-ounce) can tomato paste
½ cup steak sauce
⅓ cup cider vinegar
¼ cup sugar
¼ teaspoon red pepper flakes
3 pounds country-style pork ribs
2 cups cooked kidney or pinto
   beans
1 medium-size onion, diced

Step 1 Pour the tomato sauce, tomato paste, steak sauce, vinegar, sugar, and pepper flakes into a slow cooker, and stir them together.

Step 2 Wash the ribs in cold water and lay them side by side in the slow cooker. Push them into the sauce until covered. Set the cooker on low and cover. Cook all day, 5 to 9 hours. After 5 hours, the ribs are tender and well cooked. After 9 hours, the meat falls from the bone.

Step 3 About 30 minutes before serving, stir in the beans and diced onion. If the heat is low, the onions will get hot but will not cook. Finally, before serving, skim any excess fat from the top of the pot.

Variation: Lower the heat of the sauce by omitting the red pepper flakes.

Breaded Pork Chops

Fried pork chops are a tradition related directly to hog killing and mountain living. Years ago, eating pork started with raising a pig. The cooking is far less complicated than dressing, breaking down, and cutting up a whole hog. Serving pork chops is eating "high on the hog" and that means the loin. Today, however, rather than killing a hog, most mountaineers go to the big market and select chops from a meat counter.

At home they prepare them in many different ways. An elderly mountain cook recently told me that she fries the chops, sets them aside, and makes a brown pan gravy. She then places the chops in a casserole dish, covers them with the gravy, covers the casserole with foil, and bakes the chops 1 or 2 hours. Then, she said, the meat is so tender, it falls from the bone and melts in your mouth. The gravy adds both moisture and flavor.

According to Wayne T. Rutherford, the former Pike County, Kentucky, Judge/Executive, his mother fried her chops and then dipped them in whipped egg and fried them again. As in the recipe below, some cooks prepare pork chops like cutlets, battering them and then frying. Mountain cooks might place the chops on a warmed serving platter and offer them for breakfast with bacon, fried eggs, fried potatoes, orange juice, and biscuits and gravy. At dinner, the chops might be served with scalloped potatoes, fried apples, and creamed cabbage.

PREPARATION TIME: 15 minutes
START TO FINISH: 15 minutes
YIELD: 4 servings

4 center-cut ½-inch-thick pork loin
    chops
3 tablespoons oil or fat
½ cup flour
1 tablespoon salt
¾ cup water, coffee, or chicken
    stock

Step 1 Wash and pat dry the pork chops. Preheat a large cast-iron skillet over medium-high heat for 3 minutes. Add the oil or fat to the skillet.

Step 2 Using a gallon-sized sealable bag, combine the flour and salt. Slide the pork chops into the bag, seal, and tumble, rolling the bag until the chops are covered with flour.

Step 3 Lift the chops from the bag, shake off the excess flour, and set the chops in the pan. After about 2 minutes, turn the chops. Fry ½-inch-thick chops until the juices run clear, the meat feels firm, or if you cut a chop in half, a slight bit of pale pink in the thickest part turns brown. Over medium-high heat this should take about 2 to 3 minutes on each side. Some cooks use a digital read-out thermometer and lift the chops from the pan when they reach 150°F. Thicker chops require more time, but too much cooking dries out the chops.

Variation: Fry the chops without the flour coating.

Souse

Souse is a cold cut or a head cheese made with pork meat and gelatin. The preparation renders, preserves, and embellishes the head, cheeks, snout, underlips, brains, tongue, heart, liver, and feet—pork parts that are available at hog-killing time. Souse can be served as an appetizer on lettuce with liver sausage, carrots, celery, and pickles.

Butchers sell whole hog heads that weigh 10 to 12 pounds, or they cut it in half, top to bottom or front to back through the center of the snout and sell halves. In place of the red bell pepper, use onion or whole kernel corn. Include the tongue as it is a favorite part and adds both firmness and moisture to the souse. To make the recipe you boil twice, chop, chill, and slice. It's not hard.

PREPARATION TIME: 30 minutes
START TO FINISH: 10 hours
   intermittent or 2 days
YIELD: 1½ pounds headcheese or
   12 (2-ounce) servings

½ hog head (5 pounds)
1 red bell pepper (1½ cups) diced
1 teaspoon ground sage
1 teaspoon salt
¼ teaspoon ground pepper
⅛ teaspoon ground cloves

Step 1 Wash the half head in hot water, place the entire half in a large saucepan, cover it with water, bring it to a boil, reduce the heat, cover the pan, and simmer 4 hours.

Step 2 Refrigerate the pan, broth, and head overnight. Then, pull off the meat, separate the skin and fat, and remove the tongue. (This process is easier than taking the meat from a chicken.) Dice the meat and tongue. In addition, dice about ⅓ cup of skin with a thin layer of attached fat. This moistens the souse.

Step 3 Simmer the broth about 4 hours or until it is reduced to 3 cups. As it simmers, skim the fat and bubbles. Remove all the fat.

Step 4 Combine the diced meat, broth, red bell pepper, sage, salt, pepper, and cloves. Boil 5 minutes or until the bell pepper is tender. Pour into a 9×4×2-inch loaf pan. Cool in the refrigerator 2 to 3 hours or until firm. As the gelatin cools, push the red bell pepper off the surface and back into the souse.

Step 5 When the souse is cold and firm, immerse the outside of the loaf pan in hot water for about 45 seconds. When the gelatin loosens around the edges of the pan, turn the souse out onto a cutting board. Chill again, and then slice, seal, and refrigerate.

Variation: Souse Sandwich. Slice and use on a sandwich with a slice of sweet onion, tomato, and lettuce. Add mayonnaise and mustard. Serve for lunch as an open-faced sandwich with coleslaw and potato salad.

Grilled Lamb Chops

Starting with a quality cut of chops, cooks use high heat to singe the edges, and then after cooking the meat over medium heat, they often serve the chops pink. Too much cooking dries them out. To control the cooking time, some cooks press a cooking thermometer probe into the center of one chop, and grill until it reaches 135°F to 160°F, depending on their preferences.

Serve these chops on a warmed platter with grilled vegetables. Offer stuffed baked potatoes and green beans. Offer sides of bread, coleslaw, and red wine. (See Chapter 8 for a discussion of lamb and wool on mountain farms.)

MEATS
AND FISH

PREPARATION TIME: 20 minutes
START TO FINISH: 30 minutes
YIELD: 4 servings

8 lamb chops, 1 to 1½ inches thick
  or about 2 pounds
oil
salt

Step 1 Place the grill rack 4 inches away from the heat source. Preheat the grill 10 to 15 minutes on medium high.

Step 2 Take the chops from the refrigerator and wash them under cold water. After drying them coat them with oil.

Step 3 Arrange the chops on the grill rack and cook 5 to 8 minutes per side or until meat is brown on the outside, soft when pressed, and pink inside. Remove one chop, cut it to the center, and look at the meat. It should be pink or darker, depending on your preferences. Do not overcook—too much cooking dries the chops out. Sprinkle with salt.

MEATS
AND FISH

Pies & Cakes

Sweet Potato Pie

Tasting this pie at a church dinner, second grader Lily Castle Tidwell closed her eyes in rapture and said, "This isn't pie, this is heaven." And she is right, in comparison to squash or pumpkin pie, this mix of sweet potato is more substantial, and the sweet potato yields a fuller, more complete, more dense, and even richer taste. The pie is usually prepared from October through the winter when sweet potatoes are in season. In addition, in the fall, candy corn is used to add a crisp yellow and orange garnish to the white pillows of whipped cream. See Chapter 5 for a discussion of sweet potatoes.

PREPARATION TIME: 55 minutes
START TO FINISH: about 2 hours, plus
    3 hours cooling time
YIELD: 8 servings

For the pie filling:
2 pounds sweet potatoes, ends
    removed, washed, and
    quartered
1 cup heavy cream or milk
1 ½ cups brown sugar
3 large eggs
½ teaspoon cinnamon
¼ teaspoon ginger
¼ teaspoon nutmeg
¼ teaspoon allspice

For the pie crust: ·
1½ cups flour
¾ teaspoon salt
½ cup ice cold lard, butter, or
    shortening
1 large egg
about 3 tablespoons ice water

For the garnish:
1 pint heavy cream
½ cup sugar
2 teaspoons vanilla
8 pieces of candy corn or small
    pieces of sweet potato

Step 1 Boil the sweet potatoes until tender, about 25 minutes, then drain, peel, and mash them. Set aside 2 cups of potatoes (you will have some left for a small lunch).

Prepare the crust:

Step 1 Move the oven rack to the lowest third of the oven and preheat the oven to 450°F. Select a deep-dish, 9-inch pie pan. Cut two large pieces of waxed paper, and have handy a rolling pin and instant flour.

Step 2 Using a pastry blender and a medium-sized bowl, mix the flour and salt. In small pieces, add the lard, butter, or shortening. Blend until most pieces are the size of peas and a few are as big as kidney beans.

Step 3 Use a fork to incorporate the egg into the flour mixture, then slowly stir in the water. The crust will look crumbly, but it should be moist enough to come together.

Step 4 Dump the mixture onto waxed paper, draw into a ball and flatten. Sprinkle with instant, quick-mixing sauce and gravy flour. Place the other sheet of waxed paper over the disk and roll the crust. When the crust is about half the size needed, remove the paper, sprinkle the dough with instant flour, replace the paper, and finish rolling the crust. Using the instant flour makes it easier to roll the crust.

Step 5 Transfer the rolled dough to the pie pan, shape it to fit, and crimp the edges.

Prepare the pie:

Step 1 Drop 2 cups of cooked sweet potato, the cream or milk, sugar, eggs, cinnamon, ginger, nutmeg, and allspice into the bowl of a food processor or mixer and blend until smooth, and then scrape the filling into the pie shell.

Step 2 Bake the pie 20 minutes, or until the crust starts to brown, then reduce the heat to 350°F and bake an additional 30 to 35 minutes, or until a toothpick inserted into the center comes out clean. The center of the pie should be firm and not jiggle. Cool.

Prepare the whipped cream:

Step 1 Place the bowl and beater of an electric mixer in the refrigerator. After 15 minutes or when they are thoroughly chilled, add the cream (it too must be chilled), sugar, and vanilla. Beat on high until the mixture becomes thick, falls in globs, and has a slight gloss. Refrigerate.

Garnish the pie:

Step 1 When the pie is cold, garnish it with eight pillows of whipped cream, reserving the remaining whipped cream to be offered at the table.

Variations: For a festive look, scoop the whipped cream into a pastry bag equipped with a star tip, and pipe the cream onto the pie, forming eight large swirls. Top each swirl with a piece of candy corn or a mallow (sugar candy) pumpkin. You can also substitute vanilla ice cream or dessert topping for the whipped cream.

Buttermilk Pie

This pie can be served at room temperature or chilled, and, like other transparent pies, it can be stored in the freezer for 6 months. However, do not freeze the pie after topping it with the whipped cream and bananas. If you omit the whipped cream topping and if the top of the baked pie is light in color, broil the pie a few seconds or until the surface changes from beige to gold. Sprinkle with grated nutmeg.

PIES AND CAKES

PREPARATION TIME: 30 minutes
START TO FINISH: 1¼ hours, plus 2
    hours cooling time
OPTIONAL TOPPING: 15 minutes
YIELD: 8 servings

For the pie:
1 (9-inch) pie crust, not a deep
    dish 9-inch crust
¼ cup melted butter
¾ cup sugar
2 large eggs
2 tablespoons all-purpose flour
1 cup buttermilk
1 teaspoon vanilla

For optional topping:
1 cup heavy cream
2 tablespoons sugar
1 teaspoon vanilla
1½ large very ripe bananas or 2
    cups blueberries or raspberries

Step 1 Preheat the oven to 400°F, and bake the crust until it browns on the edges, about 10 to 15 minutes. Remove the crust from the oven and set aside.

Step 2 Reduce the oven temperature to 300°F. Beat together the butter, sugar, and eggs, and then add the flour. Stir in the buttermilk and vanilla. Pour the filling into the pie crust, filling it up, but allowing enough space so that it will not spill when carried to the oven.

Step 3 Bake until raised and bubbly in the center, about 45 minutes. Cool and then refrigerate for 2 hours.

Step 4 For the optional topping, chill a large bowl and beater in the refrigerator. Pour the cream, sugar, and vanilla into a mixing bowl and beat with an electric mixer on high until thick. It will stand in sharp peaks. Spread sliced bananas or other fruit over the top of the pie and cover with whipped cream.

Chocolate Chip Pecan Pie

This pie is delicious with whipped cream or vanilla ice cream and fresh fruit or berries.

PREPARATION TIME: 15 minutes
START TO FINISH: 1 hour
YIELD: 8 servings

2 large eggs
1 cup sugar
1 cup light corn syrup
¼ cup melted butter
2 teaspoons vanilla
¾ cup chocolate chips
1 ½ cups pecan pieces
1 unbaked 9-inch pie crust

Step 1 Preheat the oven to 375°F. In a large mixing bowl beat the eggs and add the sugar, corn syrup, butter, and vanilla. When these are fully mixed, stir in the chips and pecans.

Step 2 Pour this mixture into the pie crust and bake about 55 minutes, or until raised in the center. Remove from the oven and cool on a wire rack.

Gingerbread Patties with Light Butter Cream Frosting

This small cake, or maybe we should call it a cookie, is not only pretty with its dark brown edges, buff body, and white frosting, but it is also a gingerbread in the finest of Medieval traditions. For Thanksgiving place a mallow (candy) pumpkin on top or randomly add corn candy. For Christmas add tiny bits of red and green maraschino cherries. At other times of the year, decorate the patties with thin strips of sliced crystallized ginger and nut pieces. This sweet treat is a delicious complement to morning coffee or late-night TV. Hold the peanuts and savor the gingerbread with a crisp red apple.

This small recipe can easily be doubled. Consider the frosting optional—the patties are good without it. Please note that if the frosting gets warm, the butter breaks or melts causing trouble so keep it chilled or below about 65°F.

PREPARATION TIME: 20 minutes for
   the cookies; 30 minutes for the
   frosting
START TO FINISH: 2 hours
YIELD: 36 patties

For the gingerbread patties:
3 cups flour
1 tablespoon ginger
1 teaspoon baking powder
1 teaspoon cinnamon
½ teaspoon cloves
1 cup sorghum molasses
⅔ cup brown sugar
½ cup (1 stick, ¼ pound) butter,
   softened
2 large eggs

For light butter cream frosting:
5 tablespoons flour
1 cup milk
1 cup sugar
1 cup (2 sticks, ½ pound) unsalted
   butter, softened

Prepare the patties:

Step 1 Heat the oven to 350°F and grease four large cookie sheets.

Step 2 Combine the dry ingredients: flour, ginger, baking powder, cinnamon, and cloves, and set aside. In a large bowl, cream the molasses, brown sugar, butter, and egg. Combine the dry ingredients with the creamed mixture.

Step 3 Drop 9 soupspoon-sized batter mounds on each cookie sheet and bake about 8 to 10 minutes, or until the edges brown and the tops darken slightly.

Step 4 Remove from the oven; cool 1 minute; transfer to cooling racks; cool completely.

Prepare the frosting:

Step 1 Three hours or more before frosting the patties, prepare the flour paste. Away from the stove and in a cool medium-sized saucepan, combine the flour and the milk. Start mixing with just ¼ cup milk. Stir and whisk until the flour is completely dissolved, adding the milk slowly. Over medium heat, bring the mixture to a boil, stirring constantly as you cook. Boil 1 minute. Refrigerate about 3 hours or until completely chilled.

Step 2 When both the cake patties and paste are cold, use an electric mixer to beat together the sugar and butter. Beat until creamy, white, and a bit fluffy. Slowly add the cold paste, and again beat on high until fully mixed, smooth, and of spreading consistency. Continue beating until the frosting stands in peaks and the grains of sugar are dissolved. To assist with the mixing, use a rubber scraper to push the frosting into the beaters.

Assemble the patties:

Step 1 Frost each cookie, but let the brown edges show. Garnish the tops with nuts, candy, ginger, or maraschino cherries. Store at a temperature below 60°F.

Scripture Cake

You can serve this cake plain with milk, hot coffee, or hot tea or, like pound cake, with a scoop of vanilla ice cream and a whiskey-honey-raisin sauce or even whipped cream. You can also treat it as a quick bread and spread it with butter or cream cheese. But the flavor is very delicate, so do not serve scripture cake with other cakes or pies as they will overpower it. (See Chapter 10 for the scriptures used in this cake.)

PREPARATION TIME: 35 minutes
START TO FINISH: 2 hours 20 minutes
YIELD: 30 servings

3½ cups flour (I Kings 4:22)
2 teaspoons baking powder
(Amos 4:5)
1 teaspoon cinnamon
(Exodus 30:23)
1 teaspoon nutmeg
(II Chronicles 9:9)
½ teaspoon allspice
(II Chronicles 9:9)
½ teaspoon salt
(Leviticus 2:13 or Mark 9:50)
2 cups figs (Nahum 3:12)
2 cups raisins (I Samuel 30:12)
2 cups slivered almonds
(Numbers 17:8)
1½ cups butter, softened
(Judges 5:25)
2 cups sugar (Jeremiah 6:20)
6 large eggs (Isaiah 10:14)
½ cup honey (Exodus 16:31)
1 cup milk (Judges 4:19)

Step 1 Preheat the oven to 300°F and grease three 9×4×2-inch loaf pans. Line the bottoms and sides with waxed paper and grease again.

Step 2 Mix, sift, and set aside the dry ingredients: flour, baking powder, cinnamon, nutmeg, allspice, and salt. Chop the figs to the size of raisins or a bit larger. Toss the figs, raisins, and almonds with ¼ cup of the dry ingredients until they are coated.

Step 3 Using a large mixing bowl, cream the butter and sugar until light and fluffy. One at a time, mix in the eggs. Add the honey. Add the dry ingredients alternately with the milk to the egg mixture, beginning and ending with dry ingredients. Using a spoon, stir in the fruits and nuts.

Step 4 When fully combined, pour and scrape the batter into the prepared pans. Bake until a toothpick inserted at the center comes out clean, or 1½ to 1¾ hours. Cool in the pans 10 minutes, lift to wire cooling racks, and pull off the waxed paper. Cool fully before slicing.

PIES AND CAKES

Buttermilk Pound Cake

The key to success with this recipe is to watch the baking. Less baking results in a cake that is more moist. Some cooks even serve it warm from the oven. Be careful as there is a fine line between raw and moist. Most chefs want to have the dough fully cooked; however, if it is a bit less cooked it will be moist, chewy, and, for many, quite pleasurable. Either way, pound cake is delicious with fresh sliced strawberries, peaches, blueberries, or blackberries and whipped cream. Or you can serve it with boiled custard (see the recipe in the next section) or vanilla ice cream and chocolate sauce. See Chapter 10 for a discussion of pound cakes.

PREPARATION TIME: 20 minutes
START TO FINISH: 1½ hours
YIELD: 18 servings

2 sticks (1 cup) butter, softened
3 cups sugar
4 large eggs
1 teaspoon vanilla or almond
    flavoring
3 cups all-purpose flour
¼ teaspoon baking soda
1 cup buttermilk

Step 1 Heat the oven to 350°F and grease and then flour a large tube pan.

Step 2 Cream the butter and sugar. Add the eggs, one at a time, and then the vanilla or almond. Measure the flour and whisk the soda into it. Then, add the flour mixture alternately with the buttermilk, beginning and ending with dry ingredients. Transfer the batter to the prepared pan and slide the cake into the oven.

Start watching after 1 hour, and take the cake from the oven as soon as it shows the slightest sign of being cooked. A thin knife pressed through the crack in the center will come out almost clean. Bake about 1 hour 10 minutes. Immediately, turn the cake onto a wire cooling rack, remove the pan, invert, and cool.

PIES AND
CAKES

Fresh Apple Cake with Black Walnuts

Summer or winter, this cake is time-tested and popular. Fresh apple cakes are filling, scrumptious, unencumbered, sweet, black walnut-flavored and brownie-like in texture. Fresh from the oven, the cakes are crunchy on the outside and moist on the inside. Black walnuts give this cake its special flavor, but it can also be made with walnuts or pecans. Some cooks include cinnamon, allspice, raisins, coconut, rolled oats, and butterscotch chips. You can serve the cake like a brownie, eating out of hand without any topping, embellish it with a generous topping of vanilla ice cream, hot sorghum, and black walnuts, or offer it with whipped cream or a buttermilk glaze. With 10 ingredients and one baking step, this recipe is moderate in difficulty. Allow time to soften the butter, prepare the apples, and cool the cake.

PREPARATION TIME: 20 minutes
START TO FINISH: 65 minutes
YIELD: 12 servings

2 large apples
1 cup (2 sticks 1 cup) stick-style
   margarine, softened
2 cups sugar
3 large eggs
1 teaspoon vanilla
2½ cups all-purpose flour
1 teaspoon baking powder
½ teaspoon soda
½ teaspoon salt
1 cup black walnut pieces

Step 1   Preheat the oven to 350°F and grease and flour a 13×9×2-inch baking pan. Peel, core, and slice the apple into ¾-inch pieces to equal 2½ cups. Set aside.

Step 2   Cream the margarine and sugar, and when they are well mixed and a bit white, mix in the eggs, one at a time. Add the vanilla.

Step 3 Sift together the flour, baking powder, soda, and salt. Stir this into the butter mixture. The batter will be thick. Using a rubber spatula, fold in the apples and walnuts.

Step 4 Scrape the batter into the prepared pan and bake until it has browned across the top and a toothpick inserted into the center comes out clean, or about 45 minutes. Cool ½ hour and cut in 12 pieces.

Healthy Alternatives: Replace the margarine with canola oil. You can also change the cake by replacing half of the oil with applesauce, and if salt is a problem, omit it.

Dried Apple Stack Cake

Serve this cake with whipped cream, vanilla ice cream, or hot sorghum. If the cake is dry, moisten it with a topping of caramel sauce, spiced applesauce, or cider jelly. For snacks or breakfast, heat single slices in a toaster oven. The results smell like ginger-cinnamon toast with apples.

Use 5 cups of apple butter or prepare the recipe for dried apple filling. If you don't have pure sweet sorghum syrup, use molasses or dark corn syrup. Finally, if you have six 9-inch cake pans, you'll be able to bake the layers at one time, but it's more likely that you'll have to reuse the pans once or twice to bake all six layers.

This 13-ingredient cake combines three recipes: apple filling, cake layers, and glaze. In the process you'll boil, purée, mix, roll, cut, bake, pour, and spread. You might make the filling on one day, bake the cake and spread the filling on the second day, and let the cake rest the third day. Before serving, boil and spread the glaze or sprinkle powdered sugar. For a complete discussion of stack cakes, see Chapter 10.

PREPARATION TIME: 1½ hours to make the filling and bake the layers; 15 minutes to stack the layers and spread the filling; 20 minutes to boil and spread the glaze.

START TO FINISH: 14 to 26 hours

PIES AND
CAKES

YIELD: 1 large six-layer cake. Ten might eat a whole cake, but this recipe is better divided into about 20 servings, and don't forget Francis Collier's advice, and "Eat until your belly is content."

For the dried apple filling:
5 to 6 cups home-dried (very dry) apples
4 cups water or apple cider
1 cup sugar
1 teaspoon ground ginger
1 teaspoon ground nutmeg
Or, use 18 ounces of commercial, soft-dried apples and 4 and ¾ cups of water.

For the stack cake:
5 cups plus ¼ cup all-purpose flour, divided
½ cup sugar
2 teaspoons baking powder
2 teaspoons ground ginger
1 teaspoon cinnamon
1 teaspoon salt
1 cup melted shortening
1 cup 100% pure sweet sorghum
2 large eggs
2 teaspoons vanilla

For the sugar glaze:
1¼ cups sugar
⅓ cup water
¼ cup shortening or ½ stick butter
1 teaspoon ground ginger
1 teaspoon vanilla

Prepare the apple filling:

Step 1 Prepare the filling first so that it will be almost cool when you spread it on the layers.

Step 2 Bring to a boil and then simmer the apples, water or cider, and sugar for 30 minutes. Stir to combine fully. To save time, pressure cook the apples 10 minutes; however, when using a pressure cooker, be sure the apples are covered with water before putting on the lid.

Step 3 Stir in the ginger and nutmeg. Using a mixer, food processor, or potato masher, break up the apples until they are the consistency of applesauce. The filling needs to be moist but not runny, and thick but not dry. Add water to yield 5 cups of sauce. Cool.

Prepare the cake:

Step 1 Preheat the oven to 350°F and grease two, three, or six 9-inch cake pans.

Step 2 Measure the dry ingredients: 5 cups flour, sugar, baking powder, ginger, cinnamon, and salt into a very large mixing bowl or tub and whisk them together.

Step 3 Make a depression or nest in the center of the flour mixture and pour in the shortening, sorghum, and vanilla. Crack the eggs and drop them in. Whisk the liquids until well mixed. Now, with clean hands mix the dough ring by ring, slowly incorporating the flour into the wet ingredients as you would for bread. When the dough is dry enough to handle and roll with a rolling pin, stop adding flour. Some may remain in the bowl. If the dough becomes too dry to come together, moisten it with water. If it is too moist to roll, add flour.

Step 4 Roll the dough into a log and cut it into 6 equal-sized parts of about 8 ounces. Round the pieces into a ball, and roll them in the extra ¼ cup flour.

Step 5 Even though traditional mountain cook, Francis Collier, says, "You need a number 10 iron skillet because the cake wouldn't taste the same if baked in Silverstone," the following also works. Roll out each layer to 8 to 9 inches in diameter. Fold or roll the layers onto the rolling pin and lift each into a 9-inch nonstick baking pan. Unroll the dough and pat it evenly across the bottom, repairing breaks as you pat and pressing the dough to the edge of the pan. Bake about 12 minutes, or until the layer is brown on the edges and lightly brown across the top. Repeat for each layer. Remove the layers from the oven and flip them onto cooling racks. When the layers are cool, spread the filling and stack the layers.

Assemble the cake:

Step 1 Place the first layer on a cake plate and spread 1 cup of apple filling over the layer. Repeat this with each layer. Do not spread apple filling on the top layer.

Step 2 Let the cake stand 6 to 12 hours at room temperature. This allows the moisture from the apple filling to soak into the layers. Refrigerate for 12 to 36 additional hours before serving.

Prepare the sugar glaze:

Step 1 Combine the sugar and water in a small saucepan set over high heat. Bring to a boil, reduce the heat, and simmer for about 8 minutes or until the mixture reaches the soft ball stage or 234°F to 236°F.

Step 2 Remove from the heat, slice and stir in the shortening or butter and then the ginger and vanilla. Pour the glaze over the cake, starting at the edges and dripping it down the side. To make drip lines down the side of the cake, tilt the cake 45 degrees off the work surface and pour slowly. Finally, cover the top of the cake with the remaining glaze, spreading it with a knife. Reheat the glaze as needed to soften.

Variation: Party Stack Cakes. After rolling the dough to 3/8 of an inch, cut it into rounds with a 2-inch biscuit cutter. Bake on cookie sheets or parchment-covered cookie sheets, and stack the "cookies" three high with apple filling between the layers. Drizzle with glaze. Let stand 12 hours.

PIES AND CAKES

Desserts, Candy, & Tea

Bread Pudding

Many mountain cooks prepare pudding with biscuits. Some use day-old, crusty buttermilk biscuits while others use any leftover breakfast biscuits. Biscuits are available at many fast-food restaurants as well as the frozen section in most markets.

PREPARATION TIME: 15 minutes
START TO FINISH: 1 hour 15 minutes
YIELD: 6 servings

3 large eggs
¾ cup sugar
1 teaspoon vanilla
3 cups milk
6 large biscuits, about 3 inches
     wide and 1 ½ inches high
¼ cup raisins
cinnamon sugar

Step 1 Slide a pan of hot water large enough to contain a 2-quart casserole into the oven, and preheat the oven to 325°F.

Step 2 Break the eggs into a mixing bowl, and whisk in the sugar and vanilla. Stir in the milk. Cut the biscuits in thirds and spread them into the casserole. Sprinkle the raisins over the biscuits. Pour the milk mixture over the biscuits, and place the dish in the hot water bath.

Step 3 Bake until the custard is set near the center. A cake tester inserted near the center of the custard should come out clean. Allow 1 hour or more.

Step 4 Smooth any bubbles on top of the custard and sprinkle with cinnamon sugar. Serve warm or at room temperature with boiled custard.

Banana Pudding

After almost 50 years of popularity, banana pudding has become a classic with many variations. What follows is an old-fashioned custard-based banana pudding. Since its humble beginnings in the 1940s to its appearance on boxes of Nabisco Nilla Wafers, to its transformation to instant pudding mixes, this dessert is an American home food of the best sort. The current edition of *The Joy of Cooking* calls banana pudding an American-grown trifle (English pudding). Others compare it to banana cream pie.

With a custard to cook and a meringue to beat and bake, this pudding is fairly difficult to prepare.

PREPARATION TIME: 1 hour
START TO FINISH: 1 hour
YIELD: 10 servings

1 cup sugar
⅓ cup all-purpose flour
2½ cups milk
4 large eggs, separated and at
    room temperature
2 teaspoons vanilla
40 (6 ounces) vanilla wafers
4 (1½ to 2 pounds) ripe bananas
4 ounces marshmallow cream

Step 1 In a medium-size cold saucepan combine the sugar with the flour. Slowly whisk in the milk, and then cook over medium heat until the mixture bubbles 1 minute.

Step 2 In a small bowl whisk the egg yolks until smooth. Whisk about ⅓ of the hot milk mixture into the yolks, and then return this to the saucepan. Cook, stirring constantly, until the yolks thicken and the temperature of the custard reaches 177°F. When cooked, the custard will coat the back of a wooden spoon. Do not let the mixture boil. Stir in the vanilla. Cool for 15 minutes.

Step 3 Line the bottom of a small (6-cup or 6×10-inch) casserole dish with 12 vanilla wafers, and slice 2 bananas lengthwise over the wafers. Stir the custard and pour ⅓ of it over the wafers. Repeat, adding 12 more vanilla wafers and 2 bananas. Press 10 wafers into an upright position around the sides of the dish. Position these wafers so they touch the sides of the dish. Top with the remaining custard.

Step 4 Preheat the oven to 450°F. To prepare the meringue topping, beat the egg whites until frothy, and slowly beat in the marshmallow cream. When these are fully mixed, stiff, and stand in peaks, spread the meringue over the pudding, sealing it to the standing vanilla wafers. Using the back of a spoon, draw the meringue into peaks. Garnish by pressing 6 vanilla wafers across the center of the pudding. Bake 3 minutes, or until the peaks of the meringue brown.

Step 5 Serve warm or cold in small dessert bowls.

Apple Crisp

Mountain cooks bake this sweet apple and oat mixture in a tin, and it comes from the oven much like a pie filling. Some call it apple betty. Historically, mountaineers made these crisps by layering sugar, spiced fruit, nuts, and buttered bread crumbs, and baking them in a hot oven. The dish is served as a pudding, warm in custard dishes, and topped with vanilla ice cream, heavy cream, whipped cream, *crème anglaise*, and, of course, a few extra nuts. With seven ingredients and one baking step, this recipe is moderate in difficulty. The time-consuming parts are preparing the fresh apples and baking the crisps 40 minutes. For the nuts use hickory nuts, walnuts, or pecans.

DESSERTS CANDY & TEA

PREPARATION TIME: 20 minutes
START TO FINISH: 60 minutes
YIELD: 6 servings

1 cup rolled oats
1 cup brown sugar
½ cup nut pieces
½ cup all-purpose flour
1 teaspoon cinnamon
6 tablespoons melted butter
4 medium-sized apples

Step 1 Preheat the oven to 350°F, and select an 8×8×2-inch baking tin.

Step 2 Mix the oatmeal, sugar, nuts, flour, and cinnamon in a medium bowl. Stir and mix in the butter. Set aside.

Step 3 Wash, peel, core, and cube the apples to make 4 cups. Stir the crisp mixture into the apples, reserving ½ cup for topping. Spread into the baking tin, press the mixture down, and top with the remaining crisp mixture.

Step 4 Bake 30 minutes and press down again. Bake 10 additional minutes, or until the apples are cooked through. When cooked, the edges will brown a bit, the apples will be soft, and a few bubbles will appear.

Pawpaw Custard

With five ingredients, making this custard is moderate in difficulty, but first, you have to find and ripen pawpaws. Then, separate the pulp, blend the ingredients, and finally, bake using a water bath. Bake the custard in custard cups, casseroles, or pie crusts. For a discussion of pawpaws, see Chapter 9.

PREPARATION TIME: 25 minutes
START TO FINISH: about 4 hours
YIELD: 8 servings

> 3 to 4 ripe pawpaws
> 1 cup milk
> 1 cup heavy cream
> 3 large eggs
> ¾ cup sugar

Step 1 Select 8 custard cups. Preheat the oven to 325°F and pre-pare a water bath. To prepare the water bath, boil 2 quarts of water, and select a baking pan that will hold the custard cups. Cover the bottom of the pan with a dishcloth.

Step 2 Using a food mill, separate the pawpaw seeds and skin from the pulp. Measure and set aside 1 cup of pawpaw pulp.

Step 3 With a blender or food processor, combine the ingredients as you add them, beating together the milk, cream, eggs, sugar, and pawpaw pulp. Pour the mixture into the custard cups, and place the cups on the dishcloth in the pan. Pour the boiling water around them, bringing the water ⅔ up the side of the cups.

Step 4 Bake for 40 to 50 minutes or until a knife inserted near the center comes out clean. Remove from the oven just before the custard is set in the center. The custard will continue to cook. Do not allow the water bath to boil during baking. Cool and then cover and refrigerate.

Healthy Alternative: Replace the cream with skim milk or fat-free evaporated skim milk. Use two eggs.

Peach Cobbler

While French food is supposed to be the best, this mountain cobbler is not only much like a French clafouti, but it tastes better.

The miracle of this recipe is that as the ingredients bake, the butter and peaches come together to form a flavorful crusty shell around a soft center. The trick to achieving that result is not to stir the butter or peaches into the batter. After pouring the peaches over the batter, some cooks sprinkle them with cinnamon, mace, or even pecan pieces. The dish can be served warm or

DESSERTS
CANDY & TEA

cold in cereal bowls with a scoop of vanilla ice cream. On the second day, reheat in the oven and sprinkle with powdered sugar. To make this dessert you will wash, slice, and boil peaches or, as suggested in the variation, use a can of prepared peaches. Then, you will stir batter, bake, and cool.

PREPARATION TIME: 20 minutes
START TO FINISH: 55 minutes
YIELD: 10 servings

2 pounds fresh and very ripe
   peaches
1¾ cups sugar, divided
1 stick (½ cup) butter or
   margarine
1 cup self-rising flour
1 cup milk

Step 1 Heat the oven to 350°F and select a 13×9×2-inch baking pan.

Step 2 Either peel or leave the skin on the peaches and wash and slice them to equal about 4 cups. Place the peaches in a saucepan with 1 cup of sugar. Stir, cover, bring to a boil, reduce heat, and then simmer 2 to 3 minutes.

Step 3 As the peaches cook, melt the butter. Set aside. In a medium bowl, combine the remaining sugar, self-rising flour, and milk. Mix well. Pour the melted butter into the baking pan. Pour the flour mixture over the melted butter, but do not stir, allowing the butter to remain around the edge of the pan. Add the cooked peaches and all the syrup to the center of the pan, and again, do not stir. Gently spread the peaches over the top of the batter.

Step 4 Bake until the cobbler is cooked to the center (firm, not runny) and brown on top, or 30 to 40 minutes. Cool 30 minutes or more.

Variation: Canned Peach Cobbler. When peaches are not in season, make this recipe using 1 32-ounce can of peaches in sweet syrup. Do not cook the peaches. Use all the syrup. Reduce the sugar to 1 cup and stir it into the batter.

DESSERTS
CANDY & TEA

Boiled Custard

Boiled custard is a cooked sauce or drink. Mountaineers call it float, and when cooked and cooled, the sauce is thick, rich, and sweet. The French call it English custard or *crème anglaise,* and they use it as a sauce as well as the base for floating islands.

PREPARATION TIME: 15 minutes
START TO FINISH: 15 minutes
YIELD: 6 servings

1 quart milk
4 large eggs
1 cup sugar
2 teaspoons vanilla

Step 1 Warm the milk in a large saucepan set over medium heat. As the milk warms, combine the eggs, sugar, and vanilla in a large bowl. Pour half of the hot milk into the egg mixture, blend, and return this to the saucepan.

Step 2 Over medium heat, cook the egg mixture to 175°F or until the custard thickens and coats the back of a wooden spoon. If it curdles, blend or strain it. Cool until serving.

Bourbon Balls

Bourbon balls are made by forming centers and then dipping them in melted chocolate. They should be served on the second day, after the flavors have ripened. With six ingredients and two steps, making the recipe that follows is moderate in difficulty.

PREPARATION TIME: 1 hour
START TO FINISH: 2 hours
YIELD: 50 to 60 pieces

Chocolate coating:

1⅓ (8 ounces) cups semisweet
   chocolate pieces
1 ounce paraffin (just less than ¼
   a block Gulf sealing wax),
   chopped

For the bourbon candy centers:

1½ cups pecans
5 tablespoons bourbon
½ cup melted butter
1 pound sifted confectioners'
   sugar

Step 1 Drop the chocolate and paraffin into a double boiler over hot, not boiling, water.

Step 2 Cover two cookie sheets with waxed paper. Using a grater or food processor, grate or pulverize the pecans and mix them into the bourbon. Add the melted butter and then stir in the confectioners' sugar. Mix thoroughly and drop by teaspoonfuls (about 1 inch in size) onto waxed paper, then roll them in the palm of your hands to shape into balls. If the candy is not stiff enough, stir a bit more powdered sugar into the cream mixture or refrigerate a little longer. Refrigerate for 25 minutes. When the candy centers are cool and firm, roll and round the pieces a second time.

Step 3 When the chocolate mixture has melted, stir it up. Keep the melted chocolate over low heat while you dip the candy. To dip the candy, select a spoon and a fork with long and wide tines.

Step 4 Use the fork and spoon to roll the candy centers in the chocolate mixture. Rest the dipped piece on the fork, and tap the fork handle on the edge of the pan, forcing the excess chocolate to drip back into the pan. Slide each piece back onto the waxed paper.

Step 5 Refrigerate another hour or so, and then loosen the candy from the paper. Store covered in the refrigerator or freezer.

DESSERTS
CANDY & TEA

Peanut Brittle

This candy is heavy on nuts and light on sugar—in fact, it's mostly peanuts. You can make a tasty peanut brittle using only half the nuts, but many people prefer this peanutty peanut brittle.

Be careful to buy unsalted and not coated peanuts. Many dry-roasted peanuts are snack foods with coatings, and these glazes cause problems.

PREPARATION TIME: 15 minutes
START TO FINISH: 1 hour
YIELD: 60 pieces or 1¾ pounds

1½ cups sugar
½ cup corn syrup
1 (16-ounce) container (3 cups)
    unsalted dry-roasted peanuts
⅛ teaspoon (2 pinches) baking
    soda

Step 1 Lightly grease a 13×9×2-inch baking tin or a large baking sheet.

Step 2 Stir the sugar and syrup into a very large microwave-safe container until fully mixed—the syrup should coat the sugar.

Step 3 Microwave on high for 7 minutes. Pour the nuts on top of the syrup and microwave on high for an additional 3 minutes or until mixture begins to develop light caramel color. Cook based on color, not time. Do not let it darken because it will continue to cook after you remove it from the oven.

Step 4 A pinch at a time, sprinkle the soda evenly over the candy. Stir until fully mixed and the large bubbles are gone. The candy will foam with tiny bubbles, and it will lighten in color. This may take ten strokes or half a minute.

Step 5 As you pour, scrape, and spread the candy onto the prepared pan, be careful and use two potholders to protect your hands. The mixture is hot. Use the bottoms of two tablespoons to finish spreading the candy.

DESSERTS
CANDY & TEA

Step 6 Cool on a rack for 40 minutes or more. Remove the block of candy from the pan and break into 1- to 2-inch pieces. Store in an airtight container.

Cream Praline Fudge

When made with brown sugar, the flavor is sharp caramel; however, with this recipe, the white sugar allows the flavor of the pecans, butter, and cream to dominate. Covering the sugar syrup with a lid for 3 minutes steams the sides of the pan and removes the sugar crystals.

With six ingredients and one cooking step, making this candy is easy; however, the temperature has to be measured, and at the end stirring smoothes the candy. Make this candy on a dry day.

PREPARATION TIME: 20 minutes
START TO FINISH: 3 hours
YIELD: 2½ pounds or 16 pieces

1 cup heavy cream
1 stick (4 ounces) unsalted butter
2 tablespoons light corn syrup
3 cups sugar
2 teaspoons vanilla extract
3 cups pecan halves or pieces

Step 1 Select an 8×8-inch baking tin.

Step 2 Place a three-quart saucepan over moderate heat and stir together the cream, butter, and syrup, stirring until well mixed. Add the sugar and stir until combined.

Step 3 Bring the syrup to a boil and cover the pan. Turn the heat to low, boil the syrup 3 minutes, and remove the lid. Do not stir. Raise the heat to medium-high and place a candy thermometer in the pot. Do not stir.

Step 4 When the temperature reaches the soft ball stage or 234°F, remove the pot from the heat. Do not stir until the fudge feels just a bit warm or reaches 115°F. Cooling may take 2 hours. Stir in the vanilla and pecans. Continue to stir until the candy loses its shine and is smooth, not grainy, on the tongue.

Step 5   If at any time the candy gets too hard to work, warm it on the stove. Turn the candy into the pan, and press it flat and into the corners. If some fat separates, absorb it with a paper towel. Cover with plastic wrap. Cool and cut into pieces. Wrap each piece in plastic wrap and place in an airtight container.

Peanut Butter Fudge

Mountaineers today make this fudge because peanut butter—not chocolate, vanilla, or caramel—is the most popular candy flavor. They might whip up a batch for a birthday, Thanksgiving, Christmas, the Fourth of July, or any other day of the year.

If you follow these directions carefully, the fudge will be smooth and creamy, not grainy. Grainy fudge, unfortunately, is worse than soup that curdles or scrambled eggs that are too dry. Smooth fudge, on the other hand, is a sweet and supreme confection. This fudge is so smooth it is almost sticky.

When cooking this recipe, try not to grill chicken, watch a movie, or talk on the phone, because if you do, you'll miss or mess something. To save the trouble of wrapping each piece, cut the 8-inch square into four pieces and wrap them in plastic wrap. Keep the fudge sealed because it dries out quickly. Now get out a saucepan and start cooking.

PREPARATION TIME: 30 minutes
START TO FINISH: 2½ hours
YIELD: 25 pieces or 2 pounds

4 cups granulated sugar
1⅓ cups milk
½ cup light corn syrup
1 cup creamy peanut butter
2 tablespoons butter
2 teaspoons vanilla

Step 1 Grease an 8×8×2-inch baking tin. In a 4-quart saucepan set over medium heat, stir together the sugar, milk, and corn syrup. Stay with your candy now, and bring it to a rolling boil. Reduce the heat to low-medium, and cover the pan for 3 minutes. This washes sugar crystals from the side of the pan. Remove the lid and raise the heat to medium. Now sit down and watch your candy. Like you watch a crackling fire, enjoy the bubbles, but do not stir them. Cook the syrup without stirring to the soft ball stage or 240°F.

Step 2 Remove the pan from the heat, and do not stir, shake, or jar the pan. Do not allow dust to fall into the pan. Cool till the pan feels hot or to 110°F, 1 to 2 hours.

Step 3 Stir in the peanut butter, butter, and vanilla. Stir until the candy begins to thicken and loses its gloss. This fudge has a short stirring time, however, too little stirring at this point will yield a granular product. Turn the candy into the prepared pan, and with greased fingers press it flat. If it gets stiff, add a bit of heat and press the candy out and into the corners of the pan. Seal with plastic wrap.

Step 4 Cool and cut into 25 pieces, making four cuts in each direction. Seal the candy in plastic.

Healthful Comment: Each piece of fudge has 106 calories and 3 grams of fat and that's not bad for such good candy.

Sweet Tea

On one hand tea is a universal drink, but on the other hand, the way Southerners serve it has become a sign of both Appalachia and the South. Iced sweet tea and "iced tea-un" or unsweetened tea are common daily fare, and if you order them in other regions of the country, you may be surprised because sweetened tea may be unfamiliar to the kitchen staff.

Note that orange pekoe tea is a blend of Ceylon teas. The leaf is orange in color and the blend is the most popular tea in the United States. In place of loose orange pekoe tea, use 4 tea bags. For "iced tea-un" omit the sugar.

PREPARATION TIME: 8 minutes
START TO FINISH: 15 minutes
YIELD: 8 servings

2 cups fresh water
¼ cup tea leaves or 4 tea bags
¼ cup lemon juice
3 cups ice
cold water
⅓ cup sugar

Step 1 Boil the water in a non-aluminum saucepan and add the tea leaves or bags. Reduce the heat and steep the tea, simmering for 7 minutes. Strain the tea leaves and pour the tea into a pitcher.

Step 2 Add the lemon juice, ice, cold water, and sugar to make 2 quarts. Stir until the sugar dissolves.

Step 3 Serve with extra sugar and lemon wedges. Serve as the primary beverage for breakfast, lunch, afternoon tea, or dinner.

Festivals and Events

Pride, history, imagination, and modern culture converge during community festivals, and some of them are named for food. Today, many communities celebrate their heritage with street fairs, food booths, exhibits, contests, music, and parades. These gatherings draw together entrepreneurial and creative spirits to present a show that must include food. But what food? While the following list is far from complete, some almost-iconic Appalachian foods such as ramps, apples, and sorghum have become the focus of festivals.

Apple Festivals

Every Appalachian state from New York to Georgia features an apple festival. Communities schedule the festivals from the time the trees bloom in the spring until well after harvest. The North Carolina Apple festival is typical.

North Carolina Apple Festival
This diverse community festival in Hendersonville had its beginnings in the 1930s and has been held annually since 1947. The festival dates correspond to the early harvest of mountain apples, and the festival is held on the last weekend in August, which includes the Labor Day holiday. The character of the four-day festival is seen in events such as the Apple Recipe Contest, Apple Orchard Tour, Street Fair, Railroad Days, Robot Fightin' Time, Lion's Club Big Apple Country Breakfast, and the King Apple Parade, which starts with an Antique Aircraft Flyby. Finally, the festival offers the Mineral and Lapidary Museum Display and a Gem and Mineral Spectacular that features dealers selling gems, minerals, fossils, and jewelry.

Write P.O. Box 886, Hendersonville, NC 28793, call 828-697-4557, or click on *http://www.ncapplefestival.org/*.

Banana Pudding and Dollywood

As Dolly Parton, the country music singer, stated recently before a worldwide audience, "The only thing more American than apple pie is banana pudding." At Dollywood and Pigeon Forge, Tennessee, banana pudding is on the menu. See the Desserts and Candy section for the recipe.

Dolly Parton's Dollywood is a theme park that offers country-style entertainment and crafts as well as rides that thrill, soak, and excite. The park is a showcase for the Smoky Mountains, offering mountain food, dance, and events. Musicians and artisans ply their trades. Attendees can dine at the Backstage Restaurant and Grandstand Café, or they may go to the Sausage Works, Frosted Nuts, or Pork Rinds for some down-home Appalachian food.

Contact the Pigeon Forge Department of Tourism, P.O. Box 1390-I, Pigeon Forge, TN 37868, or call 800-251-9100 or email *www.dollywood.com.*

Black Walnut Festivals

In 1954, Spencer, West Virginia, began celebrating the black walnut with a community festival. The festival includes a beauty queen, auto show, long-distance Nut Run, fireman's competition, art and photography show, and gospel sing. In recent years the town added the Black Walnut Bowl football game played by the high school teams from Spencer and nearby St. Albans. In Appalachian Ohio, just west of the Ohio River, Switzerland Township of Monroe County has also celebrated black walnuts. In 2003 both festivals were held on the second weekend in October. Among the events in Switzerland Township are a horseback cattle-pinning contest, walnut log judging, and rolling pin throwing, as well as a banjo and fiddle contest.

For the West Virginia Black Walnut Festival call 304-927-5616 or look at *http://www.wvblackwalnutfestival.org/.* For the Switzerland of Ohio Black Walnut Festival call 740-472-0169 or look at *http://www.travelohio.com/.*

The Blue Ridge Parkway

Operated by the National Park Service and built by the Civilian Conservation Corps in the 1930s, this small highway connects the Shenandoah National Park in Virginia with the Great Smoky Mountains National Park in North Carolina. Its more than 450 miles follow the ridges of the Appalachians, Blacks, Craggies, Pisgahs, Balsams, and Great Smokies. The Blue Ridge Parkway attracts cyclists, hikers, tourists, bird watchers, and photographers. Many of the bridges, walls, and overlooks are in the original style as the highway has not been widened or updated. Because of low speed limits and many newer highways nearby, those living in the area generally do not use the parkway for travel.

For general parkway information, call 828-298-0398 or visit *www.nps. gov/blri.*

Chicken: World Chicken Festival

In the 1940s, Colonel Harland Sanders of Kentucky Fried Chicken (KFC) opened his first chicken restaurant, an endeavor that eventually made him one of the most recognized figures in the world. Sanders' first restaurant was in Corbin, Kentucky. Today London, Kentucky, a nearby town, celebrates the founding of KFC with the World Chicken Festival or WCF. The four-day event is held each year in late September. The festival offers exceptional entertainment on four big stages and attracts more than 250,000 visitors. As the weekend progresses, attendees can sample chicken from the world's largest skillet, run in the Run for the Roast, compete in the Children's Chicken Dance, and prepare a dish for the WCF Cook-Off. The WCF also features the Chick-O-Lympics, Golf Scramble, KFC Hot Wings Eating Contest, Colonel Sanders Look-Alike Contest, and many other "egg-citing" events.

The 14th WCF was held in London, Kentucky, in 2003. For further information call 800-348-0095 or write to the World Chicken Festival, 140 West Daniel Boone Parkway, London, KY 40741. Click on *http://www. chickenfestival. com/*.

Cornbread: National Cornbread Festival

People who have a passion for cornbread attend the National Cornbread Festival, or at least visit the web site at *http://www.nationalcornbread. com/*. Since 1997 folks in South Pittsburg, Tennessee, have used the last weekend in April to celebrate cornbread and cast-iron cookware with a cornbread cook-off, Cornbread Alley, iron skillet motorcycle run, road race, band contest, and carnival. At Cornbread Alley you can purchase all kinds of cornbreads including ones made with sweet potato, beans, chicken, fruit, chili, ham, and broccoli. The festival's web site offers almost 50 cornbread recipes, as well as directions for preparing dishes such as Indian bean bread, coal miner's pie, cheesy potato corn cakes, and chicken asparagus cobbler.

For further information write to the National Cornbread Festival, P.O. Box 247, South Pittsburg, TN 37380, or call 423-837-0022.

Dinner on the Grounds

While dinner on the grounds is a church event, many music events are similar and open to the public. *The Blue Ridge Music Trails* is a book title and web site that tracks about 160 music venues that are open to the public. The music includes bluegrass, old-time, country-and-western, gospel, and blues. Many of the events include food and some are associated with dinner on the grounds. In other cases, the music supports the food as is the case with the Sorghum Molasses Festival in Amherst County, Virginia; Hall's Barbecue in Yadkin County, North Carolina; the Downtown Street Festival in Galax, Virginia; and the White Top Mountain Ramp Festival in Grayson County, North Carolina. Also of interest is the Shape-Note Singing at the Cullowhee Baptist Church in Jackson County, North Carolina. *Blue Ridge Music Trails* includes sites within about 25 miles of the 469-long Blue Ridge Mountain Parkway.

For contact information, dates, and directions look at *Blue Ridge Music Trails: Finding a Place in the Circle*. Fred C. Fussell. Chapel Hill, North Carolina: The University of North Carolina Press, 2003, or click on *http://www. blueridgemusic.org/*.

Grits Festivals

The community of St. George, South Carolina, celebrates grits with the World Grits Festival in April of each year, and across the state line in Warwick, Georgia, folks turn out to celebrate the National Grits Festival.

The Warwick festival, also in April, includes a beauty pageant, grits cook-off, contests, and entertainment. In both communities, folks eat grits year-round and at any time of day, but at the Warwick festival the Martha White Grits Cooking Contest and the Grits Eating Contest heat up the competition. Over in St. George, in addition to Martha White, sponsors include Quaker Oats and John Deere.

By unanimous resolution, the state of Georgia has declared Warwick to be the Grits Capital of America. To join the fun contact The National Grits Festival at *http://www.gritsfest.com/*, phone 229-535-6670, or the World Grits Festival at *http://www.worldgritsfestival.com/* or phone 843-563-7943.

Moonshine Festivals

While it is illegal to buy or sell moonshine, communities in Alabama, Georgia, and Ohio celebrate their relationship to the brew with festivals. On the third weekend in May, folks gather in New Straitsville, Ohio, for music, local history, and flea markets, and they sell moonshine burgers, moonshine pie, and moonshine doggies. In the Deep South near Stevenson, Alabama, in McMahan's Cove, concerned citizens gather to celebrate life and raise money for scholarships. Georgia, too, has a festival. Every October since 1968, "stilltenders, barbacks, and liquorheads of every ilk come down from the Georgia hills to celebrate the blinding brew. . . ." At the Mountain Moonshine Festival you'll find cloggers, clowns, gospel singers, an Elvis impersonator, and a real still. Vintage Fords and other restored cars memorialize the drivers who outran the police to transport moonshine during Prohibition.

Moonshine Festival, NSBA Box 38, New Straitsville, Ohio 43766; phone: 740-394-2838.

McMahan's Cove Moonshine and Muscadine Festival, Jackson County, Alabama.

Mountain Moonshine Festival, Dawsonville, Georgia; Phone: 706-265-6278; or visit *http://www.motorsportamerica.com/banners/moonshine.html.*

Peanut Festivals

For the recipe contest at the first Plains Peanut Festival in September of 2000, First Lady Rosalyn Carter submitted her peanut brittle recipe, but she did not win. The $250 grand prize went to Ms. Brooks for her Georgia gold peanuts, a recipe for candied peanuts with gold luster. While the Plains peanut festival is not the oldest, it may be the most famous. Across the state in Sylvester-Worth County, the Georgia Peanut Festival was established in 1963, while over in Dathon, Alabama, the nine-day National Peanut Festival got its start in 1938. In Suffolk, Virginia, The Peanut Fest has been held since 1977 and includes the gooberland family area and the world's largest peanut butter sculpture. Indeed, every Southern state has a peanut festival.

To enter the Plains Peanut Festival recipe contest contact The Peanut Institute, P.O. Box 70157, Albany, GA 31708; phone 888-8PEANUT or check their web site at *http://www.peanut-institute.org/.*

Suffolk Peanut Fest, P.O. Box 1852, Suffolk, Virginia 23439 1852; phone 757-539-6751 or *http://www.suffolkfest.org/.*

Poke Sallet Festival

Harlan, Kentucky, is home to the annual Poke Sallet Festival, a gathering that offers bluegrass music, a Choo Choo Train, and a homecoming pageant. During the four-day event, groups such as the Lion's Club, Jay's Restaurant, the Boardroom Restaurant, and Town Site Restaurant sell poke sallet. The Harlan County Health Department gives free health tests, and civic groups sell hotdogs. The Zeta Beta Club sponsors the Little Feet Street Race, runners compete in the Run for the Hills, and Hospice offers a health walk. Festival bingo is organized by the Harlan Revitalization Association. Car collectors gather at the Village Mall, and craftsmen demonstrate their skills in wood, clay, and fiber. So, even if you don't eat poke, this series of events organized around poke sallet may offer something of interest.

For information call the Chamber of Commerce at 606-573-4717 or go to the Harlan County web site at *http://www.harlancounty.com/*.

Pittsburgh Irish Festival

Irish stew is at least a small part of the Pittsburgh Irish Festival held each year on the second weekend of September at Station Square in Pittsburgh, Pennsylvania. The three-day event celebrates Irish and Irish-American culture from both historic and contemporary perspectives. The festival brings together art, history, patron saints, dance, sports, language, and music. The music and dance entertainment schedule is extensive, and the events are supported by vendors who such sell Irish foods as soda bread, Limerick limeade, corned beef and cabbage, corned beef sandwiches, shepherd's pie, fish and chips, Dublin Coddle, Irish coffee, scones, and shamrock cookies. Guinness, Harp, Bunratty, and Meade sell beer.

For further information contact the Pittsburgh Irish Festival, P.O. Box 81173, Pittsburgh, PA 15217 or call 412-422-1113. Visit *http://www/pghirishfest.org*.

Pork: Virginia Pork Festival

Enjoy the combination: five bands and 20 tons of pork. The Virginia Pork Festival is a four-hour event held in Emporia, Virginia, on the second Wednesday in June. For 26 years, this community of 6,000 has attracted about 15,000 pork aficionados from New York to Florida. They come for the music, and they sample some 30 different pork dishes prepared by civic groups including Greensville Ruritan Club, Hospice, Shriners, and fire departments.

For further information contact the Virginia Pork Festival, P.O. Box 1001, Emporia, VA 23847; phone: 800-482-7675 or click on *http://www. va-porkfestival.com/*.

Ramps: Feast of the Ramson

The annual ramp feed and festival held at Richwood, West Virginia, claims to be the biggest and oldest of the many ramp dinners held in Appalachia. The Richwood Chamber of Commerce and the National Ramp Association sponsor the dinner, and they hold it at the Richwood High School cafeteria on the third or fourth Saturday in April from about 11:00 a.m. to 3:00 p.m. The feast also includes a display of arts and crafts at the Richwood Junior High gymnasium.

See *http://www.richwoodwv.com/ramp.asp* or call the Chamber of Commerce at 304-846-6790.

Sorghum Festivals

At sorghum festivals scattered around the mountains, groups gather to celebrate fall and to make sorghum. At these festivals you'll see stacks of bright green sorghum cane stalks waiting to be hand fed into a sorghum press and boiled into syrup. Farmers and civic service clubs sell sorghum and many foods they make with it.

Since 1967 the West Virginia Molasses Festival has been held annually in late September in Arnoldsburg of Calhoun County. The three-day event is described as a "sticky time for all." Call 304-655-8350 or visit *www. wchstv.com/traveling/000928.html.*

West Liberty, Kentucky, Sorghum Festival featuring a mule-drawn cane mill has been held annually since 1970. Go to *http://www.cityofwestliberty. com/sorghumfestival.htm* or call 606-743-2300.

Blairsville, Georgia, Annual Sorghum Festival since 1969 in October has featured biscuit eatin', log sawin', rock throwin', and pole climbin' contests as well as square dancing and golf. Go to *http://www.blairsville. com/sorghum.asp* or call the Blairsville Jaycees at 706-745-4745.

Foods, Terms, and Expressions

You can buy many of the foods defined in this glossary from vendors listed in the next section, Mail-Order Sources, page 303.

Apples, Dried: Home-dried apples are very dry and the flavor is concentrated. When making dried applesauce, dried apple stack cakes, and fried apple pies, some traditional mountain cooks used dried apples. A bushel of fresh apples yields about 3 pounds of dried apples.

Beans, Green Beans: A classic mountain vegetable. The popular Appalachian varieties are different from the small, soft, uniformly shaped beans that are sold frozen or canned. Robust mountain green beans include varieties such as Kentucky Wonder, Romano, white half-runner, and white McCaslan. All of these mottled beans are thick, full seeded, and meaty with little resemblance to either tender snap beans or tiny French *haricot verts*.

Beans, Fall Beans: With the arrival of peanut beans, October shellies, October reds, greasy cut shorts, colored greasies, and fall white half-runners, the green bean season renews itself. Like summer beans, these beans are cooked with salt pork until they split open and turn a drab olive-green color.

Beans, Shelly: Shelly beans or shellies are mature beans of any variety. They are picked when the seed has enlarged and the pod has started its decline. These shelly, shell, or shelled beans are mixtures of pods and seeds. This stage of development borders on dry beans, but holds onto some green bean characteristics.

Beans, Shuck Beans: Shuck beans, shucky beans, and leather britches, as mountaineers call them, are mature, dried green beans. The beans are dried and sold on strings, three to four feet long. To cook shuck beans, cooks soak the beans 12 or more hours, and then boil them with a piece of salt pork or a couple of smoked ham hocks. Today, mountaineers prize shuck beans for their concentrated flavor.

Beans, Soup Beans: The term "soup beans" is another name for dry pinto beans as well as the name of a mountain bean soup. Mountaineers cook these beans with pork flavoring.

Beechnuts: The American beech produces the beechnut used in cooking. The American beech is also called the "lovers tree" because young people often carve their initials on the smooth, gray bark. Beechnut trees are part of the beech family, which encompasses 100 North American species, including the chestnuts, oaks, chinquapins, and tanoaks. Highlanders eat beechnuts raw or cooked and use them in any recipe that calls for pecans. These nuts are especially good when substituted for pecans in pecan pie.

Black-seeded Simpson Lettuce: A popular early season leaf lettuce.

Black Walnuts: Black walnut trees grow from New England across the northern states to Minnesota and south from Texas to Florida. In the mountains, they prefer cool damp valleys, but they also grow in the open.

Black walnuts are a strong-flavored and oily nut. The nut is almost round, and has a green husk and a strong, corrugated shell. Popular recipes that include black walnuts are black walnut sugar cookies, chocolate fudge, fresh apple cake, and the popular black walnut cake.

Blades: Colloquial for onion or corn leaves. Mountaineers eat onion blades in the spring, and, during the summer, folks sit outside and watch the fireflies flicker as the corn blades reflect the moonlight.

Bolted Corn: Ground corn or cornmeal that has been processed to remove the hull.

Butternuts: Closely related to black walnuts, butternuts are also called oilnuts, yellow walnuts, and white walnuts. They do not grow much south of Tennessee.

Butters: Apple, peach, or pear butters are thick, concentrated fruit conserves. Hill folk spread them on buttered toast or biscuits and use them to fill fried pies, stack pies, and stack cakes.

Cast-Iron Cookware: Any saucepans, Dutch ovens, camp ovens, fryers, skillets, kettles, stove broilers, griddles, biscuit, or muffin pans made of cast iron. Cast iron is a durable alloy of iron, carbon, and other elements. Cast-iron cookware is heavy, and it improves with use.

Cast-Iron Skillet: This heavy frying pan is made of thick cast iron. As cooking surfaces have evolved from hearth to stovetop to glass top, these skillets have maintained their popularity as standard cookware. Mountain cooks use them to sear, fry, blacken, and bake, continuing a centuries-long tradition. Cast-iron skillets are available with or without covers in 6-, 8-, 11-, and 14-inch diameters.

Cathead Biscuits: Large, uneven, hand-pulled drop biscuits. Some see the shape of a cat's head in the biscuits. Other biscuits are uniformly formed with a biscuit cutter.

Chickentoe: The common name for tanglegut and spring-beauty, *Claytonia virginica*. An early wild spring green that foragers add to salads and serve with soup beans.

Chow Chow: A mixed vegetable relish made with cabbage, onions, green tomatoes, green beans, corn, and cucumbers.

Chuckwagon: A beef sandwich made with hamburger or cubed steak and served in mountain restaurants.

Cold Pie: *See* Pie, Cold.

Corn Cutter and Creamer: This tool cuts, creams, and grits corn from the cob. With the creamer attachment, the corn is cut, scraped, and shredded, forcing the milk out of the kernel and making gritted or creamed corn. With only the cutter blade, the tool removes whole kernels.

Corn Dodgers: Cornmeal dumplings cooked in water.

Corn, Gritted: *See* Gritted Corn and Gritted Cornbread.

Corn, Roasting Ears: Roasting ears are young, not-filled-out fresh sweet corn. John Parris in *Mountain Cooking* says that "If you can get some roastin'-ears, you've been to the garden and picked some fine corn." Mountaineers look forward to the roasting ear season, and at the post office or in church, if you listen closely, you'll hear them comment, "It's roastin'-ear time."

Cornmeal: Ground, dry, white or yellow corn. Millers make cornmeal in fine, medium, or coarse grinds. When labeled "stone-ground," the meal includes both germ and hull.

Cornmeal Mix, Self-Rising: Self-rising cornmeal mix is a combination of cornmeal, flour, salt, and leavening. Unless labeled otherwise, self-rising cornmeal mix is made with enriched, degerminated, and bolted cornmeal. Every mill prepared a different mix, but typically millers added 1/2 cup all-purpose flour, 1 1/2 teaspoons baking powder, and 1 teaspoon salt to 1 cup of cornmeal.

Cornmeal, Stone-ground: Millers make stone-ground cornmeal in water-powered gristmills with whole kernel (not degerminated or bolted) corn. They reduce the corn kernels to meal when they roll them through two round stones. If the meal is labeled "bolted," the hull has been removed.

Cornpone: Cornbread batter. *See* Pone.

Country Ham: To make country hams, farmers dry-cure fresh hams in flaked salt, sodium nitrate, sugar, and seasonings. These country-cured hams are not soaked in brine. After dry-curing the ham, farmers rinse off the salt and some smoke the ham for anywhere from a day to a week or maybe two. Then the hams hang for one, two, or three years.

Crackling Cornbread: Cornbread made with cracklings or bacon.

Cracklings: Cracklings or cracklins are crunchy fibrous morsels. When farmers render or boil lard from pork fat, they end up with two products: lard and cracklings. The cracklings are a snack eaten out of hand.

Cream: Fresh milk separates into cream or top milk and fat-free milk. Heavy cream has from 36 to 40 percent butter fat. In the mountains, cooks use the word "cream" to refer to evaporated canned milk. Today, cream often means evaporated skim milk.

Cream-Pull Candy: A firm, white, cured candy that is cooked to the hard ball stage and then pulled until it stiffens. The pulling adds air to the candy and then after it cures or stands for about 12 hours, it becomes firm and crumbly. The candy is flavored with vanilla, mint, or chocolate and kept fresh by being dipped in chocolate. Also called marble-top candy because it is cooled on a marble slab.

Cushaw Squash: Also called green-striped cushaw, this smooth-skinned, hard-shelled, winter squash is shaped like a yellow crookneck summer squash, but larger. Cushaw squash weigh between 10 and 25 pounds, and they ripen in the fall. As they would with pumpkins and other winter squash, cooks use these squash when the flesh is firm and the shells are hard.

Cushaw Squash, White: White cushaw squash is a rare, smooth-skinned, hard-shelled, and ivory-colored winter squash. The squash is similar in texture and taste to green-striped cushaw. White cushaw is shaped like a pumpkin, but more squat and larger, weighing up to 30 pounds.

Delights: Layered portable casserole desserts with a bottom crust. The layers consist of fruit and puddings as suggested by names such as blackberry delight, raspberry delight, chocolate delight, and dirt pudding delight.

Dippy: *See* Soppy.

Dirt: Mountain cooks use the word "dirt" to describe some chocolate desserts such as dirt pudding. Mud also means chocolate, as in Mississippi mud pie.

Dried Apple: *See* Apples, Dried.

Dried Green Beans: *See* Beans, Shuck Beans.

Dry Beans: *See* Beans, Soup Beans.

Fat Back: *See* Salt Pork.

Fiddleheads: When ferns sprout in the spring, they send up coiled shoots or fiddleheads. The ostrich fern is a popular variety, but mountain foragers know that any tender fiddlehead is good in a pot of greens or an herb salad. Ostrich fiddleheads are dark green and almost as thick as a pencil.

Flour, Instant: Also called quick-mixing flour or sauce and gravy flour, this granular flour absorbs hot liquids. When sprinkled over a boiling sauce, the liquid absorbs the flour without forming lumps.

Flour, Self-rising Flour: This mixture of wheat flours includes baking powder and salt. Mountain cooks use it to make biscuits and other baked goods.

Foxfire: A term from late Middle English referring to the organic luminescence from a group of widely distributed fungi, some of which grow in

Appalachia. Also the name of an education organization located in the mountains of northeast Georgia and established by Eliot Wigginton.

Goober Peas: Raw peanuts.

Green Tomatoes: Hard, green, and immature, these tomatoes are 2 to 3 inches across. They are available all summer, but they are common in the fall, and some produce stands sell them all year. Highlanders serve green tomatoes sliced and pickled, as part of a relish, in green tomato pie, and as fried green tomatoes.

Grits: Any coarsely ground or cut grain such as corn, rice, or barley, but in the mountains the term refers to hominy grits or grits made from corn hominy. They are served boiled or fried for breakfast or as a side to meat and eggs. *See* Hominy.

Gritted Corn: This corn is too mature to eat fresh but not dry enough to shell. Appalachian gardeners cut gritted corn from the overripe corn on the cob using a large-holed grater or creamer.

Gritted Cornbread: Made with gritted corn, this cornbread is a moist, pudding-like cornbread with a solid crust.

Grubbing: Mountaineers grub for poke, which means they dig the roots from the ground with a heavy shovel or mattock when weeding the garden. They might also grub poke and plant the roots in the basement to harvest the stems in the winter.

Ham, Country: *See* Country Ham.

Hickory Nuts: The hickory nuts most often used in cooking are shellbarks, shagbarks, nutmeg hickories, and mockernuts. The shellbarks are as large as walnuts and rather sweet. As a group, the hickories are part of the walnut family and include 20 or more varieties, most of which produce edible nuts. Many of these large deciduous trees grow in the Appalachian Mountains.

Green hickory wood chips are a favorite for barbecue and smoking. Wood manufacturers use dry hickory wood to make tool handles and sports equipment.

Hominy: Hominy is tender cooked corn, one of the first foods colonists learned about when they came in contact with Native Americans. To make hominy at home, mountain cooks boiled dry white or yellow corn with lye or lime and removed the hull and germ. Today, they serve hominy as a breakfast grain or side dish vegetable. Millers make hominy grits.

Hominy Grits: *See* Grits.

Kieffer Pears: A hard, rough-skinned, old-fashioned pear variety that is crunchy, juicy, and slightly sweet. These pears lend themselves to poaching, baking, and pear honey, and even though they don't compare in taste to soft-flesh pears, many people enjoy them fresh from the tree.

Lard: Rendered pork fat. While 1 tablespoon of butter contains 100 calories and 31 milligrams of cholesterol, 1 tablespoon of lard has 115 calories and 12 milligrams of cholesterol.

Lean: The thin strips of red meat in pork side meat or bacon.

Likker: *See* Pot Likker.

Linn Honey: Honey made from the fragrant flower nectar of the July-blooming American basswood trees, members of the Linden family. May be sold as basswood honey. The honey is light in color, runny, and mild. In terms of flavor, linn honey is a fast, immediate sweet, and it has no sharpness or aftertaste.

Loosen: To thin. Mountain cooks loosen mayonnaise and breakfast gravy with milk.

Middling Meat: Also called salt pork or smoked side meat. Butchers cut it from the pork belly, and like bacon, the cut is mostly fat.

Molasses: Molasses is a colloquial term for sorghum syrup or 100% pure sweet sorghum. Molasses is also a sweet by-product of cane sugar production. *See* Sorghum Syrup.

Moonshine: Illegally distilled liquor or corn whiskey; any smuggled liquor. Related terms include: *Distilling,* the process of boiling the fermented mash to evaporate the liquor. *Mash,* a mixture of sprouted corn or ground dry corn and water that ferments. It usually includes about 80% ground corn and some barley, rye, sorghum syrup, or sugar. *Prohibition,* a government law that makes the production and sale of alcoholic beverages illegal. National Prohibition is a reference to the eighteenth amendment to the U.S. Constitution, which was the law from 1920 to 1933 and did not allow the production or sale of alcoholic beverages. Prohibition caused a significant increase in moonshining. *Proof,* a measure of alcoholic strength. Moonshine proof is typically 100, meaning that the beverage contains 50% alcohol. By comparison wine is 13% alcohol or 26 proof. Proof is twice the percent alcohol. After the last run, moonshine is too strong, and the moonshiner tempers it or waters it down to reduce its strength to about 100 proof. *Revenue agent,* in reference to moonshine, Alcoholic Beverage Control officers who find and arrest moonshiners and confiscate their whiskey, mash, stills, and vehicles. *Run or A Run*, to evaporate the contents of the still one time. *Still,* copper pots or other large vessels; a chamber where liquid is heated and vaporization occurs. Moonshiners used several kinds of stills, with the pot still being most common. Also, the entire apparatus used for making moonshine. *Worm,* copper condensing coils; a cooling device for condensing vapor that comes from the still; a 16- to 20-foot-long copper tube coiled and placed in a barrel. Cold water passes around the worm to cool steam from the still. Moonshine runs out the worm, through filters, and into a jug.

Morels: Also called dry land fish or hickory chickens, this pitted, spongy, cone-shaped mushroom pushes up from the soil in late spring. Mountaineers treasure morels for their woodsy, nutty, fish-like flavor. These mushrooms are related to the popular French truffle.

Mud: Mountaineers use the term "mud" to refer to chocolate as in mud pudding or Mississippi mud pie.

Muddler: A round-bottomed masher, like a potato masher but much smaller. This silver tool is used to mash mint leaves in the bottom of mint julep cups.

Mush: Mush and polenta are boiled ground corn. Mountain cooks prepare mush with fine-, medium-, or coarse-ground corn.

October Beans: A fall green bean.

Oil Cakes: Mountaineers prepare prune cakes, pumpkin layer cakes, and many others with oil. They use corn oil or safflower oil, not butter or lard, and as a result the cakes feel smooth and moist.

Pawpaws: A sweet wild fruit, similar in texture and diameter to bananas but shorter in length and with large seeds. The fruit grows on small understory trees and ripens in the fall. It is most flavorful after the skin turns brown.

Peanuts, Fresh: Called green peanuts, raw peanuts, or goober peas, these peanuts are fresh from the field and neither dried nor salted. Used to make boiled peanuts. *See* Lee Bros. Boiled Peanuts in the Mail-Order Sources.

Pecans: Pecans are soft native Southern nuts. While pecan trees grow in open fields, on fence lines, and as far north as Northern Kentucky, they prefer a warmer climate and grow well in low, damp areas.

Persimmons: This fruit ripens in the late fall. Unlike the foreign imports, wild Appalachian persimmons are small and have many seeds. Ten or more pumpkin-sized seeds are in each quarter-sized fruit. They should be orange and they are gathered after a good frost, one that goes down to about 25°F. When the persimmons have frozen hard, they are sweet, and some mountaineers will stand under the tree and enjoy them just like the possums do. To remove the seeds and skin, cook the fruit, and press it through a food mill.

Pie, Cold: A cold pie is an overnight shortcake. To make cold pies, cooks split leftover biscuits, cover them with berries and sugar, and place them in a pie safe for the night. By the next morning the ingredients have come together and the day-old biscuit is a soft, sweet treat.

Poke: A wild perennial potherb that sprouts in the spring and early summer from a large tuber. Because pokeberries, poke roots, and the mature plants are poisonous, mountain cooks prepare only the young, tender shoots. Writers who compare poke to asparagus fail to recognize poke's special tenderness, succulent texture, and mild flavor.

Pone: A pone or corn pone is a "loaf" of cornbread. However, unlike loaf bread, mountain cooks bake pones in round skillets and cut them into wedges like pieces of pie. A corn pone is also a small, round piece of cornbread about the size of a biscuit.

Potherbs: *See* Wild Greens.

Pot Likker: Pot likker, or pot liquor, is the broth left after boiling cabbage, turnips, greens, or other potherbs with pork. Mountaineers serve this broth with cornbread, and they prize it for its flavor.

Raccoon: A smooth, sweet wild game.

Ramps: Wild leeks (*Allium tricoccum*). Depending on the geographic region, ramps are in season from January through May. Not usually as strong as garlic, but similar, ramps are prepared fried, boiled, dried, salted, and in jelly.

Red-eye Gravy: A broth like an *au jus*. After frying country ham, mountain cooks deglaze the pan with coffee, Pepsi, or water to make red-eye gravy.

Rolled Dumplings: *See* Slick Dumplings.

Salt Pork: Also called fat back, white bacon, fat pork, side meat, middling meat, and sowbelly, salt pork is salt-cured pork fat often streaked with lean. Fat back and other cuts of pork fat may or may not be salt cured. While bacon is smoked, salt pork is not.

Sassafras Tea: A tea made from the roots and root bark of sassafras. In the early history of this country, people drank the tea as a tonic. Today, the FDA requires that safrole, the active ingredient, be removed.

Self-Rising Cornmeal Mix: *See* Cornmeal Mix, Self-Rising.

Shelly Beans: *See* Beans.

Shuck: The outside covering of corn or beans. Mountaineers use corn shucks to make cornhusk dolls and bean shucks to prepare shuck beans. Dry bean pods are shucks or shucky beans.

Shuck Beans: Also called shucky beans. *See* Beans, Shuck Beans.

Skillet Cornbread: Also known as a pone, this cornbread is baked in a round cast-iron skillet.

Slick Dumplings: Like a large flat noodle, these dumplings are usually unleavened. To make them, mountain cooks roll the dumpling dough out like a piecrust and then cut the dumplings. They boil slick dumplings in a sweet or savory broth. The favorite mountain dumpling dish is chicken and dumplings.

Slick Runner Dumplings: *See* Slick Dumplings.

Slurry: A suspension or mixture of solid particles and water. In the Appalachian coalfields, mined coal is moved in a slurry. To make a slurry, coal is mixed with water and kept moving. Slurry is also another name for a cold roux, a mixture of flour and water with which cooks thicken a hot broth.

Soppy: "Soppy" and "dippy" are colloquial terms for milk gravy, squirrel gravy, and sausage gravy. Mountain cooks make these gravies with milk, flour, and pan drippings, and they serve them over biscuits.

Sorghum Syrup: Mountain cooks refer to this sweetener as sweet sorghum, pure sorghum, or sorghum. It is important to distinguish between sorghum syrup (100% pure sweet sorghum) and sugar cane molasses. Both sorghum syrup and sugar cane molasses are liquid sweeteners made from tall, corn-like plants. Molasses, however, is made from cane sugar plants. Sorghum syrup is made from sweet sorghum plants. Here in the mountains the terms are used interchangeably, and this is confusing.

While molasses is a by-product of sugar production, sorghum is an end product made by pressing the juice from sweet sorghum and boiling it into a concentrate. Sorghum syrup has a sweet, distinct, and slightly burned flavor; molasses is stronger in flavor, more bitter, and less sweet.

Soup Beans: *See* Beans, Soup Beans.

Sourwood Honey: Honey gathered from the flowers of sourwood trees is prized by Southern mountain cooks. This honey is ready in mid-July, and it stores longer than many other honeys.

Souse: Also known as headcheese, this gelatinous cold cut is served sliced. Mountain cooks make souse from the pig's head and feet and mold it in a loaf pan.

Stack Cake: An apple and ginger-flavored cake made with 4 to 12 layers. The layers are like big cookies and are covered with dried-apple sauce, apple butter, or peach butter. After the cake is assembled, it stands for about a day to absorb moisture from the filling.

Stack Pies: Made with fresh fruit or apple, peach, or pear butter, these double-crust pies are thin, perhaps only 1/2 inch thick. Single pies are comparable to fig or apple newtons, but because highlanders served them stacked up, maybe eight high, the pies were called stack pies.

Stone-ground Cornmeal: *See* Cornmeal.

Tanglegut: *See* Chickentoe.

Trout, Smoked: Smooth, salty, and full-flavored, this trout has a flavor and texture between fresh baked trout and smoked salmon.

Turtle: While old-time mountaineers used box, snapping, soft, or hardshell turtles, today snapping turtle meat is available boneless and trimmed ready-to-eat.

White Cushaw Squash: *See* Cushaw, White Cushaw.

Wild Greens: The term used to describe greens picked in the spring. Also called potherbs. When the winter fades and greens begin to grow, mountaineers go out and pick poke, chickentoe, fiddleheads, and other edible wild plants.

Yard Birds: Chickens, ducks, and geese that live and grow in the yard around the house. Yard birds are similar to the free-range chicken.

Yellow Walnuts: Also called white walnuts, "yellow walnuts" is a colloquial term for butternuts, a member of the walnut family. *See* Butternuts.

Mail-Order Sources

When exploring Appalachian food, it may be useful to pick up the telephone and have a conversation with someone who knows it. Ask a few questions, and allow time for a chat. Many suppliers of mountain foods are friendly and like to talk about the weather, their products, and cooking. Tell them where you are from and what you are cooking.

A few hard-to-find, indigenous foods are a traditional part of Appalachian cooking, and this book would not be complete without a list of sources. To make a purchase, send a fax, click on a web site, or call in an order. To find fresh ingredients in your area, ask your produce manager or go to a small produce stand. Farmers who sell produce by the road often know where to find ingredients such as greens, pawpaws, fall beans, fresh squirrel, and raw peanuts. For a more complete list of food sources, see *True Grits, the Southern Foods Mail-Order Catalog* by Joni Miller. In 348 pages, Joni Miller presents hundreds of mail-order sources. Her book, while a bit dated, is a treasure.

Mail-Order Sources for Food Items

Apple Butter	Braswells
Apples, Dried	Apple House
Bacon, Hickory Smoked	Colonel Bill Newsom's Hams
Barbecue, Pork	Smithfield Companies
Beans, Dried	Mountain Sunshine Farms
Beans, Shuck	Apple House; Floyd Skean's Marathon
Beans, Green Fall	Any mountain produce stand
Beans, Green Half-Runner	Any mountain produce stand
Beaten Biscuits	The Jackson Biscuit Co.
Beets, Pickled	Braswells
Biscuit Mix	White Lily Foods
Black Walnuts	Sunnyland Farms
Blueberries, Dried	American Spoon Foods
Blueberry Spoon Fruit	American Spoon Foods
Boiled Peanuts	Lee Bros. Boiled Peanuts
Bourbon Balls	Ruth Hunt Candy

Bread and Butter Pickles	Flag Fork Farm
Buffalo	The Buffaloguys.com
Butters, Apple, Peach, Pear	Gallery Crafts
Cast-Iron Cookware	Lodge Manufacturing Co.
Chicory Coffee	Community Kitchens
Chow Chow	Colonel Bill Newsom's Hams;
	Flag Fork Farm
Cinnamon Lollipops	Ruth Hunt Candy
Coffee	Community Kitchens
Corncob Jelly	Gallery Crafts
Cornmeal, Stone-Ground	
White or Yellow	The Old Mill;
	White Lily Foods
Cornmeal Mix, Self-Rising	The Old Mill;
	Weisenberger Mills
Country Ham	Smithfield Companies;
	Colonel Bill Newsom's Hams
Cracklings	Poche's Meat Market
Cream-Pull Candy	Ruth Hunt Candy
Cushaw	Mountain produce stands
Damson Plum Jelly	Gallery Crafts
Fat Back	Mountain Sunshine Farms
Fiddleheads	Earthy Delights
Flour	White Lily Foods
Fruit Butters	Gallery Crafts
Gift Baskets	Flag Fork Farm
Goober Peas	*See* Peanuts, Raw
Grits, Stone-Ground	Callaway Gardens;
	Weisenberger Mills
Green Tomatoes	Reynolds Produce;
	Greens markets and produce stands
Hickory Nuts	American Spoon Foods
Hominy	Lee Bros. Boiled Peanuts
Honey	Mountain State Honey Company;
	Gallery Crafts
Jellies	Gallery Crafts
Leather Britches	*See* Beans, Shuck
Linn Honey	Mountain State Honey
Middling Meat	*See* Salt Pork
Moonshine Jelly	Gallery Crafts
Morels	Earthy Delights;
	American Spoon Foods

Pawpaws	Floyd Skean's Marathon; Reynolds Produce
Peanuts, Boiled	Lee Bros. Boiled Peanuts
Peanuts, Raw	Gallery Crafts
Pecans	Sunnyland Farms
Pickles	Gallery Crafts
Pinto Beans	Mountain Sunshine Farms
Poke	Floyd Skean's Marathon
Pork Barbecue	Smithfield Companies
Pork Rinds, Fried	Poche's Meat Market
Preserves	Gallery Crafts
Ramps	Cherry River Food Land; Ramps, From the Seed to the Weed; Earthy Delights
Raw Peanuts	Gallery Crafts
Relish	Gallery Crafts
Rock Candy	Braswells
Salt Pork, Fat Back, White Bacon, Side Meat	Mountain Sunshine Farms
Sassafras Tea	Pappy's Sassafras Tea
Self-rising Flour	White Lily Foods
Shuck Beans	Floyd Skean's Marathon; Apple House
Sorghum	Colonel Bill Newsom's Hams
Townsend's	Sorghum Mill
Sourwood Honey	Mountain State Honey; Gallery Crafts
Spices	Penzeys Spices
Trout	Salmolux
Venison	Broken Arrow Ranch
Wild Boar	Broken Arrow Ranch

American Spoon Foods, Inc.
Justin Rashid
P.O. Box 566
Petoskey, MI 49770
Phone orders: 888-735-6700
Customer service: 800-222-5886
Web site: *http://www.spoon.com/*
American Spoon Foods, Inc., was founded in 1982 by Justin Rashid and
Larry Forgione to encourage the use of native American foods. In the
early years, Rashid foraged for mushrooms and marketed many natural
wild foods. American Spoon now sells a full line of Native American foods

including nuts, dried fruits, preserves, sauces, marinades, relish, morels, butters, and dressings that promote regional American recipes and ingredients. One of their trademark products, Spoon Fruit, is a line of about a dozen different spoonable fruit preserves, sweetened only with concentrated fruit juices. Request their tasteful, hand-painted, all-color 30-page catalog.

A.M. Braswell, Jr. Food Co., Inc.
P.O. Box 485
Statesboro, GA 30459
Phone: 800-673-9388
Fax: 912-489-1572
Web site: *http://www.braswells.com/*
Since 1946, Braswells has offered low prices on jams, jellies, preserves, butters, relishes, pickles, and chutney. Braswells offers apple butter, pickled beets, and green tomato relish. They are also a source of rock candy on a stick, and their philosophy is to "create homemade quality foods that will take you back in time."

Apple House
Sam and Brenda Holbrook
P.O. Box 745
Coburn, VA 24230
Phone: 276-328-3575
No web page
The Apple House sells dried and pickled beans, dried apples, kraut, hot kraut, homemade apple butter, pickled corn, squash pickles, sweet dill pickles, chow chow, hot chow chow, cucumber relish, and Mullin's barbecue sauce.

Order half-pound bags of dried apples, shucky beans, or dried beans, but Sam cautions that they are available for about nine months. He is not in the mail-order business, but if you telephone with a request and then send a check or money order in advance, he'll ship by UPS. Add postage and handling.

Broken Arrow Ranch
Mike Hughes
P.O. Box 530
Indian Creek Road
Ingram, TX 78025
Phone: 830-367-5875
Web site: *http://www.brokenarrowranch.com/*
The Broken Arrow Ranch sells free-range venison, antelope, and wild

boar to both chefs and consumers. The meat is of extremely high quality. The ranch is located in the Texas hill country and the owners harvest axis deer, fallow deer, and sika deer as well as antelope and wild boar. The company sells a variety of cuts of venison including fillets, loins, patties, stew chunks, sausage, and bulk ground. They also offer wild boar and antelope boneless leg roasts.

The buffaloguys.com
Ken and Peter
P.O. Box 74
Elk Mountain, WY 82324
Phone: 888-330-8686
Fax: 785-899-5804
Web site: *http://www.thebuffaloguys.com/*
This relatively new company fills orders for bison Monday through Wednesday and ships the product frozen and on dry ice. Their price sheet and web page list more than 40 buffalo cuts and products from tenderloin buffalo steaks and rib roasts to Mexican Buffaloaf to old-style buffalo jerky. The company's recipe booklet lists the USDA values for saturated fat in a buffalo rib eye steak—about 70% less than that of a beef rib eye.

Callaway Gardens Country Store
Pine Mountain, GA 31822-2000
Phone: 706-663-5100
Web site: *http://www.callawayonline.com/*
Located in the foothills of Georgia's Appalachian Mountains, Callaway is a large family vacation destination, complete with cottages, villas, a 14,000-acre nature preserve, and seven restaurants. The resort includes pools, lakes, ponds, golf courses, gardens, butterfly center, circus, horticultural center, and biking and hiking paths.

Callaway is also an educational organization and a subsidiary of the Ida Cason Callaway Foundation. It serves as the southern location for the PBS show, "The Victory Garden." You can visit Pine Mountain (southwest of Atlanta) and sample Callaway's old-fashioned, full-flavored Speckled Heart Grits, or you can order the grits by mail.

Cherry River Food Land
Norma Hess
Cherry River Plaza
Richwood, WV 26261
Phone: 304-846-6238
Web site: *http://www.shopfoodland.com/*

This grocery store sells ramps when they are in season, February through April, by the pound, peck, half bushel, or bushel, and the store assures high quality. Cherry River Food Land is a supporter of the annual Richwood Ramp Feed that serves a ramp dinner to about 2,000 and is held each year in early April. Food Land ships ramps throughout the continental United States. Early in the season, the plants have fewer greens and more bulb, and later in the season the greens are more dominant. The price is dependent on size, with larger ramps being less expensive.

Colonel Bill Newsom's Hams

127 N. Highland Avenue
Princeton, KY 42445
Phone: 270-365-2482
Web site: *http://www.newsomscountryham.com/*
Since 1917 at the Old Mill Store in Princeton, Kentucky, the Newsom family has sold aged Kentucky country hams as well as other products such as ham glaze, country sausage, and hickory smoked bacon, Kentucky sorghum, relish, preserves, and chow chow. Since 1975 when James Beard, an American foods author from Portland, Oregon, first visited and wrote about their hams, other chefs and gourmands from around the world have come here. Wolfgang Puck, for example, is a regular customer. Today, a Newsom granddaughter, Nancy Mahaffey, operates the business.

Community Coffee Company

P.O. Box 2311
Baton Rouge, LA 70821
Phone: 800-525-5583
Web site: *www.CommunityCoffee.com/*
Almost 90 years old, The Community Coffee Company is the largest family-owned retail coffee brand in the United States. On their web site, you'll find The New Orleans Blend, a mixture of Arabica coffee and imported French chicory, a coffee that is similar to one made in Appalachia 75 years ago when supplies were short. Through their web site you can also buy the popular Dark Roast Community Coffee, mocha java blend, and, for a Southern flavor, the Louisiana Blend or the Magnolia Blend.

Earthy Delights

1161 E. Clark Road, Suite 260
DeWitt, MI 48820
Order: 800-367-4709
Phone: 517-668-2402

Web sites: *http://www.wild-harvest.com/*
http://www.earthy.com/
Earthy Delights is a source for fresh morels, fiddleheads, and ramps, and the calendar on the web site shows when each is available. For example, they have ramps in March and April and fiddleheads in May and June. Earthy Delights is not a retail store, but rather it serves home cooks and chefs with mail orders.

Flag Fork Herb Farm, Inc. The Garden Café
Mike and Carrie Creech
900 North Broadway
Lexington, KY 40505
Phone: 859-233-7381
Fax: same number
No web page
This restaurant, sales area, and small farm are located in a 1790s home on one acre on the north side of Lexington's downtown historic district. Products include plants, rural crafts, country furnishings, and mountain foods such as bread and butter pickles, grits, 100% pure sweet sorghum syrup, and chow chow. Of special interest are the tea mixes and bourbon cocoa mix. Their gift baskets include tea, popcorn, and Bybee Pottery, as well as other mountain foods.

Floyd Skean's Marathon
903 N. Lake Drive
Prestonsburg, KY 41653
Phone: 606-886-0630
No web site
Floyd Skean's Marathon is a one-stop deli market, service station, and produce stand that sells poke, pawpaws, creasy greens, and green tomatoes. They also sell greasy beans, mustard, kale, dried beans or shuck beans, and cushaw. During the fall season, Manager Sandy Smith will mail non-perishable foods such as cushaw squash and shuck beans. Regarding poke Smith says, "Sure we sell it—both stems and leaves—but it will not ship. Stop by during May."

Gallery Crafts
Western North Carolina Farmers Market
Box 7–570 Brevard Road
Asheville, NC 28806
Phone: 828-251-9692
No web page

For relishes, butters, pickles, jellies, jams, preserves, honey, and conserves, Gallery Crafts is hard to beat. They sell apple, peach, apple-cherry, pear, and pumpkin butters, and, with 36 different flavors of jelly and 28 preserves, Gallery's is a valuable source for special items. You can order moonshine, onion, sassafras, or hot mustard jelly. The price list also includes such jellies as bottled hell, damson plum, corncob, and honey mustard. Starting in July, Gallery sells sourwood honey, and later in the fall they offer raw peanuts.

Gurney's Seed and Nursery Co.
110 Capital Street
Yankton, SD 57079
Phone: 605-665-1930
Customer service: 605-665-1671
www.gurneys.com
For flowers, fruit trees, garden seeds, and grasses, you can shop on-line or by catalog at Gurney's. Select from ground covers, vegetable seeds, plant foods, and spring bulbs. Among their most popular seeds are Kentucky wonder pole beans, medley hybrid summer squash blend, and the sweet success hybrid cucumber. But Gurney's also sells some of the old varieties favored in the mountains, including black seeded Simpson lettuce and cushaw squash.

The Jackson Biscuit Company
Judy and John Jackson
725 Terry Drive
Winchester, KY 40391
Phone: 859-745-2561
Web site: *http://www.jacksonbiscuit.com/*
Searching the web for beaten biscuits yields a variety of recipes and several mail-order sources, but in Kentucky Judy and John Jackson are a favorite source. They bake the biscuits fresh for each order, and they charge a reasonable price. While the Jacksons have owned this company since the mid-1970s, Nancy Eleanor Jones operated it for about 40 years before them, and the company has a future because John Jackson, Jr., is helping out. The Jacksons pride themselves in the fact that by making and selling these biscuits, they preserve a Southern craft and support Southern hospitality. The Kentucky Department of Agriculture recognizes and licenses the business.

Jesse Stuart Foundation, Inc.
1645 Winchester Avenue
P.O. Box 669

Ashland, KY 41105
Phone: 606-326-1667
Web site: *http://www.jsfbooks.com/*
Chartered in 1979, the Jesse Stuart Foundation preserves the writings of
Jesse Stuart and other Kentucky and Appalachian authors. The foundation is a regional press, and its list of in-print titles is more than 500
strong, including 51 titles by Jesse Stuart. As was true for Jesse Stuart, a
major focus of the foundation is the support of education and the sale of
educational materials. As a cultural center, the foundation also promotes
regional culture through videotapes, dramas, and presentations for
school and civic groups. It also offers a number of Appalachian cookbooks including a popular family memoir, *The W-Hollow Cookbook,* which
features the recipes of Stuart's extended family.

The John C. Campbell Folk School
One Folk School Road
Brasstown, NC 28902
Phone: 800-FOLKSCH
Web site: *http://www.folkschool.org/*
The catalog of the John C. Campbell Folk School lists a faculty of more
than 500. They teach week-long and weekend classes at the residential
campus in rural western North Carolina. Classes reflect on the current
cultural, folkloric, and artistic orientation of America as well as the Appalachian region. A typical semiannual catalog lists more than 50 music
classes as well as large numbers of classes in basketry, blacksmithing,
clay, cooking, jewelry, painting, quilting, woodcarving, woodturning, and
woodworking. The school also offers classes in writing, folklore, sewing,
leather, and lace. Of particular interest here is the fact that the school
has a new cooking studio and offers classes such as artisan breads, Asian
appetizers, pasta by hand, French cooking, European pastries, Shaker
cooking, Appalachian cooking, and North Carolina foodways.

The Lee Bros. Boiled Peanuts Catalogue
Matt and Ted Lee
P.O. Box 315
Charleston, SC 29402
Phone: 843-720-8890
Web site: *http://www.boiledpeanuts.com/*
Matt and Ted Lee are food writers and purveyors of a few special South-
ern foods, including boiled peanuts, lady cream peas, whole white hom-
iny, real peach syrup, and fig syrup. Their catalog and web site feature
peanut boiling equipment such as a schoolhouse dipper, boiling kettles,
and long-handle spoons. They sell The Lee Brothers five-pound sacks of

boiled peanuts (ready to eat or freeze) as well as The Lee Brothers Boil-Your-Own Peanuts Kit and Roddenbery's Canned Green Boiled Peanuts. Their web page provides a description of boiled peanuts and instructions on serving.

Lodge Manufacturing Company
P.O. Box 380
South Pittsburg, TN 37380
Phone: 423-837-7181
Web site: *http://www.lodgemfg.com/*
Since 1896, Lodge Manufacturing has been making cast-iron cookware in the hills of eastern Tennessee. Joseph Lodge settled in the Sequatchie Valley because he appreciated its beauty and found the valley to be the perfect place to build a home, raise a family, and develop a foundry. Today, Lodge makes about 140 different cast-iron products including skillets, chicken fryers, oval casseroles, Dutch ovens, drop biscuit pans, and cornbread pans shaped as wedges, muffins, cornsticks, and cacti. Price lists and color brochures are available.

Mountain State Honey Company
Paul and Alisa Poling
Route 1 Box 46
Hambleton, WV 26269
Phone: 304-478-4004
Email: *alisapoling@hotmail.com*
Paul Poling tends about 600 beehives. During a good season and with close management, he and his wife, Alisa, are able to rob the hives of about 20 tons of honey. The Polings collect tulip poplar, basswood, goldenrod, autumn olive, wild flower, and sometimes locust and sourwood. You will have to ask for linn honey, and remember that because of changing conditions, this delicacy is not available every year. The Polings sell their honey in various containers: salt shakers, honey bears, mugs, squeeze bottles, pint jars, and quart jars. They sell honey mixed with nuts, as honey mustard, in the comb, and as stix or straws.

Mountain Sunshine Farms
Western North Carolina Farmers Market
Nancy Carlson
Box 4
570 Brevard Road
Asheville, NC 28806
Phone: 828-258-3969
Web site: *http://www.mtnsunshinefarms.com/*

Mountain Sunshine Farms sells 25 kinds of dried beans, 20 cheeses, and some pork products including salt pork, bacon, and fat back. They ship via UPS. For recipes and products click on their web site.

The Old Mill
175 Old Mill Avenue
P.O. Box 266
Pigeon Forge, TN 37868
Phone: toll free 888-453-6455
or toll: 865-453-6455
Web site: *http://www.old-mill.com/*
Located on the Little Pigeon River in Pigeon Forge, Tennessee, this mill was built in 1830. Among the mill's many products are flours, meals, and grits as well as cornbread, biscuit, and pancake mixes. The water-powered mill produces high-quality yellow and white stone-ground cornmeal, much as it has for 173 years. Today, tourists flock to The Old Mill's restaurant, bakery, creamery, and candy kitchen. Request a catalog.

Pappy's Sassafras Tea H & K Products, Inc.
10246 Road P
Columbus Grove, Ohio 45830
Phone: 877-659-5110
Web site: *http://www.sassafrastea.com/*
H & K Products is a family-operated manufacturing business that has been selling sassafras tea since 1962. Now in the third generation, manager Jeff Nordhaus sells sassafras tea and green tea concentrate. H & K makes tea concentrate from the Cambrian layer of select sassafras root bark and offers Pappy's Sassafras Concentrate Instant Tea by the bottle or by the case.

Penzeys Spices
Bill Penzey
P.O. Box 924
Brookfield, WI 53008
Phone: 800-741-7787 or 262-785-7676
Web site: *http://www.penseys.com/*
Penzeys is a family business, and through their detailed and friendly catalog they sell about 300 herbs, spices, and spice blends. The catalog also includes recipes, information about spices, and updates on world politics that affect the spice trade.

Penzeys sells arrowroot, sesame seeds, single-strength vanilla, and ground extra fancy China Tunhing cassia cinnamon. With a full page describing 13 different cinnamons, four pages for peppercorns, two pages devoted to curry powders, fresh ground ginger, and the best spice prices, Penzeys free catalog helps keep fresh spices in many home kitchens.

Poche's Meat Market
Floyd Poche
3015-A Main Highway
Breaux Bridge, LA 70517
Phone: 337-332-2108
1-800-3POCHES
Web site: *http://www.pochesmarket.com/*
Poche's Meat Market and Restaurant makes and sells pork cracklings, white pork sausage called boudin, and churice, an unsmoked marinated pork sausage. They also make andouille, tasso, crawfish boudin, chaudin, and stuffed beef tongue. When the store opened in 1962, boudin and cracklin were the only items served. Poche's cracklin is what mountaineers call fried pork rinds because it includes fat fibers, skin, and meat. Floyd Poche supplements his price list (see the web site) with a booklet of recipes, a history of Poche's, music, streaming video, movies, fish-n-camp, and product descriptions. Poche's has a ten-pound minimum order.

Ramps, from the Seed to the Weed
Glen Facemire, Jr.
P.O. Box 48
Richwood, WV 26261
Phone: 304-846-4235
Web site: *http://www.rampfarm.com/*
Glen and his wife, Norene, offer a complete line of ramp products and some of the best mountain courtesy in West Virginia. At the peak of the ramp season in March and April, Glen sells fresh ramps. He also processes and sells dried and pickled ramps as well as ramp jelly, ramp salt, bulbs, seeds, and postcards. Check out his web page and his ramp cookbook. Glen accepts mail orders only.

Reynolds Produce
Bonnie and Clifford Reynolds
673 Bypass Road
Pikeville, KY 41501
Phone: 606-437-7821
No web site
Now in its second generation, Reynolds Produce sells garden seed, onion sets, produce, dairy products, candy, and pickles. Throughout the summer and fall, they sell many varieties of green beans, cucumbers, apples,

and peaches. Their trade in pickles may be 40 to 50 cases per month. Their special produce items include green tomatoes, raw peanuts, peanut beans, potatoes, and sweet potatoes. They are not in the mail-order business, but they will ship green tomatoes during the cold season.

Ruth Hunt Candy
P.O. Box 265
Mt. Sterling, KY 40353
Phone: 859-498-1676
http://www.ruthhuntcandy.com/
Since 1921, Ruth Hunt and those who have followed in her kitchen have been making a line of traditional Southern candies that include bourbon balls, cream pull candy, cinnamon suckers, and nut clusters. They also make a Blue Monday candy bar which is a smooth, chocolate-covered, cured cream or cream pull candy. They also sell official Churchill Downs milk chocolate bars and Kentucky Derby mint julep glasses.

Salmolux Inc.
Steve Hobson, National Sales Manager
P.O. Box 23910
Federal Way, WA 98093
Phone: 253-874-2026
Fax: 253-874-4042
No web site
German born, George Kuetgens founded this value-added seafood processing company in 1988. Most of their products are raised on Scottish and Norwegian fish farms, and shipped to Federal Way, Washington. Salmon is Salmolux's primary product, but the company also sells trout, halibut, baby coho, whitefish, patés, fish salads, chowders, salmon mousse, and salmon hams. Smoked salmon and smoked rainbow trout fillets are among their more popular products.

The Smithfield Companies
Peter Pruden
P.O. Box 487
Smithfield, VA 23430
Phone: 800-628-2242
Fax: 757-357-5407
Web site: *http://www.smithfieldcollection.com/*
Formed in 1925, the Smithfield Companies prepare and sell country hams such as Amber Brand Genuine Smithfield Hams (aged 12 months) and Joyner's Red-Eye Country Style Hams (aged 70 to 90 days). Both styles are dry-cured, but Joyner's is less salty and less dry. Smithfield is the

leading producer and processor of pork in the United States. Order country ham, sausage, barbecued pork, and deviled ham. Order whole hams or as little as 2 pounds.

Sunnyland Farms, Inc.
Jane and Harry Willson
Albany, GA 31706-8200
Phone orders: 1-800-999-2488
Phone inquiries: 1-800-365-3371
Web site: *http://www.sunnylandfarms.com/*
The Sunnyland Farms plant and shipping center sits in the middle of Sunnyland's 1,500-acre pecan tree grove. The family-operated business has a beautiful catalog featuring pecans and other nuts and fruits. Among their more than 100 different products, the Willsons sell nuts such as black walnuts, peanuts, cashews, and pecans. They sell pecans in the shell, raw, toasted, sugared, spiced, and salted. The catalog offers family stories, employee introductions, and detailed product descriptions. When you order, Jane and Harry send a free, 32-page Nut & Fruit Booklet packed with recipes and information about nuts and fruit.

Townsend's Sorghum Mill
Danny Ray or Judy Townsend
11620 Main Street
Jeffersonville, KY 40337
Phone: 859-498-4142
No web site
Danny Ray Townsend is now the fifth generation of Townsends to make sweet sorghum on the family farm in Montgomery County, Kentucky. The Townsends grow and process 30 acres of sorghum using both mules and a tractor to power the mill. Then, using a continuous evaporator, they reduce the juice to sorghum syrup over a wood or natural gas-fired furnace.

The Townsends sell sorghum by the pint, quart, and five-pound tin. They also sell a 300-recipe sorghum cookbook, *Sorghum Treasures,* published by the National Sweet Sorghum Producers and Processors Association. Order by phone or request a price list. No fax or credit cards.

Weisenberger Mills, Inc.
P.O. Box 215
Midway, KY 40347
Phone: 859-254-5282
Toll free: 800-643-8678
Web site: *http://www.weisenberger.com/*

Since 1865, the Weisenberger Mills of Scott County, Kentucky, have been grinding grains for their customers. Today, the Weisenbergers sell 70 products and ship around the world by UPS. Among their special products are spoonbread mix, white and yellow self-rising cornbread mix, pizza crust mix, self-rising white flour and yellow stone-ground grits, bread flour, and all-purpose flour.

The White Lily Foods Company
P.O. Box 871
Knoxville, TN 37901
Phone: 800-264-5459
Web site: *http://www.whitelily.com/*
The White Lily Foods Company carries some of the world's finest baking ingredients. White Lily was established in 1883 and is still producing flours, mixes, and meals in downtown Knoxville. Company literature calls White Lily "the staple of the South," and indeed its flours are responsible for the fine light biscuits that mountaineers treasure.

Bibliography

American Home All-Purpose Book: Your Complete Guide to Successful Cooking. New York: M. Evans Company, Inc., 1972.

Anderson, Jean. *The Grass Roots Cookbook.* New York: The New York Times Book Co., Inc., 1977.

Anderson, Jean, and Elaine Hanna. *The New Doubleday Cookbook.* Garden City, New York: Doubleday & Company, 1985.

Angier, Bradford. *Field Guide to Edible Wild Plants.* Harrisburg, Pennsylvania: Stockpole Books, 1974.

Arnow, Harriette. *The Dollmaker.* 1954. New York: Avon Books, The Hearst Corporation, 1972.

Bailey, Lee. *Country Desserts, Cakes, Cookies, Ice Creams, Pies, Puddings, & More.* New York: Clarkson N. Potter, Inc., 1988.

Barter Theater Board of Directors. *Barter Seasonings.* Olather, Kansas: Barter Theater, 1993.

Bartlett, Virginia K. *Keeping House: Women's Lives in Western Pennsylvania.* Pittsburgh, Pennsylvania: Historical Society of Western Pennsylvania and The University of Pittsburgh Press, 1994.

Beard, James. *American Cookery.* Boston: Little, Brown and Company, 1972.

Beattie, L. Elisabeth, Editor. *Savory Memories.* Lexington, Kentucky: The University Press of Kentucky, 1998.

Beck, Simone. *Food and Friends, Recipes and Memories from Simca's Cuisine.* New York: Penguin Books, 1991.

Belk, Sarah. *Around the Southern Table: Innovative Recipes Celebrating 300 Years of Eating and Drinking.* New York: Simon and Schuster, 1991.

Birchfield, Jane. *Words from an Old Wife: Tips and Tales from Great Aunt Jane.* Philadelphia: Possumwood Press, 1991.

Bittman, Mark. *How to Cook Everything: Simple Recipes for Great Food.* New York: Macmillan, 1998.

Blaustein, Richard. *The Thistle and the Brier: Historical and Cultural Parallels Between Scotland and Appalachia.* Jefferson, North Carolina: McFarland & Co, Inc., 2003.

Bogle, Anna Ellis. *Sitting Down to the Table: A Collective Memoir of Appalachian Food.* Amherst, Massachusetts: Self-published thesis, Hampshire College, 2000.

Boni, Henry, and Patricia Klavuhn. *The Johnstown Area Heritage Association Cookbook: Ethnic Recipes of Johnstown*. Johnstown, Pennsylvania: Johnstown Area Heritage Association, 1989.

Brands, Joy, and Cookie Daugette. *Not Just Another Peanut Butter Cookbook*. Foley, Alabama: Underwood Printing, 1983.

Brooks, Maurice. *The Appalachians*. Boston: Houghton Mifflin Co., 1965.

Brown, Roger Lyle. *Ghost Dancing on the Cracker Circuit*. Jackson: University Press of Mississippi, 1997.

Bryan, Lettice. *The Kentucky Housewife*. Cincinnati, Ohio: Shepard and Stearns, 1839. Facsimile Edition: Columbia, South Carolina: University of South Carolina Press, 1991.

Bucek, Jay, Editor. *Somethin's Cookin' in the Mountains: A Cookbook and Guidebook to Northeast Georgia*. Clarksville, Georgia: Soque Publishers, 1984.

Campbell, John C. *The Southern Highlander and His Home*. New York: Russell Sage Foundation, 1921.

Carson, Sam, and A.W. Vick. *Hillbilly Cookin 2*. Sevierville, Tennessee: D & F Sales, Inc., 1972.

Caruso, John Anthony. *The American Frontier: America's First Surge Westward*. Knoxville: The University of Tennessee Press, 2003.

Child, Julia, and Simone Beck. *Mastering the Art of French Cooking,* New York: Alfred A. Knopf, 1961.

Child, Julia, and Simone Beck. *Mastering the Art of French Cooking,* Volume Two. New York: Alfred A. Knopf, 1970.

The Cincinnati Cookbook: Household Guide Embracing Menu, Daily Recipes, Doctors Prescriptions and Various Suggestions for the Coming Generation. Cincinnati, Ohio: The F.C.H. Manns Co., 1908. Facsimile Edition: David E. Schoonover, Editor. Iowa City: University of Iowa Press, 1994.

Claiborne, Craig. *Southern Cooking*. New York: Random House, Times Books, 1987.

Coe, Sophie D. *America's First Cuisines*. Austin: The University of Texas Press, 1994.

Connor, Phyllis. *Old Timey Recipes*. Winston-Salem, North Carolina: Old Timey Recipes, 1985.

Constantz, George. *Hollows, Peepers, and Highlanders: An Appalachian Mountain Ecology*. Missoula, Montana: Mountain Press Publishing Co., 1994.

Consumer Guide. *Favorite Brand Name Recipe Cookbook*. New York: Beekman House, 1981.

Corn, Elaine. *Now You're Cooking: Everything a Beginner Needs to Know to Start Cooking Today*. Emeryville, California: Harlow & Ratner, 1994.

Corriher, Shirley. *Cookwise: The Hows and Whys of Successful Cooking.* New York: William Morrow and Co., 1997.

County Federation of Home Demonstration Clubs. *Good Victuals from the Mountains.* Asheville, North Carolina: The Inland Press, 1951.

Couplan, François. *The Encyclopedia of Edible Plants of North America.* New Canaan, Connecticut: Keats Publishing, Inc., 1998.

The Courier-Journal Kentucky Cookbook. Edited by John Finley. Louisville, Kentucky: The Courier-Journal and Louisville Times Co., 1985.

Cox, Beverly, and Martin Jacobs, *Spirit of the Harvest: North American Indian Cooking.* New York: Stewart, Tabori, & Chang, 1991.

Cunningham, Rodger. *Apples on the Flood: The Southern Mountain Experience.* Knoxville: The University of Tennessee Press, 1987.

Dabney, Joseph E. *Smokehouse Ham, Spoon Bread, & Scuppernong Wine: The Folklore and Art of Southern Appalachian Cooking.* Nashville, Tennessee: Cumberland House, 1998.

Davidson, Alan. *The Oxford Companion to Food.* Oxford: Oxford University Press, 1999.

DeRosier, Linda Scott. *Creeker: A Woman's Journey.* Lexington, Kentucky: The University Press of Kentucky, 1999.

Deskins, William David. *Pike County—A Different Place.* Pikeville, Kentucky: Printing By George, 1994.

Dorton Freewill Baptist Church, Dorton, Kentucky. *Come and Dine!* Kearney, Nebraska: Morris Press, 2002.

Drake, Richard B. *A History of Appalachia.* Lexington, Kentucky: The University Press of Kentucky, 2001.

Dull, Mrs. S. R. *Southern Cooking.* New York: Grosset & Dunlop, Inc. 1968. (First published in 1928.)

Dwyer, Louise, and Bil Dwyer. *Southern Appalachian Mountain Cookin.* Highlands, North Carolina: The Merry Mountaineers, 1974.

Dyer, Ceil. *Best Recipes from the Backs of Boxes, Bottles, Cans and Jars.* New York: Galahad Publishers, 1989.

Egerton, John. *Southern Food: At Home, on the Road, in History.* New York: Alfred A. Knopf, Inc., 1987.

Egerton, John. *Side Orders: Small Helpings of Southern Cookery & Culture.* Atlanta: Peachtree Publishers, Ltd., 1990.

Ekfelt, Lynn Case. *Good Food Served Right: Traditional Recipes & Food Customs from New York's North Country.* New York: Traditional Arts in Upstate New York, 2000.

Elkhorn Old Regular Baptist Church. *Let Freedom Ring: Recipes from Elkhorn and Friends.* Jenkins, Kentucky, 2002.

Emery, Carla. *Old Fashioned Recipe Book: An Encyclopedia of Country Living.* New York: Banton Books, 1977.

The Encyclopedia of Appalachia. See Haskell.

Escoffier, Auguste. *The Escoffier Cookbook: A Guide to the Fine Art of French Cuisine*. New York: Crown Publishers, Inc., 1969.

Facemire, Norene. *Ramps A Cookin'*. Richwood, West Virginia: The Facemires, 1993.

Farmer, Fannie Merritt. *The Boston Cooking-School Cook Book,* Eighth Edition, revised by Wilma Lord Perkins. Boston: Little, Brown and Company, 1947.

Farr, Sidney Saylor. *More Than Moonshine: Appalachian Recipes and Recollections*. Pittsburgh: University of Pittsburgh Press, 1983.

Favorite Recipes Press. *The Illustrated Encyclopedia of American Cooking*. Nashville: Favorite Recipes Press, The Southwestern Company, 1972.

Fernald, Merritt L., Alfred C. Kinsey, and Reed C. Rollins. *Edible Wild Plants of Eastern North America*. Mineola, New York: Dover: 1996.

Fisher, David W., and Alan E. Bessette. *Edible Wild Mushrooms of North America*. Austin: University of Texas Press, 1992.

Flexner, Marion W. *Cocktail-Supper Cookbook*. New York: Bramhall House, Inc., 1955.

Flexner, Marion W. *Out of Kentucky Kitchens*. With a preface by Duncan Hines. New York: Franklin Watts, Inc., 1949. Also, Lexington, Kentucky: The University of Kentucky Press, 1989.

Folk Festival Cookbook. Binghamton, New York: The Community Folk Festival, 1950.

The Foxfire Book: Hog Dressing, Log Cabin Building, Mountain Crafts, and Foods, Planting by the Signs, Snake Lore, Hunting Tales, Faith Healing, Moonshining, and Other Affairs of Plain Living. Eliot Wigginton, Editor. New York: Anchor Books Doubleday, 1972.

Foxfire 2: Ghost Stories, Spring Wild Plant Foods, Spinning and Weaving, Midwifing, Burial Customs, Corn Shuckin's, Wagon Making, and More Affairs of Plain Living. Eliot Wigginton, Editor. New York: Anchor Books Doubleday, 1973.

Foxfire 3: Animal Care, Banjos, and Dulcimers, Hide Tanning, Summer and Fall Wild Plant Foods, Butter Churns, and Ginseng. Eliot Wigginton, Editor. New York: Anchor Books Doubleday, 1975.

Foxfire 4: Fiddle Making, Springhouses, Horse Trading, Sassafras Tea, Berry Buckets, Gardening, and Further Affairs of Plain Living. Eliot Wigginton, Editor. New York: Anchor Books Doubleday, 1975.

Foxfire 5: Ironmaking, Blacksmithing, Flintlock Rifles, Bear Hunting, and Other Affairs of Plain Living. Eliot Wigginton, Editor. New York: Anchor Books Doubleday, 1975.

Foxfire 6: Shoemaking, 100 Toys and Games, Gourd Banjos and Song Bows, Wooden Locks, a Water-Powered Sawmill, and Other Affairs of Just Plain Living. Eliot Wigginton, Editor. New York: Anchor Books Doubleday, 1980.

Foxfire 8: Southern Folk Pottery from Pug Mills, Ash Glazes, and Groundhog Kilns to Face Jugs, Churns, and Roosters; Mule Swapping and Chicken Fighting. Eliot Wigginton, Editor. New York: Anchor Books Doubleday, 1984.

Foxfire 11: The Old Homeplace, Wild Plant Uses, Preserving and Cooking Food, Hunting Stories, Fishing, and More Affairs of Plain Living. Edited by Kaye Carver Collins, Lacy Hunter, and Foxfire Students. New York: Anchor Books Doubleday, 1999.

Foxfire Book of Appalachian Cookery, The Regional Memorabilia and Recipes. Edited by Linda Garland Page and Eliot Wigginton. New York: Anchor Books Doubleday, 1984.

Foxfire Book of Toys and Games, The, Reminiscences and Instructions from Appalachia. Edited by Linda Garland Page and Hilton Smith. New York: Anchor Books Doubleday, 1985.

Franey, Pierre, and Richard Flaste. *Cooking in France.* New York: Alfred A. Knopf, 1994.

Frazier, William C., and Dennis C. Westhoff. *Food Microbiology,* Fourth Edition. New York: McGraw-Hill Book Company, 1988.

Fussell, Betty. *I Hear America Cooking: A Journey of Discovery from Alaska to Florida—The Cooks, the Recipes, and the Unique Flavors of Our National Cuisine.* New York: Viking Penguin, Inc., 1986.

Gates, Henry Louis, Jr., Editor. *The Collected Works of Effie Waller Smith.* New York: Oxford University Press, 1991.

Gibbons, Euell. *Stalking the Wild Asparagus.* New York: David McKay Company, Inc., 1962.

Glasse, Hannah. *The Art of Cookery Made Plain and Easy,* First Edition. London: Mrs. Ashburn's China Shop, at Fleet and Dish, 1747. Facsimile Edition: Totnes, Devon: Prospect Books, 1995.

Glenn, Camille. *The Heritage of Southern Cooking.* New York: Workman Publishing, 1986.

Green, Dymple. *Persimmon Goodies.* Mitchell, Indiana: Dymple's Delight, no date.

Gregg, Cissy. *Cissy Gregg's Cookbook and Guide to Gracious Living.* Louisville, Kentucky: The Courier-Journal, 1953.

Gregg, Cissy. *Cissy Gregg's Cookbook.* Louisville, Kentucky: The Courier-Journal, 1959.

Gunderson, Mary. *American Indian Cooking Before 1500: Exploring History Through Simple Recipes.* Mankato, Minnesota: Capstone Press, 2001.

Hamel, Paul B., and Mary U. Chiltoskey. *Cherokee Plants and Their Uses— A 400-Year History.* Asheville, North Carolina: Hickory Printing, 1975.

Haskell, Jean, and Rudy Abramson, Editors. *The Encyclopedia of Appalachia.* Knoxville, Tennessee: The University of Tennessee Press, in press, 2006.

Hayes, Irene. *What's Cooking for the Holidays*. Hueysville, Kentucky: The T.I. Hayes Publishing Company, Inc., 1984.

Hayes, Irene. *What's Cooking in Kentucky*. Hueysville, Kentucky: The T.I. Hayes Publishing Company, Inc., 1982.

Herbst, Sharon Tyler. *The New Food Lover's Companion: Comprehensive Definitions of Nearly 6000 Food, Drink, and Culinary Terms,* Third Edition. Hauppauge, New York: Barron's Educational Series, Inc., 2001.

Houk, Rose. *Food and Recipes of the Smokies*. Gatlinburg, Tennessee: Great Smoky Mountains Natural History Association, 1996.

Island Creek Baptist Church. *Our Daily Bread*. Collierville, Tennessee: Fundcraft Publishing, circa 1995.

Johnson, Arlene, Alvin Little, Virgil Mullins. *Newsome Branch Kitchen Kanfusion: From the Descendants of Henry and Martha Ann Isaac Mullins*. Olathe, Kansas, 1992.

Jones, Loyal. *Appalachian Values*. Ashland, Kentucky: The Jesse Stuart Foundation, 1994.

Junior Charity League of Monroe, Louisiana. *The Cotton Country Collection*. Monroe, Louisiana: The Junior Charity League, 1972.

Junior League. *Smoky Mountain Magic: A Superb View of Treasured Recipes*. Johnson City, Tennessee: The Junior League, 1960.

Junior League of Jackson, Mississippi. *Southern Sideboards*. Jackson, Mississippi: The Junior League, 1978.

Karry, Ted. *The Sportsman's Cookbook: For the Hunter and Fisherman*. New York: Doubleday, 1961.

Kasper, Lynne Rossetto. *The Splendid Table*. New York: William Morrow and Co, 1992.

Kellner, Lynda W. *The Taste of Appalachia: A Collection of Traditional Recipes Still in Use Today*. Boone, North Carolina: Simmer Pot Press, 1987.

Kimball, Christopher. *The Yellow Farmhouse Cookbook*. New York: Little, Brown and Co., 1998.

Kimball, Yeffe, and Jean Anderson. *The Art of American Indian Cooking*. New York: Doubleday, 1965.

Kleber, John E., Editor. *The Kentucky Encyclopedia*. Lexington, Kentucky: The University Press of Kentucky, 1992.

Kluger, Marilyn. *The Wild Flavor*. 1973. New York: Henry Holt and Company, An Owl Book, 1990.

Kowalchik, Claire, and William H. Hylton, Editors. *Rodale's Illustrated Encyclopedia of Herbs*. Emmaus, Pennsylvania: Rodale Press, 1987.

Kremer, Elizabeth C. *We Make You Kindly Welcome*. Harrodsburg, Kentucky: Pleasant Hill Press, 1970.

Kremer, Elizabeth C. *Welcome Back to Pleasant Hill*. Harrodsburg, Kentucky: Pleasant Hill Press, 1977.

Labensky, Steven, Gaye G. Ingram, and Sarah R. Labensky. *Webster's New*

World Dictionary of Culinary Arts. Saddle River, New Jersey: Prentice-Hall, 1997.

LaFray, Joyce. *Seminole Indian Recipes*. St. Petersburg, Florida: Seaside Publishing, Inc., 1996.

Langman, R.C. *Appalachian Kentucky: An Exploited Region*. New York: McGraw-Hill Ryerson Limited, 1971.

Larousse Gastronomique: The New American Edition of the World's Greatest Culinary Encyclopedia. Jenifer Harvey Lang, Editor. New York: Crown Publishers, Inc., 1988.

Ledford, Ibbie. *Hill Country Cookin' and Memoirs*. Gretna, Louisiana: The Pelican Publishing Co, 1991.

Liles, Glennis Stuart, Compiler, and Chuck D. Charles, Editor. *The W-Hollow Cookbook*. Ashland, Kentucky: The Jesse Stuart Foundation, 1992.

Lively, Ruth Rohde. "Cast-Iron Cookware," *Taunton's Fine Cooking*. April/May, 1994, No. 2, pp. 50–52.

Lundy, Ronni. *Butter Beans to Blackberries: Recipes from the Southern Garden*. New York: North Point Press, 1999.

Lundy, Ronni. *Shuck Beans, Stack Cakes, and Honest Fried Chicken: The Heart and Soul of Southern Country Kitchens*. New York: The Atlantic Monthly Press, 1991.

McCulloch-Williams, Martha. *Dishes & Beverages of the Old South*. New York: J.K. Cole Studio, 1913. Facsimile Edition with an Introduction by John Egerton: Knoxville, Tennessee: The University of Tennessee Press, 1988.

Margen, Sheldon, and the Editors of the University of California at Berkeley. "Wellness Letter." *The Wellness Encyclopedia of Food and Nutrition: How to Buy, Store, and Prepare Every Variety of Fresh Food*. New York: Rebus, 1992.

Mariani, John F. *The Encyclopedia of American Food & Drink*. New York: Lebhar-Friedman Books, 1999.

Martha White's Southern Sampler. Nashville: Rutledge Hill Press, 1989.

Mickler, Ernest Matthew. *White Trash Cooking*. Berkeley, California: Ten Speed Press, 1986.

Miller, Jim Wayne. "From Oats to Grits, Mutton to Pork: North British Foodways in Southern Appalachia" in *Savory Memories*. L. Elisabeth Beattie, Editor. Lexington, Kentucky: The University Press of Kentucky, 1998.

Miller, Joni. *True Grits: The Southern Mail-Order Catalog*. New York: Workman Publishing, 1990.

Mitchell, Patricia B. *Grist Mill Quick Loaf Breads*. Chatham, Virginia: Sims-Mitchell House Bed & Breakfast, 1991.

Mitchell, Patricia B. *Sweet 'n' Slow: Apple Butter, Molasses, and Sorghum Recipes*. Chatham, Virginia: Sims-Mitchell House Bed & Breakfast, 1988.

Montgomery, Michael. "The Idea of Appalachian Isolation." *Appalachian Heritage,* Vol. 28, No. 2, Spring 2000, pp. 20–31.

National Sweet Sorghum Producers and Processors Association. *Sorghum Treasures, A Compilation of Recipes—Old and New.* Audubon, Iowa: Jumbo Jack's Cookbooks, 1991.

Netzer, Corinne T. *The Complete Book of Food Counts*, Third Edition. New York: Dell Publishing, 1994.

Nickell, Estelle B. *My Favorite Molasses Recipes.* West Liberty, Kentucky: Estelle B. Nickell, 1981.

Olney, Richard. *Simple French Food.* New York: Macmillan Publishing Company, 1974.

Olson, Ted. *Blue Ridge Folklife.* Jackson, Mississippi: University Press of Mississippi, 1998.

Paget, Ruth Pennington. *The Edible Tao: Munching My Way Toward Enlightenment.* New York: iUniverse, Inc., 2003.

Parloa, Maria. *Miss Parloa's Kitchen Companion: A Guide for All Who Would Be Good Housekeepers.* Boston: Estes and Lauriat, 1887.

Parris, John. *Mountain Cooking.* Asheville, North Carolina: Asheville Citizen-Times Publishing Co, 1978.

Parris, John. *These Storied Mountains.* Asheville, North Carolina: Asheville Citizen-Times Publishing Co, 1972.

Patton, Floy Russell Shain. *Favorite Foods by Floy.* Morehead, Kentucky: Floy Russell Shain Patton, 1992.

Picayune Creole Cook Book. The editors of Picayune, Compilers. New Orleans: Picayune Publishing Co, 1900.

Pikeville Cheerleaders. *How to Feed a Panther.* Kearney, Nebraska: Morris Press, 1998.

Pikeville United Methodist Church. *Heavenly Fare.* Olathe Kansas: Cookbook Publishers, Inc., 1993.

Plante, Ellen M. *The American Kitchen 1700 to the Present: From Hearth to Highrise.* New York: Facts on File, 1995.

Plemmons, Nancy and Tony. *Cherokee Cooking: From the Mountains and Gardens to the Table.* Doc Bill Thomas, Editor. Gainesville, Georgia: Bill Thomas, 2001.

Porter, Mrs. M.E. *Mrs. Porter's New Southern Cookery Book and Companion for Frugal and Economical Housekeepers.* Philadelphia: John E. Potter and Company, 1871.

Preston, Ruth Stambaugh. *Hoop Skirts & Leather Britches: An Autobiographical Cookbook.* Venice, Florida: Self-Published, 1992.

The Progressive Farmer Southern Country Cookbook. Edited by The Progressive Farmer Magazine, Lena Sturges, Foods Editor. Birmingham, Alabama: The Progressive Farmer Company, 1973.

Purdy, Susan G. *A Piece of Cake.* New York: Collier Books, 1989.

Randolph, Mary. *The Virginia House-Wife*. Washington, D.C.: Davis and Force, 1824. Facsimile Edition: Columbia, South Carolina: University of South Carolina Press, 1984.

Rennick, Robert M. *Kentucky Place Names*. Lexington: The University Press of Kentucky, 1984.

Rice, June. *Common Sense Cooking: For the Cook on the Run*. Paintsville, Kentucky: Common Sense Books, 1992.

Robinson Creek Old Regular Baptist Church, Robinson Creek, Kentucky. *Robinson Creek Old Regular Baptist Cookbook*. Kearney, Nebraska: Morris Press, 2001.

Rodale's Illustrated Encyclopedia of Herbs. Claire Kowalchik and William H. Hylton, Editors. Emmaus, Pennsylvania: Rodale Press, Inc., 1987.

Root, Waverley, and Richard de Rochemont. *Eating in America: A History*. New York: The Ecco Press, 1981.

Rombauer, Irma S. *A Cookbook for Girls and Boys*. Indianapolis, Indiana: The Bobbs-Merrill Company, 1946.

Rombauer, Irma S. *The Joy of Cooking: A Compilation of Reliable Recipes with an Occasional Culinary Chat*. Indianapolis, Indiana: The Bobbs-Merrill Company, Inc., 1946.

Rombauer, Irma S., and Marion Rombauer Becker. *Joy of Cooking*. Indianapolis, Indiana: The Bobbs-Merrill Company, Inc., 1973.

Rosengarten, David. *Dean & Deluca Cookbook*. New York: Random House, 1996.

Ross, Elizabeth. *Kentucky Keepsakes*. Kuttawa, Kentucky: McClanahan Publishing House, Inc., 1996.

Sauceman, Fred W. *Home and Away: A University Brings Food to the Table*. Johnson City, Tennessee: East Tennessee State University, 2000.

Scalf, Henry P. *Kentucky's Last Frontier*. Pikeville, Kentucky: Pikeville College Press, 1972.

Schneider, Sally. "April in Helvetia." *Saveur*, No. 5. New York: Meigher Communications, March/April, 1995.

Scully, Virginia. *A Treasury of American Indian Herbs: Their Lore and Their Use for Food, Drugs, and Medicine*. New York: Crown Publishers, Inc., 1970.

Sharpe, J. Ed, and Thomas B. Underwood. *American Indian Cooking & Herb Lore*. Cherokee, North Carolina: Cherokee Publications, 1973.

Shelton, Ferne, Editor. *Southern Appalachian Mountain Cookbook: Rare and Time-Tested Recipes from the Blue Ridge and Great Smoky Mountains*. High Point, North Carolina: Hutcraft, 1964.

Simon, Andre L. *A Concise Encyclopedia of Gastronomy*. Woodstock, New York: The Overlook Press, 1981.

Sinclair, Charles. *International Dictionary of Food and Cooking*. Middlesex, England: Peter Collin Publishing Ltd., 1998.

Smith, Effie Waller. *See* Effie Waller.

Sohn, Mark F. *Education in Appalachia's Central Highlands*. Pikeville, Kentucky: Self-Published, 1986.

Sohn, Mark F. "Food and Cooking," Section Editor. *The Encyclopedia of Appalachia*. Haskell, Jean, and Rudy Abramson, Editors. Knoxville, Tennessee: The University of Tennessee Press, in press, 2006.

Sohn, Mark F. *Hearty Country Cooking: Savory Southern Favorites*. New York: St. Martin's Press, First Griffen Edition, 1998.

Sohn, Mark F. *Mountain Country Cooking: A Gathering of the Best Recipes from the Smokies to the Blue Ridge*. New York: St. Martin's Press, 1996.

Sohn, Mark F. *Southern Country Cooking*. Iowa City, Iowa: The Penfield Press, 1992.

Sokolov, Raymond. *Fading Feast: A Compendium of Disappearing American Regional Foods*. New York: Farrar, Straus, and Giroux, 1981.

Sokolov, Raymond. *Why We Eat What We Eat: How the Encounter Between the New World and the Old Changed the Way Everyone on the Planet Eats*. New York: Summit Books, 1991.

St. Francis Episcopal Church. *Saint Francis in the Kitchen*. Greensboro, North Carolina, Self-Published, 1974.

Steelesburg Extension Homemakers Club. *Appalachian Heritage Cookbook or The Steelesburg Sampler*. Blacksburg, Virginia: Pocahontas Press, Inc., 1981.

Stuart, Jesse. *Head o' W-Hollow*. Reprint of the E.P. Dutton 1936 Edition. Lexington, Kentucky: University Press of Kentucky, 1979.

Stuart, Jesse. *The Chronological Bibliography of Works by Jesse Stuart*. Ashland, Kentucky: Jesse Stuart Foundation.

Sturdivant, E.N. and Edith. *Game Cookery*. New York: Outdoor Life, 1967.

Sturges, Lena E. *For the Love of Cooking*. Birmingham, Alabama: Oxmoor House, Inc., 1975.

Tannahill, Reay. *Food in History*. New York: Stein and Day Publishers, 1973.

Tates, The. *Hillbilly Cookin: Mountaineer Style*. Sevierville, Tennessee: C & F Sales, Inc., 1968.

Taylor, Joe Gray. *Eating, Drinking, and Visiting in the South: An Informal History*. Baton Rouge, Louisiana: Louisiana State University Press, 1982.

Thomas, Doc Bill. *Northeast Georgia Cuisine: The Foods and Flavor of Northeast Georgia Revisited with a New Perspective*. Gainesville, Georgia: Bill Thomas, 1999.

Thorne, John, and Matt Lewis Thorne. "The Irish and Potatoes," *Simple Cooking*, Issue 38. Steuben, Maine: John Thorne, April, 1994.

Tyree, Marion Cabell. *Housekeeping in Old Virginia: Contributions from Two Hundred and Fifty of Virginia's Noted Housewives, Distinguished for*

Their Skill in the Culinary Art and Other Branches of Domestic Economy. Louisville, Kentucky: John P. Morton and Co., 1879. Facsimile Edition: Louisville, Kentucky: Favorite Recipes Press, Inc., 1965.

Ulmer, Mary, and Samuel E. Beck, Editors. *Cherokee Cooklore: To Make Bread.* Cherokee, North Carolina: Mary and Goingback Chiltoskey and The Stephens Press, Inc., 1951.

Waller, Effie. *Rhymes from the Cumberlands.* New York: Broadway Publishing Co, 1909. Reprinted by Intrinsic Publishing Corp, Pikeville, Kentucky, 1987.

Waller, Effie. *Songs of the Months.* New York: Broadway Publishing Co, 1904. Reprinted by Intrinsic Publishing Corp, Pikeville, Kentucky, 1987.

Williams, Cratis D. *Southern Mountain Speech.* Berea, Kentucky: Berea College Press, 1992.

Williams, Cratis D. *The Cratis Williams Chronicles: I Come to Boone.* David Cratis Williams and Patricia D. Beaver, Editors. Boone, North Carolina: Appalachian Consortium Press, 1999.

Woman's Day Encyclopedia of Cookery. 12 volumes. Eileen Tighe, Editor. New York: Fawcett Publication, Inc., 1966.

Yates, Augusta. *Key to the Pantry: Choice, Tried Recipes*, Second Edition. Richmond, Virginia: The Hermitage Press, 1907.

About the Author

As an 11-year-old Boy Scout, Mark F. Sohn cooked near his home in the hills of western Oregon. Over an open fire and in the shadows cast by tall Douglas firs, he baked biscuits, simmered stew, and scrambled eggs. That was the beginning of a life-long passion for cooking, which continued in 1987, when he studied culinary arts at L'École de Cuisine, a school in Paris, France, owned by Pierre Cardin and Maxim's Restaurant.

Mark Sohn, Ph.D. and Professor of Educational Psychology at Pikeville (Kentucky) College, is a foods author, recipe developer, newspaper columnist, cooking teacher, food stylist, and photographer. His food interests combine history, culture, and cooking. He serves as the food and cooking editor for *The Encyclopedia of Appalachia,* which is to be published by the University of Tennessee Press in 2006. Since accepting that position in 1998, he has written about 20 articles on Appalachian food for six other encyclopedias, including the *Oxford Encyclopedia of American Food and Drink, Scribner's Encyclopedia of Food, The West Virginia Encyclopedia,* and *The Encyclopedia of Southern Culture.*

Sohn is from a family of cooks. As a young man, Sohn's father, Fred, worked in Germany as a flour miller, test baker, and cereal chemist. Today, Fred is a meticulous avocational bread baker, and Mark's mother, Frances, cooks everything else. Sohn's four brothers also preserve, cook, bake, and critique food. The whole family is fascinated by food, and each is quick to defend a favorite recipe or argue the merits of a particular restaurant.

Mark Sohn is married to Katherine Kelleher of Greensboro, North Carolina, and he and Kathy have two grown children, Laura, a fund-raiser, and Brian, a teacher. Both children enjoy cooking and sometimes use their father's recipes.

To his credit, Mark Sohn has written about 1,200 published recipes, and he produced and demonstrated cooking in more than 450 cable-access television food shows. His 1996 book, *Mountain Country Cooking: A Gathering of the Best Recipes from the Smokies to the Blue Ridge,* was a 1997 James Beard Foundation nominee for Book of the Year in the category Food of the Americas. Sohn's other cookbook is *Southern Country*

Cooking, published in 1992 from Penfield Press, and for 16 years he wrote a weekly recipe and food culture column for the *Appalachian News-Express.* His recipes have appeared in magazines including *Saveur* and *Southern Living,* and his food photography has been featured in regional art galleries.

For further information visit *www.marksohn.com.*

Index

For definitions of particular terms, refer to the glossary starting on page 293.